JUST DON'T TURN AROUND . . .

JUST DON'T TURN AROUND . . .

Yan P. Bielek

To order additional copies of this book, contact:
Xlibris Corporation
1-888-795-4274
www.Xlibris.com
Orders@Xlibris.com
41532

CONTENTS

I dedicate this book to my wonderful wife Nora.

Chapter One

Time to make Decision

Monday 18 May 1983

That Monday started like any other Monday before it. The alarm clock rang at about 5:30. I had a quick shower and breakfast. An early morning look out the window warmed my soul a bit. A few small trees that were edging a tediously grey street and the parking lot across the street seemed to wake and spring to life. It was the middle of May and fresh green leaves invited a flock of the town's sparrows. Chirping over each other, the two biggest males could not come to an agreement over which one was the most beautiful and deserved the attention of all sparrow princesses. I was standing at the window, holding the cup with both hands and drinking a slowly cooling tea.

A few weeks ago, I had sent out an application and other papers to ICI Company in England. As I had heard from Mr. Jicha, the manager of ICI division in Brno, ICI management was considering opening another division in Bratislava, which could cover business interests in Slovakia. My interest in being employed at ICI Company was welcomed with much enthusiasm, the decision moving slowly but certainly to my advantage. A lot of weight was given to the fact that I had a Masters degree in chemical technology as well as a great deal of knowledge of the English language. According to what I had heard during a phone call with Mr. Jicha last week, the business manager from England had planned his trip to Czechoslovakia for the second week of June. My interview with him was scheduled for that week. I had heard that I had a ninety-percent chance of obtaining a position with ICI; a successful interview with the business manager had been considered to be critical. Initially, I would have just been alone at the Bratislava division to cover all of Slovakia, which could have meant a lot of traveling. If I could prove successful in increasing sales, then I would be promoted and be in a position of hiring more employees and would become the head of Bratislava's division. I was looking forward to that challenge, knowing that it would not happen easily.

I was determined to keep learning English; regular trips to England could be very helpful in that endeavor. I understood there was a lot of studying needed in order to learn and remember all the details about ICI products that would make me a real technical sales expert. Everything looked so promising, it was hard to believe. Like a dream . . .

A glimpse at my watch brought me back to reality. Already it was half-past six and it was time to hit the road and go to work. I quickly finished my tea.

"It is good that we have a car," I thought, because I would not make it on time by traveling in overcrowded buses from Petrzalka. Out of the corner of my eye, I could see the car was still where I had parked it last night, in the lot across the street.

I ran down the stairs, crossed the road, rushed to the parking lot, quickly jumped in, and started the car. I did not expect any troubles because the car was only two months old. It was a red Skoda L-105, a very modest car which did not attract thieves. They preferred luxury models, or at least those with a larger engine. A one-liter, four-cylinder engine with four gears was not an exciting option for thieves who would be trying to outrun a pursuing Member of Public Safety—what they called police officers those days. The majority of car thieves were young people, often teenagers. Teenagers would be absolutely much more attracted to showing off in front of peers in a car not so modest. This logic, that brought us to selecting such a car, also gave me a warm satisfaction. Not that a bigger engine or otherwise more luxurious car would not feel more pleasing inside. Under the given conditions it has been an ideal choice. I shook my head subconsciously:

"No, we can not afford a different vehicle."

Slowly exiting from the parking lot, as I had to pause to let a bus go by, which was crowded by the less fortunate ones that had to travel to work by bus, I caught sight of Comrade Stromcek, the chairperson of my company's Communist committee. A malicious smile ran across my face, but immediately afterwards I felt a freezing chill down my spine and the hair on my neck stand up. Comrade Stromcek had noticed me and shot me with a radioactive look. I have already lost the battle; I was being "pampered" to work in a car and he, the big comrade, must crush himself in a bus. I tried to find an excuse for myself or at least a convenient explanation for when I would be called to a Communist committee in the future. I was trying to make myself believe that, after all, he also has a car, but apparently was saving money for gas, or maybe . . . possibly this way he became "one of the many," an intimate closeness of man to man that was requested by the doctrine of Communist ethics. That was a logic that nevertheless I never understood. Fully absorbed by questions for which I could not find answers, I did not notice that there was only one left turn and I would be at my destination.

"If only parking was planned for the people with cars and not for filling a column in a table at a regional committee of the Communist party!" I thought. I ran up and down a couple of adjacent streets and by a bit of luck I found a parking spot. I glimpsed at my watch one more time and I found I only had eight minutes to punch in. I ran towards the company entrance and punched my time card at 6:55. Consequently, I made it on time . . .

I was not yet sitting down in my office when the telephone rang:

"Good morning, this is Jan Bielek"

"Good morning, just a friendly reminder, meeting begins at 7:30 in the vice-president's office," said my boss's secretary.

I was glad I had a few minutes to prepare some documents; I scribbled some remarks in my notebook, at the same time trying to ignore the ringing telephone and depended on Ms. Jarmila to pick it up.

"She is a wonderful woman," I thought, because the telephone stopped ringing, but in a moment, I heard a signal from Ms. Jarmila. It must be something important because I know Ms. Jarmila well. She knows that I am just preparing for an important meeting, and would take a message to give to me later on.

"I picked up the telephone, introduced myself after saying "Good morning" and recognized the voice of Karel Jicha from Brno's division of ICI Company.

"Good morning, this is Karel Jicha, ICI. I have the official decision of our company. It has been decided to hire engineer Jozef Dobos from Brno. Bratislava's branch will not be opening."

I opened my mouth to say something, but words were stuck in my throat. It seemed to me like a strike below one's belt, somehow my thoughts and mouth stopped collaborating. Finally, my mouth closed and somehow I yielded an answer:

"But Mr. Jicha, when we talked about the position of technical sales representative for ICI Company last time, you felt strongly that I had a ninety-percent chance of getting it. Right now you are telling me that the position was given to someone who had a ten-percent chance."

"Mr. Bielek, I am telling you that this was the official decision," insisted Mr. Jicha.

"What are the unofficial reasons for my non—acceptance?" I tried from another end.

"I cannot say that indeed. I got a direct command not to say," kept on mister Jicha.

The term "direct command" returned me from the world of dreams back into hard reality. "Direct command"; this can have only one source— Communist party involvement. I tried to change the tone of our conversation to a more personal, less official one. I laughed a little bit and said quietly:

"Mr. Jicha, I fully understand that the ruling is definitive and nothing can be done to change it. Without consequence between us, tell me, what in fact happened. How is it possible that the ninety-percent chance I once had wasn't enough to win the contest?"

"Well all right, Mr. Bielek," as he changed his tone.

"Only between us and everywhere else I will deny that I have said anything like that. Our director was called from your regional Communist party committee and he was ordered to deny the position to Jan Bielek at the ICI Company. The Communist Party also forbade the opening of Bratislava's division," said Mr. Jicha and his voice was very weak, hardly audible on the telephone.

"Thank you, thank you very much," I said very quietly and hung up the telephone.

Ms. Jarmila opened the door to my office.

"Mister Bielek, you have to go to a meeting with the vice-president . . . ," she stopped in the middle of her sentence when she noticed I was still holding a dead telephone, with my eyes closed and with a helpless expression on my face. After a brief hesitation she said:

"For God's sake, Mr. Bielek, somebody died?"

"Just now I was informed from Brno that something died inside of me," I said, opened my eyes, took my note book and files and, as I passed by her, made a mental note of her uncomprehending face and sight. They were saying:

"This young man has just gone crazy."

With my head sagging, drowned in thoughts about the sheepishness of myself and the mighty strength of the Communists, I walked in the back yard towards the vice-president's office. I did not even notice that I was already there, just a few steps to the main company's entrance. Suddenly, I caught sight of two black shoes and black pants walking toward me. I lifted my head and Comrade Stromcek stood in front of me; the sight of him startled me into consciousness and, having been brought up by my mother always reminding me that I must respect older people, I let him go by waiting on the side until he passed.

"Good morning," I greeted the comrade, as he walked by me without so much as an answer; only the nod of his head indicated that he acknowledged my presence. For a second, he threw another radioactive look at me. I let him pass by and at the same time thought that these types of people are most likely excluded from non-written laws that rule us, the common people. They could come in half an hour late and nobody had the authority to question them or demand reasons from them.

"It has been unlikely that traveling by bus and the intimate proximity to others is what made them untouchable'," I thought. More likely, it was the Communist ID card, nicknamed the "red booklet." I come to work on time every day, but I was not "one of them" and at the same time I was perceived quite brash and "pampered" to be riding to work in my own car. I started to worry that the "justifying Communist's arm" will be falling on me very soon. As I entered the vice-president's office, not one of my colleagues lifted their eyes from their notes; only the vice-president pointedly lifted his left arm and looked at his watch through his glasses, then over his glasses at me:

"So, we can finally start our meeting." His face was markedly red, despite the fact that fluorescent lighting drifted all colors into blue-green. I said in a weak voice:

"Excuse me, I had a long distance call."

As usual, a meeting originally planned for an hour, took the whole morning. I could hardly pay any attention to what was happening during the meeting. More or less there was nothing to pay attention to. Department managers were not capable of leading their departments. They were managers because they were members of the Communist party. Among them, I was the only non-member sticking out like a sore thumb. The capability of a particular manager was judged according to how many problems he brought along to a meeting and how long he was able to talk about them. Problems were essentially not solved; they were just discussed at a meeting. Sometimes it seemed to me that problems were, in fact, a result of the existing political system and solving them could put Communism out of business. Frequently, I just looked around and wondered how it was possible that I ended up among them. Every now and then, I had a feeling that I had done something really bad in my life and now I was being punished for it. What was my big sin, I could never successfully find out. My memory was evidently slipping, or I had been delinquent in my early childhood because, no matter how hard I tried, I could not remember my sin. Thank God even party members needed to eat; otherwise meetings would never end. Noon approached slowly; otherwise, the endless string of yesterday's problems would never be finished. Today's problems will be endlessly chewed over again during a future meeting. Next time, there would be a very slight change. More or less the same thing was always spoken about over and over again. It seemed to me like the same song, but on each occasion played in another key. The difference was that the average song lasted for three and a half minutes; these meetings lasted three and a half hours.

I used to go to lunch to a corporate dining room that was outside of the company in a next-door building, about two hundred meters further down the street. The dining room was one of the "achievements" of Communism. The building in which the dining room was located was very poor and there was not a lot of imagination needed to name it "Miserable." It did not look any better from inside. The dining room was a long rectangular area with paint peeling off the ceiling. Some spots on the ceiling were covered with stains of various origins. Some of them were left by rainwater that seeped through the roof. Others were the result of non-existing ventilation. It was achieved by opening windows that could not open enough in summer or close enough in winter. In summer it would be unbearably hot inside, and what else but unbearably cold in the winter. Vapors from cooked food would find their convenient place on the ceiling and from there they would come down only when the original white paint peeled off and dropped down on our food. The aesthetics of the dining room were justified by red flags, signs like "With the Soviet Union For Ever" and pictures of Lenin, Marx, and Engels. These decorations were ideal because they could organize Communist party meetings there without any preparation. The tables and chairs were most likely the cheapest pieces of furniture that money could buy. Wooden tables were covered with Formica and uncomfortable wooden chairs made unpleasant screeching noises with the smallest movement on the floor. The floor was created by smooth ground concrete and polished cobblestones from concrete were the only decoration which the owner was willing to pay money for.

All of that was under the thumb of **ROH** (Revolutionary Labor Movement), which also paid for some of the food. Together with what we paid, the meals should have been nicely covered. Thus, we should be given superior food. As with most other folks, I seldom had a good meal there. The Theory of Relativity was applied fairly well, depending on only how the comparison was done. The quality of that food and home-cooked food could not even be compared. And we are again at theory of relativity, which also depended on how one cooked at home. To me, the bottom line was very simple; the majority of meals I did not finish and went back to work hungry. What happened to me many times was that I turned around right after entering the room because I did not like the aroma that filled the air. Following a look at a platter, I gave up and did not bother taking the platter or tasting the food. I turned around and went back hungry. I would rather choose hunger than tempt fortune with my health, not even mentioning that I completely lost my appetite.

When exiting the dining room, I met my boss vice-president, whose last name was Flak. We were walking side-by-side on the sidewalk and he, without saying anything about the day's beautiful weather, started:

"I am giving you some advice; do not drive to work in your car!"

In the first moment, I did not understand what in fact he was talking about because I kind of expected comments on today's nice weather and how comfortably warm it was. Then I remembered the radioactive look comrade Stromcek gave me this morning, when he noticed me behind the wheel, while he was hard-pressed in the overcrowded bus. Still, a bit surprised by his demand, I replied with a simple question:

"Why?," I asked.

"Because people do not like it. I am giving you important advice . . . If you don't want to involve yourself with a lot of trouble, immediately stop driving to work with your own vehicle," said my boss.

The imperious tone of his voice surprised me and, at the same time, made me angry. I stopped walking and stood directly in front of him. He stopped walking also and did realize what was going on. I did not give him more that half a second to assess the situation and in a very resolute voice, looking squarely into his eyes:

"The vehicle in which I drive to work has been bought with our own money. Gas that I pumped into it last night is also bought with our private money and, as long as this stays this way, I myself and I alone will decide when and where I drive that car."

My answer surprised him very much, his face reddened and his eyes were saying:

"What an impudent guy is this young man!"

He opened his mouth, but when he saw an angry expression on my face, he did not find the guts to say anything further. At that moment, I turned around and without saying another word continued on my way to the office. Comrade Vice-president was left standing alone at the sidewalk. He was turning around and wondering whether someone else could hear our dialogue, primarily my very bright and loud finish. When he was convinced that nobody could hear us, he continued on his way. He was satisfied and happy that his authority had not been compromised.

I walked through the company backyard toward my office and felt a diminishing level of adrenaline in my blood. Despite the courage that I had shown a few seconds ago, I was not quite sure about winning that fight.

"Maybe now they will call me to the almighty company's Communist-party committee and I'll be given a warning for my cheeky behavior to comrade vice-president. Nobody is going to listen to my voice because decisions about many private issues were made by those others," ran through my mind; however, I decided not to abandon my way of thinking.

"Nobody is going to decide about private issues, especially when I am paying for them, or that come from our family budget," hummed in my head.

It was almost unbelievable that there was so much controversy about driving or not driving to work in my own vehicle.

Payday was usually a bit different than other days; one could even feel pleasant feelings and expectations in the air. Plans of how to spend the money were usually nicely shaped long before the actual payday. Money in cash was handed to every employee neatly bestowed in an envelope. Bills were organized from the biggest values to the smallest; there were even coins to the last penny.

A narrow and very long paper slip which was called "the payroll slip" was printed with all itemized numbers from the pay book. At the very right end of the slip was printed the net pay after all deductions. Someone once said that that was the only day when we worked for money; all other days we worked for free . . .

I heard a knock on my door and just before I was able to say:

"Come in," the door flew open and technician Anna handed me my envelope without a word.

I did not have a chance to say "Thank you" and the door closed behind her. She was gone . . .

I took a look at the envelope and at first sight it was clear that something wasn't right. Hand scripting on the envelope said:

"Federation of Czechoslovakia—Soviet Union Friendship—60 crowns"

"It must be some sort of mistake. Indeed I am not a member of the federation," I thought.

The majority of people called the federation "Russian Friend." I recounted my money and found out that 60 crowns was really missing from the envelope.

I knew that Anna was a member of the federation and was also in charge of collecting membership dues.

"I will hold on until she disperses all the pay envelopes and then I will speak to her about the mistake and she will return my money," I thought.

"By mistake you took out money from my pay for "Russian Friend. I'm not a member," I said jokingly to Anna, as she returned to her office after dispersing the pay envelopes to all the people in our department.

"Of course you are . . . since yesterday you have been a member."

"I don't remember filling out or signing an application yesterday," I glimpsed at her with a bit of amusement.

"Yes you are too, because yesterday the management of the company decided that all supervisors from group leader up must be members of the federation."

"As far as I know, the Federation of Czechoslovakia Soviet Union Friendship is a voluntary organization and there is no "must" joining," I said.

"I guess you know how it goes around here," she tried with a bit of sarcasm and at the same time put herself in a good light.

"I know . . . even still, I'm not a voluntary member and want my money back," I responded with a bit of irritation.

She opened the top draw of her desk and from an envelope marked 'Membership dues ZCSSP' took out 60 crowns and handing me the money. She noted:

"I don't know whether you are doing the right thing . . . you may get in a lot of trouble for this . . ."

"Don't worry, I know what I am doing and I am already looking forward to facing my next problem," I responded to her with a lot of amusement and left for my office. I sat back at my desk, took out the pay envelope from my briefcase and, as I was stashing my money back in the envelope, I was weighing the possibility of whether really top management had decided about the mandatory membership in "Russian Friend" for all supervisors. That federation was not very popular among the people; therefore, no one would be very surprised that they used new and different ways to make membership grow. Maybe that has just been her trick of how to "obtain" more members and become very popular with management. I never did hear how this mandatory membership came to be, but I never heard about my membership in ""Russian Friend" again.

When I was promoted to be manager of the technical-organizational department in January 1981, I had no idea into what kind of spin I was actually tumbling. Maybe it was because I had been young then—only 29 years old. Maybe I was impressed by reaching a promotion about which several fifty-year-olds around me only daydreamed. They would not reach that kind of promotion before retirement and they looked at me with much jealousy. Like one of my friends told me back then—I became a "big boss" at a young age. The hook was in the fact that I wasn't a member of the Communist party and being promoted I became a member of the company management. It did not bother me and I thought my promotion came as a result of my education, and my technical and managerial capabilities. The others did not deny my accomplishment in any way, but somehow were bothered by the fact that I was not a member of their "golden umbrella"—the Communist party. Officially, it was called Communist dominance; therefore, all managers at the company level had to join. Every quarter they were sending statistics to the regional Communist committee and I, as the only non-member, spoiled their average. The Communist dominance requested one-hundred percent; well thanks to me they had only ninety-nine percent, so I was sticking out like a sore thumb. Thanks to an order "from the top," a merry-go-round started, which one could name "How to Drive Jan Bielek into the Communist Party." I thought I knew the situation in that country and how people acted. I was born under that regime, survived the Pioneer Organization, Czechoslovak Union of Young, even the Socialist Youth Union; consequently I had experienced and witnessed all sorts of things. But what was done to "drive one into the party" was too much even for someone with all my experience. I felt like someone who had gotten mixed up in the Mafia; now it was time to prove to the Godfather, that I was ripe to join his excellent organization. Getting out was impossible; just like someone who did not resign alive from the Mafia, it was impossible to break away from the post of manager for the technical-organizational department. Godfather would make an example out of my case that would speak loudly to all people around and even my family would pay for it dearly. Well, the chase has only started and I've already heard from my family members:

"How is it possible that you don't want to join the Party? You should reconsider that. Don't you know the membership brings along benefits which otherwise you don't get?"

They had no idea what other things the membership would also bring. Maybe they knew, but **the sparkle** of obtaining all benefits obliterated their eyesight, deadened their hearts and souls. They were willing to sell themselves in the hope of a quick acquirement of tangible advantages. For me to become one of them, it meant throwing away all moral values and becoming a hypocrite that, without a conscience, agrees with everything requested "from the top," and additionally, becomes a rat who will destroy the lives of people who disagree with Communism, and who have no courage and no power to do anything about it. Now I was getting myself into a similar situation because I was married and had two small children. Refusal or scorning membership in the Communist party meant that I would be "black-listed" as a dissident and would never get employment at a level of someone with a Masters degree and virtually until retirement would perform labor, like sweeping courtyards or digging trenches. My wife Nora was a teacher at a middle school and she was already experiencing problems with her employment. She was transferred from school to school and didn't stay anywhere for more than two school years. With my name on the "black list" she could have definitely "hung up teaching" and just like me until retirement would not get fair employment. Not to mention that our academic diplomas would become useless pieces of paper. Our children were just little then; nevertheless, they would not be admitted to any middle school. All universities would become unreachable for them. The Communist Mafia would not stop only at my closest family members. They would follow up with my parents, siblings, and in-laws, as well as other distant family members. Thinking about the terrible situation, I was not surprised that the other people did not have the courage or the power to stand up, lift their heads up and start acting up to their best conviction and conscience. Fundamental principles of self-preservation brought everyone into the realization that the right time had not come yet; there was nothing that could be done. The best way was to shut your mouth, tuck your tail between your legs, and become accustomed to the situation. The ordinary citizen just waited until the time came when all that would be gone and people would again exist like people.

People were riddled with fears and waited for someone else who would fight for them. The more I was meditating about the inconclusive situation, the more I was confident that there must be some sort of solution. After all, I would not live my entire life with a bent backbone and without indication of resistance against evil and do what was required. Every day we were forced to do something against our own will and convictions and at the same time pretend everything was OK. The realization of my future threatened and scared me.

"No . . . no . . . something must change . . . We cannot live this way any longer," I thought frequently; however, I didn't know what. I speculated about leaving the country. If caught making plans or leaving the country, it was punishable by law at 10-15 years in prison. Every—one who helped or just knew about it and did not inform the government was, according to the law, considered an accessory to a crime, punishable by incarceration too.

A few times I talked to Nora about my contemplation and she immediately terminated our discussion with saying:

"I am not going to sleep under a bridge with small children and therefore we are not going anywhere."

Evidently, she was more afraid of not having a roof above our heads in a foreign country than the fact that the idea was illegal. "Driving into the Party" business was a very well fabricated network of new obligations. The most important goal was the brainwashing of a candidate and at the same time consistent, gradual involvement of an individual into the Communist Mafia. If somebody had some moral principles at the beginning, after a few years there was nothing left. Prospective party members started getting new duties. At first little ones just to see if one becomes frail enough and when everything proceeds as scheduled, some duties got bigger and bigger and after some time one's moral retrocession became impossible.

I did not get a chance to catch my breath yet and found out that one of my new mandatory duties would be attending all Communist-party meetings. It was mandatory or else. My first such meeting was planned, so I had to go. I arrived a little early, I sat down at a table in the last row, very close to the exit and got a wrenching feeling of being somewhere where I did not belong. I was quietly watching people already in the room, as well as those were just coming in. Somehow, I could not believe that all those people had already lost a sense of justice, truthfulness, and human dignity. All those people were a part of the ten percent of the total Czechoslovakian population that lost their own face and joined the Communist party. They became an accessory to the terrible government bringing the whole country into complete misery, both spiritual and economical. I was looking at their faces, but none of them seemed to be shamed. Just the opposite—both men and women were in a very good mood and, for a moment, I thought they were looking down on me. They were the chosen ten percent of the population who made decisions for the rest—the ninety percent of the population. What the rest will be or will not be doing, will or will not think and what kind of face the rest will be wearing all the time. It had to be a happy face!

I knew most of those people and became sick to my stomach because most of them were just right-down stupid. Without the "Red Booklet," they would not find a significant job and would be destined for poverty, hunger, and misery. Now they were members of the Communist party; they were chosen and made decisions. It appeared to me that they thought they were destined to become a part of the nation's history.

During my childhood years, my father used to say:

"There are some limits to human ingenuity. Geniuses may reach an IQ of 190, maybe 200; on the other hand, there is no limit when it comes to human stupidity. When you think you have heard and seen it all, another idiot comes along to top all the others."

I started smiling unconsciously when thinking which one of them would achieve the highest negative IQ number.

The meeting room was a large one filled with smaller tables for four and larger tables for eight. In front there was a big desk and podium occupied by ten of the most important of the chosen ones; left of them there was a podium with a microphone. The front of the podium was decorated with a huge flowerpot with no flowers. Czechoslovakian and Soviet flags were pushed into the soil and sticks created a big V. The wall behind was decorated with a big sign "With The Soviet Union Forever."

What the sign meant was not quite clear because it was missing a verb. I used to see the sign on a building from my childhood. Ever since I learned to read, I have wondered why the inventor of the sign omitted the verb. Did he make it purposely to try to entertain the nation? Or was he trying to point out to the nation that the top Communist leaders did not master the Slovak or Czech languages and never actually figured out the missing verb. I never found out who was the funny inventor. The sign was never fixed and could be found in the original funny form everywhere. During my childhood, some friends and I we were making fun of it. One of us read:

"With The Soviet Union Forever"

Another one would add immediately after:

"To Hell."

We had to do it very carefully and make sure no one from the chosen was listening. If someone reported our play to StB (State Security) it would bring our family, mainly our parents, big troubles. The Godfather did not allow anyone making fun of him!

A set of three huge portraits of Lenin, Marx, and Engels were hanging right under the funny sign along with a big five-pointed red star created by ten red fluorescent tubes. Sometimes people called it "Red Lamp," which was an analogy to the "Red Lamp District" in the middle of Amsterdam . . .

A cheap plaster bust of Lenin to the very left finished the decoration of the room. It was also a constant reminder of the Soviet presence.

Two of my friends, both named Peter, came to the meeting shortly after me. They joined me at the table. Just like me they were not members of the party but they were recently promoted and found themselves in the same situation as myself. The Godfather has been watching them with one eye. They had to be very careful not to make a mistake that would be disliked "up there" and turn their life into complete misery. Somehow, we did not feel like talking and just watched what was going on around us. From time to time, we made eye contact and it was very clear that our thoughts were on the same wavelength.

It was getting close to 3:00 pm. I turned my head back to the entrance and watched a few people entering the room. I noticed Comrade Director Prazec having a last-minute talk with the chairperson of the Communist-party committee, Stromcek. When Prazec noticed me looking in his direction, he waved his hand to come see him. When I approached him, he said in an angry voice:

"Follow me . . ." and he limped in front of me while supporting his right side with a cane. We walked into an adjacent room to the meeting room that appeared to be a kitchen.

"Close the door behind you . . ." said Prazec in an angry voice. He turned to me with his angry face. His eyes looked like they were ready to shoot arrows. He stared at me and, when he started talking small droplets of saliva were shooting through the air:

"Forget the position at ICI . . . and remember you have reached a position of a department manager . . . and that's the way it is going to be from now on . . . Stop playing games with me; otherwise, you are going to be very sorry . . ." he yelled at me.

I wanted to say:

"What are you talking about? Your comrades at the regional Communist party committee **forbade the opening of Bratislava's division of ICI including, hiring me** . . ." I opened my mouth but I had been shocked by what he yelled next:

"That was the last time . . . do you understand . . . last time," I closed my mouth again. I was not afraid . . . I was just shocked at what this lousy comrade was saying. It felt like I was his slave and he was going to dictate to me what I would or would not do with my own life. My blood boiled, my face turned red, and the fingers of my right hand clenched into a fist. I was ready to punch this lousy comrade's mouth. In a fraction of a second before I hit him, I realized it would not be very intelligent or something I would be proud of in the future. One of his legs was four inches shorter that the other and he limped, supporting himself with a cane. Just poking him with a finger was enough force to make him fall down on the floor. I remembered a rule of fair play that my mom used to remind me of so many times:

"When you want to fight with someone, make sure that the other person is not smaller, lighter, much younger, older or an invalid. If you don't follow this rule, you become a coward in your own mind as well in the minds of other people."

I also came to the realization that there were crowds of StB agents standing right behind him and they did not follow the "fair play" rule at all. I did not stand a chance of winning the fight on a physical-strength level. It did not take too much time to figure out I had a very good chance of winning my fight on a mental level. In a flash of light, I saw the "Statue of Liberty" in New York and my whole family hiding in her shadow where none of these lousy Communists could reach us. After that three other flashes followed:

"Statue of Liberty . . . New York . . . USA . . ."

I heard a ringing in my ears:

"When freedom . . . then USA . . ."

In another fraction of a second, I made a definitive decision for a plan I had been thinking about more and more and which had to be thought out in every single detail. I decided to turn the play around and from now on I would be the movie director and the guy in front of me, including his peers in the other room, would follow my script. From that moment there was nothing that would overturn my decision to leave the country and go to the USA . . . and never come back. I liked the imaginary future so much that it calmed my soul. I felt the redness of my face disappearing when Prazec repeated the third time:

". . . last time . . . do you understand? . . ."

Completely calmed down with the decision about my future, I smiled and said in a very solid voice:

"Yes, that was the last time," and I was thinking . . . we will see who's going to be laughing the last laugh, but I did not say another word. Comrade Prazec was surprised by my quick agreement. He could not believe his quick and easy victory over me. He swallowed, looked at me again and tried to hide his astonishment. He surely thought he was much stronger than I . . . a little bit of yelling, spitting over me . . . and I would fold down like a folding yard stick. His face was glowing in superiority over me, there was no more anger, and his eyes did not shoot arrows anymore. He considered the case closed and said in a low voice:

"Let's go back to the meeting."

I opened the kitchen door without saying a word. Comrade Prazec stepped out and I followed him. We came back to the meeting room and I sat down at my table next to the two Peters. One Peter turned to me and, making sure no one could hear, he very quietly whispered into my ear:

"What did the old man want from you?"

"I'll let you know tomorrow," I whispered back in his ear.

It was exactly 3:00 pm and the meeting started. My new life started too. I did not remember any details from the meeting nor did I pay a good deal of attention. Nothing they said was either smart or interesting. Big comrades like Stromcek, Prazec or Flak read something they called the discussion entry. Every entry was typed up by their respective secretaries and gave the impression it had been copied from a newspaper. It did not have a head or a tail.

I liked the entry that was read by Comrade Stromcek the best because it was very entertaining. Not that it was interesting or lecturing. Poor Stromcek was very incoherent and had a hard time reading the typed text. Grammar was not one of his strong points and some of the words he could not pronounce even the third or fourth time. It was definitely the "golden nail" of the meeting. When he could not make the word out the fourth time, he looked over his glasses at the audience and said in broken Slovak:

"Aaa . . . You know, what I want say . . ."

The audience was amused as well as apprehensive. All knew that Stromcek had barely finished the fourth grade and all his effort trying to achieve something in his life without an education and intelligence brought him to the Communist party. Over there his credits were awarded because he had all the qualifications for a leading position in the party and in no time they made him the chairman of the company's chapter. The conclusion of the meeting was slowly approaching but before they voted about resolutions, non-members were asked to leave the meeting. Apparently, they feared that, if we stayed, no resolution would acquire one hundred percent of the poll; indeed in Communism, the result of the vote is always at a one hundred percent!!!! It was called democracy. The two Peters and I were not allowed to speak during the meeting; we could only listen and they warned us about that before the start. We were invited there just to see with our own eyes how the Communists ruled. We had a hard time not to laugh about it and very gladly left.

"What did the old man want from you?" Inquired Peter again.

"I'd rather tell you tomorrow," I insisted and made a hand gesture indicating too many ears and eyes around.

"What do you think about it?," inquired the second Peter and he pointed at the door we had just closed behind us. We just looked at each other and everything was clear. No words were needed. We shook our heads in amusement and were happy finally to be out of there and on our way home. I walked out to the street and was welcomed by an exquisite May Day. It was an afternoon just like out of an illustrated calendar or a travel booklet. I took a deep breath and thought how beautiful it could have been in the world without those people in the meeting room. I came to my car, unlocked the door, and sat down behind the steering wheel. Just before I started the engine, I hand-saluted and said aloud:

"Comrades Stromcek, Flak, and Prazec! I am driving myself home in a car! Again!"

I imagined how they would go home by bus and that thought made me jolly for a second time:

"It is too bad they do not live close to each other! They could ride the bus together and organize a Communist-party meeting during that time. They would have a lot of chances to re-ruminate vestigial words from the regional committee, which they repeated so frequently at work, but nobody listened to or understood them."

The drive home took only about ten minutes; however, the entire time I meditated about my new plan. Our children Peter and Katarina were only eight and five years respectively and they were too little to know about something that could possibly endanger the entire family and additionally was punishable by law. I knew they could not learn anything about my plan and Nora and I had to make sure it would stay that way. I parked the car in the parking lot, ran up the stairs to the first floor of our building and, as I was opening the door, Nora inquired:

"Hi. How did you like the meeting?"

"Hi. So, so . . . I'd rather tell you more later," I said and indicated with a gesture . . . preferably when the children would be asleep.

We knew snoops were everywhere, at every turn, as well as in every building, who listened to and wrote down the conversations of their neighbors. In a concrete building like ours it was relatively simple;, all they needed was a cup and a notebook and pencil. There was no need for any electronics, just a simple metal cup applied to a wall and an ear pressed to the cup would do the trick. There was only a four inch concrete wall without sound insulation that separated them from the conversation of their neighbors. Already as children we learned from our parents how to make sure that our private conversations did not end up in the notebook of snoops. It was relatively simple; all we needed was to turn a TV set or radio on, turn up the volume, and sit in the middle room, with our backs to the wall. This trick functioned very effectively if speakers were behind our backs and aimed at a wall behind which were snoops with cups. Our conversation must nevertheless be very quiet; we whispered because they could have been above us. The snoops then transmitted their notes to StB which was the executive power arm of the Communist party. Value and thus reward was measured according to the seriousness of the overheard, recorded, and reported activities. Reported plans on leaving the country would be high at the reward scale. StB personnel again knew what reward was worthy enough to make their snoops work days and nights. For instance, at that time it was next to impossible to obtain an apartment. There was a shortage of them and so many times a young family with children resided at one of their parents' homes for many years. Private enterprises were outlawed; the entire economy was controlled by the Communist Party and a young family had to wait on "allocation" of an apartment sometimes even up to fifteen years.

"Come back to inquire in twelve years. Maybe then we will be able to say when an apartment will be "assigned" to you," was the typical advice from government workers, when a newly married couple registered on a waiting list for apartments. Registration on the waiting list without a marriage license was beyond one's reach because by regulations a single person did not have the right to an apartment. StB agents, however, were almighty and they could move anybody from the last to the first position on the waiting list, or vice-versa. I heard about cases when snoops snitched on a member of their own families only to be "liked" by StB and to get some help in moving their position on such a waiting list.

It was nine o'clock in the evening and the children had already fallen asleep. Nora had just finished watching a movie on TV, which I somehow could not get into. I took two wine glasses and poured our favorite red wine, Nitrianske Knieza. I put the glasses on the table in the living room, turned off the TV set, and turned on Overture 1812 from Tchaikovsky. When we clinked glasses, they made a pretty ringing noise and, instead of the usual, "To our health," I said:

"To our victory!"

"To our victory?" Nora asked and looked at me with surprise.

I clinked glasses once again and repeated:

"To our victory!"

"To our victory!" Nora said resignedly and took a sip from her wine.

"When did you come up with this new toast?" Nora asked with irony in her voice after placing her wineglass on the table.

"During today's Communist meeting. I decided to leave this country," I said with a low voice, so the snoops could not hear me.

"You have gone crazy! Do you have an idea how many kinds of papers and stamps we need, in order to get out?" Nora responded with a question and, at the same time, subconsciously lowered her voice. She looked at me with concern as if she knew something wasn't right.

"Perhaps I have gone crazy, but one thing I know quite certainly. I'm leaving this screwed—up country and I want to know if you're all going with me. It's my definitive decision and I don't want to hear from you that we are going nowhere. Now make a decision whether you will go also or stay here," I said in a rush.

With one hand she grabbed the end of her chin, scrutinizing and apprehensively watching me, wondering whether I had really gone insane indeed. She looked inquiringly into my eyes and in a moment, which felt like eternity, she said:

"All right, I am going with you. But I have one condition. Only if we all go and all of us together," Nora responded definitively, at the same time raising her voice.

I put my finger to my lips and made "Pssst." Nora understood and again quietly, but definitively, insisted:

"This is my condition!"

"All right, I will arrange everything in a way that all of us will go at the same time. Right now I only have a very foggy idea how many kinds of papers and rubber stamps we need in order to get out. By the time we are actually going I will know every detail and my plan will perform like a Swiss watch," I whispered in a firm voice. She looked surprised at me and at the same time she had an expression of uncertainty in her eyes when she spoke:

"Do you really believe you can achieve that? You talk like you do not know it around here . . ." But she didn't say even a word, lifted her glass from the table, clinked it with mine and with laughter in her voice she said:

"To our victory!"

"Situation here's horrible. Someone else is always making my decisions, **as if I were a snotty boy," I said ignoring her ridicule.** Then I continued telling her about the telephone call from Brno, how Vice-president Flak forbade me to drive to work by car, as well as about Comrade Prazec when he spit anger at me and forbade me to look for work somewhere else.

"You are a grown man over thirty years old and you were born under this regime . . . ," Nora said, trying to approach our discussion from another point.

"I do not understand what you are trying to say . . . ," I interrupted Nora in the middle of her sentence.

". . . I just want to say you are already old enough to understand that this is the way it is here and you are unable to change it," Nora said, resuming her thought and continuing:

"You are aware the snoops are on every step of anybody's life and one can do nothing about which they would not know."

"You are exactly right . . . . I know snoops are at every step of our life and I am old enough to realize not to try hanging anything here. And because I was born under this regime, I have had a lot of opportunities to observe how it works. I know the situation very well; I must keep my eyes open and at the same time be a little bit smarter and more intelligent. I realize my plan is impossible to execute tomorrow or next month. It will take me at least one, maybe two years, while I piece all that successfully together," I kept on in a semi-whisper.

"I hope you are aware of the consequences, if your plan fails?" Nora looked at me with a bit of apprehension.

"I know very well what I am tampering with. I also know the both of us are risking fifteen years in prison or we are going to be shot dead at the border. I know as well that our children's lives won't be any stroll through the woods if this topples over and we end up in jail. They are only children now and know nothing about this, but even so, they will pay a big price if our plan misfires. The fact we are talking here right now and at the same time we know snoops can't hear us is already a part of our plan. All must be thought out to the last detail; we have to be a little bit smarter and cheekier than the others. Courageous ones always win the world!" I said.

"Do you have any idea, where you want to go?" Nora asked.

"To the USA . . ." I said with confidence.

"Why exactly to the USA?" Nora asked slowly and seriously.

"For several reasons: the United States is safe from Communists and, besides that, they are a multi-national country. If we were going to England, the English people would look at us as emigrants and intruders. For life in America, they are all emigrants, except for Indians. Another crucial detail is that for years I have been studying English really hard," I said

"But the children and I don't know any English at all," she said.

"I am not worried about the children. They will learn English very quickly at school. It is going to be more difficult for you. But when you think about it, which language do you know well enough that you could live in that country?" I asked.

""I know the Latin language," Nora said with laughter.

"Based on that we could go into Ancient Rome," I responded also with laughter.

"Look, when you think about it any language you choose you have to start learning from square one. I am confident that you will learn English without problems. For a family staying in a foreign country, it will be very important that at least one member of the family will manage the local language," I said with an already serious face.

"Well, how do you actually want to get out of here? How do you want to go through barbed wire fences at the border with the entire family?" Nora asked apprehensively like a mother with small children.

"Don't worry; in no instance will I follow those who tried to get over the fence with a big truck or a bulldozer. The majority of those did not make it and ended up in prison. Fences are always being improved and they become stronger and stronger. These days there are already three fences and the middle one is on insulators because it is charged with high voltage. I've heard it's up to ten thousand volts. Voltage is so high that only one touch is enough and the "escapee" is dead immediately. Two external fences are there to protect the wild animals from touching the middle fence and thereby saving them from death," I said.

"So let me understand this . . . our government protects wild animals, but people wishing to leave the country are killed with high voltage? The entire country is fortified with fence under high voltage? Well, this is in fact a big concentration camp," Nora whispered with disgust.

"Exactly; as I said before, I want to leave this screwed-up country. You will see that we are going to be successful and leave here under their noses without them realizing what is going on. We will never be messing around with fences. They can raise the voltage to twenty thousand volts. By the time they put the entire plan together, we are going to be far enough away," I completed our whispered dialogue about the future.

The wine was all gone and the clock on the wall indicated eleven o'clock in the evening. It was bedtime. Tomorrow was coming slowly but surely.

It was Friday and, as usual, I left the house early; the children and Nora were still asleep. I quietly swore at Comrade Prazec because he had ordered me to change the working time to a 6:00 AM start. Originally, our working time started at 7:00. Then I used to get up along with my family and had a chance to be with them for a moment, at least at breakfast. Many times, I came back home late in the evening, the children were already sleeping, and Nora was watching television.

I remember when the vice-president started talking during our usual meeting in his office about a change in our working hours. It happened only a few months ago and no one had any prior information or warning. It was the first topic of our meeting:

"Beginning next Monday, the working hours will be moved one hour . . ."

"That is perfect . . . starting at 8:00 is just great . . ." I interrupted the vice-president in the middle of his sentence. He looked at me with surprise and finished the sentence with a malicious smile:

". . . to 6:00 in the morning."

I lost my speech for a moment and then I asked, very confused:

"When a change is being made why not to make a change for the better?"

"So, beginning next Monday, we start working from 6:00 in the morning," the vice-president repeated and completely ignored my question.

"I would like to know anyway why to 6:00," I tried again.

"To start at the same time as the people in production and that way even out differences between production and the offices," the vice-president explained.

"Evidently, our starting an hour later than the people in production was not appreciated by them, and the office personnel became, in their eyes, something of a nobility. No, no, no . . . that must be changed!" I said with a bit of irony in my voice.

It was evident that my entry about nobility irritated him. He looked at me with a lot of anger in his eyes and added his explanation:

"It is clear to everyone that the Communist-party meetings ought to be organized after working hours and, therefore, by moving the work hours by an hour, the difference will be solved. The case is closed and I do not want to hear any more questions about it."

I finally realized we were just informed about a change and there was no room for discussion. All of a sudden, sadness crawled into my soul. I will not see my family in the morning anymore. I lowered my head, starred at my notebook, and stopped registering anything around me. I was completely immersed in my thoughts and not hearing what was going on next to me. I woke up when my name was called loudly:

"Comrade Bielek . . ."

I came back from my small world, but it must have been visible that my mind was somewhere else.

". . . innovations at TOR department . . ." the vice-president brought me back to reality.

After the meeting was all over, I went to my office, took my tea pot, went unconsciously to the kitchen and made some tea. My thoughts were completely somewhere else. I still could not believe the working hours were being moved up without any serious reason. It was decided by someone who thanks to the "red booklet" possessed absolute power—Comrade Prazec. The explanation that was offered seemed to me really childish. Comrades from production would not have to wait an hour to meet with comrades from the offices. Meetings were organized once a month; the working hours were changed for every day. There was not too much thinking needed to realize that the whole issue was more than stupid. It reminded me of a saying my father used to repeat once in awhile:

"When you think you have already seen and heard all stupidity, there is always someone who will set a new record."

I was sitting at my desk in my office and slowly sipping hot tea from a cup that came from a set with a very funny name. It was called "Onions." I did not know who came up with the name. The design on a small cup and saucer did not remind me of an onion at all. It was a blue print on a white background. Strong black tea sweetened with honey was calming my mind. My string of thoughts about onion design was mixing with a helpless feeling and sadness in my soul. A feeling of sadness was mixed with resentment about my complete powerlessness to organize my life according to my own will. A knock on the door interrupted my life opinions:

"Come in," I said loudly, and the door opened with the smiley face of Mr. Kolesar. When he noticed my face, he hesitated for a moment; his smile was gone. He entered the office very slowly and sat down in a chair on the other side of my desk. He stared at me for a long while. He put down on my desk a folder with some papers he brought with him and said slowly with a very apprehensive face:

"Jan, you are not happy here. I can see that in your eyes."

"I can see that in your eyes," he repeated and I just agreeably moved my head without saying a word. I just looked at him, thinking how much misery he had gone through here over the years. His situation has not been easy. Not even at first sight. As a young man shortly after World War II, he started working for the company when it was owned by the English parent company. In 1948, Communists chased out capitalists from the country and the company was taken from private hands into state hands, or more precisely into Communist ones. As I heard from him many times before, the situation changed from excellent to miserable within days.

Vagabonds and lazybones, as Mr. Kolesar called them, became managers and supervisors only because they had joined the Communist party. He declined to join and thereby was pushed out **"at a border"** of salary possibilities and selection for better positions.

"Mr. Kolesar, now when you are looking back, aren't you sometimes sorry for not joining the party?" I startled him with my question.

He looked at me surprised, but immediately came round and said in quite a calm voice:

"When I take a retrospective look at my life, I have to say truthfully that I am sorry. Today I didn't have to be in such a shitty situation, but could be living in retirement at a higher level, I could have had much more money. I should rather have joined that whorish party," he completed sincerely and from the bottom of his heart. I knew he meant this very seriously because his selection of words was quite different from the lexical resources he used to use during regular conversations. Rarely did he talk in this manner. All the more I realized that his glimpse at the past left him very bitter and angry. To clarify his situation, he **superadded** an example:

"Jan, they eliminated me from my position as group leader of production prep responsibility and comrade Sobotka got my position. The chair which he sat on was still warm from my ass and he, as a Communist, got the promotion to manager of the department and double pay. This regime is an ideal situation for all whores and prostitutes and all pimps and primitives. Decent and educated people have no chance here," he recapped in conclusion.

Our quite exceptional conversation reminded me of a situation four years ago when he was preparing himself for retirement. He had written numbers in a calendar, which counted down his departure. He looked forward to the day when he would not have to get up early in the morning and rush to work. As he said so many times, he would buy a newspaper in the morning instead and would read about sports. It was quite evident he was looking forward to the moment because one day he noted:

"Jan, every time I look in my calendar, I realize that the circle of people who can kiss my ass widens every day."

On the day of his sixtieth birthday, he retired from his job. We all missed him very much, especially his characteristic and uncommon sense of humor. Sometimes it appeared to me that, if someone else had said the same sentence he had said, it would not even have been laughable, saying nothing of the fact that anybody else would have gotten himself into enormous trouble.

However, he was retired for less than a half year and his financial situation forced him to come back to work and take a job as a part-timer. He was willing to accept any work in administration, so they gave him the job of taking care of paper work for design improvements and patents. He did his work very well indeed; even though he was only a part-timer, his results were much better than the results of people who used to work in the same position full time before him.

Meanwhile, I finished the second cup of tea and the caffeine I had consumed raised my mood a little bit. I was quite sure the conversation with Mr. Kolesar gave me a slightly different perspective. He could not change anything in his life; a man at pension age has already had his fate sealed. At that time, I was still young and had more than thirty-five years before my retirement. I definitely did not want to regret in the future that I had not done something I should have done, or have done what I shouldn't have done. I poured him a cup of tea and handed him a spoon and a jar of honey. Then I broke the silence with a question in casual a voice:

"I guess you would know what kind of paper work, signatures, and rubber stamps are needed for one to get through the borders?"

He looked at me with a piercing and searching stare and, without changing the tone of his voice, asked me very innocently:

"Jan, do you want to desert this country?" and without blinking he still stared at me awaiting my answer. I did not rush into answering and slowly poured the leftover tea into my cup. Only then did I say in a calm voice:

"No, not really . . . I am just thinking . . . Peter and Katarina have grown up and now they are old enough for a big and interesting trip. Nora would certainly appreciate a vacation like that. You are aware we got a car, so traveling abroad would not be a problem for us.

Mr. Kolesar still stared at me and without blink was watching my every movement. I was not quite sure I played this part of my play without a mistake, so I added with laughter:

"Now that I am a "big boss," I can also show off; we can afford a vacation in the West. I guess going to Italy wouldn't be a bad idea."

It appeared that this time I had played it perfectly because he stopped watching me so closely, the muscles in his face relaxed again, and his eyelids started closing at regular intervals. Even he started laughing at my note about being a big boss:

"You are still young, even though you are a "big boss. Enjoy the world now because, when you retire, you will not be able to afford it."

"Do you think so?," I asked with naïveté.

"Certainly not," he said quite convinced. I smiled a little bit because I was reasonably convinced I was not going to retire from that place. He noticed my smile and evidently thought I was not taking his life experience seriously enough, so he said:

"Look! Retirement is sixty percent of your average pay for the last five years of work. Today you can calculate how much money you will receive for retirement."

"Mr. Kolesar, let's not perform any calculations today. Yesterday I heard I could become the director and general manager of this place, providing I would join the Communist party. That would make our calculations very difficult and inaccurate," I said with laughter.

"Jan, is that true?" he asked with a lot of interest. It was evident he had not heard about it yet. He looked at me and said with the voice of a father who is giving his son very important advice for life:

"Jan, you do certainly join that party. You will positively not be sorry like me now, regretting for not joining the party. I should have signed the application and not stuck it in a drawer like I, STUPID BIG ASS, did. And when you become the big general manager, you will raise my pay by fifty percent, won't you?" he added without changing his voice.

"Oh yes, you can depend on it. But first we both have to wait until Prazec retires," I said.

My answer made him happy. The word Prazec woke him up from his dreams; he opened the folder with the papers he brought with him and placed it in front of me:

"Jan, please quickly sign these for me because I have to bring them to Prazec before 11:00. It is 10:50 now," he said.

I started signing the papers and he turned a page after each signature and showed me where to sign to speed up the process. In the middle of signing, I stopped, looked into his eyes and said:

"Mr. Kolesar, what we said here today will stay a secret between you and me."

"I will be quiet like a fly on a wall," he said in a low voice, confirming our secret.

I finished signing the papers and he put them back into the folder. He stood up in a hurry and, with the folder under his arm, opened the door. He was almost out in the hallway when I said:

"Let's finish our meeting at 1:00."

His head reappeared in the door and he said:

"At 1:00, here in your office." He closed the door behind him and I heard his quick steps in the hallway. He disliked being late and was very dependable. Every project he had ever worked on he had finished successfully. He did it without taking consideration for or to the complexity of a project. Very often, I was just amazed by his very precise, analytical way of thinking. Despite his sixty-four years of age, he was much smarter and quicker in making decisions than his much younger colleagues who worked full time.

At noon I went to the company dining room for my lunch. This time the aroma in the air was quite pleasing. I took a plate of pork in Sauer Kraut with dumplings on the side and ate it. I did not leave hungry like other times. I did not get as much pork as I get when Nora cooks the same kind of meal, but it was OK, it was edible. After returning to my office I brewed my afternoon tea. It was a strong black one from Vietnam. Sipping the tea from the "onion" and immersing myself in projects, papers, and deadlines I became unaware of the time and its passing. When I heard a knock on the door I glanced at my watch. It was exactly 1:00 pm.

"It must be Mr. Kolesar," I thought. The door opened and his smiling face appeared again.

"Jan, may I come in?," he asked politely. It was his habit.

"Yes, of course . . . please come in and sit down," I said with a smile. He sat down in the chair across from me and laid down a folder. He breathed in and instinctively kept straightening up the folder on my desk. He looked straight into my eyes and said in a very quiet voice to prevent someone from overhearing us:

"The first and most important thing you need is Foreign Allowance from the Exchange Bank here in Bratislava."

At that time I knew the regular banks were dealing with Czechoslovakian crowns and all other foreign money was called "Foreign Currency." How, when, and who could exchange Czechoslovakian crowns to foreign money was very complicated and regulated by many laws and regulations. According to the law, a common citizen was prohibited from owning any foreign money. Those who did not abide by the law had their foreign money confiscated by the government and the criminal was punished in a court of law. Mostly, it was a huge fine on top of having the foreign money confiscated.

"Foreign Allowance" . . . I have heard about it before but I don't really know what it is," interrupting him in the middle of his sentence.

He looked at me surprised and continued when he found out I was honest about not knowing it:

"You may know according to the law that we, the common people, are prohibited from owning foreign money."

"Yes, I know that part . . . ," interrupting him again. He went on without further interruption:

". . . and because our Czechoslovakian crowns are worth a fart abroad, you have to have US dollars.

"US dollars to Italy . . . ? They use Liras over there," I said. He smiled at me like a father smiling at a naive question of his six-year-old son and said:

"US dollars are valid all over the world and they are gladly exchanged in any country for its own money. But it is too late for this year. Foreign Allowance is here distributed only in January for the whole year."

"It is too late for this year anyway because we have already planned and purchased our vacation to Vratna Dolina here in Slovakia. It is the beginning of June now . . . ," I agreed with him.

"But do not forget that you have to apply for Foreign Allowance at Exchange Bank at the beginning of January. You are going to need a relative or at least a very good friend at the bank in order to push your application to get approved," he added very concerned.

"I think that would be the best way, but now, I cannot recall any relative or a friend working there. I have time until January and maybe I will find a cousin who works there. Also, I have to check the list of names from my class at high school. Hopefully, I will find someone who will push my application through," I said with confidence.

"The bank will make a decision on who will get the Foreign Allowance and who will not by the end of January. At the beginning of February, you will receive a letter with their decision.

"How do I figure out how much money I should fill out the application for," I asked with real interest.

"It is a very difficult question indeed. When you ask for too much, they are not going to give it to you because it is too much. If you ask for too little, the bank will give it to you but StB will not give you the passport because you will not have enough to properly represent our socialistic country in the capitalistic world at the required level," he said a bit philosophically.

"It looks like different agencies of our government behave like a bunch of jerks. How will I figure out how much I should apply for," I said with irony.

"You are a hundred percent right. They do it that way on purpose because they eliminate a lot of people from traveling to the West. Until people figure out how much money they should ask for, three or four years are gone and during that time they are not traveling anywhere," he said philosophically again.

"Mr. Kolesar, you have already traveled to the West; you should be able to advise me," I asked him directly. He looked at me with a foxy face, blinked his left eye, and inquired:

"For how many days do you want to travel?" and immediately added:

"But I advise you, do not go there for two weeks. It would be a lot of money and the bank would not give you that much."

"One and a half days by car there, a week in Italy, one and a half days going to come back home . . . ten days." I added aloud.

Mr. Kolesar tilted backwards, leaned back in the chair again, and glimpsed at the ceiling. He stayed like that a few seconds and thought; then he looked back at me, tipped himself closer toward me again, and said quietly:

"Request six hundred dollars. It will not be too much, or too little. And you will see that they will give it to you," he delivered with complete confidence.

"Will they give it me? After all I have to pay for it in Czechoslovak crowns," I noted irritated.

"Of course, you have to pay for those dollars in our crowns, but still you will be happy, like a flea in a fur coat, that your application was not turned down," chilling me with reality, and I just approvingly bowed my head. When he noticed my agreement and the resignation in my eyes, he quietly said:

"Jan, I am convinced the "Foreign Allowance" will be given to you. When you get a letter from the bank about the allotted money, you may start dealing with the papers, signatures, and rubber stamps."

"In fact, how many papers or applications are there that I need to have?" I asked with interest. He again winked at me and, with a smile of somebody who knows the situation very well, inquired:

"Do you have a valid passport?"

"I do not," I responded without hesitation.

"So, at first file an application for a passport," he said. In fact at the same time you may submit an application for the Travel Provision to the Western countries."

"What's the Travel Provision?" I inquired.

"That's a kind of official government stationery with a crest, which contains your name and is "sealed" by the government; namely, the StB. Right on the top it is titled: TRAVEL PROVISION," Without it you are barred from going to the West. Only after acquiring that piece of paper may you apply for visas," he explained patiently.

"Even though we will have a passport, which is valid in any country in the world, when we want to travel to the West, we must have a "Provision?" I asked.

"Even so, but just getting the Provision will be the most difficult for you," he delivered with a sarcastic smile, whereupon he kept on:

"To apply for the Travel Provision, you will need five signatures and rubber stamps," and at the same time, he lifted his left hand from the table with stretched out fingers and palm turned over toward me.

"Five?" I asked surprised.

"Five," he repeated with certainty and I got ready with pen and a scribbling-pad that I always kept on my desk and started making notes. Again, he turned his palm to himself and, with the fingers of his right hand, caught the little finger of his left palm and I comprehended he was beginning with the easiest obtainable signature.

"At first you will need to bring the application to the company ROH committee and ask for a signature from the chairperson of the committee. His secretary will smack the rubber stamp of the committee there right after the autograph."

"After that you will bring it to your boss, Vice-president Flak, for a signature," he said and, at the same time, he again caught with the fingers of his right hand the ring finger on his left hand.

As I finished writing in my notepad, with his right hand, he caught the middle finger on the left hand and I understood that this time it would be somewhat more difficult. He grinned and said:

"When you have the application signed by the ROH and the vice-president, you will again proceed to the company committee of the Communist party and give it to the chairman of the board for her signature. The rubber stamp will be smacked there automatically."

After that he caught the forefinger of his left hand and asked me:

"Under which district military administration do you belong?"

"Four," I responded promptly.

"So at the four you obtain permission of the military administration to travel to the West."

"I am so glad I do not need to seek permission to travel to the West from a lamp room," I said; I could not miss an ironic note, which really impressed the old gentleman strongly. As if he was fired off he tipped himself in the chair backwards so quickly that the chair was standing only on the two back legs and, at the same time, he kicked my desk from below with his knees. He slammed the palms of his hands on his thighs and, with his face rotated toward the ceiling, he was laughing like a horse. His reaction affected even me and together we laughed like a couple of horses. The noise we made was so loud that Ms. Jarmila from the next office opened the door to my office without knocking and looked inside to find out what was going on. We were so absorbed by our laughter that we did not notice her face in the door; not until she said:

". . . I only wanted to see what was going on here and whether you are both all right . . ." and her head disappeared behind the closed door again.

Mr. Kolesar tipped himself forward, his chair was back on all four legs, the palms of his hands were not slamming his thighs anymore but remained there motionless. His shoulders slowly stopped swinging up and down and his very loud laughter turned into a regular one. Both of us were wiping tears from our eyes and it took a while till we stopped completely. Only then did we realize how we must have startled Miss Jarmila: exploding from a whispered talk into a very loud laughter, and concluding with a knee kick to my desk. I could still see the amusement in his eyes when he returned to our whispered conversation:

"When you have the signature and rubber stamp from the company Communist party, then give the application for a Travel Provision to Director Prazec. I advise you to bring it yourself to Prazec." he said, and at the same time, he held the forefinger of his left hand with a closed right fist.

"Do you think he will sign it while I wait?" I asked.

"Definitely not. They will call you to a company management meeting. There all of them will nod their heads and only then the director will sign it. Don't forget that his secretary has to rubber stamp your application," he advised with the voice of someone who knows the entire process of signing and rubber stamping very well. During our entire discussion about having the director sign the application, he held with his right hand the thumb of his left one and wagged it from side to side. That could not mean anything else but that this time it was going to be really tough. I thought we were extremely lucky that there were only five of those stupid papers because I could not imagine how he could keep on counting. A smile followed my thoughts.

"If anyone from the company management shakes his head from side to side instead of up and down, we are not going to Italy," I noted ironically.

"Jan," gabbled out Mr. Kolesar, letting his thumb go. He opened his arms wide, tipped himself toward me, stared me straight in the eyes and then in a quiet voice he delivered:

"If only one single person from the crowd of people that will be around when they are going to sign and rubber stamp your application at any level shakes his head side to side instead of up and down you are going to shit and there will be no Italy. It doesn't need to be the one signing your application. One single person will be enough . . . You can go swimming in a pool at your neighbors. For that vacation doesn't need authorization from anybody."

"Consequently, the swim suit that I have got prepared to my neighbors I should not be packing in the luggage," I noted again with irony.

He laughed in amusement in a loud voice and picked up his folder resting on my desk and with the wink of his eye quietly added almost like a conspirator:

"For now, keep your suitcases in the closet because you do not have the Foreign Allowance yet."

It occurred to me that all this would not be needed if we were living in a normal country where one can travel normally. A country where people who want to travel shove their passports in their pocket with some money, money which their own government doesn't deny them, and just go; a country where one doesn't need to beg for permission to travel, starting with the janitor to the director. I didn't want to make any more ironic comments even though I had a thousand of them on my mind. That old gentleman nevertheless was not responsible for the situation in the country; he suffered his entire life for not bending his spine. I was very thankful to him for the detailed description of how to process all the papers required. I could not imagine how many years I would need in order to find out all that by myself. I knew the situation in the country with the authorities and I also knew that no official was capable or willing to advice or directly say what I learned from him. He treated me like my father and he was only about two years older than my own father.

I ran down the notes I had written down so far and said:

"It seems I will have to study my notes and then make some kind of time chart, how and when I will deal with all this."

"Of course, Jan, it is going to be my pleasure to chit-chat with you about it. However, today is Friday and in half an hour we are going home and I wanted to prepare some documents you are going to need Monday morning for the management meeting. Well, there you will be reporting about improvement proposals and inventions," he said with good manners, which long since were gone from that society. Indeed, he was brought up with good manners and being an honorable human being; values that parents would be giving to their own children.

"Of course, Mr. Kolesar, I am most grateful for the advice you have given me. Well, we still have plenty of time to cook this cake," I replied.

He took his folder, and before he went out to the hallway, he said:

"Jan, before I go home I will put on your desk a complete report that you will need for the meeting Monday morning. If we don't see each other before the day is over, I you wish a nice and pleasant weekend."

"Thank you . . . likewise, Mr. Kolesar . . ." and I could not finish my sentence because the telephone rang. They called from production and needed my immediate attention. Solving production problems has always been first and foremost on my list of important subjects; therefore, I rushed out from the office and ran to production. Production on line B was down and Technologist Vlado and Foreman Thomas were trying to figure out a solution. They welcomed my arrival with satisfaction:

"Right now we are here like the Three Kings, so we must get to the bottom of this problem," Vlado noted. Thomas looked into the production recipe and I reviewed the results from quality control. I asked the operator of line B to take another QC sample and looked at the production recipe. I handed the Sample to Vlado and asked him:

"Add 2 grams of additive AC-50 and after mixing give that to QC for rechecking."

About ten minutes later the results were available and I found out that it had been an overshot. Fortunately, that was only a small sample, not the whole lot. I pulled out a calculator from my pocket that I always carried with me and calculated the amount of additive for an entire batch, remembering to make a correction I learned from the small sample. The new results turned out all right; consequently, line B was again in operation. In Thomas's office we drew up temporary instructions for production, just in case the problem reappeared. Satisfied, we broke up our emergency meeting and went home. Busy dealing with the problem, we did not notice that it was already four o'clock. We worked in this manner for two more hours. We did not get paid for because all three of us were "administration" with monthly salaries. It occurred to me that the working time having been moved to six a.m. made it so that I lost time again. If we were still starting at seven my "overtime" would be only one unpaid hour. Shifting the start to eight, as I had wanted, would have been completely ideal today. Our building was empty, all personnel long gone home and the door to my office was locked. I unlocked the door and found the report from Mr. Kolesar resting on my desk. I did not bother reading it and picked up the telephone and called my parents-in-law, where Nora was with the children. Nora and I agreed that morning that I would pick them up by car at four o'clock. It was ten past four and I was still in my office. Nora picked up the phone, expecting my call when I did not show up at four o'clock.

"Hi, where are you?," she asked.

"Hi, in my office . . . troubles in production . . . I am going now . . . I'll be there four thirty . . . ," I tried to explain briefly.

"All right. We will meet at four thirty. You can wait for us in the car," she answered.

"Bye," I said and hung up the phone.

My in-laws lived close by, only a couple of blocks away. However, it took me about fifteen minutes to get there because I had to cross three relatively large intersections. I parked the car in the front of the building where my in-laws lived and hadn't switched off the engine yet when I noticed Nora with the children walking out from the building entrance.

"Hi . . . Hi . . ." we said to each other and they quickly jumped in the car. They buckled up and I turned on the left blinker and slowly came out of the parking spot. We went home to Petrzalka. Nora was sitting next to me and the kids were in the back.

"I guess it was a little bit busy at work today," Nora said, just before I drove the car from the parking space.

"It was OK the whole day until the very end. You know that troubles in production always start on Friday just before we are supposed to go home. I had an opportunity to chat with Mr. Kolesar about getting the papers," I said, turning my head to the right as our eyes met. I winked my right eye, turned my head back because I had to watch the traffic and then without delay noted:

"Tomorrow is supposed to be nice weather, so can we go for a walk in Sady Janka Krala." Nora understood my wink and in the corner of my eye I saw her approvingly nod her head.

"Hurrah, we heard from the back seats, as the children responded with pleasure to our plan about Saturday's walk.

Sady Janka Krala was in Petrzalka not too far from the place where we lived. It was a public park built on the right bank of the Danube River by Bratislava's City Hall in the year 1775. In an area of twenty-two hectares, they had planted eight tree alleys in a star shape and originally called it Star Alley. Following World War II, the park was named in memory of Slovakia's poet, Janko Kral, and in English it would be called Janko Kral's Alley.

The Danube is a gigantic river and the long existence of the park is thanks to the fact that the City of Bratislava originally grew on the left bank of the Danube and the right bank was accessible only by ships for centuries. The first permanent bridge that was not destroyed by high water or floating ice in the winter had not been built until the year 1890. This bridge was for a whole century the only solid interconnection of both Danube banks in Bratislava and it was called Old Bridge. Trees in the park were very old and tall and made pleasant shadows in summer months when the heat in the concrete buildings and the asphalt covered streets of the city become unbearable. There was grass below the trees and it was always maintained and mowed. gravel-covered sidewalks ran in between rose bushes, flowerbeds and fountains with water. Benches were at edges of sidewalks; some flowerbeds as well by the fountains. The park was a favorite weekend attraction for many people. One could see young couples, young families with little kids, as well as elderly people there. One side was hemmed by the Old Bridge and tower, which was once transferred to the park from the church of Klarisiek. On the other side was the Bridge of SNP (The Slovak National Uprising) and a small restaurant where they sold simple meals as well as beverages. The New Bridge as we used to call the Bridge of SNP was finished in 1969 for the 25th anniversary of the SNP. Until then the Petrzalka side of the city was connected only by Old Bridge or by a steamship, which went from one side to the other and was called "Propeller." The right bank of the Danube, beginning at the Bridge of SNP down to the Old Bridge, created a natural north border of the park. Benches were laid at the bank of the river, from which one could watch Propeller and people who came on or were leaving with the ship. The benches were favorite spots for both painters who painted Bratislava and photographers who were trying to capture panoramic townscapes and preserve them for future generations. On the other side of the Danube, there was the Bratislava Castle majestically standing on the top of a hill for many centuries. Saint Martin Cathedral in which six kings and queens were crowned towered next to the castle.

Saturday afternoon we went out on our planned walk in Janko Kral's Alley. For the kids this was a welcomed opportunity for running, walking on toppled trees or playing hide-and-seek in hollow trees. For us parents it was an opportunity to have a discussion without the kids or snoops hearing us. We walked slowly following sidewalks and keeping a constant eye on the kids, so they would be safe but have enough freedom to play just like kids of the same age would. Very quietly so nobody could hear us, we spoke about the important information, which only the day before I had learned from Mr. Kolesar:

"So, what in fact did you learn?" Nora asked.

"To tell you the truth, I learned a lot. I would need years at it, if I wanted to find out all of that alone," I responded quietly, and at the same time we looked around. We were paying attention to our kids and also making sure that no one else could hear us. Later I repeated in all details to her the entire conversation I had had with Mr. Kolesar.

"You should be more careful what you say, so that you don't have a slip of the tongue," Nora said when I finished.

"I don't think he is an StB agent. Of course, I will never tell or even indicate what plans we are contemplating. I am not so stupid," trying to suppress her fears and then I added:

"Nobody will ever know anything, including our entire family. This will stay only between you and me and we can only reveal things to the kids once we get to Vienna."

"But how do you want to assure that our children will not prematurely know about it? As a matter of fact, you know that by the time you get all the required signatures and rubber stamps, everyone at your work will know about it," Nora said. At this, both of us again subconsciously glanced back and around and, when we noticed someone approaching us, we stopped talking. We just walked side by side holding hands looking silently at each other. When they were a sufficient distance in front of us or behind us we kept on very quietly, almost whispering:

"I know what you want to say. We live in a block of apartments and everywhere around us there are 'employees' from our company," I continued in her thoughts and concluded:

"I already thought about it and I guess we still have time for these kinds of fears. Nobody from our company knows anything about our tour to Italy so far, only Mr. Kolesar. And he will keep it to himself until next year."

"Are you sure?" Nora asked with apprehension.

"Don't worry; I know him very well," again trying to suppress her fears and immediately after adding::

"If we file the application for Foreign Allowance at the start of January next year, until the beginning of February no one will know anything because we won't even be certain that it will be given to us. It would be completely useless to start the entire merry-go-round of signatures and rubber stamps if we can't get any dollars."

"Do you think we are going to have enough time to make it?" Nora asked with apprehension again.

"I think so. Look, first we must stop being constantly afraid because, as you know, the courageous ones get the world," I said quietly and at the same time tried to make my voice firm and convincing.

"It is easy for you to say . . . You know me . . . ," Nora said somewhat resignedly.

"Just because I know you, we can make a pact. You will stop being afraid all the time and believe that I will bring it to a successful conclusion. I promise you that I will clear the decks just as we agreed before." I offered with a great deal of confidence. She looked at me and asked:

"Including our children?" and made a gentle nod at Peter and Katarina who were far from us, fully occupied with a hollow tree.

"Including our children," I assured her and at the same time I felt that she had squeezed my hand a little more firmly. She tipped her head toward me and rested it on my shoulder. I kissed her hair. We came to a bench; she sat down and leaned on the backrest. I put my legs between the backrest and the seat still sitting beside her and laid my arms on the backrest. We sat in this manner side by side, each of us with our face turned to the opposite side; she watched the kids and I watched the sidewalk behind her back. It wasn't long before the kids noticed that we had sat down on a bench, so they came running to us. Katarina sat down next to Nora and Peter sat down beside me the same way as I. Markedly, he did not sit comfortably because the backrest was almost at the height of his eyes and he could not see over the bench. He laid his elbows on the backrest and his shoulders stuck in the air in the form of a capital V. He looked at me and smiled:

"Are you sitting all right?" I asked him.

"And you?" he responded with a question.

"I am seated all right. I can watch people walk by. And you?

"I do not see anything because the backrest is too high," Peter responded.

"The backrest is the correct height; it's just that you're too short," I said. My answer quite surprised him and for a while he was dumbfounded and after two seconds of thought he broke out laughing very loudly.

Sitting at the bench was very pleasant; gigantic trees with branches covered with leaves generated natural air conditioning. In a couple of days, the school year was going to end for the kids and also for Nora. Back in March we had paid for a two-week vacation to Vratna Dolina, which started a week from today on Saturday. I looked at Nora and pretended resuming our conversation:

"This week we should start packing our luggage to have it ready for next Saturday."

"Where are we going?" Katarina asked with interest. Peter didn't say anything, but only watched me with interest.

"Indeed to Vratna Dolina for a vacation," Nora responded.

"Where's Vratna Dolina?" Peter inquired.

"In central Slovakia, between the High and Low Tatra Mountains. It takes about six-seven hours of driving," I said and could see happiness from the expectations of the kids.

"Each of you can pack one small briefcase with toys, to take along. But take only what you will actually need." Nora said to Peter and Katarina, so they could share at preparations for the vacation.

"So, let's go home and we can start packing," Katarina said as she slid down from the bench, stood before Nora, caught her arm and started pulling her from the bench.

"We don't need to hurry so much; we still have a whole week to manage it," I said and then added:

"Now can we still walk along in the park? You two can talk about what toys to pack and mom and I can plan what to take with us in the big suitcases."

Peter rose from the bench like a shot, and then along with Katarina walked a small distance in front of us. They were evidently cheered up by the end of the school year and the following vacation. An automobile journey of the unknown world of Vratna Dolina appeared to them fantastic. The two of us followed them without words and held hands. We quietly thought about the kids and wondered what would be their reaction, when we told them in Vienna that we were not going back to Slovakia anymore. How would we explain to them that this, which is their home now, we would never return to again. How would we justify our leaving everything we had behind and going far out into the world where we had no family or home and our imaginations about the future were only dreams? For a while we walked like that without words, peeking ahead at the children and, after a few moments, our eyes met. Our eyes were full of tears. What luck that our children were far in front of us and they were fully absorbed in their plans to pack toys for our vacation!

After coming back home, the kids started packing their toys enthusiastically. At first they each made a big pile of toys in the middle of the room. When I noticed that in no way would those piles fit in the suitcases we prepared for them, I pulled them out of the closet and opened them next to the piles:

"Here are your suitcases. You have to reduce the piles, so your toys will fit," I said.

After seeing the suitcases, they understood the situation and reduced the number of toys. The kids started carefully packing the toys inside the suitcases. Nora and I could not resist a smile when we infrequently looked at them and observed their uninhibited enthusiasm.

During the following week, Nora prepared and packed the clothing and shoes we would need for a two week-vacation. Along with the trip, we purchased food coupons from the travel agency that were valid at any restaurant in the area around Vratna Dolina. It was a great advantage because we were not tied to one restaurant and could make trips in the whole valley. For some unknown reason the travel agency did not recognize the difference between kids and adults and sold us food coupons for four people, which meant our kids had the same amount of money as we did. It appeared to us too much; Peter and Katarina would in no way "eat" all that money. It was impossible to return unused coupons; we had to use them or lose them. We decided we would use the extra money to upgrade our dining by a notch and buy a lot of ice cream.

The week of preparation for our vacation went by really fast. Saturday morning we loaded up the trunk with luggage and left the city for the Mala Fatra Mountains. In a matter of a few hours, we were transferred from the concrete jungle of Bratislava's Petrzalka into the middle of the most gorgeous natural beauty we had ever seen. After six hours of driving, we reached our destination, Vratna Dolina. The weather was very nice and the valley invited us with its beauty immediately as the road turned into it. The cottage we stayed in was in the middle of Vratna and provided a breath-taking view of the whole valley.

Vratna Dolina is located about three kilometers from the village of Terchova and it is considered the most beautiful valley of the Mala Fatra Mountains. Vratna Dolina contains practically all natural mountain prettiness in a very small area. Mother Nature created there a lot of images—a stunning canyon with a rocky relief; one can find a plain and mountains, rich woods and ravines, majestic rocky tips of Mala Fatra's hills. A canyon called Tiesnavy with several waterfalls created by the river Varinka at the entrance of the valley is very impressive. Dolomite rocks created interesting figures called Rocky City, Monk, Camel, Five Waggoner's . . . Valley territory is bordered by a wreath of hills called Boboty, Velky Rozsutec, Stoh, Poludnovy Grun, Chleb, Velky Krivan, Kraviarske, Baraniarky and Sokolie.

The entire territory has an important place in Slovak culture because Juraj Janosik was born in Terchova in 1688. His figure, personality, idealized activity and kindness are depicted in the literature, songs and legends. His portrait as well became a central idea in folk graphic art and his idealized life has been made into movies many times. According to legends, the goods that Janosik robbed from the nobility all was given to the poor. Janosik's legend is well known in Poland and the Czech part of Czechoslovakia.

According to historical data, Janosik was enlisted in Habsburg's Royal Army between 1706 and 1708 and fought the Kurucs who were members of the armed uprising against Habsburg's Monarchy. In 1711 he became a leader of forest thugs, which robbed horse-drawn carriages of rich nobility during their journeys through wooded areas of northwest Slovakia. He was captured in the spring of 1713 and jailed in Liptovsky Mikulas. Following a two-day court, he was sentenced to death by hanging on a hook and was executed on March 18, 1713.

Every day we went out for a hike around the valley. It was July and the weather was really nice. Almost every day we had sunny weather; it rained very little. In those two weeks we crisscrossed our surroundings. During the day, it was hot; generally, we walked only in shorts and T-shirts. After sunset temperatures ran lower and shorts and T-shirts were no longer sufficient if we didn't want to shiver. In the evening, pants and sweaters or jackets were by far more comfortable. As city folk we did not know this phenomenon before. In the city there was warmth even after sunset because the "concrete jungle" held the warmth even at night. There was nothing to complain about; we were in the mountains and we adjusted quickly to the local weather.

Sunday morning, on our first day out hiking, we took the cable car from Vratna to the highest summit of Mala Fatra which is called Velky Krivan. The cable car brought us straight from Vratna, which is about 750 meters above ocean level, but not quite on top of Krivan, but only 1500 meters high. The rest of the way up to 1709 meters to the summit we had to hike. The weather was lovely; a cloudless sky and already the morning was hot. Being city folks, we planned the trip simply by riding the cable car up, then a hike to the summit, following a short walk on foot and then again by cable car down to Vratna, the entire time unaware of the local weather. Initially, everything went as planned. Early morning we came to the cable car, bought tickets and stood in line for our turn. Our tickets were round trip. We got in a cable car and, following a fifteen-minute ride up with exquisite views of our surroundings, got off and slowly hiked to the top of Krivan. We were at the highest summit and really fascinated by the panoramic views, we looked around at all the other peaks and mountains. We even walked a bit on the ridge. After a little walk we sat down for a little rest, taking a couple of pictures. It was comfortably warm; we were wearing only shorts and T-shirts. A few minutes later, while sitting down, we noticed gigantic clouds, which ran directly over us. I looked around and said:

"I guess we should go back down. I do not like those clouds."

No one argued with me and we immediately started descending to the cable-car station. The temperature sank very quickly and we started to get cold. We walked even quicker still, and when we arrived at the station, there was a heap of people. We were lucky to get inside the station building as the cable car was already stopped due to the danger of being struck by lightning. Nobody was able to descend so we just watched a quickly approaching storm. Suddenly we noticed the first lightning, how it struck the summit. We were really scared because only a half hour ago we were up there. It started raining along with the first roar of thunder and the storm lasted about half an hour. We were lucky to be inside because otherwise we have been completely wet. The cable car was still down; consequently, more and more people accumulated inside the station. Many of them did not make it inside and stayed outside trying to hide from the rain. The temperature even inside the building dropped quickly and it was obvious that we were inexperienced people from the city because all around us people put on sweaters and jackets they pulled from their backpacks. Only we were shivering and at the same time wrapped around each other trying so hard to stay warm. The storm ended as quickly as it had begun and the cable car was again in operation. In a couple of minutes, our turn came to board the car and in another fifteen minutes we were back down in Vratna. It was 2:00 pm, the storm was completely gone and we were comfortably warm again even though we still had only shorts and T-shirts on. As was originally our plan, we went to dinner at a local restaurant. Ever since this experience, we have always carried backpacks with warm clothing like all the other people. Just in case we ever needed them. However, we never needed them again on that vacation. Tuesday morning the sky was cloudy when we got up. After breakfast we came back into our room and from our window observed sheep on the opposite hill. They grazed on the hillside that served for skiing in winter. The ski-lift was at the edge of a hillside by the forest. We waited for the weather to change as it looked like a storm would start any minute now. In a little while lightning and thunder started. Everything turned dark, but only an infrequent flash followed by thunder lit up the valley. We watched from our window how the heavy rain poured from the sky and drummed on everything around, creating a loud noise. It all lasted only about twenty minutes, then the flashes and thunder ceased. The rain stopped like someone had turned off a faucet. A few minutes later the sky cleared again and the July Sun let us feel its power yet again. Nature looked washed clean and it appeared to us that the flock of sheep peacefully continued grazing the adjacent slope which was nicely washed into a cleaner white.

After those two rainy occasions the weather improved, and till the end of our stay, it was typical July weather—very hot. Despite the hot temperatures, we continued carrying our backpacks with us every day. We also continued looking at our map and planning hikes for the following days. As usual, our vacation ended too soon and, on Saturday two weeks later, we went home.

A month went by since Mr. Kolesar and I had had our detailed talk and I had written everything down about the ridiculous circus of paperwork, and often I thought of the begging for permission to travel. Heeding his advice for getting the Foreign Allowance from the Exchange Bank, I started systematically looking for family members and friends who might be working at the Exchange Bank. I had plenty of time till January, but I did not want to leave the matter for the last minute. First I made a list of my uncles and aunts, including their children, my cousins. At that time I had three uncles, five aunts and nineteen cousins. I knew them very well and was aware what kind of school they were graduated from and where they worked. Next to their names I wrote down their occupation, which sped up the process. For instance, if someone was a doctor or a bus driver, he most likely would not be working for the Exchange Bank. I glanced at my list from top to bottom and from the bottom up and found out what I had instinctively known before. No one had anything in common with the Exchange Bank. I was looking at my list with sadness and then I realized that thirteen of my cousins had been married. With a lot of joy, I wrote down the names of their spouses and my list grew by an additional thirteen chances to find someone.

However, this part of my detective work was much harder because, as we were growing up and starting our families, contacts with my cousins became less frequent. I found out with shame on my part that I did not know this part of my family so well. I had to figure out one by one what I needed, their occupation. I thought about calling my cousins and finding out. Somehow it would bring the discussion to my subject of interest. As soon as I finished thinking about it, I abandoned this plan because calling most of my cousins in a short time I had felt would be very suspicious to anyone. Suspicion had no place in my big plan. I came up with a different approach involving a coincidence very carefully prepared and planned in advance. When I talked to a chosen person, I incidentally brought our conversation to the object of my interest; for instance, I "ran into" a classmate when shopping:

"I think you live in the same building as my cousin Marian. It is unbelievable how fast time goes by! I feel like it was just a few days ago when we rode our bikes on the riverbank. We have not seen each other for years and now he has three kids. His baby son Peter is one year old and his wife Terka is going back to work. It is a big advantage she could come back to work at her building company," I nostalgically mentioned "old good times" to my classmate.

"She has never worked for a building company. Terka has always worked for a grocery market," my classmate corrected me.

"Oh . . . yes, of course you are right. She has always worked for a grocery market," I said and crossed out one of my detective cases. However, I was really surprised how much information people knew about each other when they lived in the same building. That was scary . . . . It took me ten weeks just to check out everyone on my family list and I found out with a lot of sadness that finding a family member in a bank was completely out of the question.

My next step was to start working on my classmates. It was quite obvious that the detective work I employed for my family would not be applicable for classmates. Too many classmates, so little time! I came up with a quite different method. Rather than writing anything down, I systematically organized a plan in my head to think about classmates one by one. To do that I used all the free time available to me, like sitting at a boring meeting, driving in the car, eating my lunch or traveling by train. It was unbelievable how much time I could find this way! I immediately excluded classmates from university because they were all chemists. Not one of them worked in the Exchange Bank. Using my free time, I gradually went from A to Z for the whole graduating high school class to no avail. The situation was becoming hopeless, but I refused to give up.

The following Monday I was sitting at a meeting with my boss, Comrade Flak and my comrade colleagues. Comrade Bok, the manager of the investment department was talking about his work. I thought it was going to be just another boring day. I was in my distant little world thinking about a way to find someone who worked in the Exchange Bank when Comrade Bok attracted my attention:

". . . and they send us from the Investment bank into the Exchange Bank to see Ms. Modrakova . . ."

That sentence was like lightning from a blue sky. Ms. Modrakova was Maria Modrakova, my classmate from driving school. All of a sudden, I realized that Maria Modrakova was in the same class of driving school and I had completely forgotten about her. She still had the same last name . . . maybe she had not gotten married . . . maybe she just kept her maiden name . . . in any case I had finally found the human being I had been looking for. I did not write her name down; only subconsciously and now consciously I have it written inside of me. I did not react in any way or let anyone know around me that they had just reminded me of something that would completely change my life. I could hardly wait for the conclusion of that meeting and, once over, I rushed back to my office. I took out the phone book and found a number for the Exchange Bank and dialed it without hesitation:

"Good morning . . . Exchange bank," I heard from the phone operator.

"Ms. Modrakova, please," I asked very respectfully.

"Good morning. Secretary of Investment Exchange," said someone who appeared to be Maria's secretary. I was so glad no one could see me because my eyes almost popped out of my head. When I met Maria years ago she was a very modest and nice girl. I could not imagine that the next time I would be talking to her she would be a director of the investment exchange branch of a major bank. I quickly kicked up all my acting reserves and in a calm voice indicating no urgency I said:

"Good morning, this is Jan Bielek. Could I talk to Maria for a moment?"

My personal approach confused the secretary quite a bit and she just said:

"Just a moment, please," and the phone was quiet. I knew she did not hang up on me, there would be a busy signal. Those few seconds the phone was quiet seemed like an eternity. I did not know what to say when Maria picked up the phone. I covered my mouth and softly coughed and got ready to talk about anything with my calm low voice.

"Hi, Jan," Maria said with a voice indicating that my struggle finding someone I knew in the Exchange Bank was over and I had won.

"Hi, Maria," I said and, despite my deep voice, I had a hard time to hiding my excitement about talking to her.

"My colleague Bok from our investment department just mentioned your name to me," I started our dialogue on the wrong leg.

"Yes, he was here yesterday together with another guy named Blaz," said Maria a little bit officially and with disappointment.

"I am sorry, I am not calling you because of business," I said and then continued:

"I am calling you because Bok mentioned your name and it reminded me of when we were in driving school and you talked enthusiastically about working in a bank. No one from my company is aware of this phone call. I just wondered how you have been . . . I was really surprised you still have the same last name."

"I got married five years ago but I kept my maiden name. My husband's name is David and I also have a three-year-old son, Jacob. You should see my family picture!" Maria said with a voice that wasn't official anymore. We talked a few more minutes before she said:

"I would gladly talk to you more, but I have a meeting to go to. Come see me in the bank when you have time and you're going by. But call me first, so we can plan a small meeting."

"I will call you and we have to get together so that we can catch up a little more about things we couldn't today," I said at the end of our phone call.

I stopped at the bank many times, and every time it was a pleasant meeting. Maria mostly talked about her family and showed me her newest family pictures.

Saturday 24 September 1983

It was a Saturday night, the kids slept and it was raining. As usual, the TV program was not worth watching. Nora and I sat in our living room lighted by the aquarium in the corner. We poured our favorite red wine, lifted our glasses and clinked:

"To our victory" as we got used to saying in the last few months.

The two-week vacation in Vratna was over and a new school year started on September first. The year was slowly but surely coming to the end and it was time to intensively start working on the following Orwell's year 1984. I strongly believed that a year later we were going to be somewhere else. Nora still subconsciously believed we would not be successful in the complicated system of applications, permissions, approvals, signatures and rubber stamps. As Mr. Kolesar said a while ago:

". . . if only one single person from the crowd of people that will be around when they are going to sign and rubber stamp your application at any level shakes his head side to side instead of up and down you are going to shit and there will be no Italy . . ."

I tried my best to continue according to advice that was given by my father a long time ago:

"When you are looking at a forest from a distance, it seems to be thick and solid. But when you come closer, you realize there is a lot of space between the trees. If you try to run ahead in a straight line, you will hit a tree very soon. However, if you are aware of every single tree ahead of you, all you need to do is deflect a little bit from a straight line and you run through the forest in a very short time because you are running in almost a straight line."

Already a long time ago, I thought it would be wise to sell some items from our apartment. This would not only give us more money to leave with, but also less stuff to leave behind. I felt a little sorry about it; some things only hold value for their original owner. Fortunately, communism created a society with a chronic shortage of goods and therefore the value loss was not so catastrophic. I could see very often that some articles were worth more money on the black market than when they were brand new. The shortage of goods created a situation where people had a huge amount of cash on hand and carried the cash with them. If they found some articles they had been looking for a long time, they had to buy them immediately. There was no time for thought or hesitation; everything had to be thought out before they "discovered" the wanted article. The whole situation was so complicated that so many times we had to have a family member or at least a friend among the store clerks just to be able to get anything new. Free market did not exist, so people made their own with used goods.

"We should start selling some articles from this apartment that we are not going to need anymore," I said shortly after we clinked our glasses.

"What do you mean exactly?" Nora asked very pragmatically.

"Of course only such items that are not obvious when someone enters the apartment and cannot see them; for instance, the moped which will be sitting in the basement until the next spring will not be obviously missed by anyone. Or the Black & Decker drill with all the attachments I bought so far," I said and felt a sharp pain in my chest because it was a complete set I had been putting gradually together for some time. Some of those parts I received as presents for birthdays; others were Christmas presents. It took me years to complete the set.

"The drill?," asked Nora with irony in her voice and then she added:

"What are you going to say when a family member asks you to fix or drill something? It is going to be suspicious to everyone."

"I would not be afraid at all of being suspicious. We can say we have sold it because now there is a new and bigger model on the market and we want to buy it. Do you know what your mother will say when she learns about it?" I asked.

". . . Jan needs a new drill AGAIN . . . ," Nora spit out really quickly.

"That's right . . . do not worry . . . ," I said and added to her answer:

"So, any of those things we are selling due to a purchase of a new model, we just have to say so in agreement. We have to inform our kids about it. They will be the first ones to see something being sold. We have to include them in our plan.

"Which plan is on your mind?" Nora asked with suspicion.

"Look," I said and added:

"We tell them that we are selling those things because we want to buy new ones. And also advise them not to discuss the matter with anyone else. Only in case someone should ask them and even in then just say as little as needed. If someone starts asking persistently, just advise the person to come to us. At least we are going to know who is "sniffing" around . . .

"I am getting an impression that your plan is getting quite devilish," Nora said with sarcasm.

"I am glad you noticed," I said with satisfaction and added:

"I guess you know me. When I start something it is worth every penny."

". . . just because I know you . . ." Nora said.

In the meantime, we both finished our first glass of wine and I poured another one and we clinked glasses with the traditional:

"To our victory," and continued:

"Now we should make a list of items we are going to sell. Not on paper, just in our minds. It wouldn't be Ok if a list like that gets into the wrong hands.

"So, start with the list," Nora encouraged me.

"I would start with items we would not sell under any circumstances. It is everything anyone can see after entering the apartment."

"Furniture, carpets, refrigerator . . . ," Nora started the list.

". . . and also glasses, plates and others on display in furniture shelves or behind glass doors. But everything that is behind solid doors we can include in our list," I added to her list.

"No clothing," Nora said.

"No clothing. But we have some fur coats which we are going to need for the following winter and no one will buy them in the spring. Either we sell them now or after this winter we will forget about them like a lot of other things," I added.

"We cannot sell the fur coats because it would be suspicious to everyone. We can wear them just like we did any other winter and after winter is over I will bring them to the cleaners for summer storage. Shortly before we cross the borders, I will mail the receipts to my brother's wife Anka. By the time she gets the receipts, we are going to be far away and she can pick them up," Nora said and looked at me with a big smile.

"Do you think they will give them to her?" I asked

"Of course they will give them to her. Nobody checks who brings the receipt. The rule is "you have the receipt, you get the stuff." And besides that you are aware she and I get confused very often. When I ask her to pick up Katarina from kindergarten, teachers give her to Anka because they think it is me.

"What a pity it doesn't work that way in the family too," I said with a lot of sadness in my voice. Nora did not say anything, she picked up a pillow from the sofa and hit my head with it with full force. I pretended nothing happened and continued:

"I have a feeling that devilish planning is contagious," I said, hugging her with my both arms and kissing her.

"So now let's make a list of things we are going to sell. It is our "invisible furnishing," I said and started with the list:

"Moped, Black & Decker drill with all the accessories, the second film camera, typewriter, sewing machine, aquarium . . . ," at which I stopped. It wasn't just the aquarium, but also the stand, electronic heaters, lights, filtering system with electronic heating for filling the aquarium with water at the right temperature and so on . . . Every piece was made either with my own hands or made by someone else following my design. It was my hobby and I enjoyed doing it. Still, the system had not been finished to my latest imagination.

"Aquarium? It is the first thing you see when you enter our living room," Nora said and then added:

"How are you going to explain it is gone? No one will believe you are in the process of making another bigger one."

"No, I am not planning another one. Since I have been a department manager, I do not have enough time for it and the aquarium is turning ugly. I do not have time to finish everything I have planned. Besides that, you are planning to buy a cabinet for our crystal glasses and put it in the aquarium's spot," I said with confidence.

"That sounds really reasonable. I guess you have an answer for everything," Nora said.

"That's what I call "the right-play directing." You've got to have an immediate answer to everything, but you have to play it just right. Do not rush with an answer; speak calmly as if you are just saying it incidentally. Just like I am doing it now. An answer played this way is trustworthy," I tried to play trustworthy.

Nora softly coughed, made a trustworthy face and imitating my voice started:

"Ever since he became a department manager, he doesn't have time for his aquarium . . . ," Nora did not finish the sentence and both of us started laughing.

"That was perfect . . . but without the laugher at the end," I said honoring her endeavor to play trustworthy. She continued in the same voice:

". . . yes, Mr. Movie Director, without the laughter at the end . . ."

In the course of a few months, we easily sold all our "invisible" furnishings. The solvency of all the buyers and their hunger for black-market goods worked in our favor. We were completely surprised that we did not miss anything and went on comfortably with our life. We received such a huge amount of cash that originally we did not know what to do with it. We used the cash for paying off all our loans from the banks, so they would not be transferred to our co-signers. They would swear at us for the rest of their lives if confronted with paying off our loans. They were our friends and our conscience would not allow us to leave them with such an ugly disappointment.

The end of the year 1983 slowly approached and with it also our last Christmas and New Year's Eve, party in Czechoslovakia. In this manner our pleasure of the holidays and the good feeling for a happy and successful year was blended with the feeling of sorrow, that this was the last in the region, the only one we knew as our home. On the other hand, I was charmed with the uncertainties of the future, which was for us "in the stars" and on which we would have to work hard. I was not afraid of the difficulties that we might encounter abroad. It was already a better alternative than to let someone else control your life and at the same time throw away all your dreams, pride and freedom of thinking, as well as being. Every time I recalled how the communists manipulated my entire life, my yearning to go away and never return increased.

The endeavor to get out of there was a result of the long-term process, which started August 21, 1968. Our early morning was disrupted by the presence of army tanks in the city streets and, in the first moment, we did not know what it all meant. Then I remembered that by about two after midnight I was awakened by a noise in the streets, which was quite reminiscent of army tanks. I stared into the darkness and at the same time thought what kind of stupid idea it was from our army.

"As if they could not plan army training exercises somewhere outside and not in the center of the town," I thought. About half an hour later, the noise ceased a bit and I fell asleep again. It did not occur to me to look out a window because my room had windows facing the back yard. My father and mother had windows from their bedroom into the streets, but somehow I didn't want to go through their bedroom and disturb them in their sleep in the middle of the night. Neither had I imagined that they did not sleep for a long time and also did not understand, what in fact was going on. At about six in the morning, I was awakened by a radio that was on in the kitchen. It was strange to me why my parents would be listening to the radio so early. They had never done it before. Through the wall I could not understand what the speaker had been saying, but by the tone of his voice, I recognized that his speech was full of emotions. I got up from my bed and walked over to the kitchen where mother and father were sitting in their pajamas at the table, smoking. They sat there quite noiselessly; my father had a very sad expression on his face and my mother quietly wept. The dense smoke in the kitchen, which could be cut with a knife, was blended with the emotional voice from the radio, which served exact information about the movement of the Soviet Army on the Czechoslovak territory. I looked apprehensively at my father, and after a few moments, he said:

"The Soviet Army has occupied our country . . ."

"Soviet Army?" I asked with a lack of understanding and immediately raised a question:

"Why? This country has been a part of the Soviet block since 1945."

"Russians did not like what's been done by Dubcek, so they have come to make orders of their own," my father responded.

"They did not have to use the army to achieve that. Indeed, they have another two thousand KGB agents in Prague who are called advisers. They could have quietly "taken care" of Dubcek in the manner they had used on other people till now," I added pragmatically, because I knew the situation in the country well.

"Apparently they could not . . ." father said and then added:

"The situation in this country was slowly slipping out of their hands, so they sent their army."

"And what was the Czechoslovakian Army doing when the Soviet Army just took over our territory. How is it possible that they don't fight against the aggression of foreign forces?" I asked with logic which was allowed by my age—seventeen years old.

"Our army got an order from Prague not to combat the soviets. Allegedly it is too small to rise into battle with the Soviets," Father repeated very quietly what I had heard on the radio many times before, but in a more emotional execution.

"The Czechoslovak army did not fight in 1939 when Hitler sent the Wehrmacht into the still free and sovereign country. Likewise, it capitulated without fighting. Then what do we have this army for when it never fights?" I asked with my seventeen-year-old logic.

"I have already told you before that it is impossible to fight against such predominance. Not against Russians, not against Germans," he said self possessed.

"Yes it is possible. If someone gives up without a fight, he loses completely. When he starts fighting, there is always a chance he may win. If someone really wants to fight and he puts everything into it, he has already won half the battle. And last but not least, sometimes it is better to die standing up than to live life on your knees," I said.

My last sentence really made a huge impact on my father. He threw his cigarette into the ashtray, jumped off the chair and started yelling at me at the top of his lungs:

"Now listen to me really carefully . . . I forbid you to get involved in this problem . . . and you are grounded for the whole next week. I will not allow you to sacrifice your life."

Mother started crying much more and this time it wasn't a quiet weep. She repeated a single sentence over and over:

"My little Janny, I do not want you to die . . . My little Janny, I do not want you to die . . ."

After that very unexpected reaction of my parents to anything I said, I realized further discussion did not stand a chance and I went back to my room. I lay back on my bed and stared at the ceiling. Two sentences roared in my head like a needle stuck in a groove:

"What kind of country is this? . . . Why do they always give up without a fight . . . What kind of country is this? . . . Why do they always give up without a fight . . . ?"

The second part of my emigration thinking was my "English Experience," which was a stay in Great Britain from June to August 1969. I traveled there based on a government treaty of a student exchange between Great Britain and Czechoslovakia. During the stay, we were accommodated in an international student camp where we worked during the day picking fruits and vegetables on a farm and, at night we had English courses. Among others there were students from France, Germany, Belgium, Holland and other European countries, as well as black students from Uganda or Arab students from Egypt. With the money we made picking strawberries, gooseberries, pears or apples we paid for our room and food at the camp. It wasn't luxury accommodations by any means and fully reflected the level of our income. The food was typical English and it did not compare with my Slovak menu at all. I ate very little, and within three months of being in Britain, I lost 10 kilograms (22 pounds). When my mom saw me for the first time after coming back home, she folded her arms into a prayer and started to cry. A few moments later, she decided to fatten me up to my original weight. My reasoning with her that my travel to England was for study purposes and not for increasing my body weight was completely pointless. I was very grateful for the opportunity to stay in England for three months despite the fact that my income was just enough to cover my accommodations and food. My parents would not be able to afford my stay in Great Britain from their income.

On top of studying English, I had an opportunity to meet students from different corners of the world and realize through my own experience that most of them were the same kind of human as myself, without any bearing on the language they spoke or the color of their skin. Thanks to a common language we were just learning, we spoke to each other about our home, parents, customs and religion. So many times, we got carried away by our discussions that we did not realize it was already one after midnight. We got up at five and after breakfast we started picking fruits at the farm at six.

Our British hosts were very nice to us. The students from Czechoslovakia, especially, held an unusual interest for them because what had happened in August 1968 to our country was still fresh in their memory. When we told anyone we were Czechoslovak, in abbreviation Czech, they were ready to help us do almost anything. Many Brits asked me directly whether I was going back home or staying in Britain. They also explained what kind of studying opportunities were available to me or how they would help if I decided to stay. My emigration thinking had not ripened yet because, despite many tempting offers of help, I went back home in August.

It did not take long till I realized I should have listened to my British hosts. The situation in Czechoslovakia worsened every day, thanks to the Soviet pressure and native collaborates. Only then when I was looking at the situation at home from a historical perspective did I realize how the situation was getting better and we could "breathe easier" at the beginning of the sixties. It was quite evident in the culture, politics, traveling and even everyday life. When Dubcek came in January 1968 and started his "program of reforms," it was in reality the end of "breathing easier." Soviet invasion and the following "sovietization" of everything around us killed the last hope for a better life ever.

Somehow, I rather felt than knew I would not stay in the country. However, it took a long time until my emigration thinking ripened completely. It happened in May 1983 when the communists directly affected my life and "machinated" my position at the ICI Company. Then I decided that against all odds I would not stay there and remembered the words I had said to my father right after the Soviet invasion:

"Rather die standing up, than live on my knees!"

Just shortly before Christmas, I went to see Maria at the Exchange Bank. I was just going by and the Christmas spirit was felt everywhere. So I bought her a small present. It was a very enjoyable visit, we talked about hearsays in our families and I also remembered bringing the latest pictures of my family.

She showed me her most recent Christmas card with a picture of her family that she had already mailed a hundred of to everyone in the family and to all friends . . . I was going to receive mine in a couple of days.

I hesitated if I should ask her about my "Foreign Allowance" or should just leave it for the next time. Finally, I got some courage and asked her:

"I hate to bother you, but I just remembered, if it isn't a big nuisance for you to help me get the "Foreign Allowance."

"Not at all. When you stop by next time, just bring your filled application to me and it is done," she said and winked at me with her right eye.

"It is done . . ." I heard repeating inside my head and I was really happy.

Regardless of my solid decision to leave the country, the closer it came to the end of the year the more emotionally I looked at everything around me. Every family member, every matter and episode would subconsciously call a single scheme:

"This is the last time . . . I will not even have a chance to say Goodbye."

I knew it would pass right after the New Year as I got more strength and enthusiasm for achieving more than last year. Now I needed to pick up my pieces and find a motive to move me forward and turn down my emotions. I felt it had to be something rational and solid. I was sitting in the living room and overheard a fairy tale Katarina was listening to from a tape. It was about a little girl that was trying to escape from a frozen country running via a high ice bridge. A good fairy was helping the little girl by encouraging her:

"Just don't look down because you will slip and fall back."

In that moment it came to me:

"Just don't turn around, keep going forward; otherwise, you will fall back."

It was exactly what I needed to balance my spiritual stability in the most difficult situations. From that moment I would silently say to myself:

"Just don't turn around . . ." and was able to overcome almost anything on my way to the world.

Chapter Two

Time to Get Serious

Wednesday February 8, 1984

I came home from work and after opening the door found Nora standing behind it with a finger on her lips, indicating to me to keep silent and she was showing me a letter from the Exchange Bank. The children were in their room with the door wide open and that's why she did not want to attract their attention. I looked at Peter and Katarina playing in their room and then calmly and quietly asked:

"Did we . . . ?"

"Yes," Nora said and I asked:

"How much?"

"Six hundred," Nora said and it was quite obvious she had a hard time hiding her excitement. I just added very quietly:

"Put it on the refrigerator in the kitchen and we can look at it in more detail later on."

We could hardly wait till we finished eating dinner and the kids went to bed. We wanted them to be saved from the details, because when they did not know anything, they could tell it to nobody. A few months ago, we had made a decision to do everything so they would know the least till the last moments. They were too small to be able to understand the complexity of life in these given circumstances, and if our plan came out OK, we would need not trouble them with explaining and telling them what they could say and where. At about nine in the evening when we were sure that the kids were asleep, we again sat down in the living room. We turned on Tchaikovsky with the speaker turned at the wall behind us so snoops could not hear our conversation. We both read closely the letter which stated that the Exchange Bank decided to allot 600 dollars to us for the purpose of traveling to the west in the calendar year 1984. Two hundred dollars would be paid to us in cash and an additional four hundred in American Express traveler's checks. Before leaving, we had to pick up the dollars at the Exchange Bank after paying a money order to the bank for 24,600 Czechoslovak crowns. For that time it was a decent amount of money, but fortunately for us, it wasn't a problem because just recently we had sold the "invisible" furnishings from our apartment.

"It seems my plan is slowly taking off and now let's get going," I said, invigorated by the first achievement.

"Do you have any time schedule? I mean what you will be doing and when," Nora asked.

"Roughly, however the details still had to be thought out at every step. Above all, I must be ready with all alternatives," I noted pensively.

"I thought you had only one alternative," Nora noted.

"Of course, with reference to leaving from here, I have only one alternative. I am working on a trip to Italy, but when we come to Vienna, we are not going any further," I said and then added:

"When talking about alternatives, I am referring to looking out for all the "gimmicks" anybody might make up and somehow precluding them."

"Such as what?" Nora asked with interest.

"Such as . . . I've heard that sometimes people, out of jealousy, will try to ruin, or completely prevent someone from traveling, so they call customs and say that the Bielek's want to escape from the country . . . Customs officers at the border will take all our papers and send us back home . . . ," I said.

"Customs officers do not verify anything? How can they know that the one calling is telling the truth?" Nora poured out.

"Look, customs officers will not bother with verifying anything. In addition, the call from the envious people can be anonymous. For them the simplest thing to do is send us home and take no chances that one day somebody will accuse them of neglecting their duties," I explained.

"But how do you prevent that?" Nora asked and immediately responded resignedly:

"There is no way of preventing that!"

"Of course it can be done, only I must prevent a possible caller from calling my play," I responded with a smile.

Nora tipped toward me, looked straight into my eyes and inquired with interest and a little bit of irony:

"Yeah? How?"

"All right," I said and glimpsed at the door to make sure that the kids did not wake up in the meantime. Then I stood up, added a bit of volume to Tchaikovsky because they had just played a quiet passage of the symphony and quietly said:

"We will never talk to anybody over which border we are crossing into Austria. Everybody knows that we live in Petrzalka, around three kilometers (two miles) from the nearest border, but we are not going to use it. For safety's sake."

"So which way?" Nora asked.

"So far I am planning to cross over by Znojmo," I said.

"But it will look strange to the customs officers. They will certainly be interested to know why we didn't go through over in Petrzalka," Nora said.

"It will be certainly their first question at which time I will have an answer in my passport even with a date stamp," I said with the certainty of someone who knows what he is talking about.

"Hmmm?" Nora opened her mouth with misunderstanding.

"All right, I am not going to stress you anymore, so here is the whole story," I said and then explained:

"It's a well-known fact that the Italian embassy in Prague loses applications for visas quite often and I want to use that to our benefit. I will purposely apply for our visas late, just in time to fit my plan. Accordingly, the time lapse between applying and receiving information from the embassy is about five weeks, so five weeks prior to our departure, I will take a few vacation days and go to Prague. I will apply for visas for all of us and then they will mail us a letter saying we can either mail our passports to them or pick up our visas at the embassy. When we get the letter we all take off to Prague and from there we make a short cut trough Znojmo into Austria. As you know, the first question of Czechoslovakian customs officers will be why we did not go through over in Petrzalka, because our address is printed in our passports. I will tell them that the Italian embassy lost our applications and we had to do it over again. So, we received our visas only yesterday and we are now taking a short cut through this crossover into Austria and it is much closer to Italy, rather than going all the way to Petrzalka," I explained and then asked:

"What is the customs officer going to do?" and immediately answered my own question:

"He will turn pages in the passports to the visa section and find that we have really received our Italian visas only the day before."

"And what if he calls the Italian embassy?" Nora asked.

"He will not for several reasons. First of all the rubber stamped date on our visas will tell him exactly what I have already told him. Secondly, if he does call them, what is he going to ask them? Whether it is true they lost our applications? Or when did we get our visas? Clerks at the embassy are not going to waste their time with him and he knows it," I said with much confidence.

Nora was quiet, thought for a little while if the plan had any flaws, and then she said:

"It seems to be a good plan."

I agreeably nodded my head and added:

"It is a good plan and it will work under one and only one condition. If no one ever knows which crossover we are going to use. This is just between you and me. If anybody asks about it, the answer is:

"Through Petrzalka. Well, we live just three kilometers from the crossover to Austria."

"Of course," Nora said and added:

"This is just between the two of us."

After so much whispering, our mouths went dry, so I poured red wine into two high glasses. Then I turned the LP with Tchaikovsky on the other side and after our traditional:

"To our victory", I continued whispering:

"We started our talk at the end. So let's go from the beginning. Tomorrow morning I will go to StB passport department and get applications for passports and Travel Provisions. After filling them out, we have to start running around for signatures and rubber stamps in order to be ready for traveling in July."

"Do you want to go in July?" Nora asked and then stated:

"I would like to go in the second half of August."

"Why?" I asked.

"I want to celebrate Peter's birthday here. Let the grandparents enjoy his company one last time," she explained and I said:

"I think it would be too much of a psychological burden. The whole family will be present, nobody will know anything, only two of us would be thinking about that occasion being the last one. We should try avoiding situations where big emotions are involved, because a very difficult test of our state of mind is still ahead of us. Anyway, it is too soon to set a firm date. For now let's say from the middle of July till the end of August. We are going only for ten days . . . we'll see how soon we are going to have our papers.

"During the weekend we should fill out the applications and Monday start running around for signatures and rubber stamps," I continued.

"What papers do I need," Nora asked.

"Exactly the same as I. The only difference is you are not an army reservist, so you do not need permission from the Regional Army Headquarters . . . One more detail. Children are not going to have their own passports because they are too small and only one of us can have them both listed in the passport. Usually mothers have their kids . . ."

". . . of course I agree," Nora said before I finished my sentence and then added:

"We should be filling out the applications during weekend nights. First, we should go out with them on weekends and then . . ."

". . . good idea . . . they should not see what we are doing," I finished her sentence this time.

The record with Tchaikovsky finished playing and we finished our glass of wine. It was time to go to bed . . .

Monday morning I went to the passport department to pick up forms for passport applications and Travel Provisions. I had to go to the regional passport department because everything was organized by regions and StB workers made sure we understood they were the masters of each situation. The forms were printed for particular regions and it was a waste of time trying something that we were not told to. I did not expect this "circus" (that's how I called it) would be simple. The Communists with a lot of help from StB created different categories of travel and they were all constantly afraid that most of the nation would leave the country, so they purposely made traveling abroad, especially traveling to the West, so complicated that most people just gave up before they got anywhere.

In the passport department, in a relatively small hallway, there was a huge number of people standing in triplets and the row snaked in every possible direction, filling the room to capacity. They all looked very tired and their faces told of the many, many hours that they had been standing there. I was looking around and trying to find the end of that line when someone spoke to me:

"Hi Jan, what are you doing here?"

I turned my head to where the voice was coming from in the crowd of people and found a classmate from high school. I was glad I had found someone I knew and could talk to for a few moments and maybe find out how that circus functioned. He was dressed up like he was going skiing. He was wearing a heavy sweater, a flannel shirt, and instead of regular pants, heavy gauge sweat pants. His feet were inside heavy winter boots and his top was covered by a substation winter jacket used for skiing at subzero temperatures. A sleeping bag and a backpack were lying next to his feet on the floor. He was holding a hiking water bottle and most likely the backpack was filled with food for the whole day.

"He must have slept outside in front of the building to be able to get in on time," ran through my head. I said to him:

"Hi Lubo," I am trying to find the forms for passport applications and Travel provisions. And you?"

"I am trying to hand in my completed application and I have been standing here since one in the morning," he said and then he kept on:

"You got something relatively simple. You will go to the end of this hallway and on the left side there is a little window. There you request forms for your application. It will be worse when you come back with them. Do you see those people around here? Those are the ones, who came to stand in a line before two in the morning," he patiently explained to me. I looked at the side where he showed me, it was actually the end of the line.

"At two in the morning?" I asked in disbelief:

"Well, it is one o'clock in the afternoon. That means that they have been standing here eleven hours and are they quite at the end?"

"That's what I am trying to explain to you. If someone comes here about two in the morning, he has no guarantee that he'll get in. The ones who come later have no chance," Lubo explained patiently.

"Accordingly, you have been here for twelve hours and still you have a mound of people in front of you. Do you have a prospect at all that today you will get in?" I asked with interest.

"Of course, right now they open the office after lunch break and around three o'clock I should be inside with my applications. Remember, the sooner you come here, the sooner you will get in the office," he added yet.

"And where in fact are you traveling?" I asked.

"I'd like to go with my wife and kids to Paris," he responded quite composedly and I was thinking that if I should lower myself this way every time when I wanted to travel, I would rather go to hell. Only once in my lifetime I was willing to undergo all that misery making sure that I was doing this for the last time as well. I looked back and it seemed to me almost impossible that somebody would be able to enslave hundreds of the people in this manner, submissively standing there like a flock of sheep and patiently waiting for their turn, to get into the office and an StB worker to check their applications. Lubo observed me and then, as if he read my thoughts, he added:

"I entirely understand your shock, but believe me, after some time you get accustomed to it. When you come here the third time, it will not affect you so much."

I looked at him and said:

"So, then we will meet here again and compare our experiences."

Following a short "Bye-Bye" I left him and went to the end of the hallway, approached the small window and asked for application forms. Behind the small window was sitting a very unsympathetic StB worker. Politely, like my mother always taught me, I said:

"Good Morning. Two forms for a passport and provision to the passport." The worker looked at me and without greeting me he said in incorrect Slovak:

"Citizen ID . . ." I passed him my ID book and he asked:

"Name?"

That trick had been already known to me. He was not curious about my name; it had been written inside of my identity book. He tested me, if I was going to include my title "engineer" in my name, just like it was written in my identity book and routinely used in day-to-day life. I knew that if I wanted to come out amicably with this type of government officer, I must never mention it. Those guys were all very simple; largely they had not graduated from the ninth grade of primary school and they became very touchy when someone had an academic degree. Even so, they were always sovereign masters of every situation; they suffered from a deficient education and inclusion titles like Ing., Dr. or Prof. in someone's work title irritated them like a red flag at a bull in an arena. Knowing the game I said:

"Bielek, Jan," whereupon he scrutinized me and then the photo in my identity book, in order to make sure it was really me. Afterwards, he started browsing through and again asked:

"Address?"

I told him our address and he compared it with what was written in my identity book. Afterwards he still browsed through for a moment but did not question anything else. Apparently he had already verified that I was the one pictured in the book and not a secret agent of some capitalist country. After a few moments, he placed two forms in the little window, on top he put my ID book and in an impersonal voice and in incorrect Slovak he ordered:

"Next!"

I took my hard-earned pile of blank forms and ID book and still politely thanked him. He did not answer. Good manners apparently were not his strong suit, although they requested good manners from their slaves, us the ordinary people.

I came out from the building and still could not believe what I had seen inside that building. That was waiting for me after my application was signed by the company and army headquarters! I took a deep breath of cold February air. The hand came to my mind which Mr. Kolesar was holding in front of my face with his five fingers spread out and I said quietly just to myself:

"Now, let's get going"

Waiting lines in the hallways and in front of StB buildings were the largest ones I had ever seen. Average waiting time was between twelve to fourteen hours. Passport office hours were 8:00 to 12:00 am and 1:00 to 4:00 pm. The waiting line in front of the building started forming long before midnight, and when someone came there after 2:00 am, he had almost no chance of getting inside the passport office of the almighty officer that day. When the almighty opened the entrance door shortly before eight o'clock in the morning, only then did people come out of blankets and sleeping bags and slowly enter the building. They slept outside on the sidewalk just to get permission to travel. The almighty just eyeballed the crowd, and when he estimated it was enough for him that particular day, he just stuck his arm into the crowd and said:

"Everyone from here till the end of the line can go home."

And people tilted their head with sadness and without a word of protest went home. They knew any sign of protest or just a question would be brutally punished. The lowest sentence would be "black list of passports" which meant a lifetime denial of a passport. The top sentence, as usual was death. StB workers were armed and they did not hesitate to use their guns. Their brutality was very well known and I have never heard about a citizen winning his argument with StB. However, many times I heard about those who lost their argument. They were all dead.

I was thinking on my way to the car:

"I have to go through all that misery of long waiting as well. Fortunately, by the time I got all the signatures and rubber stamps it was going to be June. I will not have to wait outside in freezing temperatures like my friend Lubo. By that time, it should be comfortably nice and warm. I hope . . ."

I jumped into the car and hurried to work. The lunch break was already over. When I walked inside our building, I was welcomed by Mr. Kolesar:

"Jan, did you get your foreign allowance from the bank?"

"Yes, as a matter of fact, I did," I said and added:

"I just came back from the passport department with forms. When I look at all those pages, I can hardly believe we will travel anywhere this year.

"It is only the beginning of February. You've got plenty of time till summer. I think you'll get it all done by then. Fill them up very soon and start with signatures here," he encouraged me.

When Nora and I took a look at all those long pages, we decided not to wait until the weekend to start filling them out. The following few nights after the kids were already asleep, we would fill out the passport and Travel Provision applications. Every form had four pages with columns and rows for writing in personal information. It was so much information that for a few moments we could not believe everything that was needed just to travel. The filling out was very slow because we had to be careful not to make a mistake. Nothing could be crossed out, corrected, erased or covered with corrective fluid. When the StB workers found a mistake or the application was messy, they yelled at the person and threw him out. That was their famous approach . . . The whole process had to start from the very beginning, begging for a form at the little window at the end of the hallway.

"I am glad they do not need my shoe size on this application," I vented my frustration with a sarcastic remark and we both started laughing. After a moment of laughter, we relaxed, clicked our wine glasses "To our victory" and continued filling out the forms. Wednesday night we had everything done and Thursday morning we took the forms to work for signatures and rubber stamps.

First thing in the morning, I went to the company ROH committee. I knocked on the door and heard a secretary's voice from inside:

"Come in."

I went in and after saying "Good Morning," I laid the application in front of her on the desk. The secretary looked at it, lifted her head and looked me straight in the eyes:

"Mr. Bielek, so . . . you want to travel to Italy."

"Yes, I would like to take my wife and children for a vacation," I said making sure I employed my calm and balanced voice. She stared at me for a moment and said:

"ROH committee has a planned meeting two weeks from next Monday. I will pass your application to the chairman of the committee and she will sign it after approval from the committee.

The chairman's door was cracked opened and I looked at it and noticed the boss sitting at her table and reading a newspaper.

"She is preparing a discussion entry for her committee," I thought but did not say a word. When we made eye contact, she got up and came to me. Before she had a chance to say anything I said:

"Good morning."

She completely ignored my greeting, shook my hand and said:

"Honor Work, comrade engineer."

"Honor Work, comrade chairman," I responded to her greeting and as it was custom for a real communist shook her hand. Afterwards I asked a bit less officially:

"How are you?"

"Very well," she answered quickly and asked me:

"And you?"

"Thank you, I am fine," I said and asked her:

Would you be so kind and let me know when my application will be ready to pick up?"

"I will call you," she said and I thanked her again:

"Thank you. Honor Work!" and went back to my office. During my walk to my office, I was thinking how quickly I had switched my greeting to "Honor Work" and also how long the whole process of signing would take if just the ROH needs over two weeks for one signature and rubber stamp. And more or less from that moment, my application would be "chewed over" at a meeting of the company committee; every employee would know that my family wants to go on vacation to Italy. I remembered how Mr. Kolesar told me, if only one single person turns his head differently, we are going to . . .

"We'll see," I said to myself and was ready to come up with a solution if that was to happen. For now, the only thing I could do was calmly wait. However, I was quite sure that shaking hands with the ROH chairman and the comrade's greeting "Honor Work" made a very good impression.

Saturday immediately after lunch we all went for a walk on the promenade by the Danube River. The weather was picture-perfect just like from a brochure: blue sky and warm sunny day. We walked on the sidewalk against the flow of the river and I remembered it was a beautiful day such as this on our wedding day, almost exactly nine years ago. The restaurant called Fishermen's Guild was only a short distance from us on the right side. Above us, high on the top of the hill was Bratislava's Castle and down under the castle was the Fishermen's Guild in which our wedding party was held. Nora apparently thought about the same thing I did. We walked side by side and held hands. Peter and Katarina ran in front of us like little kids and for a few moments we were walking in this manner silently. She too looked at that side and then our eyes met and she said:

"Do you remember? It's been already nine years . . . I can hardly believe how fast the time flies."

"I do remember," I said and then added a little philosophically:

"Sometimes it seems that time flies just like water in a river. You don't stop water or time."

We kept walking against the flow of the Danube, which was very low as usual this time of year. The waters of the Danube are supplied mostly from melted snow from the Alps and it was still freezing there. On our left side there were about three-foot-high concrete walls, which bordered the rocky bank of the river at the level of the sidewalk. The walls served as flood protection, when the Danube was high, and they were about eighteen inches wide and on top of them they had a little slanting concrete shelter. Many children with pleasure ran on the top of the walls while parents held them by the hand. Very often a child let the parent's hand go and kept running on the wall. The parent then apprehensively started running beside the wall trying to catch a fly-away, because from this side there was a sidewalk, but from the other side there was a very steep rocky cliff, and then only water. The falling of a child down on the rocks was very dangerous and falling in waters was almost certain death by drowning because the river flowed too fast and additionally it was about one third of a mile wide. Fortunately, about every 150 feet, the wall was interrupted with a scenery platform. The platform was at the level of the sidewalk and it was in the shape of an oval balcony, which was fringed with a wrought-iron railing. A fly-away had to jump down from the wall and was caught there by the parents. It was a pretty view at the river from the balconies, of the ships that sometimes went by, as well as at the other side of the river. From there it was a good view for kids too; they could see everything without the risk of falling from the wall. Petrzalka was at the left side and right in front of us, behind the river, were big patulous trees of Sady Janka Krala. Behind the river on the right was a road going to the border cross-over into Austria, which was "forbidden fruit" for us. I looked at that side and at the same time contemplated on a little hill on the other side of the Danube which was called Berg and was only around two and a half miles from us. So close and at the same time so far. Only to be able to get to Berg!

We knew very well that all movement at the promenade was closely watched with binoculars by the border guards. Years ago while still students, Nora and I went there for a walk. It was July then and it was very hot in the city; temperatures climbed over 86°F. A pleasant cool air was coming off the river water, so we jumped down from the wall to the rocky cliff. We wanted to sit down on the rocks and just watch the water while cooling down. We barely sat down and a fast boat with a submachine gun with armed guards came next to us. They aimed submachine guns at us and ordered us immediately to climb up to the sidewalk and stay behind the wall. There was nothing else to do but just obey the order! We were climbing up and those two from the boat watched us until we got behind the wall. Only then did they return to the other bank of the Danube.

Even though we knew we were being observed with binoculars at a sidewalk behind the wall, we were quite secure, and so the walk was a superb opportunity for us to have private talks without risk of being listened to by somebody else. I used a moment, when the kids were quite far away from us and they could not hear us, to quietly say:

"Thursday morning I brought my application for a signature to the ROH committee and it was so ridiculous how they observed me when inquiring whether we wanted to go on vacation to Italy. I hope they did not believe that they could read something off my face."

"They ask everyone a question and at the same time watch him to see if he becomes tense," Nora replied composedly.

"I believe, if somebody has such weak nerves that he becomes nervous at the first question, he should not start any games," I responded.

"You know that people are different," Nora said and then she added:

"Who should be nervous here are people like the chairperson of ROH. If she signs an application and then the person doesn't return here, she's got a problem. They would be calling her at committees . . ."

"I don't think so. That's why she needs the committee meeting. She will have someone to make a record of the meeting, where it will be written down that the whole meeting unanimously agreed with her signature. The responsibility thereby falls down on all of them, not just on her," I said and then added smilingly:

"ROH signature for me is all set."

"Hmm? How come?" Nora asked and I described in detail how we greeted each other with comrade chairperson and at the same time shook hands. We laughed our heads off at my greetings of "Honor Work" and Nora said:

"Just be careful, so those comrades don't think you are mocking them."

"No. Don't worry . . . "Honor Work" is "Honor Work" . . . As a matter of fact it's their most famous greeting," I said and added:

"As you may know when I was a boy 1 was a member of the Children's Broadcasting Studio. For a real acting career my acting was not very good, but for ordinary life it is more than I need. I think that it'll be sufficient for all comrades."

The children noticed our laughter so they ran toward us again. I waited till they approached us and could hear our conversation. I started with a joke, which I heard years ago:

"How do you put four elephants in a car?"

Both of them looked at me and I could see in their eyes:

". . . well, this isn't laughable at all . . ."

"Well, after all two in the front and two in the back," I said and they first looked at me and then started laughing. They ran away from us again and we heard how they repeated:

". . . two in the front and two in the back . . . hah, hah, hah . . . two in the front and two in the back . . ."

When they were far enough away so that they could not hear us, I kept on:

"As soon as our application is discussed at the ROH meetings everyone at your school and also in our company will know that we are going on vacation to Italy."

"Of course, you cannot prevent that," Nora said.

"Problem isn't that the people around us will know, but that our children will not. The later they learn about it the better. It would be best if they do not learn about it at all," I said.

"How do you want to accomplish that? We cannot lock them up at home and keep them there forever!" Nora said.

"I know that's impossible; it is only February now. However, we can go a long way in order to restrict their contact with people from our company and from your school. Fridays you can take them to your parents and for the weekends we can we go for walks outside of Bratislava or to my parents' cottage," I suggested a plan for the following months.

"Nevertheless, you will not be able to prevent the neighbors from asking them if they are looking forward to a vacation in Italy," Nora found a hole in my plan.

"No, definitely not," I acknowledged her logical thinking and added:

"But at least one of us will be there and then we will know who it was. You're right that this can happen but it is very unlikely. In that case we will modify our plan according to new circumstances."

I looked at my watch. It was half-past two in the afternoon and still comfortably warm. However, it was time to turn around and go back home. By the time we get back to the car, it will be four and close to sunset. The temperatures would drop down with the sunset. I called out to the kids:

"Peter, Katarina," and just when they turned, I indicated with my arm that we were going back now. They came running to us, caught our hands so that now they were between Nora and me. We walked in this manner, side by side, discussing plans for dinner.

"I want some pancakes with jam," Katarina said.

"I want some pancakes with cottage cheese and raisins," said Peter.

"So, we are going to make pancakes," Nora said and then asked me: "And what about you?"

"According to what I heard till now, two pancakes with jam, and then two with cottage cheese and raisins," I added myself to the pancake plan and the kids started laughing. Then I added a bit of my own into the dinner planning:

"After pancakes we can drink rose hip tea with honey."

The following Monday after handing in my application to the ROH, the telephone in my office rang immediately after my early morning arrival. As usual, I picked it up and said:

"Good Morning. Jan Bielek" and at the same time paying attention to the balanced, deep voice that I used.

"Honor Work, comrade engineer," a female voice spoke on the other end that I recognized as the chairperson of the board of the Communist party, the highest and mightiest power in the entire company. Even Director Prazec had to go to her and "render an account" every once in awhile, which meant he had to bring a report outlining how he had fulfilled the amenable duties the party has imposed on him. Quickly, before she was able to speak I jumped in with:

"Honor Work comrade chairperson."

"Could you come to my office for awhile?" she asked very smoothly.

"Of course. When is the best time for you?" I asked without any change in my voice, even though it wasn't an easy thing to do in that moment.

"If you could come immediately," the mightiest suggested.

"Yes, I'll be in your office in a moment," I said and she did not bother anymore with the paramount "Honor Work" and hung up. I hung up as well and tried to make sense of her phone call, but I could not. I subconsciously straightened up my tie, grabbed my jacket, which was hanging on a clothes rack beside my table and quickly put it on. From my desk I quickly grabbed a notebook which I use at big meetings. The book had a leather cover with a zipper and held a pen and company business cards inside. I did not know whether I would need it, but with a book under my arm, I would look more professional. I looked through my window outside at the cold February morning, but decided against bringing my coat. It was only a short distance through the yard into the opposite building to get to the big comrade's offices.

"I can make it there without my coat," I thought and quickly ran down the stairs and came out of my building where I was welcomed by frosty air. In the first moment I was sorry for not taking my coat, but I didn't want to turn back and rather ran through the yard. I wondered what she could possibly want or whether it had anything to do with my application for the Travel Provision, which I had just delivered to the ROH a few days ago. I could find no connection, nor had I a lot of time for dwelling on it because I was already on the other side of yard. I said to myself whatever happens I must keep a cool head and a balanced low voice. I entered the opposite building, stopped outside the door of the communist board, and knocked on the door.

"Come in," spoke the comrade behind the door.

I opened the door and greeted her:

"Honor Work, comrade chairperson."

"Honor Work, comrade engineer," she said and added:

"Sit down" and with her hand she pointed at a chair opposite her, on the other side of the desk.

I sat down and she handed me an application form for Evening University of Marxism-Leninism, which was well known by the abbreviation VUML. However, ordinary people used to interpret this abbreviation as Evening Washing Brains of People. Actually, this was not a university, but rather evening courses which were lectured by people with very modest knowledge. However, these people had a great talent for repeating certain sentences and postulates, which geniuses of communism, Marx, Engels and Lenin drew up into their books. Courses were held one night a week and the whole "study" lasted for two years. I glanced over the application and looked back at the comrade. She watched me fixedly and then she said:

"I have already registered you for VUML at the District Committee of the Communist Party. Now I need you to fill out the application as soon as possible and bring it back to me signed. By tomorrow morning would be the best because the semester is starting next Monday."

"Of course. tomorrow morning I'll bring it back," I said in a voice, which spoke perhaps this:

"This is an enormous honor for me to be a student on VUML."

"VUML will be a great asset to you. As a future party member, you are certainly going to need that," she explained and I thought:

"Yet, we'll see, what the future brings," and at the same time I grinned with a smile, which spoke:

"I have been greatly delighted and can hardly wait to I become a member of this party."

"Here's a detailed program for the next semester with the time and place of the lectures," she said and handed me a brochure with roughly thirty pages. I looked at the first page of the brochure and there were lectures planned for next Monday at five in the evening. I thought how nicely they have planned and prepared the brainwashing and smiled at my thoughts. I looked back at the comrade and she evidently understood my smile as my looking forward to it. She too smiled and then she said:

"So, see you tomorrow morning."

"Tomorrow morning, certainly," I said and smiled again. By the expression on her face, I saw that I had fulfilled her expectations and she was very content with me. I got up from the chair, stepped toward the door, and prior to opening the door, greeted her:

"Honor Work."

"Honor Work," she responded and I went out.

Outside I was welcomed again by the cold February air, so I ran across the yard and in a flash was in front of my building yet again. I did not stop running when I got to the stairs. I entered my office and laid the notebook with the VUML application and program on my desk. I sat down at my desk, picked out some tea and a tea pot. I walked into the kitchen and put on some water for tea. I stood by the hotplate and in good spirits I summed up my conversation with the big comrade. I was confident that everything turned out very well and I would not have any problem with any signature on the travel provision application. A bit of acting experience would never hurt! I brought the brewed tea back into my office, poured it in my "onion" cup and added a little bit of honey. I noisily drank tea from my tea cup and it tasted very, very good. I placed the VUML application in front of me on the desk and started filling it out in between sips of tea and smiles of contentment. Even if they wanted my shoe size, it would not be disappointing for me. If they believed that my brain was washable, they were far off.

"Well, just try it, comrades!" I said to myself and for a very strange reason I was even looking forward to it. Indeed that was my only and the last opportunity to be a student of VUML. It was either now or never! The notion that I would experience it first hand and with my own eyes and ears made me quite jolly. It took me about ten minutes to fill out and sign the application. I thought about bringing the application to the comrade at her board right now but remembered we had agreed on tomorrow morning, so I put it into my briefcase and brought it home to show it to Nora.

I could hardly wait for the end of the day and to tell her about everything. After dinner that night, I took the application from my briefcase and without saying a word laid it down on the table in front of Nora. She looked at it and then said:

"So now you'll be going to VUML" and she added with a lot of bitterness in her voice:

"For two years there is going to be another day of the week you'll be home late."

"I winked at her and said:

"Half a year"

"I guess you are aware that the VUML term is two years.

I winked at her again and said:

"Half a year"

This time she got it and smiled a little bit. I did not want to continue in our discussion any longer because the kids were just getting ready for bed. We waited until they went to bed and sat down in the living room in front of the TV. The program that was just on was not very interesting, so we just used the TV set as our sound curtain. I told her every detail of my encounter with comrade chairman and by the end of my story Nora appeared to be relaxed. It became obvious that my coming home late every Monday was not so much a concern anymore. When I finished my story she said:

"Seemingly, you know how to deal with women because so far you have been successful every time."

"It may look like dealing with women so far, but from now on, it is going to be just dealing with men," I said and using the fingers on my right hand I started counting:

"My boss—Vice president Flak-man; Director Prazec-man, and District Army Headquarters very likely a man again. I can hardly believe that the chief commanding officer there would be a woman. So, the following three signatures are all men and I can assure you they are going to be just a piece of cake for me," I said and then added:

"And . . . at the StB passport department there are all men. When our applications have been signed, I have to bring them there. Those were "tough guys"; dealing with them was not so much fun.

Tuesday morning on my way to work I wanted to stop by the office of "big" comrade chairman and hand her my completed VUML application. I stopped there before coming to my office; it was 5:45 in the morning. I knocked on the door . . . and nothing. I did not hear any voice. I just looked around and decided:

"No problem, I got plenty of time and can wait for her here" and I stayed at the door. I wondered when those "Big" comrades came to work. I stood there for about five minutes when I heard steps at the other end of the hallway. I turned around and saw big comrade coming toward me. I smiled a little and greeted her:

"Honor Work, comrade chairperson!"

"Honor Work, comrade engineer," she answered and immediately after asked:

"How long have you been waiting here?"

"Only a few minutes. I would like to hand you my application as soon as possible because I know it has to be delivered to the District Committee very soon," I said and handed her my application:

"Here it is," I said very politely.

"Don't forget it is starting next Monday at five in the afternoon," she reminded me.

"No, I will not forget. I will be there Monday and quite certainly on time" I added with the highest level of enthusiasm.

"Honor Work," she said and I responded:

"Honor Work, comrade chairperson."

I went to my office. During my walk through the yard, I met a lot of employees just coming to work. I repeated so many times:

"Good morning . . . good morning . . . and also Honor Work," because I walked by Comrade Stromcek. To my big surprise, he answered me:

"Honor Work." And I finally got it. Now I understood why he never answered my greeting, or rather why he just nods his head. Greeting someone "Good morning" was not good enough for him. Quite apparently saying "Good morning" was substandard for a real communist. As my old good grandma used to say:

"One learns something every day till death."

I just could not understand why Comrade Stromcek did not answer "Honor Work" to my substandard "Good morning." I would have gotten the clue a long time ago.

It was a Monday again, but this one was a little different than others. At 5:00 in the evening, I had to go for my first lecture of brainwashing—VUML. For some strange reason I was kind of looking forward to it and the reason was I had planned to attend only for half a year, not two years. If our plan goes through, there will be no more "must" of going to brainwashing, communist meetings, not even May First parades. It was horrifying to imagine going to VUML every Monday for two years. It was a huge waste of time and seeing people I have nothing in common with was not very exciting.

The address that was written on the brochure I had known for a long time. However, I had not been in that part of the city for many years, so I could not visualize how that could be a university address. I vaguely remembered seeing apartments in the building and it looked very seasoned from the outside. I was never inside. Years ago when I was just a boy, someone told me that about a hundred years earlier it used to be a pub and prostitutes who used to entertain the customers lived in apartments above the pub. After World War II when the communists came to power, the prostitutes were chased out and they rebuilt the rest of the building into apartments only.

When I arrived at my destination, I was really astonished at how much the building had changed. The facade was completely new and I did not recognize it. I double-checked the address—it was the correct street and correct number.

I went inside with mixed feelings. I had never been inside, but when I entered the first hall this time I could not restrain myself from saying:

"Wow"

The whole inside was renovated with the best that money could buy in those days. I remembered five years of studying at a technical university; even I had been to other universities in Bratislava and had never seen anything similar. It was quite obvious who the building was renovated for and who got the money! I stood off to the side by the entrance hall very close to the wall and watched people who were coming in. Despite the hundreds of people in attendance, it took a while before I recognized anyone. However, I was glad they did not see me. I had no interest in meeting them or talking to them there.

I was already thinking about crossing to the other side of the hallway to keep my cover when a door opened just a few feet from me. The ones standing close to me started slowly entering the open door. So I went too. When I entered that room, I again could not hold myself back and not say another:

"Wow"

I was completely taken back by how huge the room I just entered was. I could not understand how a huge room like that could fit in a building with such a small street presence. There was a big blackboard on the right side, a long table and a movie screen. On the very edge, outside of the screen there was a small podium for a teacher with a microphone. From there the floor pitched upwards like in a movie theater, so people sitting in the back could see the screen over the heads in front of them. One single row was a bow shaped bench with seats for fifteen students. I counted the number of rows—there were thirty rows there.

I sat down in the center of a middle row hoping I could avoid meeting people I didn't want to meet in the entrance hallway. That evening apparently wasn't my lucky day, because a moment after I sat down, Milan Majovsky came to me and sat next to me. I couldn't pretend anymore that I did not see him, so I said:

"Hi Milan"

"I welcome you at VUML," Milan said with his typical "superiority" voice that sounded like he was the master there who was allowing me to stay.

At that point I considered our dialogue finished and pretended I was studying the VUML brochure, so that I did not have to talk to him anymore.

Milan was employed at the same company as I and he was a schoolmaster of the adjacent school to the company. Ever since he had been promoted to that position, the superiority complex had become part of his character and he treated all people like that. He thought he was a general manager of the whole company and everybody reported to him. Most people, including me, hated him from the bottom of their hearts.

Fortunately, our class started and I did not have to study the brochure anymore and listen to our lecturer. He talked about the Scientific Basis of Marx-Leninism. People capable of thinking had to be doubtful of it just from the title—there was no science in Marx-Leninism. It was just a patchwork of a few sentences which were plagiaries from books of those two pseudo philosophers and filled up with postulates from the current Highest Communist Party Committee. This was how they found an answer to everything that was going on in the country.

After two hours the lectures ended and we were divided into groups of about twenty and sent into small rooms located in the atrium of the building. When the group I belonged to found room number 23, I just turned around, looked at the atrium and could not resist laughing. The rooms used to belong to prostitutes who served their customers inside. I was really glad that Milan did not get into room 23.

When I was finally on my way home very late that night, I laughed at the fact that I was being inundated with the scientific basis of communism in the same place where a long time ago prostitutes were dispensing their services.

Another week went by and on Tuesday morning we had a "big" meeting of about fifty of the highest supervisors of company management. Among others there were also chairpersons of the communist party, the ROH and the communist youth organization. As I entered the room I heard someone calling me:

"Comrade engineer," and by the voice, I recognized it was comrade chairperson of the ROH. I turned toward the voice and saw that at the head of the table, sitting side by side, were the comrade chairpersons of the ROH and the Communist party. I approached them and greeted them:

"Honor Work."

"Honor Work," they both responded at once and then the head of the ROH added:

"Your application has already been signed; you can pick it up from my secretary."

"Thank you," I said and went back to my seat.

The meeting dragged from eight in the morning till lunch-time; the whole time I felt that the bigger the meeting the less I learned. In other words, it was an enormous waste of time. Every hour we had a five-minute break and we could grab a coffee or a tea to wake up, because most people were falling asleep during the meeting. I took a cup of tea, even though it was not the type which I was used to. I used to cook my tea in a tea pot just like any tea enthusiast. Tea at the meeting was "only" a tea bag with hot water poured over it in a mug. At twelve the meeting was finally over and I went for lunch into the company dining room, which was next door in the same building. More or less the whole management moved there and behind tables with new tablecloths just for this occasion. This time we had roasted chicken with potatoes. I had a fairly good meal and on my way back I was thinking:

"They know how to cook edible food; all that is required is for top management to be eating it that day."

Before I came into my office, I stopped by at the ROH board and picked up my signed application. I entered the building and knocked on the door of the company's ROH board:

"Come in," the secretary called from inside.

I opened the door and greeted from the doorway, which now was the practice on those premises:

"Honor Work" and closed the door behind me. The secretary was sitting behind a desk immediately by the door. She looked at me and said:

"Honor Work," and handed me the signed application.

"Thank you," I said and looked over the application. In column "ROH" I saw a signature and also the rubber stamp of the company's board.

"Pleasant journey," I heard the voice behind the semi-closed door of comrade chairperson. I didn't see her;, the door was open only about two centimeters (one inch) and the light from her window shined through. I shifted my head aside and spotted half a face of the comrade. I knew she could hear me; nevertheless, I said once more louder:

"Thank you." I waited a couple more seconds to see whether she would come out of her office, and when she did not show up, I said again louder as I exited:

"Honor Work."

"Honor Work," said both at once chairperson and secretary and I went out into the hallway. The adjacent door was the office of the highest chairperson of the Communist party. I opened my notebook, inserted my application in it and knocked at the door.

"Come in," I heard the highest chairperson from the inside.

I pushed my head in the door and said:

"Honor Work."

"Honor Work," she said and added:

"Come in and sit down," and pointed at a chair by her desk.

I sat down and she asked me:

"How was it yesterday at VUML?"

"Very good," I told a lie with my trustworthy voice and added:

"I was really flabbergasted at how many students went to that university. The choice of lecturers is in every way fascinating."

"I knew you would like it there. Bratislava's VUML has a very good reputation," she said with confidence.

"Indeed it does. I heard about it from my acquaintances a long time ago," I said in order to support her pride for Bratislava's VUML.

After that I briefly described to her what kind of lectures we had had and who was lecturing them. She was evidently satisfied with the amount of information I retained in my memory. We talked about VUML for about ten minutes when she asked:

"Did you pick up your application for travel provision at the company's ROH committee?"

"Yes," I opened my notebook and pulled out the application. When I was handing it to her I said:

"Please, here it is"

"Thank you," she said and laid the application in front of her. She checked the column with the signature and rubber stamp of the ROH and then she looked at me:

"I will bring it to the general company meeting for approval. I will let you know right after it is signed" and she stuck her hand out for a hand shake. I understood it as a signal from her to end our discussions. I stood up from the chair and shook her hand:

"Honor Work," I said.

"Honor Work" said the mightiest comrade of the company as she shook my hand. I left her office and closed the door behind me.

As I expected, after bringing my application for the travel provision to the ROH, it would be discussed everywhere and with almost every single employee of the company. After that they would start stopping in when passing inquiring about our trip to Italy. However, to my big astonishment during all that time from the very beginning of the signing circus until our departure, I ran into only a few "extra" inquisitive people. All together there were only five snoops sent by the company's ROH committee and five snoops sponsored by the company's committee of the Communist party. Maybe, just like for everything else, they had a very specific plan for that kind of activity as well. With the exception of three instances, in every case the snooping expeditions were just alike. The snooping person would just "shoot" a question at me:

"I heard you're going to Italy. Which part of Italy are you going to?" and then very carefully watch my reactions. I was always ready to answer with my balanced, deep voice:

"We would like to see the historical artifacts in Rome like the Colosseum, Pantheon or Forum Romano. Time permitting, we would like to spend a few days in Florence."

"So, I wish you a pleasant journey," they all responded exactly the same way. I thought it was some kind of code from them of approving our vacation. I don't know what kind of code they had for a denial because I never heard it. There were only two employee snoops sent by the Communist party and one sent by the ROH committee who differed from the stereotype.

The first one was my colleague, Pavol Cvrcek. We were walking side by side out of a meeting because we had our offices in adjacent buildings. He shot at me:

"The Communist party committee now wants me to approve and sign your application for your travel to Italy. But how can I know that you're going only for a vacation and won't just leave the country and never come back?"

I looked at him and again said with my balanced deep voice:

"We would like to see the historical artifacts in Rome like the Colosseum, Pantheon or Forum Romano. Time permitting, we would like to spend a few days in Florence," and then I added:

"But Pavol, if you don't trust me or you are afraid, do not sign it!"

Evidently he did not anticipate that kind of answer and he said:

"But . . . on the other hand, I don't want to screw up your application for a vacation."

"Look Pavol, think about it and only then do what your best judgment and conscience tell you to do," I advised him with my still balanced deep voice.

Pavol's face turned red as he quickly ran upstairs into his building.

The second deviation from the stereotype was Mr. Hrkulik. He had never been a Communist party member, so everyone addressed him Mr. By the way, his behavior and approach to people was much worse than many communists. It was a well-known fact that he stuck his nose into the personal affairs of other people. His wife worked in the same company and she was in the quality-control department. I knew both of them were members of the company's ROH committee, so they had to know about our planned vacation to Italy. They never had any children, so they both placed all their energy into collecting and spreading rumors. Their whole life revolved around those two activities and that was the foremost reason for both of them being members of the committee. Being there, they could work on their hobby during working hours and with a lot of help from the rest of the committee. He pulled a trick on me previously tested on other people.

A long time after the ROH committee signed my application, he stopped me in the yard and very casually asked me:

"What are your plans for a vacation this summer?" and he watched me very suspiciously as I responded.

"Well, Mr. Hrkulik, you must know about it. Both you and your wife are members of the company's ROH committee. They signed my application for travel provision to Italy more than a month ago," I said with my balanced and deep voice. It was obvious I surprised him with my answer. He definitely didn't expect that kind of reply; his face turned the color of Bordeaux red and he could not come up with a retort. It took him a little while to get his speech back and asked what all the others had before:

"Which part of Italy are you going to?"

I got a feeling all those people were sent to me by the same agent and he was most likely mentally slow when he is unable to teach them better inquiries. I kept my face straight and again answered with by balanced deep voice:

"We are most interested in the historical artifacts and so far we are planning to visit Rome and Florence. If we have enough time, we will go to other places. When I come back, I will tell you all the details of the trip and show you pictures. I will be taking some slides, so if anybody is interested, I can bring the slide projector in."

"I wish you a pleasant journey then," Mr. Hrkulik said and we went our separate ways. On my way I was wondering why those committees did not hire people with better acting capabilities. Just one question or response that is not in their script and the agents' faces turn red and they cannot continue in their mission. On the other hand, the big advantage was on my side.

The third extraordinary and a little bit interesting deviated snooper was our neighbor Hana Klúbešová, who lived with her partner in the apartment above us. Hana had a very interesting deviation of another kind, but this did not have anything to do with our vacation, so I would preferably skip this part. That could be material for another story. As a snoop sent by the Communist party, she sharply watched what was going on in our place and I was quite sure that she tried listening to our conversations as well. This task was probably given to her due to the fact that she was a member of the Communist party. Hana, as well as her partner, worked for the same company as I did, such that it was not difficult for them to monitor when I came home late due to a business trip or VUML seminars. We were not big buddies with them, we did not visit each other, and I did not long to spend more time with them than was needed at work. Hana pretended to be Nora's best friend and sometimes she came over when we were both home, but usually she picked a time when I was not at home. The second Monday night that I was at VUML, she utilized for her snooping duty and came to Nora "for coffee." When she walked inside, she very carefully studied whether something in our apartment was missing; selling furniture and other fixtures was the typical sign in apartments of people who intended to flee the country. We had expected this kind of visit by someone, so she did not find anything extraordinary. When this part of her mission failed, she came up with a somewhat shrewder plan. She watched Nora very observantly and without consequence she spit out:

"Last summer my brother fled also with his entire family."

"I did not know that you had a brother," responded Nora composedly and then again with a calm voice she added:

"We have never met him."

Hana started to flush, maybe from surprise, maybe from anger that neither of her attempts to get to the truth paid off. Then she got up the courage once again and naively inquired of Nora:

"Could you leave just like that?" and at the same time she again carefully tracked how Nora would react.

"I don't know, I've never thought about it," Nora said again very composedly and then popped in a counterattack:

"Did you know that your brother was preparing to flee?"

"No, I did not know," Hana responded shakily, at the same time her face turned red and very fixedly peeped in her coffee mug, which she stirred nervously.

"And where's he right now?," Nora asked with interest.

"Right now he is in a refugee camp in Traiskirchen in Austria, but he will be there only until he gets asylum in Australia," Hana said.

"He could not go directly to Australia?" Nora asked.

"No. It doesn't work that way. One can emigrate only through a refugee camp," Hana said.

"Why exactly to Australia?" Nora asked.

"I don't know; according to the letter he wrote me, he wants to go to Australia," Hana said.

Nora saw she was winning this fight, so she kept on:

"Did they leave any furniture behind?"

"I don't know . . . I have not been to their apartment yet," Hana tried telling a lie very amateurishly, during which time her face turned red again. She still nervously stirred her coffee and then added:

"Their car is still parked in front of their house. It is very similar to the Skoda car you have, only it is about two years older."

Nora laughed and said:

"Now you are going to have a car too. You and Jan can alternate who will drive the car to work. At least we save some money for gas."

"It will take a long time till our family gets some of the possessions that were left behind by my brother . . . about two years," Hana said uncertainly. Then she looked at her watch, quickly finished the coffee and said:

"It is getting late. I have to go home."

"Come for coffee again sometime. Can we speak more about your brother?," Nora said as she closed the door behind her.

It was Thursday, March 22, and I arrived in my office about half an hour early because I wanted to prepare for today's meeting in silence. It was still dark outside; everywhere around was quiet and I was writing something when suddenly my phone rang. The shrill ring of the telephone in the absolute silence frightened me in such a way that I stumbled backwards away from the phone. I looked at the phone and wondered who could be calling so early in the morning. Then I looked at my watch and it occurred to me that this must be the mightiest comrade chairperson from the general company board of the Communist party. It took me about five seconds till I picked up the phone and until then it loudly rang into the silence.

"Honor Work, Jan Bielek," I introduced myself, because I expected it would be the comrade. The other end of the line was quiet for a moment and then a strong female voice spoke:

". . . and since when do you answer the phone in this manner?" By the voice I recognized it was my mother.

"I thought it was going to be a call from a big comrade of the Communist party committee, so I wanted to salute her at the proper level," I said and then added:

"Hi, mom."

"Hi," mom said already in another voice and then inquired:

"Janny, I still have some belongings in our apartment, which I would like to get moved by car into our cottage. Could you come Saturday morning?"

"Where are you going to be Saturday morning? At the cottage or in the apartment?" I asked. "At the cottage," mom responded.

"OK, so first I will drive Nora and the kids to the cottage and then you and I will go to the apartment in Bratislava to pick up your things."

"What time will you come?" mom asked.

"Around ten o'clock," I answered.

"That's fine. But you don't have to hurry. I have already put everything in boxes, so it will not take a long time to load them in the car," mom said with concern about her grandchildren not being wakened too early in the morning.

"Bye, see you then," she said.

"Bye," I said and hung up.

I was just about finished with my notes when I heard it was getting quite busy in the hallway. My fellow workers were coming to work and their voices resonated in the hallway. Thursday, they used to say, was "Sundaying" and scrimmaged planes for the weekend. My quiet half hour was coming to an end, so I took the teapot and went to the kitchen to brew some tea. When I started sipping some good-smelling tea with honey, I would be able to concentrate much better and could tune out the noise around me.

I came back to my office with freshly brewed tea and I poured it into my "onion" cup. The nice aroma of jasmine tea filled the room as I scooped some honey into it and started stirring. I sipped a little bit of tea and looked out the window. I could see the early morning rising Sun and the deep red color indicated a beautiful day. Maybe a few days from now I will be able to smell the coming spring in the air. I liked that part of year when nature was waking up to new life. I also remembered it had been more than two weeks since I had dropped off my application to the mightiest comrade and had not heard anything from her yet. There was nothing I could do about it but just keep waiting.

Saturday morning we woke up around eight o'clock. Nora went to the kitchen and started making breakfast, I took a shower and put my flannel shirt and jeans on. I was pulled into the kitchen by the very nice smell of a freshly prepared breakfast. The aroma of coffee mixed with the aroma of fresh brewed tea and both were overpowered by the tasty smell of pastry. I sat down next to Nora. We were slowly eating our breakfast and silently talking about the day ahead of us.

"I will drive you and the kids to the cottage and then my mom and I will go to the Bratislava apartment to pick up their stuff," I said.

"Should I go with you to help with the loading?," Nora asked.

"Mom said it was only a few things. I can manage that by myself. I'd rather you stay with the kids and grandpa at the cottage," I said and then added:

"As I know my mom, we will need extra room in the car to squeeze those "few" things in."

The kitchen door opened and Katarina's ruffled head popped in.

"What are you doing?," she asked and at that moment Peter's ruffled head appeared in the door above Katarina's.

"We are having breakfast. Come in and sit down and eat as well," Nora said and the kids ran inside the kitchen still in their pajamas and jumped into their seats.

"Where are we going today?" Peter inquired before he took a bite from his pastry.

"Right after breakfast we are all going to grandma and grandpa's cottage. When you are done with breakfast, get dressed quickly and we can go," I said.

"Hurray!" they both yelled at once and started rushing with their breakfast.

"Do not rush your meal because you may start choking. Dad said you should get dressed quickly, not eat quickly," Nora said.

"If you want to take some toys with you, put them into the backpack," I said after a little while.

At nine o'clock we were all ready for our trip to see grandma and grandpa at their cottage in Vysoka pri Morave. A few minutes later, we were already in the car going to Vysoka. Because it was Saturday, the roads were not busy, so we arrived at the cottage shortly before half past nine. My father was already standing on grass in the front waiting for us. He did not wait until I drove up closer and helped him with opening the gate. By the time I got close, the gate was open. I drove through it and stopped on the parking spot in front of the garage. Before we managed to jump from the car, he closed the gate behind the car. A while ago I tried to talk him out of opening and closing the gate and said I could do it myself.

"That's no problem. I love doing it," my father said and I could see from his face that if I insisted on opening and closing the gate myself, I would spoil his joy of our visit to their cottage. It was his way of saying without words he was looking forward to seeing us. So, I let him manage the gate and he did it every time we arrived or left.

We got out of the car and were welcomed by a warm and wonderful March morning. The smell of spring in the air was quite obvious; grass in the yard was fresh green. As usual, it was very quiet there, only infrequent roosters' "crowing" from a distance or a dog barking interrupted the silence. Life "flowed" somehow more slowly in the village and that was the main reason why my parents considered more and more about moving there and selling the apartment in Bratislava.

Mom was ready to get going, so we jumped in the car and took off to the apartment in Bratislava. Just as we turned the corner away from their cottage, mom said:

"You should not wake the children up so early in the morning. It would be just fine if you came a little later"

"We did not wake them up. We got up at eight and Nora prepared breakfast. We just started eating when their heads popped in the kitchen door," I said and then added:

"You should have seen their burst of excitement when we told them we were going to Vysoka.

We were driving through Stupava when mom said:

On our way back, I want to stop in that store," and pointed at the grocery market on the right side.

"OK, if it fits in the car," I said.

"I am sure it will fit. I don't have a lot of shopping to do, just some mineral water and beer, because they are too heavy for me to carry on the bus," mom said.

My parents never had a car, which wasn't a problem in the city. They did all their shopping in stores that were just on the other side of the street or in another street around the corner. Everywhere else they went by public transportation. Since their retirement, they have been more inclined to live in a village. If they could buy everything they needed in a local store, they would carry their goods on a bicycle. The problem was when they had to go to another village or town; that's when traveling by bicycle was too much for them, at which point their only other option was to use a bus or a train.

"Look mom. If you ever need to shop for something like that, make a list. When we come, I will drive you to the store and help you with shopping. We come to your cottage almost every weekend," I said.

"Thank you, Janny," mom said. Every time she wanted to express how much she loved me, she would call me by this nickname.

In a little while we were already parking in the back yard of their apartment building. We rode the elevator to the fourth floor, even though I preferred using the stairway. Mom unlocked the apartment and we went in. Right in the hallway behind the door there were boxes and bags which we had to move to Vysoka. When I spotted that huge pile, I thought we would need an inflatable car in order to fit everything.

"I hope we can fit it all in," I said and started bringing the boxes into the elevator. Mom then rode the elevator down and I went down by the stairs. We brought everything in the yard next to the car and I started loading the boxes in.

"I'll go get the rest of it," mom said and went up. When she came back down, I had already loaded everything in the car and the car was full, including the back seats and trunk. What she brought down now would not fit in the car. No matter how much I tried to push it in. I had to unload almost everything and start loading it back in by sorting the boxes by size and optimizing any free volume in the back seats and the trunk. After half an hour, everything was in but one bag filled with balls of knitting yarn, which I could not get in. I knew that bag was very important to my mom and there was no way we could leave it there.

"Mom, sit down in the passenger seat," I said after awhile and buckled her up when she sat down. I laid the bag with the yarn in her lap and asked her:

"Now, turn the bag, so it is not in sight" and closed the car door from the outside. I jumped in the car and we went back to the cottage. We were laughing about the fact that we had never traveled in a car like that ever before.

When we were going through Stupava I suggested:

"There is no way that we will be able to squeeze in the shopping you talked about. Let's go to lunch now and after we can go back to Stupava for shopping.

"OK, it is going to be better with an empty car," mom said and I could see she liked my idea better. We came to Vysoka and dad was waiting outside and ready to open the gate. When I pulled in with the car, Nora called out to us:

"Let's go eat now. I have just finished cooking lunch."

I opened the passenger door of the car, took the bag from mom's lap and only then could she get out of the car. In the meantime, dad closed the gate, and when he noticed how mom was exiting the car and how much stuff was inside, he made a comment:

"Oh, my God! How much stuff did you push into the car?"

Mom gave dad a dirty look and said:

"Let's go eat now; we can unload the car later."

We all came into the kitchen to eat the meal mom started cooking in the morning and then Nora finished while we made the trip back and forth to Bratislava. We could tell everyone liked the meal because everyone was too busy eating to talk.

Tuesday we had another meeting of the whole technical division in the office of Vice president Flak. We all came down at seven in the morning and the meeting was, as usual about nothing. I maintained a look of interest and attentiveness, even though my mind was completely elsewhere. I listened only betwixt and between. So as not to give the impression that I wasn't listening at such an important meeting, I made notes in my notebook, which I always carried along for meetings. Then I left those pages in the notebook as my important notes and carried them from meeting to meeting. It was already the last week of March; therefore, almost half of the six months, which I had "planned" for getting all signatures, papers and documents. If we wanted to leave in July, all I had left were April, May and June. For the circumstances, it wasn't too much time; in the course of the last six weeks, I had obtained only one single signature—from the ROH. I was still waiting for a call from the mightiest comrade communist. Then I remembered that foreign allowance from the bank is valid until the year end and the travel provision will be valid for a grant period ten days following six months. The day count starts from the day when we cross the border into Austria.

"Well, I still have nine months in order to make the whole plan happen. We can go to Italy for Christmas! If someone is inquisitive and asks why, I will tell him Italian weather in July is very hot and winter is by far more comfortable for seeing historical remains because over there it does not snow and freeze," I envisioned and at the same time I unwarily grinned. Fortunately my head was pitched over the note book and I pretended to be taking down some notes. No one noticed my grin, only Pavol Cvrcek, who was sitting opposite me and was just telling a story about somebody who wanted to save money and instead of carbide saw blades he bought only ordinary ones for repairing wood parquet floors. However, every time they hit a nail with the saw, they had to replace the entire blade and thereby spent five times more money. Apparently, he believed I laughed at his story.

The meeting ended around eleven and I went to my office. I stepped out into the hallway and looked back at the other end, where the office of the mightiest comrade was. For awhile I hesitated, but then I just kept going my way. I opened the door, which led outside from the building and I felt a light breeze from a pleasant March day. As I was about to step out, the mightiest comrade came walking in. I took a step back and held the door open, so she could step in:

"Come in . . . Honor Work," I said.

"Honor Work. Do you have five minutes right now?" she inquired when she stepped into the hallway.

"Of course," I responded.

"So, come with me," she said and I followed her in the hallway. When we arrived at her office, I said:

"Excuse me," and I opened the door for her and entered the office after her.

"Sit down," she said and pointed to a chair I had occupied a few times before. She walked around her desk from the other side and sat down in her armchair.

"I would like to apologize," she said and; then she kept on in a quiet voice:

"Your application has been signed since last week, but I did not get a chance to call you. My mother died and I had to leave in a hurry for her funeral," and she handed me the application.

"Sincerest condolence," I said in my deep voice and added:

"That's OK. Historical monuments, which we want to see have been standing at the same place for thousands of years. They will look the same if we see them a week later."

Comrade grinned and said quietly:

"Thank you"

"I thank you too," I said.

"Now you have to excuse me, I have to take care of the mail that has piled up here for the last week," she said and stuck out her hand.

I stood up and shook her hand and said quietly:

"Honor Work."

"Honor Work," she said also quietly and I left her office. When I was in the hallway I looked at my application and found a signature and date stamp in column "ZV KSC"—March 20, 1984. It was Tuesday last week.

I was walking by the office of my boss Vice president Flak and I thought his signature was the next one I would need. After knocking on the door and entering the office of his secretary Mrs. Landinova, I asked her to put my application in the "signature-needed" book. When I handed it to her, she put her reading glasses on and started reading the document. Then she looked above the glasses at me and inquired with a smile:

"Oh, so you want to go to Italy for vacation?"

"Yes, I am just surprised you do not know about it. It has already been signed by ROH and KSC (Communist Party of Czechoslovakia)," I said.

She winked at me with one eye and said:

"I have better friends, just hold on" She returned the application to me and knocked on the boss's door. Then she opened the door a little bit, stuck her head in and asked the boss:

"Comrade Engineer Bielek is here and he would like to ask you for something. I heard the boss's voice, but did not understand what he said. Then she opened the door wide and asked me:

"Come in, please"

I entered the boss's office which I had just left about twenty minutes ago. Mrs. Landinova closed the door behind me. The boss was still sitting at the head of a huge long table for twelve people used for our meetings and for study,

"I would like to ask you for a signature on my application for travel provision," I started from the door. He just waved his arm, indicating for me to come in and his arm stayed in the air waiting for me to hand him the application. When I approached him, he pointed to a chair, asking me to sit down, again without a word. I sat down in my usual seat where I sit during meetings, the first seat at his right side. He laid the application in front of him on the table, replaced his reading glasses and studied it for a moment. When he came to the end, he looked at me above his glasses, as was his custom. Without saying a word, he pulled a pen from his jacket pocket and signed my application.

"Mrs. Landinova," he yelled across the long room and her head showed up in the door.

"Please, put here a rubber stamp" he said much quieter, and when she approached him, he handed her the application.

"Thank you," I said very surprised with the fast pace of this particular signature process.

Boss immersed himself again in his papers, which he was studying before I came in and after my "Thank you" he just looked at me again above the glasses and said:

"Good bye."

"Good bye," I said and walked into the office of Mrs. Landinova. I waited for her until she placed a rubber stamp and after another "Thank you" and "Good bye" I went back to my office. This time it was nice and warm, so I did not rush through the yard. Just an hour ago, I had planned the trip to Italy for Christmas and now it looked like it was going to be in July as planned.

I came back to my office and I sat at the desk. The nervousness I had felt just an hour ago was completely gone and I felt great again.

"It is somehow still going according to my plan," I thought; so far, I already had three signatures and would be able to make it in summer. Encouraged by the success, I picked up the phone and called Director Prazec. The phone was picked up by his secretary named Marika:

"This is director's secretary, yes please."

"Good morning, this is Jan Bielek," I said and then asked.

"Is comrade director around?"

"Yes, but he is having a meeting right now. What would you like?" Marika asked.

"I would like to give him my application for travel provision," I said.

"I am just looking into his organizer . . . come here Thursday at nine," she said.

"Yes, Thursday at nine," I repeated after her and then added:

"Thank you." Marika did not answer but just hung up the phone.

I put the receiver in front of my face, gave it a dirty look and then hung up. I wondered if common courtesy was not required from people who got so high on the throne of fame and power. Despite this little incident, I felt just great when hunger started poking me with petite horns. I looked at my watch—it was five after twelve. I went for lunch to the company dining room.

Thursday shortly before nine, I knocked on the door of the director's secretary.

"Come in" I heard Marika saying from the inside and I entered the room.

"Good morning," I said to Marika and she replied:

"Comrade Director is expecting you. You can go in."

I walked through the huge room called the secretary's office. It appeared to me bigger than our whole apartment, where the four of us lived. I guess it was designed by a different designer and paid for out of a different pocket. I came up to the door behind which was Director Prazec. The door was slightly open and I tried to knock on it, but I did not know how. The door, including the frame, was covered with red leatherette and a thick layer of sound proofing underneath it. I hesitated for a moment, trying to find a spot I could knock on when I heard the director from inside:

"Come in."

"Honor Work," I said, leaning inside the doorway.

"Honor Work. Sit down," the director said and pointed to a chair opposite him. I handed him the application and sat down. He did not look at it and asked:

"Italy is in your plans."

"Yes, we would like to see some historical artifacts," I answered and he was looking at me with a penetrating stare and then asked:

"Is a visit to the Vatican in your plan too?"

"No. My wife and I have not discussed it yet," I said with a balanced voice.

"So, you are going to visit historical artifacts," he said with a voice suggesting to me to forget about visiting the Vatican at all.

"So far we have talked only about Rome and Florence," I added. He completely ignored my last sentence and said:

"Before I put my signature down, it must be unanimously approved by the company's highest management. Marika will let you know when you are to come to that meeting. I understood he was all done with me for now and he was sending me back to Marika, so I said:

"Thank you and Honor Work" and I walked back to the door. When I walked up to the door, I heard Prazec's voice:

"You can leave the door open."

"Comrade Director advised me that I should come to the next high-management meeting," I said to Marika. She opened his organizer and said:

The meeting is Monday, April 16 at eight. Your application should come up in the program around eleven. Come here at ten forty-five," she said and wrote my name in the organizer at 11:00.

"Thank you and see you then," I said and went back to my office. During my walk, I calculated how much time Prazec needed for a single signature. Almost four weeks! I remembered our discussion with Mr. Kolesar. It was quite clear already then that this signature would be the most difficult or at least would take the most time. I knew the highest-management meetings were held every two weeks. Marika put my name down, not for the next meeting, but for the following one. Apparently, their agenda was completely filled up. Five vice presidents and two comrade chairpersons, ROH and KSC, had to nod their heads in order for Prazec to put his signature down. I was wondering again how many times the same person must nod his head till I get authorization to cross a border. If someone were to put an extra topic into their program to nod heads and put down a signature, would that be too much for them and deplete their resources? No, the whole circus of begging and signing was made deliberately complicated to turn people away from traveling to the West. That was telling me quite clearly how much people would love leaving the country and also how difficult and laborious it was for the government to prevent them from running away. For now, there was only thing I could do: just wait.

Beautiful weather was forecast for Saturday April 7, so we decided to spend the whole day at Vysoka. When I called my parents Friday and let them know we were coming, my mom said:

"Come over. We are looking forward to seeing you. Your father wants you to help him build a shelf in our pantry."

We left our apartment right after breakfast and arrived at the cottage about ten. Dad waited for us outside, as usual, and opened the gate as soon as he spotted our car coming around the corner. The spring welcomed us as soon as we got out of the car. All the trees were blossoming and the grass had already turned a dark green color.

The kids jumped out of the car like a shot and ran into the shed to pick up their bicycles. A long time ago, dad jokingly called the shed Pavilion C and the name stuck. It has been called "SE" ever since. We did not see the kids for a long time; they were brought back to the yard by hunger shortly before lunch. All that time they rode their bikes in the streets surrounding the block of houses in which the cottage was located.

On the left side, there was a work area with a smooth concrete surface and in the middle of it was neatly sorted wood for the shelf rack. There were also a hand saw, square, tape measure, hammer, nails and other material needed to build a shelf rack. I changed into my working pants and shirt and both of us, my dad and I, started working on the project. First, we measured the pantry that had been completely emptied and I drew a simple one-dimensional layout on a piece of paper. We sat down outside at a table with the layout on the top to make the design for the rack. Nora came out of the house with a tray containing two open beer bottles and two drinking glasses. We were just pouring beer into our glasses when Mom came out and saw us sitting down with beer bottles in our hands. She started yelling:

"You have not done anything and you are already drinking beer."

"Mom, we are sitting down because we are drawing a design. We are drinking beer because our throats dried out from designing so hard," I said jokingly.

"I just want to say you have not done anything," mom said angrily back to me.

"Mom, first we have to draw a design. As you may know, it is better to measure twice and cut once, than the other way around. Do not worry; the shelf in your pantry will be done today," I continued in our dialogue. She did not say anything but just waved her hand and went inside again. Together with Nora, they were cooking today's lunch in the kitchen and we had to go by them many times on our way to the pantry, measuring and installing the shelves.

After measuring out and completing the sketch, we cut with a hand saw the support construction, as well as the shelves. I measured and sawed, dad held the pieces of wood or plywood for me to make my sawing easier. By the time we had lunch, the whole support construction was assembled and most of the shelves tightly nailed in. After lunch we had a small break with beer, but this time mom did not object at all. Actually, she looked quite satisfied, because occasionally out of curiosity, she peeked in the pantry and saw how much we had completed. Afterwards, we had yet to finish four missing shelve, and festively with beer in our hands, we handed the pantry over finished and ready to use. This time, mom was completely satisfied; even she admired us:

"Well, you have done it very nicely," and she did not mind beer in our hands, which we drank for the final building approval of the pantry. Mom with a smile on her face started laying everything back in the pantry and we helped her with objects that were too heavy for her. All the things that were in the pantry before piled up could now be nicely and neatly stored on shelves. Following a successful building inspection of the pantry, my father and I put away remnants of wood and tools. Nora swept up sawdust, and so, before sunset the backyard was completely back in order. We were sitting outside in the back yard and drank our afternoon coffee and tea. The kids were exhausted from biking, and sat next to us and ate cake, which grandma made for them. When mom came out in the back yard again and noticed how nicely we had cleaned up everything, she suggested:

"You should stay here until tomorrow as well. You don't have to go home tonight. The children will sleep in the living room and you two may sleep

in 'B',"; that's what they called the bedroom, which was next to the garage."
This part once father jokingly called "Pavilion B" and the name stuck.
Peter and Katarina were just finishing the cake and the two simultaneously
shouted out:

"Yes. Hurray."

Nora and I just looked at each other and, stimulated by the "hurray" from
our children, we just nodded. It was very comfortable there and we did not
have a different program for Sunday. It was not necessary to talk us into it.
As we finished our coffee and tea, Katarina suddenly rose, as if remembering
something and ran inside. It did not take long and she rushed outside with
her toy backpack. She put it on table and took out a box of cards.

"Let us play cards. Who will play?" she asked.

"I," the grandparents and Peter raised their arms.

Katarina put her backpack down on the grass, removed the cards from
the box and handed them to Peter.

"Now you are going to shuffle and I will deal."

Grandma and grandpa moved with their chairs to the edge of the table
to sit opposite Katarina and Peter who took their cards from the table and
started organizing them in their hands. The two of us remained sitting on a
bench and observed the gamblers with interest. They played cards for about
an hour and then recalled that it was time to watch fairy tales on TV. All
four stepped inside and turned on the TV set. We saw through a window
how their faces were lit up by the twinkling light of the TV screen. The Sun
descended in the sky, reddened from the sunset as twilight slowly fell. We
observed the sunset and didn't want to go inside. It was getting colder and
we began shivering, so I suggested to Nora:

"You bring two blankets and I will open a bottle of wine with two tall
glasses."

In a moment we met at the bench again. Nora laid one blanket on the
bench and I poured wine into glasses. We sat down, covered ourselves with
a second blanket and clinked glasses:

"To our victory!"

"How is it with your application?" I asked, whispering after a moment.

"It is already signed by the principal, ROH as well as KSC. Right now,
it should be at the City Hall School Department waiting for the signature of
the school superintendent," Nora said and then asked:

"And yours?"

I told her in detail my experience of collecting the signatures and then
said very quietly:

"After Prazec's signature I will need one more from Army Headquarters and yours need be signed only by the school department. So far, it looks like we should be able to make it."

TV fairy tales were over and it was time for the kids to go to bed. The two of us still sat on the bench outside, covered with a blanket. Grandma came out of the house and when she saw us still sitting there, said with laughter:

"Look grandpa, how they are sitting there!"

We saw my father getting up from his chair in front of the TV and come out. When he came up to the outside door, he turned a switch and the outside light mounted on the house lit up.

"Dad, turn off the light. You are attracting mosquitoes," I said and he turned the light off. Then he came out with confused blinking eyes in the darkness till he saw us. Then he grabbed mom around her shoulders and pulled her inside. We heard him saying:

"Leave them alone, they need some time to talk."

It was Monday April 16 and I was waiting in the Director Prazec's secretary's office. I arrived there at exactly 10:40 as Marika had suggested. She asked me to sit down in a chair by the coffee table, which was to the right of the entrance door. Other visitors were served coffee there, but evidently I wasn't a visitor. I was just an ordinary "waiter" for the director's meeting and that's why no coffee was served to me. I looked at the clock hanging on the opposite wall. It was 10:45 now. I knew it would take a lot of time to get behind the door covered with soundproofing and red leatherette. If that happened before 11:15 it would have been a complete miracle. And that society could not believe in miracles. They were forbidden.

Marika was far away from me on the other side of the office and kept herself really busy. She either made phone calls or typed something on a typewriter. I tried to speak a few words with her just to make my waiting go by a little faster and I seized an opportunity when she finished a phone call and was quietly turning pages in some book:

"The last weekend did not turn out very nice. It should rain during the week, not on the weekend."

"Yes, it rained . . ." she did not finish her sentence and the phone rang again. She picked up the phone and said:

"This is director's secretary, yes please." And then she answered very briefly:

"Yes, April 20 . . . no . . . yes . . . yes . . . no . . . eight-thirty" and hung up. I waited until she might look at me and finish the sentence. She ignored me completely and sat down at the typewriter again. I realized there was no chance of killing any time by a dialogue with Marika. I opened the notebook, which I carried with me all the time and pretended to be studying my notes from the meetings. From time to time, I looked at the clock on the opposite wall. Time crawled with a snail's tempo.

The red leatherette door opened and I looked at the clock again. It was 11:27, so I waited there, bored to death, forty-seven minutes. The miracle did not happen. After all, atheists did not believe in any miracles. Prazec's head appeared in the door and he said:

"Janny" and his head disappeared again. I was shocked in the first moment how he addressed me. At any other occasion he addressed me very officially "Comrade Engineer." Addressing me by my first name was a good sign because only communists did it among them. I quickly closed my notebook, stood up and hurried toward the leatherette door. I entered the room and started with comrade's greeting:

"Honor Work" and changed my face to a courtesy smile.

"Sit down," Prazec said and pointed to a chair at the right end of the table. He was not on "first-name terms" with me as is the custom among the communists. After all, I was not a communist.

I sat down and looked at the faces of the people sitting there. I used all my internal strength to make myself calm and balanced and kept a friendly smile on my face.

"The next item on our agenda is Jan's application for travel provision in Italy. So, what do you say? Do you agree with an approval? Prazec asked and went from face to face and watched which way every head swung. I watched every head along with Prazec. Every head turned from up to down and back and I just remembered what Mr. Kolesar had said half a year ago:

"Jan, if only one single head . . ."

The director picked up a pen lying on the table next to my application, lifted both his arms high above the table and asked one more time:

"So, is it yes?" and I joined his stare from face to face again and watched them swinging from up to down and back. Then he lowered his arms back on the table and signed the application. He picked it up and said:

"So, Janny, have a pleasant journey" and handed me the application.

I stood up and took my application from him. Before I left the room, I looked at the faces and said:

"Thank you, comrades" and walked to the door. I heard Prazec saying:

"Janny, ask Marika to stamp it."

I turned around in the door and said:

"Honor Work" and walked into the secretary's office. I placed the application in front of Marika and said:

"Rubber stamp, please." She reached over and turned a carousel holding about twenty different rubber stamps, took one of them and looked at it. Then she carefully pressed the stamp against an inking pad and then also carefully pressed it on my application. She double-checked if it was legible and handed me the application.

"Thank you and see you later" I said, and very carefully placed that bloody valuable piece of paper into my notebook and went to my office.

I came back to my office and found a little piece of paper on my desk with a message:

"Joe B.'s birthday is today—the big 50. Let me know when you are going to have a minute, so we all can go congratulate him" and initials J.R.

I laid my notebook on the desk and went to Mrs. Jarmila's office. I entered her office and sat down at the desk which used to be mine, before I became a "big boss" with my own office.

"So, its Joe's big fiftieth today," I said.

"Boss, when are you going to have a minute, so we all can go together and congratulate him? Mrs. Jarmila said and then added:

"I have already bought a flower bouquet."

"I just came from the director's office, and to the best of my knowledge I do not have any more meetings today" and I looked at my watch. It was five to twelve. She looked at her watch and said:

"I will call Mirka and ask her to hold Joe in his office under a false pretense. Lunch break is coming in a few minutes, so we can go there together, stop in his office and surprise him with our congratulations."

"I am in . . ." I said and went back to "myself." I could hear voices of people gathering in the hallway. In a moment I saw the body contours of Mrs. Jarmila through the matte glass in the door and heard her voice:

"Boss . . ."

I came out into the hallway and she handed me the bouquet. I looked at the flowers and then at the entire group and asked:

"I think it would be better if the flowers were given to Joe by a woman. I guess he would appreciate them much more if he gets kissed by a woman, rather than by me."

"You are the boss, so the flowers belong in your hands and you ought to give them to him. We, the women, will take care of all kissing," she said and the whole department blew up into laughter.

I took the flowers, went downstairs and then out of the building. The whole department walked behind me. This way we all went together as planned by Mrs. Jarmila. During the walk, I was putting together my speech and congratulations and I was sorry for not preparing something nice and funny ahead of time. Quietly, like a bunch of rebels, we walked into Joe's office. He heard some noise behind his back and stood up and turned around. I handed him the bouquet and before I had a chance to say anything, he started:

"Mirka asked me to take a late lunch break because Engineer Bielek was coming to see me with a very important investment plan . . ." and the whole group blew up in loud laughter again. I waited until they calmed down and said:

"Dear Joe. In the name of the whole group, let me wish you a very happy, healthy, successful and love-filled twenty-fifth birthday. For another fifty years, I wish that all your dreams, desires and daydreams, regardless of how big, little or secret they may be are fulfilled" and shook his hand. At my term "secret," again they all blew up in laughter and then every one of them shook his hand and added his or her wish. At the end Joe said:

"Thank you all for congratulations and I invite you into the company's club for Friday at four o'clock."

"Thank you too," we heard from the group many times after.

I thought the worst was already behind me; now all I needed was only to obtain a signature from District Army Headquarters. Not in my worst nightmares could I envision what kind of tailspin they had prepared for me, which would make this one out of five signatures, the hardest. I picked up the phone and called information at Army Headquarters:

"Army Headquarters Four," spoke a female voice.

"Please, when do you have office hours?" I asked.

"For what purpose?," inquired the voice.

"Signature on application for travel provision," I responded.

"Monday and Thursday from 8:00 to 12:00," the voice said.

"Thanks," I said and the person on the other side hung up.

It was Monday afternoon, so I decided to go next Thursday and took a day of vacation for that day. I arrived at District Army Headquarters Bratislava IV before eight in the morning. I waited in the car until they opened for office hours. At exactly eight, I got out of my car and went through the parking lot toward the entrance till I came to the entrance where two army reservists already stood waiting. The door was still closed I did not know those two, so I stood in line at the door behind them. In about ten minutes the door opened and we got inside in the same order as we had stood outside. Arrows on the wall pointed us to the desk-room door and the first of us entered inside. I was quite happy, that at least here, at the Army Headquarters, people did not stand in line for fourteen hours, although it was a little bit strange that the first of us did not come out even after about twenty minutes. One signature and one rubber stamp could not take so much time! When he came out, we could see on his face that he hadn't done so well. The line in the hallway grew relatively quickly. I looked behind me and saw about forty guys who needed a signature for some kind of document. The one in front of me entered the office, and soon after that, he came out. It was my turn now.

"Honor Work," I said and the captain sitting behind the desk said: "Military booklet."

I handed him my military booklet and at first he looked at me, then in the booklet as if comparing my face with the photo inside. Apparently, in order to eliminate the chances of some spy from the enemy world of capitalism intruding into the Czechoslovak People's Democratic Army, he continued browsing through the whole booklet, and when he came to the end, he asked: "What do you have?"

"Signature for my travel provision application, comrade captain" I said and handed him the paper form. He read through the application and said:

"Oh, no, no, no. We need you here" and stood up from his desk and walked to a typewriter, which was on the right side under a window sitting on a small table. He inserted a paper form and then slowly with only one finger on his right hand pecked into the keyboard and used his left hand to turn the drum on the typewriter. Occasionally, he looked into my military booklet and copied something from it. I stood there without a word and observed what he was doing. I stood at his desk, He was far away from me and I had no notion what all that meant. About ten minutes later, he drew the form from the typewriter and sat down behind his desk, where he was before. The form, which he had typed out so laboriously, he laid on his desk and put my military booklet on top of it. I still stood at his desk and saw him, how he signed my application, then wrote the date and added a rubber stamp as well. He looked at me and said:

"Comrade Lieutenant, before you go on vacation to Yugoslavia, you have to go for thirty five-days of military exercise" and handed me back my military booklet, the application and a form, which he had just typed out."

"Yes, comrade captain," I said in "military style" and I just had a feeling that I heard something, which in no way was in the line of signing my application. Subconsciously I felt that it was some sort of new tailspin. I looked at the form and there it was written in a bold font: Draft Notice. I looked at him and he ordered:

"In the morning of April 30 you'll be reporting for service at the military base 1022 in Levice. Drive on," the captain ordered and I submissively, like it was written in all military handbooks, went out of the office. This latest development of events surprised me so much I did not get to tell him about his error. We were dealing with my vacation to Italy and not to Yugoslavia. I uncomprehendingly looked into my application and in column "Trip Destination" was clearly and legibly written—Italy. I did not understand where he came up with Yugoslavia. Apparently, according to some military doctrines, which I did not know about Yugoslavia was the same kind of capitalistic enemy for the Czechoslovakian Army as Italy. Maybe it was only a cover name from his last military training, where Italy was called Yugoslavia, in order to confuse imperialist secret agents. In any case, I had no intention of entering that office again to try to fix the mistake. I was only a lieutenant in the reserve and proving to a captain of the regular army that he had made a mistake could not be very wise. The application was already signed and it was clearly written on it where I was going to travel. Following a moment of hesitation, I stepped out to the exit door. I did not register guys in the hallway and did not know how I got to the car. I opened the door, sat down in my vehicle and leaned my head back on the headrest. I felt that the adrenaline level was higher than usual and my head buzzed:

". . . right now, when I've got all my signatures, they summon me for an exercise. After five weeks, when I come back home, they will tell me that I came in touch with top-secret military documents and that I can't I travel to the West for at least the next five years . . ."

I had the feeling that my plans were demolished and all I had worked for until now would fall down like a house of cards. If I continued my thoughts in that direction I would go into a state of panic. No, no, no, I said to myself in spirit, echoing the words of comrade captain and, immediately after, I recalled:

"Just don't turn around . . ." and I took a deep breath. I looked at the application again. It was signed just the way I had filled it out—for a trip to Italy. I smiled and said very quietly:

"We will see . . ." and I buckled up and started the engine. I knew I was going to make up something, but right now I did not know what. For the moment I had to preserve my cool head and go on with my analytical thinking. According to the date on the Draft Notice, I had to get in April 30 and return home June 4. The passport department of StB needs eight weeks to issue a passport with travel provision and now it was April 20. Plenty of time! Just keep a cool head! We can travel even at Christmas, I remembered again. When I came back home, I opened a bottle of beer and poured it in a genuine beer stein. I walked through the hall into the living room and laid the beer stein on the coffee table, turned on the stereo and tuned to station Ostereich III. They just played hits from American "Top 40." I sat down in an armchair and put my feet up on the coffee table. I slowly sipped from the beer stein and became absorbed in American music. Every now and then, I captured English lyrics and strove to understand them.

"Some time from now I will have similar problems like those they sing about in the radio now and I will be laughing at today's," I thought.

I just finished my beer, when I heard someone opening the door to our apartment. I looked at my watch; it was half-past eleven. It occurred to me that it must be Nora and I remembered that Thursday was her short day. I went out toward the door to welcome her. As I hugged her, she noticed something wasn't right.

"Did they sign it?," she asked.

"Yes, they did," I answered.

"What is the problem then?" she asked.

"Start warming up lunch and come in the living room. We can talk about it," I said.

Nora went to the kitchen and I returned to the living room. About twenty minutes later, Nora entered the living room with a tray, on which there were knives and forks, two plates with the pork and sauerkraut meal with dumplings. She grabbed one plate and put it in front of me:

"Ah, so you're sipping beer here," she said with laughter and put down the other plate with cutlery opposite me and sat down on the sofa. We started eating, and after a few moments, she quietly asked:

"So, what exactly is the problem?"

"The application was signed, but at the same time they shoved in my hand a draft notice for an army exercise," I said.

"What?" Nora asked as she did not understand and then added:

"For how long?"

"For five weeks and I have to be there next Monday April 30," I said and then spoke in detail about my experience with comrade captain at the District Army Headquarters. As I concluded the army story, she thought for a moment and then she said:

"That means that at the beginning of June you should be home already. It's not too bad."

"By timing this doesn't look very bad, but I have got some fears that they'll pull a trick on me, about which I've heard. They summon a guy into the army and when he returns home they take his passport away because now he knows about some top secret and they prohibit him form traveling for three to five years," I said my fears to her.

"What is such a big secret they tell to someone, that he can't travel because of it?" Nora asked naively.

"It doesn't matter what it is. They are not going to bother with substantiating their actions. They simply say that right now he knows some top secret and take his passport away," I said and the room turned quiet. Only American music from the Austrian station interrupted the silence.

"What will you do then?" Nora asked after a few moments and then she added:

"April 30, you must be with the army in Levice."

"Yes, I cannot avoid that. I must report to service in Levice maximum twenty-four hours after the term on the draft card. In order not to attract any attention to myself, it will be best if I show up on time," I said and then he kept on:

"Not reporting to service in the army could be the biggest mistake I could ever make. I can't even say, that I did not get the draft notice because they stuck it in my hand. After three days they start looking for me. Finding me would not be a big problem and then they would put me in jail."

"So then, what are you going to do?" Nora asked again.

"I don't know yet. I know one thing, that April 30 about 8:00 in the morning I will be at Army Base 1022 in Levice," I said.

"I will be home for a few more days before I go to Levice, so I must bring both applications to the passport department. Where's your application right now?" I asked.

"Last Tuesday we had a meeting in the principal's office at which time I asked her about it. She said that all three signatures from the school were done a long time ago and now my application has been lingering at the school department for three weeks. The superintendent of the school department did not get a chance to sign it yet," Nora said irritated.

"Tomorrow is Friday, so ask at school, whether they have received your application back," I said.

"All right, I will ask," Nora said and then she added:

"In a moment Peter will be out of school. Let us go to meet him there and then we will pick up Katarina from kindergarten. We can go for a walk" and she started putting empty plates and flatware on the tray.

"That's a good idea. Let's go," I said and turned off the stereo. Suddenly, it turned completely quiet in the room. Subconsciously, I looked to the left, where there used to be a big stand with my aquarium. I realized that the air pump, which used to bubble air through the water, had always created a quiet noise shroud. Right now it was completely quiet; noise was gone along with the aquarium and fish. Only the impressions in the carpet by the wall indicated that once there was something there.

We went outside and slowly walked towards Peter's school, which was in the next street over. We held hands and walked silently, only sometimes our eyes met. It was pleasant warm weather and took us only about ten minutes to get to the school. We stood at a curb by the fence, in order for us to be out of the way of the flocks of kids, which tumble out of the school. Peter came outside among the last from his class and he was quite delighted to see us. He did not expect to see me at all and inquired:

"Dad, why are you also here?"

"I took a day of vacation because I had to go to Army Headquarters," I said.

"Why did you have to go there?" Peter inquired.

"They gave me a draft notice," I told only a part of my business from the Army Headquarters visit.

"Yet again?" Peter inquired and then added:

"Well, you have just recently been in the military service."

"Yes, two years ago," I said.

"How frequently does one serve in the military?" Peter inquired.

"They say once in five years, but that is neither law nor rule. When you are a soldier in reserve, they can call on you when it suits them" I tried to explain to Peter.

We came up to kindergarten, where Katarina was. Nora stepped inside and Peter and I sat down on a small wall outside the kindergarten.

"May I go with you sometime?" Peter inquired.

"I think this time it will not be possible, because I will not be here in Bratislava, but I have to go to Levice," I said.

"Well, before you were in Bratislava twice; why is it that you have to go to Levice right now?" Peter inquired.

"I am afraid we will never learn that," I laughed at his curiosity. At first he looked at me uncomprehendingly and then he started laughing too.

Nora and Katarina appeared outside from kindergarten and came to us. For Katarina the little wall was too high for her to sit on. She stood beside me with her back to the wall, put her hands on the edge of the wall and jumped up on the wall. Completely happy that her maneuver was successful, she looked smilingly at Peter and then at me.

"So what? Are we going somewhere, or will we sit here on the wall?" Nora asked.

"Let's go to Sady Janka Krala," Katarina said.

I looked at the sky. The sun was shining nicely, but the sky to the south was covered with dark clouds. It looked like in a couple of hours it might rain.

"By the time we get there, it's going to rain. We must come up with something closer," I said.

"Let us go to the race track," Peter said.

"How do you know it's going to rain?" asked Katarina.

"Do you see the clouds there behind those houses?" I said and pointed to the south.

"In about two hours it's going to rain," I added.

The children peeked to that side; even Nora turned just to see incoming rain.

"Let us go to the race track," Nora said and the kids jumped down from the wall. Katarina sprang to her mother from the right side and held her hand. The two of us were walking behind them. When we were crossing the road, I held Peter by his hand. Once we crossed the road, the kids walked in front of us. The race track was only about a twenty-minute walk from the house where we lived. We also walked by the building, in which Nora's brother lived with his wife Anka and their daughter Petra. That building was about halfway between our house and the race track.

"Let us go visit Petra," Katarina said and came running to mom, as we walked beneath their windows. She was pulling both moms' arms in the direction of the entrance to the building. Nora looked at her watch and said:

"They won't be home yet. We can stop by on our way back."

Katarina ran closer toward the building and looked up at the apartment windows where her cousin lived. She placed her right hand to her forehead to avoid the Sun shining into her eyes, looking up into the windows, trying to detect if any one of them was home yet. The windows on the second floor, where the family lived, were closed and the curtains from the inside shaded the view from the outside. After a few seconds, Katarina comprehended that mom was without a doubt right and came running back to us. We kept on walking on the sidewalk to the race track and, after a couple of minutes, we approached Peter's School. Pupils still walked out in flocks from the school and some of them didn't go home, but stayed in the school yard.

"Peteeer, Peteeer," we heard someone shout from the back yard. Peter turned after the voice, waved his arm and shouted out:

"Hi."

We saw a boy who lived in a nearby building from us come running up to Peter and whisper something in his ear. He concealed his mouth with his right hand, so we could not hear him.

"Tomorrow. Right now we are going to the race track," Peter said and joined us again. We came close to a road that was dividing us from the track.

"Do not cross the road, but wait for us," Nora said, when the kids impatiently started running in the direction of the track. They ran down to the end of the sidewalk and stopped at the curb. They turned toward us and waited. Behind them was a relatively busy road and beyond that road the race track. When we came to them, we held their hands and crossed the road. Once on the other side, they were free again and they could run all the way to the stockade, which separated the track from the audience. It was Thursday and jockeys with horses were preparing for Saturday's races. Right now they were taking only training rides, horses had no numbers and the betting office was closed. We stood behind the stockade and spent about half an hour observing the training. Horses of various colors ran in front of our eyes and their riders drove them as if they had a real race.

I looked at the sky. Dark clouds slowly but surely approached us.

"We should go back so the rain doesn't get us on the way, because we will get soaked to the bone," I said.

The children, with conniving eyes, glanced at the clouds and Nora said:

"Let's go, we can stop by at Miso's." (her brother). The children did not rebel that we were pulling them so soon from the racing and they came with us. We crossed the road together and walked in the direction of the building where my brother-in-law lived with his family. We were just outside the building when it suddenly got very dark and the first flash lit the sky. Somewhere in the distance, there was a clap of thunder and the first big droplets of an April storm started falling. We started running to the house and weren't inside under the entrance for a minute when a dense downpour started. We quickly ran inside and through the open entrance watched the downpour outside. The downpour was so dense that we could see only at a distance of a couple of meters. People who were still outside also ran to take cover inside. We went up the stairs because we did not like using the elevator. The elevators broke down very often and it happened frequently that someone got stuck for a few hours till he was rescued. Besides that, walking up the stairs was good exercise.

It was Friday afternoon and I was sitting in my office and glancing through books with chemical formulas and technological processes. I compared data from the last ten batches and strove to find a reason why production never stayed within the allowed ranges used for final inspection of the product. I was so absorbed that I did not notice the phone ringing. Following a knock on the door, the head of Mrs. Jarmila appeared in it:

"I don't want to disturb you, but your mom is on the phone," she said and her head disappeared again. I picked up the phone with my right hand.

"Hi mom," I spoke into the phone and with my left hand I held the book of technological processes, so it would not close.

"Hi Janny," mom said and then she continued:

"Your father and I have decided that we are going to permanently move to the cottage and would like to ask your help moving some belongings."

"When," I asked.

"This weekend," mom said.

"If nothing extraordinary happens, I should be going home at 2:30. Do you have those belongings ready to go?" I asked.

"Yes, I do," mom said.

"Then I can come over today. I should be there a few minutes after that," I said.

"OK. I'll be waiting for you. Bye," mom said.

"Bye," I said and hung up. I took a single sheet of paper and inserted it into the book so I could free my left hand. I looked at my watch. It was 2:25.

"I won't be able accomplish too much today," I said to myself and tidied up papers and books on my desk. I took my briefcase and keys and went to my parents' house. The traffic wasn't too bad and in a couple of minutes I was in their apartment. Mother and father were waiting for me and the belongings that needed to be transported were neatly stored in suitcases and boxes in their hallway.

"It is not too much in volume, but those suitcases and boxes are a little too heavy," dad said and then added:

"For us it would be a problem to transport them to Vysoka by train."

"Don't worry about it. I will drive them down there," I said and grabbed the two largest suitcases. Mom opened the elevator door and my dad and I transferred everything into the elevator. Two of us went down by the stairs and mom rode the elevator along with the load. When the elevator reached the ground floor, we unloaded the stuff in the hallway. I grabbed again the two largest suitcases and brought them to the car in the back yard. I laid the suitcases next to the car and opened the trunk. After I put them in the trunk, I turned around and dad was behind me handing me boxes. After a few minutes, everything was in the car and we went to Vysoka. Dad was next to me in the passenger seat and mom behind me. The seat next to her was completely stuffed with boxes.

It was Friday a few minutes after three and the traffic was getting heavy. It took us a bit longer to come to a sally road behind the city because cottage-dwellers rushed as soon as possible to "slip out" out of the city. I drove only four kilometers on the highway and took the next exit. From there it was only a fifteen-minute drive and we were at Vysoka by the cottage. I parked the car the closest to the gate so we did not have to carry everything too far during unloading.

"I'll open the big gate, so you can drive the car into the back yard?" father inquired.

"I don't think we are going to need that. As soon as we unload everything, I have to go pick up Nora and the children," I said and started bringing the stuff inside the back yard. Meanwhile, mom opened the cottage entrance door, so I brought those two heavy suitcases inside and left them in their living room. When I returned to the car, everything was unloaded and placed in the back yard. I looked at my watch and went into the kitchen to use the phone. I dialed the number to my parents-in-law.

"Yes. Please?" Nora spoke into the phone.

"Hi," I said.

"Hi. Where are you now?," she asked.

"At my parents' cottage," I said.

"What are you doing there?" she asked.

"I drove my parents with some suitcases here," I said.

"Are you coming to pick us up?" she asked.

"Yes, I am calling you because I want you to wait for me in case I get held up in traffic," I said

"We will wait for you. Let your parents know we are coming tomorrow. Bye," Nora said.

"Bye," I said and hung up.

Dad and mom were in the back yard smoking cigarettes. They stood there silently and I could see on their faces that these surroundings suited them better than the apartment in the city. It appeared to me that the village somehow relaxed them. In the city they were quite dismal; now they were smiling.

"I am so glad that we are here again," mom said between two "inhales" from her cigarette.

"Now I am going back for Nora and the children. We will all come back here tomorrow," I said.

"Are you going to stay for Sunday as well," dad inquired.

"I don't know yet. It all depends on the weather. So far it is pretty, but if it rains on Sunday, we would rather go home," I said.

"Say 'hello' to them from us," dad said.

"We are looking forward to seeing you," mom said.

I walked to the entrance and they walked behind me. When I got to the car, I looked back. Mother and father stood in the gate, waved their arms and almost at once said:

"Thank you."

"You are welcome. We will come tomorrow. Bye," I said and sat down behind the steering wheel. I started the engine and waved back to them through the open car window as I drove away. At a curve I looked in the rearview mirror. Both of them still stood in the gate and waved their arms.

Saturday morning all four of us went to the cottage. The weather was nice and the kids were looking forward to riding their bikes throughout the village. It looked like we were going to stay for Sunday as well. When our car got around the corner from the cottage, we saw dad, as he again waited outside. He watched the curve and as soon as he saw our red Skoda car, he opened the big gate for us to enter the back yard with the car and park inside. Nora and the children got out, I opened the garage door and put the car in. Grandma came out from the kitchen to the back yard and Peter and Katarina came running to her. When they got close to her, grandma bent over and both of them hugged her around the neck.

"What are you going to have for breakfast?" grandma asked.

"They have already had breakfast at home. Do not give them anything because they will not eat lunch," Nora answered instead for them. The three of them pretended they never heard Nora and went inside into the kitchen. In a little while, the kids came out holding chocolate bars in their hands. Grandma preferred not to come out this time. Nora looked at me with a face saying:

"Now it is your turn to say or do something."

I winked at her and very quietly, so only she could hear me, I said:

"Let it go. By lunch time they will run all that out by riding their bikes. I took our bags out of the car and carried them into the bedroom in "B" pavilion. I heard Nora yelling across the back yard:

"Janny, would you like some tea?"

I stuck my head through the bedroom door and yelled back across the back yard:

"Yes." I put our bags in a closet and came to the kitchen. Nora was measuring coffee grinds into a coffee maker and water for my tea was boiling in a teapot on the stove. Mom was sitting at the kitchen table and a cigarette that she had just finished was being squashed in an ashtray by her finger. Mom blew the smoke through an open window outside and said:

"For lunch I cooked some pork with potatoes. If you prefer rice, you can cook it now."

"I think potatoes are fine for us," I said.

Through the open window we heard grandpa with Peter and Katarina pulling their bikes from a shed. Grandpa's head showed in the window and he asked grandma:

"Would you like your bike as well?"

"Yes," grandma answered out the window and she turned to me:

"Now I will go shopping to the local store and the kids are going with me. We'll get a little exercise on our bikes."

"Watch out for cars so you don't get hurt," grandpa said through the open window.

Without saying a word, grandma gave grandpa an evil look and without a word he walked back to the shed for grandma's bike. Mom came out to the back yard and in a moment we heard her organizing the other bikers coming with her. She used to be a math teacher at middle school and her sonorous voice could handle thirty children without a problem. We knew our two kids would not be a problem for her at all.

Father pulled out a watering hose and went outside to the back yard behind the fence to water the grass. He carefully tracked mom and the kids on their bicycles until they disappeared from his view and watering was just a maneuver to cover his worries. He stood there a long time and watered the grass. Every now and then, he watched the curve.

Nora and I sat at the kitchen table and the coffee aroma was mixed with the tea aroma. Nora stirred her coffee with a spoon and I slowly slurped my hot tea. For our ears, used to the rush of a city, it was unbelievably quiet there. I reached behind me and turned on the radio. There was a speaker with Slovakian news, so I tuned the radio to another station. They just played hits from the international top shows.

I put my cup down on the table and observed how a thin pillar of steam rose from the surface of my hot tea. At a height of about half a meter above the cup, the steam suddenly lost its speed and the upside part of it turned into the shape of a question mark.

"Did your application come back from the school department?" I asked.

"No. It did not come back. Otherwise, I would have given it to you. The principal called the school department, and the secretary told her that comrade superintendent has not had a chance to sign it," Nora said.

"Monday I'll go to the school department and stay there till he signs your application. Within a week I am going to military service and it's high time that I bring our applications to the passport department," I said.

"Do you think he will sign it," Nora asked.

"I am positive," I said with self-confidence.

"What if he calls your father?" she asked.

"And he will ask him what. Whether I am his son?"

"No. He will call him and tell him he is signing your application for travel to Italy. Your father doesn't know anything about it," Nora said with apprehensions and then added:

"It will be suspicious to him that your father doesn't know anything about a trip like that."

"He will not call," I said composedly and then explained:

"At the school department they know father's phone number for the apartment in Bratislava. If the superintendent calls there, no one will pick up the phone because both parents are here now. No one at the school department knows they moved here."

"What if they meet each other somewhere in the city?" Nora asked with concerns.

"I think you are just making some needless worries. The world admires courageous ones!" I said. I clinked my tea mug against Nora's coffee mug and said:

"To our victory!"

"To our victory!" Nora said.

We finished our drinks and I said:

"I have already taken vacation days for Monday and Thursday."

"What is Thursday for?" Nora asked.

"Yes, Thursday I want to go to the passport department. They say it takes eight weeks to issue a passport," I said.

Nora thought for a moment and then she said:

"By the time the passports are ready, you should be back home from the army."

"I'd like to know what kind of "shanty" they are preparing for me in the army," I mused.

"You have been there three times already, so you should know how it goes," Nora said.

"Yes, but before my draft notices came home by regular post. This time they shoved it into my hand when I asked for a signature on my travel provision," I said.

"Maybe you just showed up there when they were getting ready to call a lot of reserves," Nora said to ward off my fears.

"I would be glad if it was just like you say," I said and added:

"I told you how my late draft notice was laboriously made out by a captain as I stood in his office. Using a typewriter is generally done by young soldiers, not captains."

We heard father walking in the back yard; therefore, we aborted our conversation. We still sat at the kitchen table with our mugs in our hands. Dad entered the kitchen, took a look at us and inquired:

"Why are you sitting here so quietly?"

"I was given a draft notice for military exercises," I said.

"For when?" dad inquired.

"I am starting a week from next Monday," I said.

"Didn't you serve in an exercise just a few years ago?" dad inquired.

"Yes. You are right. That's what we are talking here so quietly about," I said.

Through the window we heard mom's sonorous voice out in the street and in a moment thereafter a door creak, as when somebody opens the big gate in the back yard. Dad went out in the back yard and closed the gate after the bikers entered the back yard. They left their bicycles lying in the grass and stepped into the kitchen with their shopping bags in their hands. Peter and Katarina put their bags on the table and grandma called from the pantry:

"Bring me your shopping bags, so I can get the shopping organized on the shelves."

They took the bags and brought them to their grandmother. Peter came back to the kitchen and said:

"I am hungry."

"Me too," Katarina yelled from the pantry.

I looked at Nora and without saying a word grinned. She looked at her watch and said:

"It is still only half-past eleven. I will start heating lunch. We will have lunch in half an hour."

"Go help grandpa store the bicycles in the shed," I said and Peter and Katarina ran outside. I walked out after them and observed how they had the storing process nicely systematized. Katarina held the door, so it would not close. Peter and grandpa together pushed the bicycles one by one into the shed and then stored them neatly next to each other. When it was all done, Katarina closed the shed door. When bicycles were stored we all went under the pear tree and sat down on a bench. From a distance we could hear barking dogs and cocks crowing.

"How did you like today's shopping on bicycles?" I asked.

"Fairly well . . . ," said Peter briefly.

"Grandma was on her bike first, then it was me and Peter was at the end," Katarina said, and then she added:

"Grandma and I went inside the store while Peter stayed outside watching the bikes."

The longest was waiting in a line outside the store. Biking back and forth took us only a few minutes," Peter said.

"Lunch is ready," said Nora called through the open kitchen window.

Peter and Katarina started running toward the kitchen like a shot. When they reached the kitchen door, grandma stopped them and ordered:

"First, you have to wash your hands."

The lunch was already on the table and we all sat down. The children started eating with a big appetite. I looked at Nora and winked one eye again. The kids had a big appetite, despite the chocolate grandma had given them this morning.

"Good appetite," grandpa said.

"Good appetite," we all said almost at the same time. After that it was quite silent; apparently, everyone liked it.

I thought why it was that I was being called into active duty the third time. It was only eight years since I had come back home after a mandatory one year of service. On average other guys were called once in five years. I guessed I had become their favorite preserver, because I did not fit the average. However, I did not say anything. It was a very nice April day and I did not want to spoil it for the whole family with something they could not help me with anyway.

Monday morning I went to the school department, which was located in the Old City Hall building in the center of the city. It was a beautiful historical building, inside of which every piece of furniture, door or built-in ceramic stove was a unique historical artifact. I knew it very well, because my dad used to work there as a curriculum supervisor. All his life, or more precisely, ever since I as a little boy, I could recall him as a teacher at the Electro-Technical Professional High School where he once taught physics. A few years before his retirement, he was offered a position as a curriculum supervisor, which he gladly accepted. I used to stop at the Old City Hall when I was going by and chat with my dad, so I knew all his colleagues, the superintendent, as well as his secretary. Sometimes he could not spend any time with me because they were all too busy, including his colleagues because they were writing a report that should have been done a long time ago.

Now I stood in the hallway in front of the office of comrade superintendent and I decided not to leave the premises until I got Nora's application signed for the travel provision and in my hand. Comrade Superintendent was in his office, but his secretary suggested that I come back some other time. I tried to explain to her that in a week I was going for army service and I had to bring our signed applications to the passport department.

"Comrade Superintendent has a very important meeting scheduled soon, and he is just now preparing for it," the secretary insisted, and I could see in her face that she did not care about my problems at all.

"That's OK, I will wait until the meeting is over," I said.

"That kind of meeting usually takes the whole morning," the secretary said and expected me to give up then.

"That's OK, I will wait until the meeting is over anyway," I said with a very mild but determined voice and a bit of a smile.

"All right, but you have to wait in the hallway," the secretary said with a forced smile.

"Yes, I will wait in the hallway," I said with a big smile.

I went out into the hallway and stood by a window, right opposite the office door of comrade superintendent. I looked at my watch; it was five minutes to eight.

"If he doesn't want to be late, it is high time to go," I thought. I knew from my dad that those meetings used to be held in the New City Hall building, which was located opposite the Old City Hall across a wonderful historical square . . . I had not finished my thoughts when the comrade's door opened. He did not pay any attention to me; most likely, his secretary did not tell him about my waiting there. I walked toward him:

"Honor Work, comrade superintendent," I said and stuck out my hand for a shake. He was quite surprised by my greeting and glanced at me with a puzzled look

"Oh . . . comrade Bielek Junior," he said, and shook my hand. The confusion from his face disappeared and he did not even stop, but just continued walking. Our hands separated after a few steps.

"I am rushing to a meeting . . ." I heard him say as he kept walking to the stairway. He did not stop or turn around, but just ran down the stairs. The noise of heels running downstairs echoed in the hallway and a few seconds later it was quiet. I was alone again, standing in the hallway, and looked at my watch. It was four minutes to eight.

"Comrade Superintendent will be tardy for the meeting," I thought. I knew eight minutes was needed to get to the mayor's big meeting room from here.

"Maybe none of those comrades show up to meetings on time. This way they show off how important they are," I thought and stood at the window again. I looked outside and saw comrade superintendent crossing the small square to the New City Hall building.

I stood in the hallway and it was quite clear to me that I would be there for hours; however, I was determined that neither one of us would go home today before I held the signed application in my hand. I was slightly irritated by the fact that my father had worked here for several years before his retirement, and now these people didn't have any consideration or humanity inside them to affix their signature on a piece of paper. That piece of paper that lowered human dignity and which did not have any justification in human society. In a free human society . . .

"The whole country is sliding deeper and deeper into stinky communistic mud and, at the same time, pretends to have the most humane government in history. Whoever is brazen and dares try to escape will end up in jail or being shot at the border. How gladly I would like to be far away from here," I thought.

I looked outside the window again. The small square was surrounded by tall buildings and the view was not very exciting. I raised my eyes above the buildings and could see a nice blue sky with puffy white clouds, majestically floating to the west.

"A few months from now, my whole family and I will hopefully be in the West and, for these comrades, I will be "uncatchable" just like those clouds," I thought and smiled unconsciously.

I remembered a story from a long time ago. It was during the time when my brother Pavol had started his first grade at an elementary school. Every time I think about it I re-live the horror in my family and a fear for my parents. It was in 1956 and I was only five years old.

My brother was at school and his teacher was giving test forms to all the pupils for their very first test. When she laid the form in front of my brother, he unconsciously crossed himself. The teacher noticed the motion and reported it to StB. Both our parents were teachers; that meant government employees. Atheism of the state did not allow any exemptions and teachers had to be an atheistic example for all people. Our parents faced immediate dismissal and they would never get decent employment for the rest of their lives. They wouldn't be able to even consider teaching again. I remember how my mom ran out crying from the apartment to see her brother, my Uncle Emil. At that time he was director of the State Educational Institution despite the fact that he was not a Communist Party member. However, he was a well-known figure for educational matters in the world; that was why communists admired him. Somehow, he persuaded StB and the School department boss that my brother did not know what he was doing. They also believed him when he said that no one in our family believed in God even though we all considered ourselves Roman Catholic. They finally said OK, but it must not happen again, because if it did, not only would my parents lose their jobs, but he would be punished as well. My family was saved.

My Uncle Emil actually saved our family from a huge catastrophe twice. It was a few months after the first one and my parents did not have a single clue about their wrongdoing. They learned about it when Uncle Emil came to us late in the night. My mom opened the door and Uncle Emil, without a greeting and with tears in his eyes said:

"Maruska, for God's sake, what are you doing? Only a few months ago, I saved your livelihood with scratches all over my body and now this?"

"Emil, what happened?" my mom asked surprised.

"StB agents came to me today and said you are propagating Christianity with a cross around your neck," uncle said.

My mom grabbed her head with both hands and her face turned red. My father watched the situation speechlessly and I could see fear in his eyes.

"But, Emil I just wore that little cross because I had a black turtle neck sweater on and did not have any other jewelry that would fit," said my mom very quietly and big tears rolled down her cheeks. The cross they talked about was a present from her mother and it was a very old heirloom cross given from mother to daughter. It was very small, less than one inch tall and its value was more in history than in size.

This time the situation was much worse. Mom was suspended without pay and she was forbidden from entering a school. My father was still allowed to teach in his professional high school, but StB agents followed him everywhere. Mom went to Uncle Emil every day and with his help they both were trying to return mom to her school. After a week of their begging and promising, StB and the school department finally agreed and mom was back at school. However, both parents had to sign an official declaration; they denounced Christianity and at the same time promised they would never ever in their lives propagate Christianity at any level. At the end of it, they swore they both were a hundred percent atheists, including their children.

I was only five years old then and could not understand a lot of these things. Among them, I was prohibited by my parents to reveal to anybody that Uncle Emil was my godfather. Only later when I was growing up did I gradually learn about terror and terrible inhumane treatment of people by the Communist Party and its power arm—StB during the 1950s. It happened quite often if someone did not behave exactly as the leading power in the country required; agents of StB dragged him out and many times the person disappeared without a trace. Justice did not exist and, if someone else asked about the missing person, he eventually disappeared without a trace too. It was not difficult to imagine how fearful people became when their names popped up on an StB list of undesirable persons. That was the fear I saw in my father's eyes in 1956. The oppressions were extremely powerful against faith and any kind of religious organizations. During that time pastors, priests, rabbis, monks and nuns used to disappear without a trace, or in a better case, they ended up in jail. Their only crime was their religion and spreading it among the people.

I stood in the hallway and was brought from the past back to reality by steps in the stairway. I looked at my watch; it was only half past eight.

"That cannot be comrade superintendent, those meetings take much longer," I thought and one of my father's colleagues came from around the corner.

"Good morning," I said when his face appeared.

"Good morning" said Mr. or rather Comrade Milan and asked:

"How is your dad doing?"

"Thank you, he is doing just fine," I said.

"Who are you waiting for?" he asked.

"For comrade Superintendent. I need a signature from him," I said.

"Comrade Superintendent is at the monthly mayor's meeting. Those meetings usually take until noon. You can go shopping in the city or just for a walk. You can catch him when you come back shortly before noon," Comrade Milan said.

"Yes, I know. But I would rather wait here. Just in case the meeting is over sooner," I said.

"Well, good luck . . . and say hello to your dad for me," said Comrade Milan and entered the office where dad used to be too.

"Thank you," I said and turned back to the window.

During the morning, I had a chance to see and chit-chat with all dad's previous colleagues. All of them asked me who I was waiting for and also asked me to say hello to dad for them. Time was running somehow faster when short chit-chats interrupted my recollections of the past that were going through my mind again.

I looked out the window and watched people crossing the little square. A big clock on a tower I could not see from the window rang its bells every fifteen minutes. I was gladly listening to its chimes because they counted down my endless waiting. Most of the time my eyes were focused on the New City Hall gate opposite me. It was almost eleven when the opposite gate finally opened and a big crowd of people came out. Among them was also comrade superintendent whom I waited for.

"How smart of me not to listen to dad's old colleagues advising me to come back shortly before noon." I thought.

In awhile, I could hear the steps and voices of several people coming up the stairs. Comrade Superintendent and another man, in this case a comrade I did not know, came from around the corner. I looked at them and did not know what to do now. They were quietly discussing something I could not understand and walking toward the office I had been waiting in front of for more than three hours. As I stood there confused, comrade superintendent looked at me, and without saying a word, he lifted his right hand with the palm of his hand facing me. I understood his signal to stay standing at the window. When the door of his office closed behind them, I looked at my watch again. It was exactly eleven o'clock.

I stood at the window for another fifteen minutes, but this time with my eyes fixed on the door, when the door opened. Those two said good bye to each other by shaking hands and a loud:

"Honor Work."

The unknown man started walking toward the stairway and comrade superintendent again without a word waved his hand at me calling me inside his office. I entered his office and he was already sitting at his desk.

"Sit down," he said when I closed the door behind me.

I sat down in a chair he was pointing to, at the same time holding Nora's application in his other hand. He studied it without a word for a minute, pulled a pen from the inside pocket of his jacket and opened it. He looked at me and said:

"I wish you a pleasant vacation" and signed the application; then he handed it to me and said:

"Say hello to your dad for me."

"Yes, thank you. I will most certainly talk to my father," I said and inserted that very valuable piece of paper into my briefcase.

"Honor Work" he said at the end. It was a signal for me I could go home now. I gave comrade superintendent a big smile and repeated comrade's goodbye:

"Honor Work."

I left his office, went up to the window and looked at the sky. Fluffy white clouds were still moving to the west,

"In a few weeks I will be there with my whole family too," I thought and smiled. I felt some kind of satisfaction in winning that struggle. Even though it was moving along very slowly just like the clouds, I was still winning. I ran down the stairs and was happy with myself as I came out into the square. I took a deep breath and went to the parking lot.

About fifteen minutes later, I was parking the car in front of our apartment building. I jumped out of the car, and while locking the door, I noticed Nora in the distance. I waved to her and she noticed me, so I stood at the car. Then she waved me to come to her.

"I can see on your face he signed my application," she said when I got close to her.

"Yes, I have it right here in my briefcase," I said and slightly lifted the briefcase in front of me.

"It is unbelievable. He sat on my application for six weeks and did not get a chance to sign it. And for you he does it while you are waiting there," Nora said turning her head in disbelief. I winked an eye and said:

"It was because of my personal charm."

"Come with me to the grocery store for shopping. You can help me with the bags," Nora said, completely ignoring my note about personal charm.

"You can tell me all the details at home," she added.

The grocery store was very close to our apartment, about fifty meters (150 feet) from our building. We shopped based on what they had at that moment, not following our list. A good sense of planning was needed for shopping because on certain days they had certain goods. Nora knew the system very well in all details. For instance, if they had fresh meat today, she had to buy it. It did not matter that we needed meat for Sunday. We had to buy pork today because it was available today and use it for Sunday.

We brought the shopping home, and while I was putting everything away in the pantry and refrigerator, Nora reheated lunch. She put it on plates and we ate it at the kitchen table.

"I still cannot believe how it is possible that comrade superintendent sat on my application for six weeks and could not sign it. He does it for you while you're waiting," Nora said, resuming where we had left off our discussion in the street.

"I told you it was thanks to my personal charm," I said with laughter.

". . . personal charm . . . that's for sure . . ." Nora laughed.

We were eating lunch and I told her in detail how I had spent the whole day's morning in the hallway in front of the office of comrade superintendent. She listened to me very carefully, and when I got to the fluffy white clouds in the blue sky, she said skeptically:

"We are not there yet . . ."

"Not yet, but we will be" I said with conviction. It was quiet for a moment and then I said:

"It is a nice day today, so let's pick up the children and we can go for a walk to Sady Janka Krala."

"OK. You go pick up Peter and I will pick up Katarina from kindergarten. We will meet at the parking lot by the car," Nora assumed managerially.

We went downstairs together and parted at the main entrance of the building. She went to kindergarten for Katarina and I went to school for Peter. I just crossed the road to the other side and saw Peter coming in between buildings in my direction. I waved to him and he waved back. I stayed at the parking lot, walked up to the car and opened the trunk. Peter just walked to me and I took his school bag and laid it inside the trunk and closed it.

"Hi, where are we going," Peter asked.

"Hi. Mom went to pickup Katarina and then we all are going to Sady Janka Krala," I said and unlocked the car. Peter sat down in the passenger seat next to me and slightly lowered the window on his side. I cranked down the window on my side all the way.

"How was school today?" I asked.

"It was fine," said Peter very briefly.

"Do you have any homework to do?" I asked.

"Just one—math," said Peter.

"You can do it when we get back home," I said.

"They are over there," Peter yelled out and pointed in their direction. Nora and Katarina stood on the other side of the road waiting for cars to go by, so they could cross the road. When they came close, Peter jumped out and said to Katarina:

"We are going to Sady Janka Krala," he said with happiness and excitement in his voice.

"I know, mom told me," said Katarina and sat in the car behind mom. Peter ran around the car and sat down in the seat behind me.

It took us only ten minutes to get to our destination and the kids happily ran out of the car. We started our walk down one of the alleys and Peter and Katarina were a little distance in front of us. They chased each other up and down a path among the chestnut trees. It was obvious they needed relaxation and running after a day spent in school and kindergarten. Chestnut trees were just blossoming and completely covered with huge clusters of flowers, their aroma was like balsam. The grass under the big trees had been mowed awhile ago and a group of young people were raking hay into piles that attracted kids like ours to jump in it.

"Now, when that we have all the signatures on our applications Thursday I will go to the passport department and turn them in," I said.

"I guess you have to go there early in the morning," Nora answered.

"Yes between one and two in the morning. You already know about half a day standing in line is needed," I said.

"The night before you should go to bed early," Nora said.

"A few extra hours should be enough for me. If I go to bed just after the children fall asleep and get up around one, I should be able to make it," I said and then added:

"I should be able to snooze for awhile outside in front of the building . . . till eight when they open."

"You should take the sleeping bag with you and snuggle up in it during the night because it might be quite cold overnight," Nora said.

"I can take a pillow. In case I doze off," I said and then added:

"I will not be able to get real sleep. I will be afraid of being robbed there."

"Do not forget the important documents . . . like the Civic ID Book or applications," Nora said.

". . . and also our pictures," I added and remembered the instructions:

"Tonight when the kids are sleeping, we should double check to see if everything is filled out according to the instructions. I don't want to wait in a line for fourteen hours and then find out something's missing. I'd rather go there a day later just to make sure I have everything StB agents will need."

Peter came running toward us and reported:

"I am thirsty."

Katarina ran up a bit behind him and from a distance shrieked:

"So am I."

"If we keep walking straight down this sidewalk and turn left at the end, we will come to a snack bar. There you can to get a lemonade or soda," Nora said and she pointed in, which direction.

The kids turned around and looked at that side.

"I'll get a soda," Katarina said.

"I see there a white building in between trees," Peter said and ran away into the snack bar. Katarina followed him immediately. We saw them running in front of us and as we approached the snack bar they were sitting on chairs at a small table with an umbrella.

"I want a strawberry lemonade," Peter said when we sat next to them on chairs. After lemonade and soda we went home for dinner. After dinner Peter wrote his math homework and it was bedtime. The children fell asleep in no time and the two of us sat at the kitchen table double-checking our applications. We carefully read again all the columns, mainly to see if they were filled out correctly. To our great surprise, we discovered that Nora's application was missing the rubber stamp of her school. The school principal had signed the application, but his secretary had forgotten to stamp beneath her signature. This tiny detail could have cost us a lot of time and extra energy if we had not seen it. Almighty StB agents sought out such details and with pleasure threw people out of their offices.

"Tomorrow I will take it to school and ask her for a stamp," Nora said.

"But I will need it back Wednesday the latest because I want to go to the passport department early Thursday morning. I've heard that there are many more people waiting in lines on Fridays. And Monday I must be at military exercises," I said apprehensively.

"I should be able to make it because tomorrow is only Tuesday," said Nora and put her application into her bag, so she would not accidentally forget it at home.

Wednesday after work there was a party, which I will perhaps never forget. My attendance at it confirmed to me even more that I did not belong there and the earlier I could get out of there the better. Director Prazec celebrated his fiftieth birthday and invited all the comrades for the festivities. I wasn't a member of the party, so I did not even assume at all that I would be among the invited guests. To tell you the truth, neither did I want to go. To my great astonishment, two weeks before the celebration, he came to my office. I sat at my desk, preparing for another meeting, as I heard his steps in the hallway. They were very characteristic because with every step the prosthesis on his knee squeaked and immediately afterwards one could hear a dreary whack with a cane on the floor. I lifted my head and listened.

"No, it cannot be the director; he would never come here in person. Always, when he needed something, he just asked his secretary, Marika, to call me by phone and I had to rush into his office," I thought. I had not finished my thoughts when his figure turned up behind the frosted glass on my door. I rose to open the door when I heard him knocking.

"Come in," I said and immediately opened the door.

Prazec entered my office and remained standing by my desk, leaning against his cane. I stood opposite him at the other corner of my desk.

"Sit down, please," I said.

"No, thank you," Prazec said and kept on:

"I came here to invite you to the celebration of my fiftieth birthday, which will be held Wednesday here in our company dining room at four in the afternoon."

"Yes, thanks for the invitation, comrade director," I said.

"Consequently, I expect you at the banquet," he said.

"Yes, I'll be there," I said.

"Once more thank you," I said, because it was clear that declining could not even be considered. Prazec turned toward the door and I opened it for him.

"See you later," he said just at the door.

"See you later, comrade director," I said and shut the door behind him. I remained standing and shook my head like someone, who momentarily misunderstood the situation. I could not get into my head his non-comradely salutation "See you later," as well as why he had put out so much effort into coming to my office in person for the only purpose of inviting me to the celebration of his birthday. I tried to recall when he was in my office last. After moments of thinking, I came to it—never!

"Why is he so anxious about my coming to his birthday gathering?" I asked myself quietly. I have never gotten an answer to that question.

Wednesday, shortly after half past three, I came to the well-known company dining room. I entered the room, looking around and looking at people standing in small groups. I could not see anyone I wanted to join when I heard a voice behind me:

"Hi Jan," I turned to the voice and saw my friend Peter.

"Let's go sit down there," he said and pointed to the middle of a row of tables.

"I was just looking to see if there were name tags. The big comrades should sit here," I said.

"They will sit over there with Prazec," Peter said and pointed to a smaller row of tables.

The tables had been placed into five long rows and on the right side there was a smaller row of tables positioned perpendicularly to the five long rows. A speaker's booth with a microphone was attached to the small row. A big sign saying "Happy 50th Birthday" was hanging right from the ceiling above.

Chairpersons of KSC and ROH were already sitting under the sign, including Comrade Stromcek. Next to him, right in the middle of that row was an empty chair. They all were wearing very important faces.

"Peter and I sat down at the spot he picked and we were discussing production problems he had as a technology manager in Plant #2. The dining room was filling up and we knew most of the people coming in; they were company employees. The ones I did not recognized were important comrades and they were seated at the table Peter had shown me previously. Prazec personally greeted them at the door and then he walked them down to their seats at his table.

Folk music from the Northwest corner of Slovakia was flowing from the speakers, which was very nice because Prazec came from that part of the country. To my great surprise, the folk music stopped playing a few minutes after four when Prazec was just showing another important comrade to his table. Peter leaned over to me and whispered in my ear:

"That's the leading chairman from the regional Communist Party committee."

The comrade sat down on a free seat just next to the middle one predetermined for Prazec, who sat down at his "front row" seat in the middle. The folk song was interrupted in the middle, and following a short break when we could hear just the background noise of the room, the Communist song called "The International" played. All the people in the dining room jumped from their seats, like they were shot at, with a lot of noise from chairs being moved on the concrete floor. The noise was so loud that for the first ten seconds we could not hear the Communist music at all. I looked at people around me and could not find any sign of shock in their faces, so I had to concentrate all my internal power in order not to blow up in laughter. When the music finished playing, they all sat down again repeating the huge noise with the chairs. I looked at people again and found everyone acting just fine. I could not believe nobody had found playing "The International" at a birthday party amusing. Or most likely they were in a situation very similar to mine and they used all their internal power not to start laughing.

After The International was over, comrade leading chairman stood up to the microphone and read from a paper, which was most likely written by someone else. I kind of expected he was going to talk about fifty years of Jan Prazec's life and, using some funny stories to entertain the audience, would turn the birthday celebration into a festive occasion. That would be most likely too much to expect from a Communist Party chairman. Instead he was reading, not with the best of Slovak language, boring achievements of Comrade Prazec in the advancement of the Communist Party and his credits for deepening the leading position of the Communist Party. It reminded me of an official speech of all general chairmen during the highest assembly party meetings or a May Day Parade. He spoke for about thirty minutes, and as it was a habit for those comrades, he did not say anything that made any sense. I was already under the impression that these people did not have any life and everything in their life revolved around Communism. When he finally finished his reading and rolled up the papers, he looked at Prazec from his speaker boot and said into the microphone:

"Jan Prazec, I wish you a happy fiftieth birthday," after which he left the booth and sat down next to Prazec. It appeared as if, only after reading through all those phrases, that he became a human again and was capable of wishing the birthday boy a happy birthday.

Now it was Prazec's turn at the microphone. He did not bring his speech written on paper, just a small card with notes he wrote down during the comrade chairman's speech. He looked at the card and answered every single phrase of the comrade with another phrase that could be found in any later newspaper. I already thought it was going to be as boring as the speech of the other guy and was getting ready to switch off my ears when he said something that attracted my attention:

". . . we must never forget where we came from and where we are going . . ."

"I do not know where you are going but in a few weeks I am going to the West, and if you knew what I know, you would poop your pants," I thought and smiled knowingly. Comrade Sobotka, who sat at the opposite seat at the same table as I, registered my smile and he smiled too.

I looked at the wall clock behind Comrade Sobotka. Prazec had already been talking for thirty-five minutes and did not say anything we hadn't heard before or wasn't boringly reprinted in newspapers. I saw a few cooks come out right under the clock, holding trays with small wine glasses filled with a little bit of wine. They walked in between the tables and placed a glass of wine in front of each person. Meanwhile, Prazec finally finished his speech and Comrade Stromcek seized his opportunity and jumped into the booth.

"Oh, no . . . not another one about achievements of Communism . . . ," resonated in my head and I smiled. Stromcek held his glass in his right hand, lifted it high in the air and, with broken Slovak language, yelled into the microphone:

"So, Jan Prazec, we wish you all health, success at work and that you would be able to stay here with us for another fifty years. Bottoms up . . ." and he poured the wine into his mouth at once. This was the first time I had ever seen him behaving like a human being, which was very nice. But people in the room started laughing and with laughter finished their glasses just as Stromcek had. I did not know what they were laughing about, but I was laughing at Prazec. After Stromcek's toast, he made a sour face and then quickly threw wine down his throat. The rumor had it that he had his eye on a higher position at the Ministry of Industry. I also did not know if Stromcek was more informed that the rest of us or it was just a play from a very simple person. It is funny that Prazec never made it to any ministry and retired as a director of that company. He did not get any help from playing The International or with phrases he had quoted in response to the phrases of comrade leading chairman.

After Stromcek's toast, we got a big bowl of beef soup for each table of four, which was very enthusiastically served to me by Comrade Sobotka. When we finished the soup, the cooks took the soup bowls away and placed a plate with fried Wiener Schnitzel and potatoes in front of everybody. It was very difficult to avoid eye contact with Comrade Sobotka during the meal. I just remembered how he had tried avoiding me in the hallway of the building we lived in. He lived there for some time with Hana Klubesova in an apartment directly above us. If we just by coincidence came out into the hallway at the same time, he stood frozen there and waited for me to exit the building first. I saw the reflection of his figure in the hallway window and he evidently thought I did not see him. Originally, I looked back shortly after exiting the building and saw that he was a short distance behind me. Later I did not turn back anymore and just laughed at him when I saw his frozen figure reflected in the hallway window.

I must have smiled unknowingly because he looked ashamed and said:

"I will stay hungry if I don't eat bread with my schnitzel and potatoes," and only then I realized what he was doing. He cut off a piece of schnitzel, poked it with his fork and, using his knife, added some potatoes next to it. He put the schnitzel in his mouth and then bit off a piece from a slice of bread. Then he chewed slowly and carefully. If he had not mentioned it, I would not have noticed. I smiled again and said:

"Every one of us has a bad eating habit," and had to use all my will to keep from bursting into laughter.

After the main dish, the cooks distributed small trays with pastries. Judging by the position of each tray, we understood one tray was meant for four, so we each took only one piece of pastry. I did not want to take another one because there were only two left. Sobotka took the initiative and lifted the tray under my nose and said:

"You take another one and I'll take the last one."

"No, thank you. I am all set with pastry for today," I said. He hesitated for a moment, and when I did not take any, he took another one and laid the tray with the last one back on the table.

People finished eating and started their conversations. The noise level in the dining room was rising very rapidly and it became impossible to talk to someone without yelling. Peter had just finished his piece of pastry when he leaned to me and asked:

"What now? Are we going?"

I leaned to him and said quietly so Sobotka could not hear me:

"Now? Nobody has left yet. Do you want to lead?"

"I have to go. I've got a date tonight," he whispered quietly with his face turned away from Sobotka.

"Let's go through the other door. It will look like we are going to the men's room. And we just don't come back here," he added.

We both turned and looked at Prazec, who was busy conversing with comrade leading chairperson. He was far away from us and he was turned the other way and could not see us. Peter gave a signal with his head and the two of us stood up like we were ordered by someone and left the room. We were glad to be out of there and after a brief "Bye" we parted ways.

Tuesday Nora brought her application form back from school, this time with the missing rubber stamp, so I could start preparing for my half a day ordeal. We told the kids I was going on a business trip to explain some of the motions and why I was not home overnight. I used to travel quite often and they did not pay attention to us.

She prepared a backpack for me with a sleeping bag and a pillow, a little bit of food and drinking water. I put together all the documents needed for the passport department. I was double-checking every item against instructions, so I didn't forget something. About 8:30, I went to bed to get at least a little sleep. I set the alarm clock for 12:30. I fell asleep relatively fast, and when the alarm clock woke me up, in the first moment, I did not understand what was going on. The hands showed 12:30 and it was still dark outside. Then I remembered that it was time to go to the passport department and quickly put a shirt on and slipped into jeans. To be on the safe side, I also took a jacket and put on sneakers. I grabbed the backpack, quietly opened the door and again quietly closed it, in order not to wake anyone. I ran down the stairs, unlocked the main entrance of the building and again locked it behind me, walked to the parking lot and stepped into the car. I threw the backpack on the seat next to me, started the car and drove on the back streets to the regional passport department, Bratislava IV. It took me an unusually short time to get there because there were almost no cars and all traffic lights were just blinking yellow lights. I parked at the nearest parking lot, took the backpack, got out of the car and locked it. Only now I felt it was rather chilly and the jacket really became useful. I shivered a little, maybe from the chill, maybe from the unusual feeling of loneliness among the high buildings. I walked in twilight toward the passport department; only streetlights lit the streets, sidewalks and houses. It was very quiet, there were no vehicles of public transportation, and I heard only my footsteps.

"The entire city still sleeps," I thought and looked at my watch. It was 12:55 in the morning. As I was coming closer to the building of the passport department, I heard somebody playing a guitar. First it was only very quiet music, which became louder with every footstep. I turned around, but could not determine from which direction it was coming. I supposed this was someone who could not sleep in one of the houses and I could hear the music through an open window. Only as I came out from behind a corner of the last house and in front of me was the building of the passport department did I find that it was coming from a crowd of people who already stood in line outside the closed building. It was there that I saw the guitarist in a crowd of about a hundred and twenty people. He played the guitar and sang very quietly, more or less just for himself. Probably many of them came there with the last trolley, which in this region used to run for the last time at about 11:30. I did not expect so many people there, but I still had a hope that today I would be able to get into the office of the almighty agent and turn in our applications.

"Good evening, or rather night," I said very quietly, almost whispering, when I walked up to the crowd of people and sat down at the end of the line. I didn't mean to wake those who slept or snoozed. Some who did not sleep also greeted me whispering or only nodded their heads. People sat down or lay down on the sidewalk next to each other. Some "sleepers" were completely bundled up in their sleeping bags and even their noses were not visible. Ones sitting down were leaning against the vacant and dark building of the passport department. Others had their legs covered with a sleeping bag or a blanket. I pulled my sleeping bag from the backpack and slipped my legs into it, sat down and pulled the zipper up. My back was leaning against the building and I had a pillow under my head to shield me from the roughness of the wall surface. My arms were hiding inside the bag and I was holding in my hands a small bag with all the paperwork and documents. I closed my eyes, but I could not sleep yet. Every minute or two there were newcomers interested in a passport joining the crowd and the waiting line was getting ever longer. I had a nice feeling it was not me at the end of the line. They sat down the same way as the others. Luckily, the building was a long one. The guitar man was still playing and singing quietly, slow and winding songs and his performance was admired by the rest of the crowd as a very good lullaby. I must have been snoozing for awhile when I was awakened by a crinkly noise. I opened my eyes and saw another newcomer at the end of the line working on his sleeping bag that looked to be a blue color in the twilight. He was pulling it from its carrying bag and that motion made a funny crinkly noise.

"That bag looks like one made for winter and he could sleep in it even on snow. Most likely he went hiking in the wintertime," I thought. It was cold now, but not even close to freezing temperature. I looked at my watch. It was 1:50

"I've already got one hour of waiting behind me," I thought. The guitar man finished his performance and pulled himself into his sleeping bag completely. It turned absolutely quiet, only seldom someone's coughing or snoring interrupted the silence. My back was getting numb from leaning against the hard stucco coating of the building, so I also slipped down into a lying-down position and slipped deeper into my sleeping bag. I laid a blanket on the pavement under my pillow. From the inside I pulled the zipper all the way up to my neck. I could not sleep, so I watched the sky above me.

It was a clear night with no clouds and the sky was covered with stars. I searched for the Big Dipper because its rear wheels gave me an idea about the position of the North Star which was a definite indication for north. I had to twist my head backwards in order to see it. The star was twinkling in the sky and seemed to be so close. It appeared to me so close I could just pull my hand from the sleeping bag and reach for it. I tried to imagine how big those stars and the whole universe really are. Our planet Earth is smaller than a poppy seed when compared to the stars and then we humans how tiny we must be living on that poppy seed. Why did we make our lives so miserable? A small group of people in this country made life for ordinary people so unbearable just for the sake of ruling them. For that purpose they picked philosophical theories employed by two French revolutions and proved, they were completely useless for real life. Those theories seemed fantastic when written down on paper because they call for total evenness of all human beings. Levelness always warms hearts by providing a platform for closeness. It just did not work in proxy because every one of us is a little different by nature, abilities, height, size, or motivation . . . Then when someone plans everything, beginning with the size of the meals, through how many pairs of shoes or the number of bedrooms in an apartment, then humans turns into a herd without a face. Furthermore, if they are told what to think, or whether to believe in God, then life in the herd becomes totally unbearable.

When I was a boy, I often contemplated what would it take for people in a herd to get fed up with the situation and organize their life according to their own will. Their lives would be governed by theories, which worked well in proxy and were corrected and redesigned throughout hundreds of years to fit the people. Not someone trying to change people to fit some theory. For examples that were close to us, all they needed was to look beyond the borders of the country . . . like Austria or West Germany. One of them was the United States where democracy has existed for more than two hundred years. It was not perfect, but maybe the best human generations could come up with.

As time went on, I realized people do have those principles. They were just hidden deep inside of them and a fear of Communist oppression prevented them from showing them out in the open. They all knew that any leader who would try to change anything would disappear without a trace from the surface of the Earth. Fear was the main force and no one was brave enough to do anything. Everyone was waiting for a miracle that would happen without their involvement. A person would join the winning miracle only when all the danger was gone. Under the given circumstances, the best choice was just running far away where the almighty Communist arm could not reach you.

Every year thousands people left this country and among those lying down in sleeping bags next to me were a lot of them just like me. They resigned their life there and decided to start a new life somewhere else. However, about half of them came back later because they could not handle a life in which nobody was making their decisions for them or telling them what to think. They came back begging and the government extensively used them as propaganda. They traveled the country, wrote articles in newspapers and tried persuading people how horrible life is on the outside and what kind of heaven on Earth it was to be home again. Those people always sounded phony and a few months later they got lost in the herd again. This time StB really made sure their life became more unbearable than ever before.

I knew that regime had to fall I just was not quite sure I would live long enough for that. However, if that were to happen during my lifetime, I would be exhilarated and would watch with pleasure as dreadful Communism fell down like a house of cards. I would enjoy it enormously no matter what corner of the Earth I inhabited at the time . . .

The noise of the first trolley coming from a distance woke me up. It was rolling on rails and its brakes made a screechy sound before every stop. When it came close to me, I could also hear its chimes and the clapping blast of closing doors. The sound was so loud it woke up everyone around me. I did not feel like pulling my arm from the warmth of my sleeping bag, so I just estimated it was 3:30 in the morning. The east sky was reddening with the rising Sun.

"I must have fallen asleep," I thought because the stars in the sky were slowly disappearing. I glanced around me. It was quite obvious no one was sleeping anymore. I made eye contact with a guy a short distance from me who was in a green sleeping bag.

"We've only got four hours till they open the door into the building," he said ironically.

"I am sure we are going to make it," I said and pulled my head back inside the sleeping bag. I did not have any interest in starting conversations with strangers. I heard and also saw how StB agents were trying to join crowds of people. They were called "provocateurs" and they usually started with a negative statement about the country or government and waited for people to join them in their opinion or information. Then a message was submitted further and problems for the people joining the dialogue started shortly thereafter. I pretended I was still sleepy, yawned and closed my eyes. The guy who was next to me on the left side joined the dialogue and I was not quite sure if he was being this stupid or was just another agent.

"Just keep on talking. I will not say another word," I thought with my eyes closed and kept quiet. Those two went on:

"Waiting for such a long time for a stupid travel provision pays off only if you do it just once in your life," said the guy next to me.

"Yes, the first and the last time," responded Green Sleeping Bag in incorrect Slovak.

"Those two are certainly agents," I contemplated. Very often they broke their cover just by speaking incorrect Slovak language. Originally, I was under the impression it was some kind of Slovak dialect. But I had been in different parts of Slovakia and spoke to many people from different parts of the country and never heard anyone speaking it but agents. I remained quiet and completely ignored their dialogue. No one else joined them, so they went silent again.

It was seven o'clock in the morning and the Sun shone down on us. I followed the example of others and took out breakfast, which Nora had prepared for me. I consumed the bread with cheese and salami, then washed it down with a bottled water. I took out my backpack from the sleeping bag, where I was hiding it overnight and packed the sleeping bag with my pillow back in it. I stood up, raked through my hair with my fingers and took a glance at myself. Jeans and jacket too were wrinkled as if somebody had slept in them. It occurred to me that right now a hot shower would feel great, but given the conditions, this was too much of a luxury. I was glad the night was behind me. I looked at the end of the line. It was about three times longer than when I came in and I didn't believe that all those people would fit into the building in the hallway.

"Perhaps they could stay waiting in line outside," I thought and glanced at my watch. It was 7:50. Around fifteen minutes later, someone from inside the building unlocked the door and walked outside. It was an StB agent, this time in uniform with rank-badges on his shoulders. He stayed standing outside and held the door open. I knew that, if I got inside the building, perhaps today I would be successful in getting inside the office of the almighty and could hand in our applications. I also knew it was not a good idea to make eye contact; therefore, I fixedly looked at the person in front of me. I walked inside with about fifty other persons behind me, when I heard:

"Stop," the agent ordered ungrammatically and then equally ungrammatically kept on:

"From here down to the end everyone can go home."

I turned my head and saw how those people submissively departed with their heads tilted downwards. I quickly turned back, so my eyes would not make contact with his. He let go of the door and stepped inside. He walked in the middle of the hallway and people avoided him like the plague so he could freely pass by. Nobody was interested in starting a confrontation. An angry expression on his face was a warning, which everyone comprehended. He entered a room on the other side of the hallway and shut the door behind him.

"He made a face, as if someone in the line had eaten his breakfast," I thought. Apparently; not even being one from the almighty brought him satisfaction in life. I looked in the hallway and just to kill some time started counting how many people were in front of me. Most of them were men, only infrequently the monotone of the line was interrupted by a woman. It took me a long time to take a count of it because the crowd was very thick and people were always moving. They stood in columns of three and the row snaked in the hallway three times from the beginning to the end. Just like I saw it when I came there to pick up the blank application forms and my classmate Lubos spoke to me. I counted 115 persons and I was number 116 in the line. The more fortunate ones, who were just outside the door of the almighty two offices, started entering inside. There were only two doors and using my watch I timed how long it took for a person to get outside after entering the door. I found out that a person was held inside from three to nine minutes, which was six on average. During lunch, between 12:00-1:00, the offices were closed because agents had their lunch break. I counted that my turn should come between two and three in the afternoon. The office hours were until 4:00 pm, so there was still a hope even if the cycle slowed down. I started thinking what I would do if I had to go to the men's room when a guy in front of me turned to me and said:

"Now I will go to the men's room for a few minutes, so please hold my spot."

"Yes, of course," I said with relief, because he in fact responded to my unmentioned question. In a moment he returned and stood in front of me. I did not say anything, only with nod of my head and a smile I let him know everything was OK.

Green Sleeping Bag tried to tie up a conversation with people around him:

"Those inside don't know how to read and write; therefore, we must wait here so long," he said and surveyed around himself, to see who would start a debate with him. I bent over my backpack on the floor and took out a book, which I carried with me for such occasions. I opened the book by the bookmark and started reading, so I avoided conversation with provocateurs. I immersed myself in my reading and subconsciously registered how the noise from the chatter in the hallway grew stronger. At first people started speaking only modestly in order to kill some time. Later, conversation became louder and louder and, at one end, a group of people exploded in a loud guffaw. I made a face that I was immersed in reading even though due to the noise I could not concentrate on reading at all. Suddenly, the door to one of the offices opened and the figure of an agent emerged who howled from the bottom of his lungs:

"QUIEEEET" and the crowd in the hallway went dead silent.

"If it won't be quiet in here I will immediately clear the hallway," he threatened in a strong voice. At that moment, one could hear a pin drop. The atmosphere in the hallway was at a freezing point and he turned around, stepped back into his office and slammed the door behind him so hard that it almost fell off the hinges. The door slam was as if someone had fired a gun. After this warning people entertained each other only by whispering. They feared that, if he carried out the threat, they would have to sleep outside the building for another night. Provocateur Green Sleeping Bag turned backwards and in a quiet voice with laughter said:

"That was a tough guy!"

In the silence of the hallway everyone certainly could hear him all right, but I did not even register if anybody spoke back to him. I read my book. At exactly 12:00, at the door at the end of the hallway, they hung up a small ticket, "Lunch Break," from outside and from the inside they locked the door. The slow advancement of the line ceased. The agents did not step outside from their offices; either they ate lunch at their desks, or they had another exit from there on the other side of the building. I took out my lunch—a sandwich, which Nora had packed in the backpack. I washed it down once more with water and resumed my reading. They reopened the door at 1:00 pm and removed the ticket from it. The line in front of me gradually reduced and, as I finally got to the door, I put my book back in my backpack and got ready with the transparent cover containing all documents. When my turn came, I stepped into the office and said:

"Good afternoon," and took all the documents out from the cover and handed them to the agent. He did not reply to my greeting and nervously shrieked at me:

"Only applications."

I quickly took the applications from the stack and handed them to him. He inspected all the columns on our applications and checked them with a pen. When he came to the end he said:

"Civic ID Book"

I handed him our Civic ID Books and he turned over pages, comparing data with the columns on the applications.

"Photographs," he ordered and I handed him Nora's and my photo.

He laid them on the applications and inquired:

"Are you traveling with children too?"

"Yes, two children," I said and handed him birth certificates of both, Peter and Katarina. It appeared to me that he smirked a bit over how quickly I comprehended his style of paper work.

"How many children do you have altogether?" he inquired.

"Two. In my wife's passport," I said and thereby I answered also his following question, into which passport the children should be written. He looked at me surprised and this time I quite clearly saw that he grinned a little bit too. I grinned as well. Our following paperwork passed quite quickly because I handed him documents before he requested them. When he got everything finished, he inserted our applications into a manila cover and at the bookmark he wrote our last name and date. He placed the manila cover on a big pile on the right side of his desk and returned my Civic ID Books and the children's Birth certificates. Then he looked at me and said shortly:

"Eight weeks" and I comprehended that we were done there. I said:

"Goodbye" and I walked out into the hallway, yet I registered how a guy who was in line behind me entered the office. I wiggled slowly among the people and left the building. The door automatically closed behind me, I breathed out with satisfaction and glanced at my watch. It was 2:55 in the afternoon.

"Consequently, I had spent fourteen hours here," I said to myself and got underway to the car. I had a good feeling because our applications were already in. They did not find any error on our applications or any other documents, for which I could have gotten thrown out. I stepped into the car, slammed the door behind me and looked through the windshield at the sky:

"Thank you, good Lord," I said this time loudly. I was so happy that I did not register my journey back home. There were two matters on my mind:

1. Hot shower.
2. Cold beer.

Nora stood at the balcony and waited for me. When I came to the parking lot in front of the house, she noticed the car and waved to me. I parked, got out of the car and waved back to her. The anticipation in her face was obvious from a distance and when I got closer she asked by swinging her head:

"Did you get it?"

"Yes, I did," I swung my head in the positive motion and her face turned into a big smile. She turned around and stepped inside. I rushed up the stairs and found her standing in the open door and she glanced at me wondering whether I was OK. She hugged me around my neck, without saying a word, dragged me inside our apartment and with her foot shut the door behind us. I dropped the backpack and when it hit the floor the buckles on the straps made a ringing sound. The ring attracted the attention of the children and they looked at us through the open door of their room. They both came running toward us. At first they did not understand what was going on and when the two of us bent down so they could reach us they both joined Nora in hugging me too.

"Hi," Nora said and the kids followed after her:

"Hi, Hi," Peter and Katarina said.

"Hi, Hi," I said and all three I squeezed with a force.

After a few moments, they let go and Nora asked:

"Are you hungry?"

"I would like some warm food with cold beer. But first I am going under the shower," I said.

"All right, go get a shower, and in the meantime, I will warm up some food for you," Nora said. By the time I was done, some warm food was on a dinner plate and a bottle of beer was standing by. In the evening, when the kids were already asleep, we sat in the living room and quietly spoke under a cover of music. I recounted in detail my experience of waiting outside the building, waiting inside in the hallway, as well as the process of our paperwork by the StB agent.

"That's horrible what one must undergo in order to get out of the country," Nora said when I finished my story.

"This is just how it was said by provocateur Green Sleeping Bag, that all this trouble makes sense only when you do it once in your life. He was right," I said.

"I hope that you did not discuss the matter with him," Nora inquired.

"No, I have already told you the story in detail," I said a bit crossly.

"But otherwise I am so glad that you see the situation here in its full nakedness," I added yet.

"I think everyone can see it, they are just afraid to say anything," Nora said pensively.

". . . and they are much more afraid of doing anything. People are afraid of everything. Fear is their motive power in life. Many of them are frightened so much they are performing self-censorship to what they are saying. Even when no one else is listening," I added.

"But I hope we will be successful without problems," Nora said meditatively.

"Just don't start with fear now. Most of it is already behind us. It cannot be without problems. Always believe I will manage everything without big problems and leave it to me," I said with determination. Nora took a deep breath and said:

"It is easy for you to say it."

"It is as difficult for me to say that, as it is for you. But you will see that one day we are going to talk about all this loudly and with laughter. There will be no need for background music either. That is what I call freedom," I said slowly and very quietly. She raised her glass with red wine that was in front of her and said:

"To our victory!"

"To our victory!" I clinked my glass against hers and added:

"Just don't turn around . . ."

"What are you going to need with you to military service?," she said as she switched to another more pragmatic theme.

"More or less only what I will be wearing, my military booklet, wallet and some money. Slightly more money than I usually carry with me," I said.

"Are you going to need any food?" she asked.

"No, I will not need any food. Monday morning I will go by train to Levice and for lunch I should already be at the army," I said.

"You always told me that food there isn't worth a lot," Nora noted.

"Yes, it is true . . . that's why I will need more money," I said.

"Tomorrow you can withdraw some money from the bank. The bank is across the street from your work," Nora said.

"I will take out some for you as well. So, you don't have to go there too," I said

The start of my military exercise approached and, according to the draft-card order, I had to spend the following five weeks there. Friday morning I arrived to work a little earlier. I wanted to utilize the morning silence and standstill in order to prepare for my five-week absence. For each division I wrote a list of things to do and discussed each list with that particular manager. Some of them made notes in their work notebooks; others just listened. Or, they just made faces as if they were listening. Comrade Vice-president Flak called a short meeting only with me for ten o'clock. He wanted to know whether the department was prepared for my long absence. I gave him copies of the lists I had prepared for the divisional managers. He carefully studied them and sometimes stopped and asked for more details. We sat behind the big table in his office and his questions appeared to me a bit ridiculous. I entertained myself with the idea: what this vice president would do when in a few weeks I would leave forever. However, everyone is replaceable. I remembered how a long time ago we talked at high school that cemeteries were overcrowded with irreplaceable people. It was cynical, but at the same time, as truthful as all teenagers before reaching maturity. Life here would go on . . . after the first shock, which usually lasts only a few days, life would return to its normal track.

Once the vice president finished reading my copies, he looked at me above his glasses and inquired:

"When are you coming back from the army exercise?"

"I will be back five weeks from next Monday, June fourth," I said and then added:

"If my tank is not destroyed and I do not fall in a war against the imperialistic enemy."

The vice president looked at me with surprise and his eyes almost popped out from their eye sockets above his glasses; then his face reddened and he started uncontrolled heehaw. I only grinned a little, and when he calmed down, I quite composedly said:

"When one goes into battle, he must consider every alternative."

The vice president laid the copies on the table in front of him, crossed his arms on his chest and started laughing again. He kept watching me above his reading glasses and he seamed to be nicely entertained. After a little while he took down his eyeglasses and put them on top of the copies on the table. He shook my hand and said:

"Then, I wish you much luck at the army," and again he grinned.

"Thank you," I said. After our handshake the vice president added:

"According to the law you have the right to some free time before your start in the army. If you still need to arrange some personal things, you may leave now."

"Yes, I have got something that I need to take care of," I said and at the same time I knew that the law said the whole day and he was giving me a few hours. I smiled and said:

"Good bye."

"Good bye," the vice president responded.

I went back to my office and took the briefcase and keys. Before leaving, I peeked into every office of my department and shook hands with everyone who was still there.

Monday morning I got up along with my family, because I didn't have to rush to work for six o'clock. I did not have to rush to the rail station because there were several trains going in that direction. Nora made breakfast and once again all four of us were sitting at the table in the morning. It was unusual, ever since they had changed my working hours to six in the morning. We ate quietly; during breakfast, no one said a word about my military service. We had already spoken about it many times before; there was nothing to ask about or add. The sorrow in the kids' eyes was quite obvious, so I said:

"In a few days, I will be back home."

"You have to go for five weeks, don't you?" said Peter.

"Yes, but before you say "quick" I'll be back home," I said to cheer them up. Nora did not say anything. When saying goodbye, I noticed tears in her eyes when hugging her. The children had tears in their eyes too when they embraced me for a farewell. I stepped out from the kitchen into the hallway and put on my shoes. They stood in the kitchen door and watched me. I opened the door and waved my hand goodbye. While walking down the stairs, I checked whether I had my wallet, military booklet, and the draft notice in my pockets. I walked out onto the street and looked up. All three stood at the balcony and waved their arms. I waved back to them again and went to the bus stop. In a couple of minutes I came to the rail station. I entered the vestibule of the railway station and looked at the board with the train departures. The next train was leaving in about thirty minutes. I did not need a ticket because the draft notice served as a ticket, so I crossed the rails in the tunnel below and came out onto the platform. I stopped in the centre of the platform and bought a journal in the kiosk for fighting off boredom on the train. I opened the journal and ran my eyes across the table of contents. No one title in the content attracted my curiosity so much that I would go on reading the article. I turned the pages of the journal and peeped at the pictures. By the time I came to the end, I found that perhaps I had thrown away money for nothing because there was nothing that could possibly have caught my interest. I rolled up the journal into a tube and looked around, searching for a wastebasket when I noticed Joe close by. Joe was one of those I had served with during my last military exercise. He stood a short distance from me and read a newspaper. I did not throw away my journal but approached him and said:

"Hi Joe. Are you going to Levice?" He gave me a startled look and then asked:

"And you?"

"Me too, for five weeks," I said.

He folded the newspaper, shook my hand and said:

"We are going to drag it out together again."

"It seems to me that we serve much too well when we get called into service so frequently," I said with irony.

"This time we should come up with some horseplay," he said with laughter.

"I am already working on it," I said with laughter too. However, I had decided that, during the entire service, I would tell nobody even the official version regarding our vacation plans in Italy, nor, what I thought about this call into service. We started to commiserate about our last military exercise, which we fought together and before we knew it the train was stopping at our platform. We boarded the train, sat down in a completely vacant compartment and kept on in our conversation. We could not understand why right now we had to go all the way to Levice and why this time we could not stay in Bratislava like last time. It would be less expensive for the military and by far better for us.

"Apparently, the army has enough money for our extra expenses and what's better for us isn't on their list of conditions for draft-notice orders," I said.

"We will learn this when we arrive there," said Joe and both of us went silent for a while. We just stared outside the window and watched the country go by that we were traveling through.

"I hope I will not have troubles with food. Lately, eating in the factory dining room irritates my stomach," I said.

"It can be also from nervousness. Do you have gastric ulcers?" Joe inquired.

"I don't know . . . . Perhaps not . . . . So far I have not seen a doctor," I said.

"If the food in the factory dining room gives you troubles, then army food won't be any better. Maybe by the end of week, when the initial rush subsides a bit at the base in Levice, you should go to the army's first-aid station. They send you to a hospital for an examination and at least you are going to know what's happening," Joe said featherlike a bit.

"I think you have quite a good idea," I said and then added:

"Also it depends on how much work they have ready for us there," I said apprehensively. I was not comfortable with the fact that someone could find peptic ulcers at my young age.

"You should go in any case and not drag out visiting a doctor," he insisted.

"If I have troubles with my stomach, I will certainly go see a doctor. Indeed, you know how it is with these kinds of illnesses. If I am not in pain and I go to the first-aid station, they will say I am a malingerer," I said.

The train started braking and in a moment it stopped; we had arrived at the first way station. Through the window we saw people boarding the train.

"Look at those three," I said and pointed at a group of three guys, who stood at the end of the line outside the car door and added:

"With haircuts like that they may only be other recruits."

"It seems that we have more company coming," Joe said with laughter.

The train had just started moving again from the way station when the three entered our compartment.

"Are you going to Levice for military service?" inquired the first of them.

"Yes," I said.

"Haircuts always give us away. We would not be good at reconnaissance," Joe said with laughter. He stood up and shook hands with our new company.

"Joe."

"Milan, George, Viktor" the new guys introduced themselves. I also stood up and shook hands with them.

"It looks like half of this train will be only recruits who are going to Levice for military service," said Viktor and he sat down beside me.

"We saw more guys boarding this train and they all had a military-style haircut," said Milan.

At the following way stations more and more guys with military haircuts boarded the train, and when we arrived at the railway depot in Levice, there were around sixty guys standing at a railway platform after the train departed. None of us knew where the army base we were going to was and we looked at one another trying to find somebody who would know which way to go. When the dispatcher clerk finished his whistle signal for train departure, he smilingly looked at us and loudly, so we all understood, waved his flapper to outside the railway station and ordered:

"Outside the railway station, turn right. Two kilometers on the left is the army base."

It seemed that to find the army base was not going to be a problem and those guys who were the closest to the railway station exit turned in the direction shown by the station dispatcher. The rest of us just followed them and in about ten minutes we saw the army base walls in the distance. We walked inside and saw the duty officers at tables outside in the back yard. Every table had a board with two letters of the alphabet: A-B, C-D . . . and we signed in according to our last name. We handed them our draft notices and the duty officers checked off incoming soldiers from their lists. After receiving uniforms and other army gear, we were sent into rooms where we placed our belongings into lockers. Right after lunch we were summoned into a conference room where the commander assigned work to us for the following week. He ordered us to prepare our troops for a full combat state of readiness. I, as lieutenant in reserve, got a tank platoon with three squad commanders and soldiers, all together ten army tanks. I was given a detailed list of my tanks and their armament, as well as technical parameters, according to which tanks were evaluated. A week later we had an inspection planned, to see if we fulfilled our duties. Following the orders I was given, I prepared a plan for every day for my soldiers and we started our work. Everything was going along very well, our tanks were getting better every day and I was very satisfied with my unit. The weekend was getting closer and also the time for the final inspection of our work.

However, the troubles with food and my stomach were worsening every day. After each meal I felt worse, so I tried eating less. I thought about the advice Joe had given me during our train ride.

"You should go in any case and not drag out visiting a doctor,"

Sunday after midnight, I was awakened by a sharp pain in my abdomen and felt as sick as never before. I lay in bed and in the first moment I did not realize where I was.

"It's time to visit a doctor," I thought when I realized I was with the army. I tried to get up. However, it wasn't so simple. I had to use all my power in order to stand up and put on my uniform. Afterwards, walking very slowly, I went to the military first-aid station. It was very quiet in the back yard and in the distance I could see sunrise colors.

"Lie down here," said the attending physician at the first-aid station and helped me climb onto an examination bench. He unbuttoned my jacket and using a stethoscope listened to my heart.

"Your heart is all right," said the doctor with relief and started inquiring about my pains. I described to him my troubles in detail and he followed examining where it hurt. He tapped a finger over his palm on the right side of my belly and in a little while he said:

"It looks like a gall bladder irritation" and he took out a vial from the drug cabinet and from it he removed three green pills. He handed me a glass of water and said:

"Swallow these pills and you will instantly feel much better."

He poured the pills into my hand, I put them in my mouth and washed them down with water. In less than two minutes I felt relief and the right side of my belly hurt much less.

"Are you feeling better now," the doctor asked.

"Yes, much better," I said.

"So, this is indeed your gall bladder," he said and then added:

"It would be the best if you got examined in the city hospital. But I cannot give you an ambulance because everything here is in such a frenzy. You'll have to take a bus."

"Do you think you can handle it by bus?" he inquired apprehensively.

"Of course," I said and added:

"I am already feeling better."

"For an ambulance you'd had to wait until the base commander signs the dispatch card order," he said apologetically.

"By then I would have already arrive there by bus as well," I said convincingly and inquired:

"How do I get there?"

"Outside the entrance to this base, there is a bus stop. Get on bus No. 23 and after two stops get off in the front of the entrance to the hospital," the doctor said and at the same time wrote a message for a doctor in the hospital.

"You will go to internal medicine and give them this message," he said and handed me a sealed envelope.

"When you get examined there, come back here. If they confirm my diagnosis, you will be sent home," he added yet.

I sat up, looked into the doctor's eyes and said:

"But I cannot go home . . . I must still finish preparing the tanks . . ."

"The army can't go into combat with someone, who suffers bilious attacks. Don't worry about it, the unit commander will assign your tanks to someone else," the doctor said.

I jumped down from the examination bench, buttoned up my shirt and jacket, put a military cap on my head and shoved the envelope with the diagnosis into the inner the pocket of my jacket. Those three little green pills the doctor had given me had taken full effect. I felt much better. The doctor also handed me a small ticket on which he wrote the name of the doctor I should see in the hospital.

"Thank you, doctor for everything," I said and walked out of the first-aid station. Then, walking slowly, I went out to the bus stop. It was early morning already and the whole base was waking up to a new day. Soldiers dressed in green sweat pants ran out into the courtyard, where they had their morning exercise. From a distance I saw how they ran and jumped according to the music and heard their distant voices. I stood at the bus stop for around fifteen minutes, till the first bus came. The bus was quite vacant, morning rush hour travel having not yet begun. I got off the bus a couple of minutes later outside the hospital and, using the orientation board in the lobby, I found internal medicine and the doctor, to whom I was recommended by the military doctor. I rode the elevator to the internal medicine floor and I handed over the sealed envelope with my diagnosis to the nurse. She immediately opened the envelope and called me inside, where they took a sample of my blood for laboratory testing. The doctor was surprised that with my diagnosis I did not get brought to the hospital by ambulance. I told him how long I would have had to wait for the commanding officer's signature, in order to get an ambulance, so I came by bus. He also asked me to lie down on an examination bench and actually repeated what had already been done by the doctor at the base. After the examination he sat down behind his desk and read over my blood analysis. He wrote out a form with my diagnosis and sealed it in an envelope. He handed me the envelope and said:

"Bring your diagnosis to the doctor at the military base and here is your prescription for pills. They are called Febichol and you'll be taking two capsules three times a day for a period of one week. The prescription may also be picked up in the hospital pharmacy on the ground floor of this building."

"Do you have a company doctor?" he inquired.

"Yes, we have a doctor in the company health centre," I responded.

"When you come back home, go see the doctor for a check-up. During the next two weeks you have to switch to a meatless and non-greasy diet," he added yet.

I thanked the nurse and the doctor for their care and on my way down to the ground floor of the hospital picked up my prescription in the pharmacy and went by bus back to the military base.

The doctor in the military first-aid station read over the diagnosis from the hospital and then inserted all the documents of my examinations into a large brown sealed envelope, which he handed to me:

"This is for your attending physician at home," he said.

"Do you mean in our company health centre?" I asked

"Yes. With this you will go into the main building of the base to the registration department, then turn in the military uniform and you will go home," he said.

"Home . . . ?" I asked.

"Yes, home. With your health condition this is the best solution. When you regain your health, you will be called for completion of the military training," the doctor said without hesitation. After updating my data at the registration department, I came back to my room, picked up all army gear and turned it in at the army warehouse, where they gave back my civil clothing. As I walked out into the back yard, I met Joe. He looked surprised at my civilian clothing and inquired:

"So, indeed you have peptic ulcers?"

"After examinations by doctors, this is a gall-bladder condition, not ulcers," I said.

He shook hands with me and said:

"Restore your health as soon as possible, I must run. Right now, I am the commander of the tank platoon instead of you" and ran away towards the tank garages. I turned that way, but he did not look back and went running to the soldiers, who were waiting for him.

I walked off the base, but I was too weak for a trip afoot to the railway station. It was ten o'clock in the morning and I had not eaten since yesterday's dinner. Even though I was as hungry as a wolf, I did not have any appetite. By bus, which had a bus stop outside of the base, I rode away into the centre of town, where there was a terminal station for intercity-connection buses. The bus stop for buses into Bratislava was immediately at the beginning and my nearest connection according to the schedule was about 1:30 pm, so I still had to wait two hours. I sat down at a bench and warmed myself in the Sun.

The trip by bus home passed very quickly because, following a sleepless night, I was really tired and, as the bus moved from the bus stop, I fell asleep. Bratislava was the final bus stop; therefore, I didn't have to be afraid of sleeping through my bus stop. I woke up when I heard:

"Get up, this is the last stop." I opened my eyes and looked after the voice. The bus driver stood above me and with his arm on my shoulder he shook me softly, so I would wake up.

"Get up, this is the last stop," he repeated when I looked up at him. I stared around and it took me a few seconds till I came round. I got up and left the bus. It was perhaps 4:30 in the afternoon when I got home, and my arrival was altogether unexpected. Nora and the children were really surprised when they heard somebody unlocking the door of our apartment. They rushed out into the hall and started peeping at a door. They had to be stricken by fear, because nobody except the four of us had a key to our apartment. In the first moment they did not even consider that it could be me. I looked inside and noticed their terrified faces. When they caught sight of my head in the door, the fear in their faces vanished and they ran over to me. All three hugged me at the same time:

"How is it possible, that you are already at home?" Nora asked.

"They sent me home for health reasons," I said.

". . . for health reasons?" Nora asked surprised.

"Yes," I said and pulled out from my pocket the sealed envelope from the military doctor. The children didn't say anything, but just followed our dialogue.

"Yesterday during the night, I felt really sick, so I went to the military physician. His diagnosis was a bilious attack and for safety's sake he sent me to the city hospital for examination. It was also confirmed by the doctor at internal medicine in Levice's hospital and he gave me some pills," I said and showed her the envelope.

"How did it happen?" Nora asked.

"I don't know . . . either food or nervousness. Maybe a combination both of them at the same time . . ." I said.

"Are you hungry?" Nora asked.

"Yes, I did not eat anything the whole day, but according to the doctor, I have to stay on a lean diet for at least two weeks," I said.

The following morning I went to see the doctor at the company health centre. Following an hour of waiting in the waiting room, I got inside and handed her the sealed envelope with my diagnosis from the doctors in Levice. She read over all my papers while I sat quietly in her office and waited. When she came to the end, she looked at me and inquired:

"How do you feel now?"

"Fairly well, ever since I began taking the Febichol," I replied.

"Yes, you have a prescription for it from the doctor at the internal medicine department in Levice's hospital," she said and looked at the papers again. Then she wrote something and, when she was done, handed me a paper and said:

"Here is a doctor's certificate for your time out of work. Inform your boss that you are going to be out of work and bring the certificate to your payroll department. Come back in two weeks for a check-up, but if you are not feeling all right or feel some sort of pain, come back immediately. If it is acute, you will have to go to the hospital by ambulance immediately."

I looked at the paper she handed me and according to it I had to stay home for "in-house healing" for another two weeks. The nurse scheduled me for a check-up on Tuesday in two weeks and handed me a little card with the date and hour. I looked at the card and said:

"Thank you and see you in two weeks at 8:30" and I went to work to see my boss. The vice president was not there because he was at the quarterly meeting. I didn't want to wait for him and just left a message with his secretary. Just a few moments before my arrival at the office, Mrs. Jarmila came to see the vice president's secretary and both were very surprised to see me so soon.

"It seems that the military food and environment are not very good for your health," the secretary said with a laugh.

"Perhaps I am too old for this kind of activity . . . they have to find someone younger as my replacement . . ." I said with a laugh and then added:

"Indeed these were my third maneuvers in the course of eight years."

"Mr. Engineer, if you still have a little time, I would like to exploit you for awhile. They sent some papers for new "measures" from the General Directorate and I didn't want to write down any dates without you. Could you dedicate me a little time?" Mrs. Jarmila asked.

"Of course. The doctor wrote me out for another two weeks. I will still have plenty of time to rest somewhat after the heavy work at the army," I said smilingly. We went together into our building. While I organized the mail on my desk, she brought about a twenty-page document from her office. Each page had about seven measures, which they sent to us from the General Directorate, in order for us to "incorporate" them in our suite and date every one of them. Officially this was called the Suite of Measures for Improvement of the Management of the Planned Economy. The title was so impractically long that everyone called it only the Suite of Measures. At the time it was a new collocation, which Communists produced at the last Grand Congress. Its contribution to the economy equaled zero and I heard it being compared to pouring stones from one bucket into another—no difference, only a lot of noise. Right now the two of us mulled aver verbal pathways without a practical meaning and tried to come up with some sort of date for it. She read a measure and I said the date. We were going forward quite quickly when, after about ten pages, Mrs. Jarmila looked at me scrutinizingly and asked :

"Mr. Engineer, so many dates for September? . . . I don't know if it's wise? When it comes to evaluating them, we'll go crazy."

Then I perceived what I had done somehow subconsciously. Subconsciously, I was certain that in September I would be far "behind the hills," but somehow I neglected that people like Mrs. Jarmila stayed there. In an entirely calm voice I asked:

"Till when do we have to incorporate all those measures?"

She turned the papers over to the last page and said:

"At the very latest by December 1986. We've got two years."

"Oh . . . I supposed this was expected to be all done by the end of this year. I am sorry; let us go once more and back to square one," I said again very composedly.

"It seems that the army service taught me to take everything "by the attack," I said still with laughter. Mrs. Jarmila rolled her eyes and at the same time flipped back ten pages of the document from the General directorate and we started from the very beginning. This time I paid much more attention that I did not disclose my big plans for a new life "behind the hills" and scheduled useless measures without suspicion.

Two weeks I stayed at home and felt very good. I got a lot of relaxation following the stress of acquiring signatures for our applications. At the same time, I could plan in detail what still needed to be arranged. I needed to pick up our passports; therefore, another sleepless night on the street inside a sleeping bag in front of the passport department and then a day-long marathon waiting in line was in the offing. There was still a threat that for some pinheaded reason we would not get the passports. Then we still needed Austrian and Italian visas. When compared to what I had already coped with, this was relatively simple. However, I was confident that just the way I succeeded until now I was going to reach my goal again.

I returned to work and I was by no means amazed that nothing changed there. Days went by with the same pace and I frequently thought it was certainly going to continue in that manner without my being there. About twice a month I went to Prague to different corporations of foreign commerce, where I arranged the shipments to our company from abroad. It was getting close to the date when it would be necessary to give in our applications for visas at the Italian embassy in order to fit within my plan. I didn't have to wait for an invitation from a corporation of foreign commerce because I got an invitation for a technical symposium, which was held in Prague at the Hotel Panorama. I viewed the invitation and my heart started rising from pleasure because the symposium was to last three days.

"Excellent, three days in Prague, this is exactly what I need," I said to myself quietly in my office and folded the invitation into my notebook. During the following meeting with the vice president, I presented the invitation card to him and asked that my travel in Prague be approved as a business trip. It did not take a long time for him to study it and he said:

"Yes, I agree."

"Luck still continued to be on my side," I thought, but I only smilingly said to the vice president:

"Thank you."

I walked through the back yard and into my office and came up with an idea, that the trip to Prague could be used for more than just giving in our application for visas to Italy. I shivered a bit by the idea, because, if I was successful, I would violate legislations and regulations about foreign currency exchange. But according to all that I had planned, the emigration of an entire family abroad, this new idea would only be a drop in the bucket. If I violated legislations and regulations about currency exchange and somebody were to find out, the punishment would only be a financial penalty. If someone found out we were "running away" from Communism Nora and I would spend fifteen years in prison. Financial penalty would be a better case scenario of the two. I did not even want to think about the worse case.

"I have been carrying a lot on my back so far and this little nothing will not harm me any more," I thought. By the time I came to my office, the idea was already a plan, which was very simple. I would give some known Austrian cash here in Czechoslovakia and he would return the money to me in Austria. I knew if the foreign visitors wanted to change their money to our crowns, the Communists would give them only fifty percent of the real value and they shoved fifty percent in their own pocket. I wanted to make an exchange at full value of their money. For an Austrian it would be favorable because he would get twice as much for his money for me it would a profitable sideline because I would have money in my pocket in Austria without transferring it over the border and the Communists would pocket no money. I thought about Mr. Kurt Schwartz. A few years ago he was in Slovakia on a business trip and I took him for dinner to restaurant Koliba. I wanted to show him something typically Slovakian and Koliba was the perfect choice. The restaurant was furnished with typical Slovak furniture, and meals and beverages were also typically Slovakian. I ordered the meals and with every one I told him how the meal was cooked and a little bit about its history. We had a wonderful time and he was completely stunned when I insisted on paying the bill. We left from there in a very good mood and Mr. Schwartz said:

"When you come to Austria, I will take you into a typically Austrian restaurant, but then I will pay the bill."

"Yes, I agree. Just to be sure, I will forget my wallet at home," I said with a laugh.

"No, you do not need to forget your wallet, I am paying in Austria," he responded also with laughter.

"All right, it is a deal," I said, shaking his hand and he went into his hotel and I went home.

I came back into my office and began studying the invitation closely. The company Mr. Schwartz worked for was listed among the participants and even his name was also listed there.

"Perfect," I said quietly with a smile and started filling out papers for a business trip to Prague for the symposium.

A few days passed and I sat on the express train and was looking forward to Prague like never before. I had ten thousand crowns in my pocket, which would give an estimated five hundred dollars in Austria after the exchange with Mr. Schwartz. Twice as much as I could get by exchanging the money through the exchange bank. Not even mentioning that exchanging additional money in excess of the approved amount by the Foreign Allowance was absolutely impossible. I thought about whether Mr. Schwartz would not be afraid of such a transaction, as well as making sure I avoided the snoops. Foreign visitors, as well as people, who came in contact with them, were very closely watched by secret agents of StB. I was on my way into a city which I did not know as well as Bratislava. I used to go there relatively frequently; nevertheless, for a consistent knowledge it was too little. I meditated about various alternatives, how and where I would talk to him, in order to evade possibilities that someone would be eavesdropping on our conversation . . . During the symposium it was impossible; too many people . . . In his room at the hotel, microphones could be installed, even cameras . . . perhaps I will not be alone with him in the car . . . Finally, I decided on a short conversation in a restaurant. I was going to be there for three days, some sort of opportunity would arise where I could talk to him at a table. I was convinced that all tables would not have microphones. According to the invitation, we would have breakfasts and dinners in a form of buffet. We would take our meals ourselves and no one was going to have seating cards on tables. I would choose my table completely at random, where nobody would be around and would start our discussion about the weather and then about the symposium. I would tell him I was going for a vacation to Italy through Austria. It was no secret, because after so many committees and signatures of people who signed our applications by now, perhaps there would not be an StB agent who would not know about it anyway. In an appropriate moment, I would ask him about the financial transaction from crowns to schillings. If he agreed, then I would shove unobtrusively in his hand the envelope with crowns, either in the elevator or in some other suitable place. In the elevator we would have to be alone and talk about weather because in the elevator there most likely were microphones. I was confident that there wasn't enough room for cameras. I considered this plan from every angle and sought for possible holes in it. I sat in a train, the distance from Bratislava to Prague being around 330 kilometers and I had plenty of time for meditating. By the time I arrived in Prague, I found no flaws in the plan, only that I would not have an opportunity or the time to make up and execute plan B, if this one failed.

"Never mind, if this fails; it is not going to be horrible because we are still going to have money from the Foreign Allowance. For plan B there is not enough time," I said to myself, as I stepped off the train.

I came to Hotel Panorama and I was given room number 538. It was almost a brand new hotel, definitely one of the most up to date in Prague. Overall there were twenty four floors, the view from my window was beautiful and on the top floor there was a swimming pool. I was sorry I had not put a swimsuit in my suitcase, so instead, before the dinner I went downtown for a walk. The historical part of the old city was very interesting. I came to The Golden Lane and in front of me there was a group of tourists. I slowed down and from a distance I listened to the Prague tour guide, who spoke English, about the history of this lane. It was quite remarkable, so I followed them a distance and carefully listened. I returned to the hotel about 5:30 and rode the elevator up to my room alone. I surveyed the area and weighed whether cameras could be in there. I found nothing suspicious and, satisfied, returned to my room. At about six I came out of my room and in the hallway pushed the elevator button. As the lift door opened, I saw Mr. Kurt Schwartz standing inside.

"Good evening, Mr. Schwartz," I said smilingly.

"Good evening, Mr. Bielek," he said smiling, and as I entered the elevator, he inquired:

"Are you going for dinner to the restaurant?"

"Yes, seems that we are lucky running into each other," I said.

"How long have you been here," he asked.

"I came into this hotel at about two in the afternoon. I dropped off my belongings in the room and went for a small walk through the old city. Have you been to The Golden Lane?," I asked.

"I've heard about it, but have not yet had an opportunity to take a look," he said.

"If you have no program after the dinner, we could go out for a small walk through the old town," I suggested.

"Only a few phone calls, but those could wait," he said smilingly and then added:

"I do not know Prague very well."

"I do only a little bit, but I may be your city guide for this evening," I said smilingly. I remembered the guide, who spoke about the history of that lane in English to a group of tourists.

"I will have less trouble translating what I know about it because only this afternoon I heard it in English," I thought for myself. I understood German relatively well, but I had troubles with speaking it, therefore for conversations with foreigners I used English. Most of them knew English relatively well. By the time the elevator came to the first floor, I decided to make a small change in my plan with Mr. Schwartz. I would not start our discussion about the money exchange by the dinner table in the restaurant, but I would utilize a moment, when we would be outside in the city. Microphones or cameras would not be in the old city!

The elevator slowed down and a big number 1 showed on the display. We were on the first floor and it was time to get off. We walked across the hallway and gave our buffet ticket to a waiter standing at the entrance to the restaurant.

We had a good time during dinner and we laughed so much our bellies hurt because Mr. Schwartz told a story about a fishing trip he had gone on with his brother. It appeared that actually the fish was catching them because in the middle of a huge lake their fishing boat turned over. They already had four fish in the boat when they caught the fifth big one. The fish was very big and when they both were pulling it into their boat, it overturned. The fish they already had in the boat ended up back in the lake, including the fifth big one and they had a hard time getting back into the boat.

I thought about poor StB agents. If they were recording our conversation they had to switch to another microphone because our dialogue wasn't good material for their reports.

It was around seven o'clock when Mr. Schwartz called for a taxi cab that drove both of us to The Golden Lane in historic Prague. We walked slowly through the lane and I repeated what I had heard this afternoon from a professional tour guide. He was really surprised how much I knew about it and, when we came to the other side of the lane, he said:

"You know so much about this place you could be a professional tour guide for Prague."

"To be a professional, I would have to study a lot," I said modestly and then we walked to Hradcany. It was already too late; Hradcany was closed to visitors. We were just looking over Prague at night and I used the moment for surveying very carefully and unobtrusively around, making sure there was no one there listening to us:

"Mr. Schwartz, I would like to ask you for a favor," I started quietly and carefully. He looked at me and said:

"Yes, I am listening."

"This year I am going with my family for a vacation to Italy. I guess in August we are going to cross Austria on our way to Italy and I would like to have a little more money with me," I said.

He looked at me with surprise and responded:

"Yes . . ."

"I would give you Czechoslovakian money here and when I come to Vienna you would give me Austrian schillings, exchange rate one to one. In this case you don't have to exchange your money here at a bad rate and I don't have to exchange my money at a bad rate in Vienna. And more or less we are forbidden from taking any money when crossing the border," I said, explaining my plan.

Now he started looking around and there was fear in his face. Evidently, he knew the situation in the country quite well.

"You give me crowns here and I will give you shillings in Vienna," he repeated like he did not believe his own ears.

"Yes, but nobody will ever know about this transaction, just the two of us. This is my suggestion and if you don't agree with it, we can both forget this discussion," I said quietly. He watched the Vltava river for awhile thinking.

"All right, I am in," he said and asked very quietly:

"How much money do you want to exchange?"

"Ten thousand, one to one. I will give you the envelope with the money at the nearest possible opportunity," I said quietly. I had the envelope in my pocket, but I did not consider the night city environment suitable for such a transaction.

"Well, we've got almost three days to complete the transaction," he said again quietly, but this time his voice was calm.

We went down to the river and at the nearest taxi terminal we hired a taxi that brought us back to the hotel. During the ride, I told him the rest of my knowledge about historical Prague, which was not too much. We came back to the hotel around nine and I was really glad about the successful completion of another part of my plan. The possibility existed of giving my money to Mr. Schwartz and not ever seeing the schillings for it was a real possibility, but I believed a very small one.

The symposium started the next day at eight in the Congress Hall of the hotel. I got there on time and registered for presentations. The first break was an hour, so I ran to the Italian embassy to give in our applications for the visas, which were filled out and signed because we had received the forms at home a long time ago. I handed the applications to the clerk at the embassy; she read them over and said:

"You will receive a letter by mail to your home about granting the visa in four to six weeks. Then you can pick them up in person or you can mail your passports here using registered mail."

"Yes, thank you," I said but there was no way I was going to depend on the post office with our passports received under such difficult scrutiny.

"I would prefer picking up the visas in person," I said.

"Of course, it is your choice. See you later," said the clerk.

"See you later," I said and went back to Hotel Panorama. By the time I was finished with the Italian embassy and I got back, it was 3:30 and I missed one presentation. However, I then stayed to the very end without missing an another presentation. Technical information was very important for a chemist no matter where he was in the world. I did not write down any notes because I knew I would not be taking them with me anyway. I listened to the presentations very carefully and made my best effort to remember just as I used to do when I was a boy. Then I was too lazy to write anything down, so I "wrote" all my notes in the memory. That way I trained myself to be able to remember huge amounts of information. Now I was doing it for practical reasons not laziness.

Another day went by and I absorbed a lot, but the envelope with the money was still in my pocket. I was in my hotel room, prepared for dinner and thought very intensively how to transfer the envelope from my pocket into the pocket of Mr. Schwartz. In the meantime, I talked to him several times during breaks in the hallway. There were too many people around to finish our business transaction. I thought about different alternatives in order to have a smooth finish; namely, no witnesses. I stepped out of my room and pushed the elevator button. When the door opened, I saw several people and Mr. Schwartz among them.

"Good evening," I said to everyone in the elevator.

"Good evening, Mr. Bielek, said Mr. Schwartz. When I got out, I waited for him by the door and asked him:

"Are you going to dinner?"

"Yes. And you?" he asked. I nodded my head and he added:

"At least we are going to have an opportunity to talk."

We went together to the buffet, placed some food on our plates and sat down at a table. Before we even started eating, he said:

"I have not yet thanked you for your guidance through the old city with the historical details."

"Oh, Mr. Schwartz, it is not worth mentioning. I really do not know too much about history," I said. He kept on without paying attention to what I said and suggested:

"What about a couple of beers after the dinner in the bar? I am buying . . ."

"I am for it . . ." I said briefly. After the dinner we went in the bar next to the restaurant.

"Kozel," I said to the bartender, ordering my favorite beer.

"Pilsner," Mr. Schwartz said.

The bartender brought our beers and we talked about our last ski trips. He told me about skiing on the slopes of the Alps and I told him about our family ski trip on the slopes close to Oravska Priehrada. I have never been a good skier, so my stories were funnier and more or less he listened to me. The night went by really quickly and after a few beers we went back to our rooms by elevator in a jolly mood. Nobody else but the two of us was waiting for the elevator and it came down empty. When the door closed, I reached into my pocket, pulled the envelope out and, without interrupting our dialogue, I pushed the envelope into his hand. He was still laughing at my skiing skills performed on a slope for small kids and pushed the envelope unobtrusively into his own pocket. The mission was accomplished.

It had been almost eight weeks since I had given in our applications for passports with the travel provision at the passport department. I was getting a little impatient and went there two days short of eight weeks as advised by the StB agent.

"Not a big deal; a day after tomorrow it is going to be eight weeks," I said to myself. I experienced first hand that such a conclusion was not a smart one. If someone said eight weeks, it was nine with a lot of luck. In no way could it be seven weeks and five days. With this wrong presumption I suffered another whole day's "shift" in a line. That was all including the arrival shortly after midnight, snoozing off in a sleeping bag and also marathon standing on line in the hallway of the passport department. When I finally got inside after fourteen hours of waiting, the almighty did not bother answering my

"Good day" greeting. Apparently, he considered that as my being forward, because if someone waited in a line for fourteen hours, it could not be a good day. He looked at me with anger and asked very abrasively:

"Last name?"

"Bielek," I said.

The almighty sat behind a desk and in the front of him were several long tables with boxes holding passports. On the front of each box, which was turned to him, was a label with the alphabet letters for the beginnings of names A, B, C . . . The boxes occupied about ten long tables. When he heard my last name, he stood up from his desk and walked to a box with B. He went up and down several times and could not find my name.

"Our passports are not done yet," I thought and went completely blank for a few seconds. It was quite clear to me now I had wasted more than half a day by waiting in line. He was not giving up yet and walked to the back of his office and looked through a pile of papers. He did not find anything, turned his head to me and asked angrily:

"When did you give in your applications?"

"April twenty sixth," I said. He sat back behind his desk, looked into his calendar and then started yelling at me:

"What the hell do you think you are doing? It is going to be eight weeks Thursday! They did tell you eight weeks, didn't they?"

"Yes," I said briefly and did not even try arguing with him. Almighty was always right and arguing with him went nowhere.

"I don't want to see you here sooner than a week from Thursday," he yelled and it was quite clear he was done with me. I walked out and this time it was I who was pissed off. First, I was pissed off with myself for making a bad judgment and uselessly wasting almost the whole day. Then I was pissed off with him for his behavior. He had no right to talk to me that way even though I showed up two days early.

I went to the car, unlocked the door and sat inside. I leaned my head against the headrest, took a deep breath, closed my eyes and said quietly:

". . . just don't turn around . . ."

I felt much better after that and went back home.

The end of June was getting close and along with it also the end of the school year. We had agreed a long time ago it would be the best to leave with the kids to grandma's and grandpa's cottage. We wanted to prevent snoops in our building from grabbing the opportunity and asking our kids about our upcoming vacation in Italy. The kids did not know anything because we never told them we were preparing a vacation. Their lack of knowledge about a vacation to the West would spark a suspicion for snoops and the whole plan could go down the drain. Only two of us, Nora and I, knew about our trip to Italy and we never talked about it to anybody in our families. We strongly believed the less they knew about it the better off everyone would be. At least they could not be charged with accessory to the crime when we left for the West.

Friday June 29th started school vacation for Nora and Peter. Katarina was in kindergarten then, but there were children left whose parents did not have vacation during school vacation. It was a big advantage for our family that Nora was a teacher at the high school because she had her vacation along with the students.

It was already a habit that every Friday Nora took the children to visit my parents-in-law. This time they went there early in the afternoon, after Nora and Peter got out of school and together they picked Katarina up from kindergarten. They went there by bus, and when my working hours were over, I came for them by car. Suitcases and bags with stuff necessary for a week stay at the cottage I already had in the car trunk. I parked in the street in front of the house where my parents-in-law lived and waited for them in the car. We were to meet there at three in the afternoon. A few minutes after three, they came out of the entrance, and when the kids spotted the car, they happily ran toward me and quickly jumped in the car. They knew we were going to Vysoka and were looking forward to school vacation outside the city, where they could have more freedom.

"You are already on school vacation," I said, when they slammed the doors behind them.

"Hurrah," they both screamed almost at once.

"And you don't have school vacation?" Katarina asked.

"No, I don't have school vacation, just a few weeks of regular vacation," I said.

"Dad must go to work, so only we will stay all week long at a Vysoka," Nora said.

"I will stay with you at Vysoka over the weekend and Monday I am going to work," I said and then added:

"Next weekend I'll come back to Vysoka."

When we arrived at the curve at Vysoka, we saw my father waiting for us. When he noticed the car he opened the big gate into the back yard. I stopped at the parking space in front of the garage, in order to unload the suitcases and bags from the trunk. Peter with Katarina rushed out from the car and ran to their grandmother, who walked out from the kitchen to the backyard.

"We already have school vacation," they screamed and both hugged grandma at the same time. I brought our baggage inside and then drove the car into the garage. Father closed the gate and said:

"I can see that the kids are quite happy about school vacation."

"They could hardly wait for it. They were looking forward to staying here at Vysoka and biking again all over the village," I said.

We sat down at a bench below a pear tree and dad showed up at the gate on the other side of the back yard and said:

"I have problems locking and unlocking that gate. Sometimes it takes me five minutes till I find the correct key position and unlock the lock."

"Maybe the cylinder lock should be replaced," I said.

"The lock on that gate has malfunctioned since the very beginning and lately grandma is unable to unlock it at all," said father.

"Because since the very beginning there was a defective cylinder lock," I said, glancing at my watch and added:

"Today it is too late. By the time I get to the hardware store in Stupava it will be closed. Tomorrow morning I will take the cylinder lock out and go buy a new one."

Nora came out of the kitchen and through the hallway door yelled:

"Dinner is on the table. Let's go eat."

We came inside and sat down at the dinner table.

"Mom, when do they open the hardware store in Stupava?" I asked.

"Tomorrow is Saturday . . . They are open between nine and two," she said and asked:

"What do you need?"

"Dad said that the gate lock gets aggravating," I said.

"Yes, I cannot even open it," mom said skeptically.

"Tomorrow morning I will take a look at it. I hope they are going to have that type of cylinder in Stupava," I said.

In the morning right after breakfast I went to the back yard. Dad was already there and tried to unlock the gate. By the time I came back with a screwdriver he had succeeded. I took the lock cylinder out and bought a new one in the hardware store. I installed the new one and the problem was solved.

During the day it was nice and warm so the children went shopping with grandma in the village by bike. Dad watered the grass and Nora and I were in the kitchen cooking lunch.

"Wednesday I am going to the passport department again. I hope this time they will be done," I said.

"When you get them call me. I want to know whether they write both kids in my passport," Nora said.

"Now we should come up with some kind of code. Just in case they are bugging the phones," I said.

"Look when we have everything, I mean passports, travel provisions and, most importantly, both kids written in my passport, just say "Got it." In case anything is missing just say "We don't," Nora said and added:

"But remember my stipulation. I am going only in case we are taking both kids with us."

"Don't worry, both kids will be written in your passport," I said with certainty.

"How do you know that?" Nora asked and added:

"We have already heard about some cases where people had one less kid written in and they left without one kid anyway and the kid stayed with grandparents. Then it took them years until they got the Communists to let the kid out of the country with a lot of help from the International Red Cross. I am not willing to let either of my kids be traumatized this way," Nora said very determined.

"We have already agreed I am working on this trip in a way that we all go together or no one goes," I said.

"You appear to me too sure. How do you know both of them will be written in?" Nora asked.

"Look, so far everything came out just the way we wanted and in the first attempt. I know it has been unbelievable. I believe everything will come through," I said and then added:

"Who is afraid should not wander into the woods."

Another waiting "shift" I planned fifteen days later in order to prevent another confrontation with the almighty. Just to be sure this time I picked Wednesday, not Tuesday or Thursday. I believed on Wednesday there would be another almighty in the office and this way I would prevent continuation of the same conflict. It was proven later that this time I made the right decision because I got the passports. The almighty found them immediately in the box under letter B. In addition I saved a half hour because this time the "shift" lasted only thirteen and a half hours. I opened the passports before stepping out. We both had travel provisions to Austria and Italy and both kids were written in Nora's passport.

"Thank you," I said and went out into the hallway. I was so happy I did not realize how I had gotten out of the building. When I was about three hundred feet away from the building, I stopped, turned around and looked at the building:

"This was the last time . . . never more . . ." I said to myself relaxed, and smiled. I found the nearest phone booth and called Nora who was still at Vysoka with the kids. I picked up the receiver, dialed the number, and when Nora answered the phone, I just said our code:

"Got it," which meant we both had passports with travel provisions and both kids were written in Nora's passport.

"Did we?" Nora asked as she could not believe.

"Got it," I said and then asked:

"How are the kids doing?"

"They are fine; they went with grandma swimming to a lake that is close by here in Vysoka. I did not go because I wanted to be close to a phone when you called," Nora said.

"What is grandpa doing?" I asked.

"Right now he is watering the lawn again," she said and then asked:

"When are you coming here?"

"Not today . . . I am just too tired. I did not get a good night's sleep during the whole night. Tomorrow is Thursday . . . Friday after work," I said.

"Get a good night's sleep and Friday you can tell me all the details. Bye," she said.

"Say hello to the kids and my parents. Bye," I said and hung up.

I went to the car and only after a short drive I realized I had won again. I don't know if it was just a strange coincidence or my destiny, but exactly Wednesday July 4th 1984 on the day of American Independence, I got the documents in my hands, on which I had worked for the last fourteen months and which would turn us, the slaves of Communism, into free people. I would not be required to beg and vilify anymore when I wanted to travel. I would just take my passport and wallet and go wherever I would like. So far it was still just a vision of my future, but it appeared to me it was now within reach. Nobody would ever make my decisions for me and when I found a position somewhere else with more interesting work, or more money or anything else, no one would make any machinations to kill it for me. And the most important of all—nobody would ever push me to join the Communist Party!

Austrian and Italian visas still needed to be taken care of, which was a very simple goal when compared with what we had undergone so far. The

Austrian embassy was located in Bratislava and it was not too much trouble to go there. One day I picked up forms and brought them home for Nora's signature. After bringing the filled out forms back and paying the fees, they gave me Austrian visas on the spot. I had to go there twice, but altogether it took me only a half hour.

The process with granting Italian visas was a bit more cumbersome because it took several weeks. The applications were already in and now we were just waiting for a letter from the Italian embassy about granting our visas.

Friday after work, I went to Vysoka. While driving the car I was looking forward to us being together again. I was already missing Nora and the kids after a week spent alone in the apartment in Bratislava. Even though I was out for almost the whole day waiting for passports on Wednesday, every day when I came back home it felt somehow empty there. In my memory I counted how much longer we had to wait for the letter from the Italian embassy granting the visas. If I remembered the clerk at the embassy all right, we should get it really soon.

On my way down to Vysoka, I stopped in Stupava's grocery market and bought an ice cream cake. When I came to Vysoka I saw Peter and Katarina on their bikes in the village. I stopped by and through the open car window I said:

"I have ice cream cake."

I drove on and saw them in the mirror turning around and pedaling toward the cottage as quickly as possible. I was just stepping out of the car when they flew in through the gate and left their bikes on the grass. They ran by Nora who came out to the back yard when she heard the car.

Wash your hands first," Nora yelled after them when they rushed inside.

I hugged her and handed her the shopping bag:

"Ice cream cake," I said.

"Now I understand what the rush was all about," Nora said and carried the cake into the kitchen. When I walked inside the kitchen those two were already sitting at the table, waiting.

After dinner and the TV fairy tale "For a Good Night," the kids went to bed. Grandma and grandpa stayed watching TV. However, they switched the set to a Vienna channel and watched an episode from a series "Kojak" dubbed into the German language. Nora and I went into the back yard and I poured our red wine into two tall glasses. We clinked our glasses:

"To our victory" and I told Nora stories associated with our passports and Austrian visas. Twilight gradually turned into darkness and our pleasant time outside was spoiled by mosquitoes. First there were only a few of them and we succeeded in getting rid of them using a fly swatter. A few minutes later there so many of them the swatter was of no avail and we had to go inside.

"Such a small aggravating nothing and it would spoil the whole evening," Nora said when we moved the chairs and glasses inside.

"Mosquitoes are the only plague that would bother you outside overnight. Without them people could spend the whole night outside," I said a little philosophically.

"I don't understand why people do not eradicate them?" Nora asked.

"They have already tried several times by several different approaches. The mosquito's capability of multiplying is so great nothing has worked so far," I said.

After getting inside, we had to liquidate with the swatter the ones that got inside with us. When I finished the stories, we went quiet for awhile and then Nora said:

"Next Saturday we should all go home."

"Why?" I asked.

"Two weeks at one spot should be enough for the kids as well . . . then Katarina's birthday is coming up the following week. I would like to take them to my parents also," she said.

"I am in . . . at least I will not be alone in Bratislava," I said.

"Grandma wants to give Katarina a school bag for her birthday," she said.

"Do you know we cannot take the school bag with us? It would be very suspicious to the customs officers," I said.

"I know, but what should I do? Grandma has already bought the bag and I can't tell her not to give it to Katarina," Nora said plaintively.

"I understand . . . ultimately we are going to leave much more behind than just one school bag," I said and added:

". . . just don't turn around . . ."

Late Sunday I drove back to Bratislava and Nora and the children stayed at the cottage for yet another week. I impatiently expected the letter from the Italian embassy about our visas. We never planned on going to Italy, at least not in the year 1984. However, Italian visas were a part of the plan and therefore we had to have them. Tuesday, July the tenth, I opened our mailbox and found there the letter I had waited for so impatiently. I did not pay any attention to the other mail, I quickly locked the mailbox and rushed up the stairs to our apartment. I slammed the door behind me, dropped all the other mail on the floor, and with my hands shaking, opened the letter from the embassy. The letter was very brief and informed me that the embassy had granted us visas and repeated what I was told by the clerk at the embassy. We could pick up the visas in person or send our passports to Prague by registered mail for the visas. I took a deep breath and said quietly with my eyes looking up:

"Thank you, good Lord!"

I could hardly wait for the end of that week so I might tell Nora about it. I didn't want to call her because we did not have any code arranged by which I could tell her what was going on. Wiretapping of telephone conversations was very common and we knew that we could use phones only for conversations that could not be of any interest to StB I had to use the first opportunity when we were together to tell her about it.

The opportunity approached right after my arrival in Vysoka on Friday when we were in the kitchen making coffee and tea. Coffee for Nora and tea for me:

"The letter from the Italian embassy, that they granted us visas, came last Tuesday," I said quietly, after I established no one could hear us.

"Consequently . . . we have everything . . . ," Nora said slowly and quietly.

"Everything," I said.

We sat noiselessly and sipped coffee and tea. Both of us thought about the fact that right now it was necessary to take the very last step, make peace with our decision and "unstuck from a chair." But we did not know that two unforeseen occurrences would accelerate the development of events by an uncommon pace.

The first of them happened immediately during the following night . . . . Shortly after midnight we were awakened by a car, which stopped directly in front of our windows. It was so unusual that both of us jumped out of bed and peeped outside through the curtain. Fortunately, in front of the cottage was a street light so we saw what was going on. A man and a woman got out of the car. Nora said whispering:

"That's Tana with her husband."

I looked at her apprehensively and she added:

". . . my colleague from the school. She said she would come to visit me sometime when she was going by."

I sighed with relief and inquired:

"At half past twelve?"

"I did not say to come after midnight," Nora said and she added:

"Who goes to visit someone at half past twelve?"

"We should go outside and ask her to come some other time," I said.

Fortunately, Tana with her husband did not use the door bell, but started throwing little stones against our window. Stones tapped on our window and Tana asked into the darkness:

"Nora, are you home?"

Nora didn't want to go out outside, turned her head, and with her finger in front of her lips, indicated to me that I should be quiet.

"In a moment they will give up and go away," Nora whispered.

"I hope they are not going to wake up my parents or the kids," I whispered.

We watched them from behind the curtain and kept quiet. They gave up in a moment, jumped in their car, and drove away.

When the silence was restored, we went back to bed and could not fall asleep. Everything happened so quickly we did not get a chance to think about it. We could not go out because we had to go through the next room where the kids and grandma were sleeping and would wake them up. That room had windows into the back yard. Dad slept on the other side in "B" pavilion and his window was also into the back yard, not into the street. Only now when we were back in bed again did we realize the sheer stupidity of the situation. We lay motionless and listened to the silence. It was very quiet; my parents and also the kids were still sleeping.

"That was a stupid idea . . . to visit someone at half past midnight!" Nora whispered with anger.

"We are lucky they did not wake up anybody else. Imagine if they just mentioned our trip to Italy in front of my parents or the kids," I said and added:

"To tell you the truth, when I heard a car stopping right in front of our window the first thing I thought was that they were StB agents."

"Such a stupid woman . . . ," Nora said repulsively.

"You should call her and let her know that, if she wants to come visit us, she should come a little earlier," I whispered.

"Screw her. If she is so stupid that she doesn't comprehend when one visits people, I am not talking to her," Nora said very quietly but decisively.

The other event happened just three days later, Tuesday. We were home in Bratislava at the apartment, it was about half past eight in the evening and the kids were just getting ready for bed. We were sitting in the living room, watching TV, when someone rang the bell at our door. We looked at each other and immediately moved our shoulders.

"If it is someone from the army, tell them I am not home right now," I said to Nora and quickly ran through the hallway into my office. Through a crack between the door and the door frame I watched Nora opening the entrance door.

"Good evening, I came here in response to your newspaper advertisement about a briefcase typewriter," said a man behind the door, when Nora cracked opened the door. The door was held by a safety chain from inside. I came out of the office and fully opened the door to an unknown man. I opened the closet and pulled out the typewriter we had already forgotten about. The man sat down on a bench in our hallway, opened the briefcase, and inspected the typewriter.

"Seems to be in very good condition," said the unknown.

"Yes, we barely use it because we bought an electric one. That's why we are selling it," I said.

"Could I see the electric one," asked the unknown.

"Of course, but that one is not for sale," I said and escorted him into the office. On my desk there was the electric typewriter, which I used for typing my translations. He looked at it and asked:

"The price listed in the newspaper is still on?"

"Yes," I said and he handed me the money, grabbed the briefcase typewriter and left.

After the unknown man left, we sat down in the living room again. After a moment of silence, when I was quite sure the unknown man was gone and the kids were asleep, I said very softly:

"We should pack up and get the heck out of here."

"Why? Nothing is pushing us out," Nora said very calmly.

"Yes, it is. To tell you the truth, when Tana and her husband came and I heard a car stopping right in front of our window, I thought they were StB agents. Now, when the unknown man rang the bell, I thought the same," I said.

"But you saw they were not agents," Nora said again very calmly.

"Yes and no. Only StB agents come in the night without announcement. We do not know who sent Tana for such an unusual visit and this guy was very suspicious because he wanted to see the electric typewriter as well," I said.

"Maybe you just see everything in black and white," Nora said.

"Maybe you are right. But when someone unexpected comes to us after dark, I almost have a heart attack every time. I don't mind it during the day, but in the dark, it is frightening for me," I said.

"But we talked about leaving after Peter's birthday," Nora said.

"You talked about leaving after Peter's birthday. I said we would go when we got all needed documents. Now we have everything, and if we wait for

Peter's birthday, someone may come and take our passports away. I've heard about cases like that happening before," I said.

"When do you want to go?" Nora asked.

"Next Monday," I said.

"Monday?" Nora asked surprised, and added:

"I would not have enough time to pack our suitcases," she said with resignation.

"Every night, after the kids fall asleep, I will help you with packing," I promised with enthusiasm and added:

"Please, do it for my sake because I cannot stand those late-night visits by unknown people. The last twelve months have been really hard on me and so far I've handled everything fine. Now it is time to pull up the anchor and set sail."

"All right, but you will help me with everything," Nora said after a moment of hesitation.

"When did I not help you?" I answered with a question. I got up from the arm chair, lifted her from her chair and hugged her:

"I have always loved you . . . and always will," I whispered in her ear with tears in my eyes.

"I love you too," she said and I felt her tear falling on my shoulder.

Shortly before leaving for the West, I had to surrender my military booklet and put it into storage. Fortunately, there were two possibilities to do so—either bring the booklet to the District army headquarters or put it into storage in a safe at our company, more precisely in the department called "Special Affairs." I had no desire to go again to army headquarters. The way they shoved me the draft notice order when I came there for a signature for my application for travel provision was still lingering in my memory.

I chose the smaller evil despite the fact Comrade Stromcek was the boss of the Special Affairs department and he was not someone I would look forward to seeing. The name Special Affairs was more or less ridiculous. It was comprised of two small rooms with a safe, which was used to hide away military booklets of all men from the company who were in reserves and were just traveling to the West. We were required to pick up the booklet from storage and bring it home immediately after returning from the West. All together there were three people employed in the department: Stromcek, his secretary, and another comrade who was Stromcek's deputy in his absence. During the booklet-surrendering ceremony they, wrote an entry into a book with a "Top Secret" sticker on its front and the traveling reservist obtained a signed and rubber-stamped receipt, which had "Secret" stamped on the top. The receipt was an ultimately important document because it was the next document the border patrol checked right after the passport. I heard about cases where someone had forgotten to surrender his military booklet and he was sent back home from the border.

In order to avoid running into Stromcek, I found out about his schedule of Communist Party meetings and secret dealings at District army headquarters. I waited until he was gone and then went to Special Affairs. On my way there I thought how ridiculous or embarrassing the name of that department was. Apparently, it was done in order to confuse secret agents from the imperialistic powers who were looking for a safe with military booklets. If they wrote "Military Booklets" on the door, most likely a group of secret agents led by James Bond would stand in the hallway and plan to get inside the safe. Because they wrote "Special Affairs" on the door, the agents never found out where the booklets were hidden and the safe was secure. Quite obviously, this very smart trick was most likely constructed by some StB agent.

I came to the door of the department above which was a sign, "Special Affairs," and next to the door a bell push button. There was a big arrow saying "Ring the bell here" pointing to the button. This was just to be sure that even people with substandard intelligence would understand to push the only button that was in the entire hallway. I had to use all my internal power not to start laughing after seeing the sign. I took a deep breath, and when I was quite sure I was not going to burst into laughter, I pushed the button. The bell, which was just on the other side of the door, rang so loud I jumped up frightened. I took another deep breath because I had a hard time holding my laughter inside. Luckily, nothing was happening for a moment and I had plenty of time to calm down. All of a sudden, a small window behind heavy bars opened in the middle of the door and the secretary's head appeared in it. This time I lost it and started laughing. I took a deep breath once again in order to keep a business approach and the secretary asked me, through the window:

"Yes, please?"

"I would like to surrender my military booklet because I am traveling Monday," I said as calmly as possible for the given situation.

"Comrade Stromcek is not here now and Comrade Korunka will be back after twelve," the secretary said through the barred little window.

"You cannot accept my military booklet?" I asked naively.

"No, because I do not have access to top secret documents," she said.

"So, I will be back after lunch, thank you," I said and went back to my office. The secretary closed the little window on the door and I could hear the sound of a security bar being pushed from inside. Now I could laugh but quietly so she would not hear me.

I could not resist turning around and looking at the door with the little barred window about 8 x 8 inches. My eyes were filled with tears of laughter.

"Little children could not have done it better," I thought.

Despite the fact that the department was on my way back from the dining room, I went back there only after the lunch break. In order to prevent myself from laughing at the childish door bell or barred little window in the door, I decided to think about a big problem I would have at the border without the slip. That idea would keep my face straight!

I pushed the button, the bell rang and I was able still to keep a serious face. The little window opened again and the secretary's head showed in it. When she noticed me, she did not ask anything and closed the window. Immediately after the door lock was unlocked and the door opened.

"Hmmm . . . the door is even locked," I thought for myself.

"Good afternoon," I said when I walked inside the room.

"Good afternoon. Comrade Korunka is expecting you," the secretary said and pointed to his office door which was slightly opened.

I knocked on the door and Comrade Korunka responded from inside: "Come in, Comrade Bielek."

I walked into his office and saw him sitting behind his desk with his arm stretched toward me. Without a word I handed him my military booklet and without a word he laid it on the desk and opened it. When he was satisfied that the picture and name inside resembled me, he closed the booklet. He slipped down to the safe, which was at floor level and built into the wall behind him. I heard him twisting the code lock and the rattling noise of the tumblers of a safe, but I could not see anything because he was covering the safe with his body.

"Everything is well thought of . . . He is covering the view of the safe with his body, so I cannot see the dial," I thought and smiled. Luckily, Korunka was turned with his back to me.

When he had closed the safe, he sat up behind his desk, and with a key he pulled from his pocket, he unlocked the left drawer of his desk. He took a book out of it with a label "Top Secret" and laid it on his desk. Still not saying a word, he made an entry into the book and replaced it immediately into the drawer. Then he pulled a different key from another pocket, unlocked the right drawer and extracted a form, bearing the word "Secret" for its heading. He filled out my name and added his signature on the bottom. Then he opened the middle drawer of his desk and took out a rubber stamp and very carefully pressed it under his signature on the slip.

"Hmmm . . . rubber stamp is not locked under a third key. That is complete irresponsibility . . . he is lucky James Bond doesn't know about this," I thought

He handed me the slip and said:

"Do not forget, you have to have this slip with you when you go through the borders."

"Yes. I will certainly take this with me. Thank you," I said and walked into the front room, which was occupied by the secretary. Yet before she unlocked and opened the door, I said out loud, so Comrade Korunka could hear me:

"Have a nice weekend."

"Have a nice weekend," they both said.

I stepped out from the top secret department and the secretary locked the door behind me. On my way back to the office, I thought what could possibly be so important in a military booklet that they stored it so laboriously. As far as I remembered, there was my picture inside, date of birth and social security number. Besides that there were my military rank and some brief and coded entries about my military training.

"Who with a sound mind would take his military booklet with him for the trip to the West? What people in the West would be interested in a military booklet? What was so secretive in those records? I was asking to myself. However; I did not find any answers.

"Maybe the Czechoslovakian army would lose a war with the West if they read from my military booklet I was a lieutenant in the reserves and on active duty I was a commanding officer of a tank platoon," I thought and started laughing again.

I came back to my office and still laughed at the childish department called "Special Affairs." I looked at my watch. It was 1:30 in the afternoon, and the last two hours I had to spend on the job there. I looked behind me on the wall where a picture of President Gustav Husak was hanging. It was a mandatory picture, which had to be in the offices of all supervisors. When I was promoted to be manager of this department, I "inherited" this office from my present boss—Vice President Flak. The picture of the president used to hang on the wall opposite me and re-hanging the picture was the first thing I had done after my arrival in this room. I hammered a nail into a wall behind me and re-hung the picture there. Since then it hung behind me and I didn't have to look at the sour face of Husak anymore. Almost everyone who came to my office took note of this change and inquired why the president was now behind my back. I patiently explained his numb look disturbed me in my work and as he hung now he could pay attention to what I write. At this opportunity I told other versions to friends and good acquaintances, which I stole from a well-known joke. The president hangs behind my back for two and a half years and no one ever told me to hang him there, where he belongs. Even Prazec, when he was inviting me to his birthday celebration, glimpsed at the picture and then at the wall in front of me. He did not understand but did not say anything either. I looked at the picture again and quietly said to myself:

"Don't worry, in a day or two a real Communist will come into this office and he will hang you there, where you belong."

I laughed and somebody knocked at my door.

"Come in," I said and Mrs. Jarmila entered the door.

"I can see that you are really looking forward to your vacation in Italy," she said a bit surprised, when she noticed a smile on my face, she added:

"Boss, just yet before you leave, we must send an evaluation of exchange credit to the bank."

"Can this wait, until I return?" I asked because I didn't want to ruin my good mood with paperwork for a bank.

"No, it cannot wait because it must be at the bank next Wednesday," she said. I looked at my watch and said:

"All right, bring it in."

Mrs. Jarmila only now let go of the doorknob and returned to her office. She left my door open and, when she came back with a pile of folders, I stood up and closed the door behind her. She laid the folders on my desk and gave me a hand-written evaluation on a piece of ruled paper. The entire evaluation was done by her and I only had to approve it. I gazed at her and thought for myself:

"Wonderful woman," but I said:

"Well, you have already done it."

She smiled and said:

"The evaluation is done; you have to approve and sign it, then it will be typed on a form from the bank," she said and then she added with laughter:

"Are you the boss, you have the signature in your pay."

"All right, let's make an agreement this way," I said and kept on:

"I will double-check what is written here, and if I agree, I will sign a blank form from the bank. Monday you retype the data from this working calculation into the form and mail it to the bank."

"Deal," Mrs. Jarmila said and I laid the paper with her calculations on my desk and began studying them. When I arrived at the end and found nothing wrong, Mrs. Jarmila placed in front of me a blank form and I signed it. When we had it all completed, I helped her with a stack of folders back to her office. I placed them on her desk and the phone rang. It was the outside line, which also rang in her office for her to pick up when I was not in my office. I picked up and said:

"Good afternoon, Jan Bielek."

"Hi Janny, my mother said in the phone.

As usual, her voice was so loud, that I subconsciously pulled the phone away from my ear and said:

"Just a moment, I am going into my office" and I put the phone down. I walked to my office and picked up the phone. This time I held the phone a bit further from my ear and said:

"Hi, Mom. How are you?"

"Fairly well. I would like to ask you whether you could drive me with some belongings on Sunday," she said.

"Of course, what is it?" I asked.

"I purchased some things for the kitchen at Vysoka. The apartment in Bratislava we exchanged for an apartment in Dubravka; now I need something to be carried from Bratislava to Dubravka and from Dubravka to Vysoka," she said.

"All right, but keep in mind that I do not have a truck. It must only be something, that will fit into a car.

"Of course," she said annoyed.

"Could we do it Saturday?" I asked.

"Saturday we are moving furniture and I have already ordered a truck and men for it. Then Sunday we could drive away only belongings which could break or be damaged in a truck," she said.

"All right; where are we going to meet?" I asked.

"If you could come for me at Vysoka in the afternoon? In the morning I have to finish a few things in the apartment in Dubravka," she said.

"All right," I said.

"Thank you Janny. Bye," she said.

"You are welcome. Bye," I said and hung up.

As I phoned with mom, I noticed through the matte glass on my door that someone waited outside until I concluded the phone call. By the figure and motions this resembled Mr. Kolesar. As I hung up, the figure outside knocked at the door.

"Come in," I said and the door opened and the head of Mr. Kolesar emerged.

"May I come in?" he inquired.

"But of course. Help yourself and sit down," I said smilingly. He sat down at a chair opposite me. It had been a long time since we had sat in this manner and he had spoken to me about how to arrange a trip to the West. Maybe he never knew how much he had actually helped me. I was most grateful to him because I had directed myself exactly according to his advice and all those papers, applications, signs, rubberstamps and dates I had gotten on my first attempt. When we talked about them, it looked almost impossible that somebody would be able to acquire all those documents without a hitch. I stared at him and wondered whether he had surmised the real intention of our journey to Italy. I could not read anything from his face. He disrupted the thread of my thought:

"Janny, I don't want to hold you up, I came here just to say good-bye and to wish you a lot of happy days in Italy."

At first, I was surprised by his words "say goodbye to you," but in no case did I want to start a discussion on this topic, so I said with a wide smile:

"Thank you, Mr. Kolesar, very much, for all the advice you gave me as well as for the effort that you made, coming here just to wish me a nice vacation. I don't know whether I would have been able to achieve it without your help."

I got up, walked around my desk, came to him and shook his hand. As he stood up, he looked into my eyes and at the same time said:

"So yet once more Janny, good luck to you . . ."

"Thank you very much," I said with great composure. He looked more emotional than I did. After we shook hands, he hugged me. Then he gave me yet a scrutinizing look and walked away. He closed the door behind him and I glanced at my watch. Already I had been there five minutes extra!

"Never mind," I said to myself. I should pick up Nora and the kids at three o'clock. The journey took only a few minutes; I still had plenty of time. I opened my briefcase to take some personal things which I didn't want to leave behind and I heard a knock on the door. Mrs. Jarmila stepped inside and said:

"I didn't want to disturb you when Mr. Kolesar was here. I just wanted to wish you a happy journey . . .

"Good journey during your vacation and I hope you will return shortly," she said with a big smile and extended her hand.

"I guess I will have to reconsider that on the way," I said also with a wide smile and, instead of shaking hands, I hugged her.

"Did you clean out the drawers in your desk?" she asked.

"No, why?" I asked surprised.

"Years ago Jozko Halenda worked here and before he left for his vacation to the West he perfectly cleared out all the drawers in his desk. And he never returned . . ."

"See, this did not appear to me. They are in the same mess as before. Now it is already too late to start with cleaning because I am leaving at this moment," I said with laughter.

"Are you sure?" she asked, and then with laughter she added:

"I was too busy with calculations for the bank and did not have a chance to check the drawers in your desk."

"Once again . . . have a pleasant journey . . ." she said and walked away. I heard how she entered her office and after a few moments saw her leaving in the back yard in the direction of the main entrance. I put my personal belongings in the briefcase, grabbed the keys and at the door I turned around for the last time. I glanced at Husak hanging on the wall, winked at him and quietly said:

"So long."

I closed the door behind me and walked in the hallway to the exit. It was so quiet there; all the offices were already vacant and I could hear only my steps echoing around. It was Friday afternoon, already after working hours and no one wasted a minute, in order to run home. As I passed over the main company's entrance, I said to the guards on duty:

"See you later," but in my mind was "So long."

It was exactly three o'clock, when I parked in front of the house where my parents-in-law lived. I turned off the engine and looked at the entrance. In a moment the door opened and Nora walked out with the children. They stopped in front of the entrance and looked around. They sought the car. Katarina had a school bag at her back and when she spotted the car she ran to me.

I got out of the car and opened a door for her. She dropped the bag from her back, caught it with both hands and raised it upwards to my face. The bag almost touched my nose and she said with pleasure:

"Grandmother gave me this school bag for my birthday."

I caught the bag, looked at it and then helped Katarina into the car. When she sat down in the car, I put the new school bag on her knees. Peter took a seat next to Katarina and it was evident that he did not share her pleasure about the new school bag. He had recently finished the third grade and for him going to school was not such a miracle as for Katarina who was going to start first grade in September. He had already forgotten that he too used to be happy, when grandmother gave him a school bag just like that for his birthday three years ago.

Nora had a very sad expression on her face, I looked at her and winked. She modestly shrugged her shoulders, but didn't say anything and even made an effort to smile. We could not speak about what we both thought, because the children were in the car with us and they still did not know about anything. We had to wait till we got back home and they were asleep. I considered proposing a small walk in Sady Janka Krala, but rejected the idea before I said anything. Her last visit with her parents was certainly full of emotion which she had to suppress inside. If she started to cry during the walk in the orchards, the children would notice even if they were far from us. Then explaining to the kids why their mother was crying during a walk in the park would have certainly been confusing. We would have to come out with some sort of deceit because it was still not the right time for telling them the truth. Children had a special instinct for sorting out the truth from deception. They would very quickly recognize what was what.

"Miro was at their parents as well and when I was leaving I asked him to stop at our place for a moment," Nora said.

I looked at her and she added:

"He arrived only a few moments before we left and we did not have a chance to talk."

"Do you know when he is coming? I asked.

He said he would leave there shortly after us." Nora said.

We came back home and expected Nora's brother Miro to show up. We were getting along with him and his wife Anka very well and quite often helped each other. This was our last opportunity to see him one more time and at least in spirit say "So long." Just like the rest of the family, he did not know about our leaving because we did not want him to be at risk of being charged with accessory to our crime—leaving the country. I was also a little bit afraid of this meeting because I was not quite sure Nora's emotions would prevail over a calm mind and she would give it away by crying.

It was almost six o'clock when Miro finally rang the bell at our door. He did not want to come inside and apologized for being so late and that Anka was already waiting for him. We just spoke a few words while he stood in the door and he promised he would come some other time. We did not want to let him know there was not going to be any other time . . . When he left, Nora came out to the balcony and waved to him as he crossed the street.

We sat in the living room, there was music playing from the stereo, and the kids were already sleeping. It was time for Nora to tell me about her last visit to her parents.

"Mom and I sat in their living room and dad watched TV with the kids. When Miro walked in, mom said out of the blue:

"Remember this very well. You are going to take care of cleaning the kitchen and bathroom and Miro will take care of the hallway and the living room."

"Did she mean you two were going to clean their apartment," I interrupted Nora with a question.

"Yes," she said and then continued:

"I just could not believe my own eyes and ears. When she repeated it again, I just thought she did not have the slightest idea I was not going to clean anything in that apartment, ever. And I laughed in spirit.

"What did Miro say?" I asked.

"Nothing. He just looked at her and did not say anything." Nora said.

"Did you tell her to clean her own house? Does she understand that the two of you have your own cleaning to do in your own apartments? Why don't you say to her that she has no right giving you this kind of work? I interrupted Nora again with my questions.

"You and I know that I am not going to do any cleaning for her. I did not want to argue with her during my last visit there. And I know Miro will go there and clean and will never say anything," Nora said.

"I am still completely stunned . . . ," I said and turned my head.

"When we were leaving, my mom asked me:

"When am I going to see you again?"

"I just said . . . as usual . . . Friday . . . but I did not say which Friday I meant," Nora said.

"So your mom technically made it easier for you . . . when she irritated you with the cleaning schedule, so it wasn't so hard to go . . . ," I said.

"It was not easy," Nora said and then added:

"When we were going down in the elevator, I had a hard time not crying. I was able to hold back just to hide it from the children."

"So, you did not cry?" I asked.

"No, I could not because the children were there," Nora said.

Sunday we sat at the table in the kitchen and ate lunch. Nora cooked the sauerkraut and pork with dumplings. Everyone liked it, so it was really quiet. I thought it was our last lunch in that apartment. I looked at Nora and could see from her face she thought about the same. When we finished lunch, Peter looked at me and asked:

"Can I go with you to help move?"

"Not this time. Grandma will be with me in the car and we will need the back seat for her stuff," I said. I could see in his face he was not happy with my answer. I caressed his head and said:

"You will have a chance to help me some other time."

I took the keys and my wallet, sat down on the bench in the hallway, put my sneakers on, and Nora said:

"Hurry up! Don't be too late."

"It should not take too long. It will mostly depend on the traffic because people will be coming back to the city from their cottages and gardens," I said.

In a little while I was out of the city and about 1:30. I arrived at the cottage. Mom prepared all the stuff in the back yard, and we were going to bring it to their apartment in Dubravka. I did not see the apartment because they had exchanged apartments only a week ago. Mom was telling me the story on the way there and in a few moments we were at her apartment building in Dubravka. The apartment was on the sixth floor and the elevators did not work. There were two of them, one bigger, for cargo; the other one smaller, which was designed to carry only three persons. We took only what we could carry and walked up the stairs. Mom stopped at the third floor and rested. It was quite obvious she was completely exhausted. She pulled a cigarette from her purse and lit it.

"Do you know why those elevators don't work?" I asked.

"Yesterday we were moving, so they turned them off," mom said.

"Hmm . . . ? There is no logic. When someone is moving, he needs an elevator. At that time he actually needs it the most," I said quite surprised.

The main office said that the elevators always break down when they are used for moving, so they'd rather turn them off. They did it yesterday and today, Sunday. The office is closed, so there is nobody to turn them on again," mom said with acceptance.

"I will never understand the local logic. The elevators should be designed in a way that they could handle moving and not be shut down for moving," I said.

I looked at mom who was just about finished with the cigarette and suggested:

"I have an idea. Give me the keys and I will run up with these things and put them in the apartment. You will follow me after you rest."

"All right," mom said and gave me the keys. I went up, unlocked the door, put everything inside and locked up again. When I came down, I met her on the fifth floor. I gave her the keys and said:

"Wait for me in the apartment. I will bring the rest of our cargo from the car."

After I walked up with the rest into the apartment, I found mom sitting at the table in the kitchen drinking water.

"How do you feel?" I asked a little scared.

"I am OK now," mom said and added:

"I am just too old for walking up stairs to the sixth floor."

"You know how your mother used to say it? She would be too old only once a willow tree grows from her butt," I said with laughter. Mom laughed too and started organizing the things we had brought into cabinets and said:

"You have not taken a look at our new apartment."

"I am going to take a look now," I said and started looking around. She joined me in a moment and showed me how she had furnished the apartment with furniture from Bratislava's apartment. When she finished the tour, she said:

"Let's go now. We still have to go to Bratislava.

We locked the apartment and went downstairs. I grabbed mom's arm, so she could walk down a little easier.

Lean on me," I said. She really leaned on me and I could feel at least half of her weight being carried downstairs by me.

We came up to the apartment in Bratislava and we lucked out; the elevator worked. First we loaded things that were going to Vysoka and then boxes with glasses that were going to the apartment in Dubravka. When we came back to Dubravka, I looked at my watch. It was 6:10 in the evening. I suggested:

"Mom, you stay here in the car and I will bring those boxes upstairs."

"No, I have to put those glasses into the cabinets," mom insisted.

I took only what I could carry in one hand and helped her up the stairs. It was much quicker, but I could carry only two small boxes.

"Mom, you do your organizing and I will bring the rest of it," I said and mom happily agreed. I had to make another three trips because I did not want to risk dropping something. The boxes contained glass and porcelain. By the time I made it upstairs with the last of the cargo, mom had already put away the stuff from my previous trips. I sat down in a chair because I was tired from the stairs. Waiting for her felt really good. When she was done, I helped her going down again. We came down to the car and I unobtrusively looked at my watch. It was 7:35 and the Sun was setting now.

We came to the cottage at Vysoka and my dad was already waiting outside. When I drove up to him, I could see his worried face:

"Where have you been so long? I thought something bad happened to you," dad said with worry through the open car window.

"Mom will explain it to you. I do not understand it either."

"This morning I was there and looked for someone who would turn the elevators on. It is Sunday today and there was no one in the office. I could not find anybody else who would turn on those dammed elevators," mom said disgustedly.

I had parked the car outside and dad was going to open the gate.

"No, you don't have to. I will bring everything inside from here," I said. He came up to the car, grabbed a package, and brought it in the back yard.

"You don't have to bring everything inside. Just leave it here and I will bring it inside later," dad suggested.

I knew father was not strong enough to lift some of those boxes, so I suggested:

"You open the door for me and I will bring it all inside, since I am already holding it, it doesn't take much more time."

This way it took much less time because mom grabbed the door for me as well and in fifteen minutes everything was inside the house. When we were all done, mom asked me:

"Would you like to eat anything?"

"No, thanks. It is getting late. I promised Nora I would not be late and it is almost nine now . . . I will drink a little bit of water," I said and we all went into the kitchen. We sat down at the table and mother offered me some food again:

"I will warm up a little bit of risotto for you I made for lunch today."

"No, thank you. A beer would be nice though," I said. Mom looked at me strictly, but before she managed to say anything, I said:

"But, I cannot now, because I still have to drive back home."

"Take a bottle of beer with you and you can drink it after you get home," dad suggested.

"No thank you. I have the same beer at home," I said and unobtrusively looked around the kitchen.

"This is the last time I will be sitting here and talking to my parents," flashed through my mind and I used all my strength not to make my thoughts obvious. I finished the glass of water and stood up. They both walked me all the way to the street . . .

"Thank you, Janny," mom said, and when I walked to the car she asked:

"When are we going to see you and your family again?"

"I don't know. I will call you," I said as calm as I could. I walked back to them and hugged both of them at once. I quickly jumped into the car because I was afraid they could see tears in my eyes. I started the engine, waved trough the open window and said:

"Good bye."

"Good bye . . . Good bye," they said and I saw them in the rear view mirror as they stood at the gate and waved. When I came out to the curve where they could not see me, I had to stop the car. I could not see the road due to the tears in my eyes. I rested my head on the seat and big tears were rolling down my cheeks. A window opened on the house I stopped in front of and an older gentleman gazed out and wondered what was going on.

"Nosy people who are trying to figure out what is going on is the last thing I need in this moment," flashed trough my mind. I took a deep breath and whispered:

". . . just don't turn around . . ."

I put the car in first gear and quickly drove away before the older gentleman figured out anything. I went back home and kept repeating over and over:

". . . just don't turn around . . ." . . . just don't turn around . . ."

By the time I got to the city, I was all right, calm and balanced. Nora stood on the balcony and waved to me when she noticed the car. I parked the car, ran upstairs, and when Nora closed the door behind me, she angrily whispered:

""You promised you would not be late . . . and it is almost 9:30 . . .

"When mom and I planned this moving, we did not even imagine that the elevators would not work," I said. She continued angrily like she did not hear me:

". . . you know we have to pack and prepare the suitcases. We are leaving tomorrow morning."

I hugged her and whispered into her ear:

"I did not expect it would take so much time. Forgive me . . . In an hour everything will be packed."

As I was holding her still around the shoulders I pulled both of us into the living room and closed the door behind us. There were four suitcases on the carpet, which we had recently bought for the trip. Using a tape measure,

I measured the trunk in our Skoda car and then we went to a store to buy a set of four suitcases, which would take advantage of the volume of the trunk. They were not too big because the trunk was quite small. However, those suitcases fit the volume perfectly.

"But you have already packed them," I said when I noticed they were all filled to the rim.

"If I had waited for you, we would not have been able to do it ever," Nora said, this time with a smile.

"Yes, we would, a little later," I said with laughter. She grabbed a slipper from a suitcase and threw it at me.

"Did you eat anything," she asked with interest.

"No, it is too late now. But I would like a beer," I said.

She rolled her eyes, and when I came back with beer, she placed in front of me a list of the suitcases' contents and asked:

"Is there anything missing?"

We went down the list item by item and added a few things. We knew we would need coats, jackets, shawls, gloves or boots for the winter. But we could not take them because it was July and it was hot. According to our official plan, we should be back home in ten days and having winter clothing in our luggage would be extremely suspicious. What was inside of those suitcases was clothing for summertime only.

Chapter Three

Time to Go

It was Monday, July 23, 1984, early morning, and I did not know why but I tried to leave before people who lived in the apartments around us would be going to work. Maybe it was because I did not want to bump into people like Sobotka, Klubesova or Cervenohlava from the fifth floor, ever again. Not only them, but all the others living on the same floor who were employed at the same company as I and were all Communists.

I parked the car next to the main entrance, so I did not have to carry the entire luggage across the street to the parking lot. However, by the time I had carried the all the luggage down and put it in the trunk, I met all those people I was trying to avoid. When everything was in the car, I went up to the apartment and double-checked if we were missing anything. Nora and the kids were ready to go on our big trip. Nora held her purse, the kids the backpack with toys and I took a bag with our passports and other documents. Nora and I looked at each other:

"So, do we have everything?" I asked.

"Do you have all the documents?" Nora asked.

"Here they are," I said and lifted the bag with them in front of me.

"Where are we going?" Peter asked.

To Prague, for a few days," I said only about part of our journey.

"Where is Prague?" Katarina asked.

"Dad goes there for his business trips," Peter jumped ahead of me with his answer.

"By car it will take us about five hours," I said.

"Are we going?" I asked.

"Yes, let's go," Peter said and Katarina opened the door and walked into the stairway. Peter followed her. Nora and I looked at each other silently and then ran our eyes one more time over everything we could see from the main entrance. Nora joined the kids going downstairs and I was the last one leaving the apartment. I locked the door and an idea flashed through my head:

"Almost everything we have worked for in the last nine years is there behind that door. Apartment, furniture . . . clothes . . . carpets . . . pots and pans and all the other dishes . . . all the books . . . everything . . . ."

I just took a deep breath and said quietly"

. . . just don't turn around . . ."

I closed my eyes for a few seconds and then ran down the stairs as fast as possible. Nora and the kids were just coming out of the main entrance when I caught up with them. It was seven o'clock in the morning. We got in the car and left by highway to Prague.

"We should be in Prague for lunch," I said just to change my train of thought.

"Where are we going for lunch?" Peter asked.

We are going to the Hotel Panorama in Prague, so maybe in the hotel's restaurant," I said.

We went through Bratislava quite quickly because rush hour had not started yet and also because I avoided places well known for congested traffic. We went on the SNP Bridge; on the right below were the orchards Sady Janka Krala and on the left, high on the top of the hill was Bratislava Castle. There were a few traffic lights on Stefanikova Street; then we came to the highway. When we drove by the exit to Stupava, I remembered my parents:

"Now they are having breakfast . . ." I thought.

Our journey on the highway went by quite quickly. The kids were relaxed and watched the country and highway surroundings. We came to the outskirts of Prague at about eleven thirty in the morning, and as we approached the hotel, I said:

"Look, there is the Hotel Panorama," and pointed to a tall building on a hill.

We drove up to the hotel about half past twelve. Driving through Prague took a little longer because even though I had been there many times before, I did not know the city well enough to avoid getting lost.

We walked up to the reception desk in the hotel:

"Good afternoon. A room for two adults and two kids for two nights, please," I said to the receptionist. She turned pages in the scheduling book and said:

"I am sorry, sir right now I have a room for four of you only for one night. If a room becomes available, I will book it for you for another night."

"Yes, thank you, so far only for one night," I said, and after filling out the paperwork, she gave us a key for room 931.

We carried the luggage up to the room and then went for lunch into the hotel's restaurant. It was the same restaurant where I recently had dinner with Mr. Schwartz.

We ordered lunch and just started to eat when Katarina asked:

"Are we going to the pool after lunch?"

She still remembered my story when I was there last time and could not go to the pool because I did not have a swimsuit with me.

"Yes, let's go to the pool," Peter added with excitement.

"Finish your lunch and we can go to the pool," Nora said decisively.

Both kids sped up eating their lunch because they could not wait to get to the pool. A pool on the twenty-fourth floor of a hotel was some kind of "never-seen" rarity even for them in those days.

"Do not eat so fast, you may choke. The pool will certainly wait for you!" Nora said.

Our lunch was finished in record time anyway and the three of them stood up from the table and went into our room for swimwear.

"Wait a minute, I have not paid for lunch yet," I said.

"You stay here and pay for lunch. We are going upstairs to the room," Nora said and the kids ran to the elevator in the hallway. I paid for lunch, and when I came up to the room, they were already waiting for me. I did not want to hold them up with changing into my swimwear, so we immediately went by elevator to the top hotel floor. When the elevator stopped, the children ran out to the pool, which was behind glass walls and we walked inside through a glass door.

"The pool is closed today because someone broke a glass cup in it yesterday. We have to pick up broken glass from the bottom of the pool," said a hotel employee.

We went back to the hallway and Peter and Katarina looked at Nora, then at me with a big question on their faces.

"We can go tomorrow," Nora said, trying to lift their spirits.

"If we get a room in this hotel for tomorrow as well," I said apprehensively and added:

"Indeed this is not the only hotel in the world with a pool. Now let's go to the city and we will see whether the receptionist will book us a room for tomorrow."

The kid's faces turned to disappointment from the closed pool, and my suggestion about going to the city for a walk did not excite them at all. I pushed the elevator button and we went back to our room. This time changing took much longer.

The center of the old city was not too far from our hotel, so it took only a few stops of the metro there. We walked on Staromestke square with the Old City Hall and also waited for the whole hour chimes in front of Orloj. The children watched the chimes and parade of apostles with interest and for a moment it seemed that they had already forgotten their disappointment about the closed pool. We walked on the other side of Vltava River on the ancient Charles Bridge. We also walked through The Golden Lane where I again had a chance to use my historical knowledge, which I had already performed for Mr. Schwartz. For dinner we stopped in a small restaurant in the old city and came back to our hotel shortly after nine in the evening.

"Nine thirty-one," I said to the receptionist and then asked:

"Did you get a room for us for another night, please?"

"No, sorry, I did not," said the receptionist and handed me the key for our room.

We boarded the elevator and there was more disappointment in the kids' faces. They did not say anything, but their mood was at a freezing point.

"There is nothing we can do; just pack up tomorrow morning and go to Znojmo," I said.

"But we have to go to the city for something," Nora said.

"Yes, it should not take too long and then we can go see the Orloj again," I said.

In the morning after breakfast, we put all our belongings back into the car and left the Hotel Panorama. We went to the Italian embassy and parked the car as close as possible to the centre of the city. The children still did not have the slightest idea we were on our way to leave the country. After a short walk we came up to the embassy and Peter read out loud the sign, which was in the Czech language written on the building:

"Italian Embassy" and then he looked with interest at the Italian flag located left from the main entrance. His sign reading stunned me and at the same time it gave me a few seconds to think.

"Dad, what are we doing here exactly?," Peter asked with a typical childlike naïveté and stared at me.

"When we were told last night at hotel Panorama that they did not have a room for us anymore, mom and I decided we were going to Italy for a couple of days. Now we are picking up Italian visas to be able to enter that country," I said.

Peter looked at Nora and Katarina and said with a big smile on his face:

"Hurray, we are going to Italy!" He lifted his arms above his head and jumped up and down with joy. Nora looked at me and smiled. We both realized now that the boy knows how to read and write and we had to include that in our plan.

"Go inside for the visas; we will wait for you outside," Nora said.

I entered the building and stood in a line, which was in front of a small window with the inscription: "VISA"

I stood in the line perhaps fifteen minutes and I got to the small window.

"Good morning," I said and handed the clerk our passports and letter about granted visas, which we received from the embassy back home.

"Good morning," she said, opened a drawer and pulled out our applications for visas that were already officially stamped. Then she opened our passports and stamped visas inside. She handed me the open passports and I quickly glanced at them. Both of them had a blue rubber stamp bearing the date: 24 July 1984.

"Exactly what I needed . . . so far all of it is working . . ." I muttered in my head.

"Thank you and Goodbye," I said in a smooth voice and walked out of the building.

"So what? Do we have visas?" Nora asked.

"Yes, we do have them and with today's date," I said and winked at her.

"Peter followed our conversation and when he heard "we do have them," he again raised his arms above his head, somewhat jumped, and said thrilled:

"We are going to Italy!"

"Now let's go for a walk in the old town and on the way we can find a restaurant where we can have lunch," I said.

"When are we going to Italy?," Peter inquired.

"Tomorrow; today it is already too late, because by the time we got to the Austrian border, it would be evening," I said.

"Why do we have to go to the Austrian border when we are going to Italy?" Peter inquired.

". . . because Italy is not a neighbor to Czechoslovakia. First we have to pass through Austria, in order to get into Italy," I shortly explained the geography. Apparently my explanation sufficed, because he did not ask any more questions. We just strolled down Staromestke (Old City) square and when the kids were quite far from us, I said quietly:

"We still have too much money."

Nora stared at me and asked:

"What do you mean . . . too much?"

"Nevertheless I have never had so much money in my wallet in all my life. But that doesn't trouble me," I said with laughter and then added:

"I know that by customs regulations we can have only three thousand crowns when crossing the border."

"Per capita?" Nora asked.

"No, for the entire family," I said.

"Is it the money we got from the sale of the "invisible furnishings"? Nora asked.

"Yes, the majority of it. I didn't want to withdraw all the money from our account in the bank, so it would not be suspicious," I said.

"Accordingly, did we still leave some money in the bank?" Nora asked and then commented:

"So, not only did we throw away a furnished apartment, but we also left some money in the bank!"

"Yes. But it doesn't work any other way," I said.

"I understand. But it irritates me that awhile ago I wanted to buy a pair of boots, but we did not have money for them. And now . . . we've left money in the bank," she said disgruntled.

"I will buy you a pair of boots in Austria," I said.

Her eyes lit up and she asked:

"Any pair I choose?"

"Any, you choose," I said.

"We should still buy the children some toys here," she said.

"I am in . . . how much each? . . . two thousand? I asked.

"No, that's too much. So it wouldn't be peculiar that we are giving them too much money for toys. A thousand each should be enough," she said.

"Then we have to buy something else," I said.

"What do you have in mind?" Nora asked.

"I don't know. We may get an idea later. You could buy a dress, suit or some other clothing," I said.

"It would not fit in suitcases anyway," Nora said.

"It doesn't have to. We are traveling with a car, so you can have that in the shopping bag on the seat or next to your feet," I said.

"I could be wearing that when we cross the border," Nora said and then asked with laughter:

"How much is my limit?"

"Keeping in mind another night in a hotel, some money for food and gas, then you can spend up to four thousand," I said.

"I have never spent so much for clothing . . . do you still have so much money?" she asked.

"Yes, I have just mentioned to you we've never had this much ever before. We should rather spend it than throw it away. We can have a maximum of three thousand with us, but they don't say what the minimum is. If we are going to have only a few hundred leftover at the border, that should be all right. After that we cannot spend it anyway," I said.

It was almost noon and we were just coming under The Prague Orloj, where Peter and Katarina had stopped a minute ago. The clockwork chimed twelve and all the apostles paraded around. The crowd of people that normally gathered before noon and waited for the show was slowly moving away. It was time to start looking for a place to eat lunch. When we wandered around in back streets, we came up to a store from the chain called Tuzex.

Communism created this chain for people receiving money from foreign countries because according to the law, citizens could not own foreign money. The government confiscated the foreign currency and gave the recipients vouchers instead, which were called Bony. They were valid up to half a year and after the expiration day, which was rubber stamped on them, they became valueless pieces of paper. Bony were un-saleable according to the sign that was imprinted on them. However, in front of every Tuzex store were several people selling Bony to anybody interested in buying them. This way all Tuzex stores turned out to be available to practically anybody despite the fact that the stores would not accept the only official legal currency—crowns. There was one big disadvantage: the merchandise in Tuzex was very expensive, making it unavailable to many people.

We stopped in front of the Tuzex store and looked at the merchandise on display. We stood there for about a minute, when an older woman approached us slowly and whispered her inquiry:

"Do you need any Bony?" and she did not look at us, but instead, carefully scanned the surroundings.

"Yes, but we don't know how much yet," I said and the older woman slowly walked away. From that moment we were her potential customer and she watched us very cautiously.

"We could buy that small radio with a tape player," I said to Nora and pointed to it in the display window.

"Are we going to have enough money for everything else after?" Nora asked.

"Yes," I said.

"So, let's buy it," Nora said, taking the kids, and all of them entered the store. I stayed outside, and as soon as I turned my head, the older woman with the Bony stood behind me and whispered her inquiry:

"How much?"

"Three hundred sixty," I said also very quietly.

"Wait here," the woman said, crossed the street and entered a gate. A moment later she came out, walked up to me and handed me three hundred sixty Bonys. I counted the money and then handed her the appropriate value in Czechoslovakian crowns and the woman again slowly walked away while constantly scanning the surroundings.

I walked inside the store and at a counter showed the sales lady which radio I had chosen. She wrote down on a sales slip the total sale value and I paid it at the register. With a sales receipt from the register I came back to the sales lady and she exchanged the slip for the radio. Nora and the kids watched with interest that sales transaction, and when I was leaving the store, they joined me. We walked out and sat down on the closest park bench, where we checked out our new radio.

"After lunch we will go into a toy store and you can buy toys for a thousand crowns. Dad will give you money for them." Nora interrupted our enthusiasm with the new radio.

The kids were still fully occupied with the radio and diligently turned knobs. They let go of the knobs, staring at me as it was too much shopping for one day. When I nodded my head, they both yelled:

"Hurray."

From that moment it was very important for them to locate a toy store and they meticulously looked around everywhere we went. Despite the fact that eating was not too important, we found a restaurant where we had had lunch and afterwards we searched for a toy store again. I even asked people walking by for the closest toy store. According to the passersby, there was no such store in the old city. I did not want to take a chance by going into a different part of Prague because traffic in large cities wasn't very fast. I suggested instead:

"Let's go rather to Znojmo. It is a much smaller city and we will be able to find a toy store much faster. Besides that, we are going to Italy, so if we do not find anything there, you can buy something on the way in Austria or when we get to Rome.

The children thought for a moment, considered my suggestion, and then Peter asked:

"Why are we going to Znojmo?"

"Because through Znojmo, there are a few good border crossings to Austria," I said.

"I want to buy a dolly," Katarina stated.

"Do you think we can find a hotel in Znojmo?" Nora asked.

"Certainly easier than in Prague. If we don't find a hotel, we will definitely see some motels on our way there. Let's go to downtown Znojmo first and see," I said.

"Let's go to Znojmo. I want to buy a dolly there," Katarina repeated when no one responded to her first statement.

"All right, you will buy a dolly," I said to Katarina and then turned to Peter:

"What do you want to buy?"

"A truck," Peter announced briefly.

"Then let us go to the car and go to Znojmo," Nora said and then turned to me:

"Do you know how we get back to the car from here?"

"Peter, you forgot to sprinkle crumbs behind us," I looked at Peter with a serious face.

"What crumbs?" Peter inquired.

"Well, just like in the fairy tale. In order to get back," I said.

Peter peeped fixedly at me and strove to find out from my face whether I meant that seriously. I smiled and said:

"When we have no crumbs, come along this way," I said and pointed to the street on the right from us. The three of them looked where I had shown them and then we set off that way. After a few moments Nora tipped toward me and asked quietly:

"Are you sure we are going in the right direction?"

I tipped toward her and likewise quietly said:

"Quite sure . . . I count on my impeccable sense of orientation."

"We have been walking in the streets of the old town for several hours. I certainly could not find the car," Nora said.

"So leave it up to me. I know where it is," I said.

We passed by some shops with clothing and we stopped in every one of them because Nora wanted to buy something. In one of those shops, she found a suit, vest and pants, which she liked. We bought the whole set and kept on walking. After about half an hour we came to a street, from where we had a nice view downward at the town. I stopped by a rail, pointed down and said:

"Do you see that red car down there? That's our Skoda car."

"Aha, there is our car," Nora said to the children, as if she had just found it.

It took us another fifteen minutes and we were at the car. After so many hours of walking, we were really happy we could sit down. I took out a road map and studied the quickest way for us to get from the centre of Prague on the road in the direction of Znojmo. The children sat in the back seat and it was quite obvious that they were exhausted. Peter looked outside the car window and yawned.

"Do you know which way to go?" Nora asked.

"Roughly, but preferably I'll take a look at a map, so we don't get needlessly lost in Prague," I said.

The road outside the city seemed very simple and without problems I headed in the direction of Znojmo. In about an hour and a half we arrived at the perimeter of town and on the way we saw three motels. I tried my best to remember their locations, so I could return to them if we found no accommodation directly in town. We also came up to a T intersection where the sign to the left showed to Znojmo and the sign to the right to Austria.

"I must remember how to get back here. Tomorrow morning, I must come here," I said more or less for myself.

"Why don't we go to Austria right now?" Katarina inquired.

I turned to the left and stopped at the road shoulder immediately behind the intersection. Before I stepped out of the car, I said to Katarina:

"Because it is getting late now. Morning is the best time for crossing borders. Besides that, we are going to have a look at toys in Znojmo" and I stepped out of the car. I surveyed the area and strove to get the best orientation, so I would not get lost in the morning. I got back in the car and drove to Znojmo.

"It looks here like the centre of town," I said, as we arrived at some historic buildings, which by their architecture resembled the Middle Ages.

"Hotel," I read on a sign as we drove by.

"Aha, those are toys," Katarina said thrilled, when she spotted a shop on the other side of the street. I parked in front of the hotel and said:

"Let us go see whether they have a room available in this hotel for us and then we will go shopping around town," I said, to the complete satisfaction of all in the car. We received a room for our last night in Czechoslovakia with no problem because the hotel was almost empty. I was really glad because we had saved ourselves from searching for another hotel in town, which we didn't know at all. This was our first and last visit to a very pretty town in Moravia, which had a very long and interesting history. However, we had not stopped there because of its historic monuments. We needed some place to sleep through the night, get up early in the morning, and cross the border into Austria. When we were given a key to our room, I looked at my watch and said:

"Let us go to downtown shopping right now. We can take the luggage from the car later."

We went outside to the street and the kids impatiently ran in the direction of the toy shops. It was five o'clock in the afternoon and shops were open till six. The children still had a full hour to pick out their new toys. It did not take them too long because, perhaps twenty minutes later, we walked out of the shop with two boxes, a truck in one of them and a plastic dolly in the other one. Each one of them held a box with the new toy in a shopping bag and in this manner we passed the historic centre of town. When we arrived back at the hotel, Nora said:

"We don't need to unload all the luggage from the car. Before we left from the Hotel Panorama, I packed all that we will need for tonight and tomorrow morning into a single bag."

"That was a good idea! So I will pull out only that one bag," I said. Nora showed me which one, I grabbed it out of the car and we went to the hotel. After the morning walk through old Prague, no one wanted to go looking for a restaurant in town, so we stayed at the hotel restaurant for dinner.

We left the hotel early in the morning, right after breakfast. I stopped at a mailbox, which was outside of town and dropped in three letters. One was for my parents-in-law; one for my parents; and one for my brother-in-law, Miro. We wrote them a short goodbye letter, but the way we wrote it was not quite clear where we went, or what was the goal of our journey. Just in case we could not get through the border, so our letters could not serve as witness documents in court. We also included a copy of the key to our apartment. We explained it was just in case of "emergency." The conclusion of the letter suggested destroying the letter and hiding the key and we would call later.

I remembered very well how to get to the border and in about ten minutes we came up to the intersection, which I tried so intensively to write into my memory just yesterday. Nora opened her purse and pulled a out a gold chain which she didn't want to leave in the apartment in Bratislava. She handed it to Katarina and said:

"Kat, put this chain on your neck" and Kat complied very enthusiastically, she squeezed in between the front seats and Nora put it on. Katarina went back to her seat, lifted the pendant in her palm to eye level, and happily looked at it.

"If someone asks you about the chain . . . you have had it for a long time. But if no one asks you anything about it, do not bring anybody's attention to it," Nora added.

"Yes," Katarina said. She was really happy about getting the chain and she was willing to say anything her mother asked her to.

"If they ask you anything at the border, answer politely, but very shortly. Do not use long-winded sentences in any case." I asked both children for this small conspiracy against customs clerks and added:

"If they ask you how long you have been preparing for vacation in Italy, just say:

"a very long time."

Both of them just nodded their heads and I continued:

"We are coming back home in ten days."

I watched the road in front of me and noticed that the bushes by the road were so thick I could not see anything else but the road.

"That cannot be an accident that the bushes are so thick," I thought and saw a toll gate in the road. There were two soldiers with automatic rifles, AK-47s, standing next to it. I stopped the car in front of the toll booth and rolled down the window. The soldier who stood on my side came up to the car and said:

"Passports, please"

I handed him our passports and the soldier standing on the other side of car lifted the gate.

Pull the car about thirty feet ahead, stop the engine and do not get out of the car," said the one holding our passports.

I followed his orders and stopped the car about thirty feet ahead and turned off the engine.

The soldier who stood on the other side of the car lowered the gate down again and watched us extremely carefully. The one with the passports brought them into a small building on the left side and handed them through a small window to someone inside. It was so quiet there we could hear the soldier's steps and whistling noise of his uniform as he walked to the building. Next to the building stood a tall guard tower with a watch guard sitting on a deck, which was about sixty feet above ground level. He had a machine gun in front of him and it was aimed at us. I looked unobtrusively to the right side. There was another guard tower and a guard with a machine gun aimed also at us. One tollgate was in front of us and other one behind us. The one behind us was a usual gate we could regularly see on roads, painted with red and white stripes. But the gate in front of us was something I had never seen before. It was built in between tall concrete walls and it was unusually big and heavy. It would open toward the car.

"So, this is the tollgate I heard about from my acquaintances who have already traveled to the West. It was known to be so strong that an army tank could not break through it," I thought.

The concrete walls were about thirty feet high and the other end was connected to barbed wire fences, which ran far into the country until they disappeared from sight. Those were the well known three layered fences surrounding the whole of Czechoslovakia. The middle one was actually under high voltage, because it hung on porcelain electric isolators. This one was protected from both sides with an "ordinary" barbed wire fence, which protected wild animals from being electrocuted. Already knowing about the electric fence. I felt like someone who was just leaving a concentration camp after a long time. I looked at Nora. She was obviously quite nervous.

"Calm down. Nothing is happening," I said as quietly as possible under the circumstances. The children sat motionless in the back seat and did not say a single word that entire time.

The steps of the soldier who brought back our passports echoed into the silence. He handed me the passports and I said:

"Thank you."

Immediately, the tank-proof gate started almost noiselessly opening towards us. It was held in position by a steel tumbler, which was about four and half feet tall and about four feet in diameter. The tumbler was protruding from a concrete block, which was a part of the wall on the right side. The front part of the gate was locked into another steel tumbler, which protruded from a concrete wall on the left side. The gate was so heavy it was moving around on two truck size tires. The tires were rolling on a concrete quarter circle, which ended about thirty feet in front of our car. I breathed out with relief, because when that contraption started moving, I thought it was going to hit our car.

The soldier who brought our passports back stood by the car and watched the opening of the big gate. When it was wide open, he handed me our passports and said:

"Start up the engine and stop over there by the customs clerks" and pointed to two figures beyond the open tank-proof gate. When the car started moving, Nora asked:

"Who were these, when the customs clerks are over there?"

"These were members of the Elite unit of the Czechoslovakian army, which is officially called the Border Patrol. They are young boys about eighteen years old and all of them are members of the Communist Party and their brains are completely washed. They are ready to shoot anyone who would try to leave the country on the spot and they are proud of it. When they succeed in shooting someone dead, they receive a monetary reward from the Communist Party and an extra week of vacation," I said very quietly.

"Who told you all that?" Nora asked very surprised.

"When I was at the army reserve exercise a few years back, one of the guys, who used to serve with the Border Patrol as a young soldier, told me," I said.

"And he told you everything just like that?" Nora asked with disbelief.

"He was drunk . . . and then maybe after twenty years his senses woke up and he needed to get it all out," I said.

We had to conclude our dialogue, even though the car was slowly moving in that freaky environment; a short distance in front of us were two custom clerks. One of them held a STOP sign in his right hand and pointed with his left hand to a concrete square, where I had to stop. I stopped the car where he had pointed and he came to my window and ordered:

"Turn off the engine."

I followed his order and he continued:

"Your passports, Travel Provisions and the slip about surrendering your military booklet."

"Good morning," I said calmly and handed him the documents he asked for. The other customs clerk still stood on the right side of the car and surveyed the inside.

The clerk who stood next to me opened the passports and started comparing our faces with the pictures inside the passports. When he was satisfied we resembled our documents, he asked:

"Why are you going to Austria through the crossing point at Znojmo, when a crossing point to Austria is less than two miles from the place where you live?"

"The Italian embassy in Prague lost our original applications for visas and we had to re-apply. Only yesterday we got the visas from them and we are going this way because it is closer to Italy or Vienna than going back through Bratislava," I said quite serenely.

The clerk turned pages in the passports and found visas with yesterday's dates. It appeared he was fairly satisfied with the results of his detective work and said more or less to himself:

"Aha . . . yes . . ." and he did not continue.

He bent his knees and peeked through an open window into the back of the car and swung from side to side, in order to make sure we were not hiding somebody else there. He counted two children and started paging through the passports again.

"The children are written up in my wife's passport," I said, in order to forestall his following the crime-hunting process.

"Where are your identity books," he inquired with a voice, which sounded, as if he wanted to say:

"So, now I've caught you."

"At home . . . in the kitchen . . . on the refrigerator," I said quite composedly because I was pretty sure that this clerk would not catch me with anything. Then I asked in a quite naive voice:

"When we travel with our passports, we don't need identity books, do we?

"No, no . . . I only wanted to know where you left your identity books," said the customs clerk and now he perused the slip about surrendering my military booklet. He studied it for a moment, then he turned it over and examined the back side. He also raised it up against the sky and peeped from the back side against the light, as if by the paper he would detect whether the slip was or wasn't a counterfeit. It never occurred to me to identify whether that slip had a watermark and now it was too late for it. The slip was irretrievably in the customs officer's hands.

"Did you leave your military booklet at military headquarters?" he inquired in the voice of an investigator who had caught a jailbird at deception.

"No. At the department of Special Affairs at our company. They locked it up in a safe," I said composedly. The customs officer didn't say anything but only nodded his head. He was annoyed that such a sophisticated trick did not work. During this entire time, the other customs officer walked around our car and he tried to find something suspicious. Every now and then he knelt down and peeped in spaces between fenders and tires. He even lay down on the ground and peeped at the car from underneath.

"This one is perhaps called Scrutinizer and this one, who gives me sophisticated questions will be perhaps Investigator," I thought and subconsciously smiled.

Investigator noticed my smile and apparently he did not know how to interpret it in any way. He watched me very carefully and at the same time he expected me to get nervous. I was very calm; their behavior did not make me anxious in any way. Customs officers were also StB agents, so I knew what to say and how to conduct myself. I had already had a lot of experience. Both customs officers recognized, that their strategy was not working, so they pulled up something better and more accomplished. At least they thought so.

"Stay in the car. Do not start the engine!," Investigator ordered and then along with Scrutinizer they both left to a small building about six hundred feet from our car off to the left. They took our passports and other documents along with them. We stayed there quite alone; it was entirely silent and there was no other car around us. On the right from the concrete surface, on which stood our car, there were long benches with shelters against rain. We patiently waited to see what would come next.

"And what now?" Nora asked quietly.

"Nothing. They said we had to stay in the car. We have plenty of time and apparently so do they," I said quietly and looked to the left. The customs officers were already inside and a window at the small building was open. Both of them sat inside and through the open window they observed us with binoculars. Apparently they believed that they were far enough away that we could not see them. They did not know about my perfect vision, so they could not include it in their game. I could see them very well and thought over my following move on the big chessboard of psychological tricks.

"Both of them sit inside of that little building and observe us with binoculars," I said very quietly, with my head rotated down and to the right at Nora, because I was not certain whether they had microphones near our car. Somehow subconsciously I felt that microphones were there.

"Why do they watch us with binoculars?'" Nora asked quietly.

"Game of nerves . . . they want to make us nervous and wait to see if we start opening bags, or try to hide something in the car," I said quietly.

"We do not have anything we should not have! How long are we going to sit here? We have been sitting here already for half an hour," Nora said upset.

"We are not rushing anywhere. We have plenty of time," I said and looked at my watch.

"Please make some sandwiches; we are going to eat now," I said loudly, so they could hear me through their microphones.

"Did you go crazy? Right now . . . you are going to eat?" Nora asked quietly.

"Yes, let's eat. The children are hungry too," I said aloud and turned my head backwards at the children. Both of them quietly nodded their heads that they were hungry too. Despite her disbelief at my idea of eating at a time like this, Nora stretched backwards behind her seat and Katarina helped her with a bag, which was sitting by her feet. Nora took out some buns from the bag and laid them on the dashboard. Then she took each bun one by one and with a knife she cut them into halves. She did the cutting down below the dashboard because her hands were shaking.

"Calm down! They just want us to get nervous," I said very quietly and in the process I bent down, as if to pick something up off the floor. I took cheese from the bag and started unwrapping it.

"It is easy for you to say," Nora said whispering still bent down and busy with cutting buns.

"I AM calm . . . ," I said.

Nora handed me a bun with cheese and ham ready to eat and I took a tasteful bite. I looked to the left and noticed customs officers walking out of the small building. I made the right move . . . Both of them came back to our car and Investigator ordered:

"Unload all luggage and put it down on those tables and all of you get out of the car!" and with his left hand pointed at the tables with the canopy roofs. I opened the trunk and pulled the entire luggage out and laid it on the tables. The bun that I barely started eating I held in my mouth with my teeth. Nora and the children got out and laid all the bags on the tables next to the other luggage I had put there.

"Open the suitcases," Investigator ordered.

The leftover bun I had not eaten started falling out of my mouth, so I handed it to Nora and opened the suitcases. Investigator picked out pieces of clothing one by one from our suitcases and with his hands felt whether he could find something stashed in the pockets. When the investigator threw everything out of the suitcases, he proceeded carefully examining each empty suitcase to see if he could find something stashed in the side pockets, or sewn under the linings. In the middle of his rummaging, Investigator looked at us and surprised us with a question:

"Are you going to go to Vatican City to see the pope too?"

"No," I said.

"Yes, "Nora said along with me. Only then I realized I forgot to speak to her about how Prazec determined for us that we were not going to Vatican City. One single detail I completely forgot about. It was already too late for any explanations, so I thought about the best possible response. Nora understood she should leave all further discussion about Vatican City to me and stayed silent.

"So, you are going, or not?" Investigator inquired and peeped at me, then at Nora.

"We don't know yet if we are going to have money and time for it. We'll see . . . ," I told the investigator.

He was satisfied with my answer, because he did not continue interrogating but continued to rummage about. Likewise, he double-checked all the bags and the last in line was the children's backpack with toys. When he took out and checked all toys one by one, he deposited them on the table, opened the front pocket of the backpack, and took out of it a little packet. Something was very tidily packaged in a handkerchief and bound with rubber bands in a crisscross fashion. He held it triumphantly in front of our eyes and asked in the same triumphant voice:

"Soooo, and what is this?" and at the same time watched us very suspiciously.

"I don't know. It must be some part of the children's toy," I said composedly.

"Who packed this backpack?" the investigator inquired.

"The children," Nora said.

Investigator slowly removed the rubber bands, laid the packet in his palm, unwrapped the handkerchief and at the same time watched our faces with one eye. It appeared to me like in a cheap opera where the king sang the first part of his aria, then he would stab his opponent with a sword and then triumphantly finish singing his aria in a higher pitch. All others on the stage stood and waited for the last note of the king's aria, so they could also stab their opponents with swords. When he finally unwrapped it he found money, which is sold with children's games. The customs officers involuntarily had to make some alterations to the scenario of this scene . . . Sword stabbing of opponents in this opera did not happen.

"Well, you see, it is money," I said with laughter and at the same time I thought:

"You idiot, if I arrange some additional money for our vacation in the West you will never find it!" . . . and thought about money, which I had exchanged with Mr. Schwartz. I looked at Nora. She laughed also.

"Unload everything from your pockets here on the table and turn the linings of your pockets inside out. Including the children," Investigator ordered.

We laid everything on the table, pulled out the linings of our pockets and observed him as he rummaged about. Handkerchiefs, which we laid there, he turned over with a pencil he took from his pocket.

"This is a very clever man . . . he observes all hygienic principles!," I thought and was also somewhat sorry that we had clean handkerchiefs. When he did not find anything in them, he caught my wallet, held it at the height of my eyes and asked like an inquisitor:

"How much money is in this wallet?"

"Six hundred dollars, from which is two hundred dollars in cash and four hundred in American Express travelers' checks. In addition, my wallet contains one thousand seven hundred fifty crowns," I said composedly. Investigator recounted the money and found that the dollars were OK. However, he found crowns short by ten crowns.

"There are some change coins . . . ," I said. He stopped me in the middle of my sentence by waving his hand and announced:

"That's all right."

He checked Nora's purse much less theatrically. He only asked how much money was there and then recounted it. It appeared to me, that he had given up and I had a very good feeling because I had anticipated this entire circus with the customs officers at the border crossing a long time ago and was really prepared for it. I had been prepared since the time I spoke to Mr. Kolesar about a journey to Italy. I was glad that I had assessed them well and they didn't disappoint my expectations. They behaved, to us, like true primitives.

"When are you coming back home?" Investigator inquired of the children with his last hope that he could find something out.

"In ten days," they both said at once and very convincingly. Investigator looked as if he was short of breath because he did not ask another thing.

While Investigator rummaged about our clothing from the suitcases, the Scrutinizer diligently searched our car. He looked in every cavity of the car, by the engine and also in the trunk; he opened every compartment he could. He also lifted the floor carpets and seat covers in the car, and knocked on the linings of the doors and ceiling . . . It took him about an hour during which time he found absolutely nothing. Frustrated and annoyed, he just scratched behind his right ear. Evidently, he had given up as well . . . without saying a word; just with his hand he motioned to Investigator that he had found nothing. The Investigator attempted a sour smile, handed me our passports and said:

"Have a pleasant journey"

"Thank you," I said for all of us and returned a smile. My smile was a genuine one . . .

They went back into the little building. I looked around and found that we were all by ourselves. No car was behind us. In this big lot there were only the four of us, our suitcases and bags with all our stuff tossed out and our empty car. We went back to the tables and started putting everything back in the suitcases and bags.

"Peter, Katarina . . . come here and pack your toys back into the backpack," Nora called to the children. They also came to the table, and when they had the backpack done, they helped us with the rest. Katarina helped Nora with folding shirts, sweaters and pants. She patiently rolled socks into balls again and Peter helped me with storing the packed suitcases and bags in the car.

"What were they actually looking for?" Nora asked quietly as we stood side by side and deposited clothing back into the suitcases.

"Money. Or something they could send us back home for," I said also quietly. It took us about half an hour to put everything back in the suitcases and bags again and then we brought them back to the car. When we had everything back in the car, we jumped in and drove off into the free world. About half a mile away were the Austrian customs.

"I hope that Austrians will not rake through all our belongings again," Nora said a bit grouchy as we moved on.

"No. By no means! Austria is a democratic country. Over there they have to treat people much more decently than those primitive Communists," I said and just drove up to a small window of the Austrian customs. Through the open car window I handed the customs officer our passports and said in German:

"Good morning"

"Good morning," said the customs officer. He took our passports and bent out his window, so he could see how many people were in the car. He opened the passports and imprinted a dated rubber stamp for our entry into Austria. He handed me the passports back and said:

"Good bye"

"Good bye," I responded to him also in German. The red and white tollgate in front of our car automatically lifted, I put the car in first gear and slowly moved forward and

WE ENTERED AUSTRIA.

We were on the road going to Vienna and it was quiet in the car. We were trying to recuperate from the shock of how they treated us at the border crossing by Znojmo. We spent two hours and fifteen minutes being degraded only because we tried to depart from "opulent" Communism and the Czechoslovak government, via StB agents who wanted to show us who was the master of the situation. Common people, as we were, meant nothing with their scale of values. Not one of us was a member of the Communist Party; furthermore; I had declined their offer to sign into that screwed party twice. By their third attempt, when Prazec said that Jan Bielek had to join the party, I preferably chose our departure from the country. Our customs clearance at the Austrian side lasted only thirty-five seconds. If in nothing else, in that experience we could behold the whale of a difference in cultural levels of the two adjacent countries.

Lost in my thoughts, I suddenly started to notice the surroundings of the country through which we were traveling. I could not spot a single gloomy, dilapidated house, which I had seen too many of on the other side of the border. Small gardens in front of houses along with lawns were "manicured" so cleanly that it was a pleasure to look at them. And then I became conscious that we were away "from there." We successfully concluded the hardest part of our great plan and inside I was overwhelmed with the feeling of pleasure. I didn't know why, but I just remembered a verse from a Czech poem, which I had to memorize as a boy in school. Right now I said it aloud with shear enjoyment:

". . . and at poplars by the rocks, a green hobbit applauds . . ."

The poem was called Waterman by Karel Jaromir Erben. It had nothing to do with running away from Communism; the poet who wrote this poem had died in the late 19th century. He was a happy fellow who knew nothing about Communism. Even the waterman in this poem was a negative figure. I just remembered this verse only because I felt like a small green hobbit, who was successful in something he had worked on for such a long time. As I finished reciting that verse, I laughed.

Nora looked at me apprehensively and inquired:

"Janny, are you all right?"

Peter stood up from the back seat, and with his hands, he covered my ears from behind and Katarina's head showed also between the front seats. She also apprehensively asked:

"Dad, are you all right?"

Only then I realized how I must have startled all of them. Never before had I spoken Czech in front of them and never reciting Czech poems, with crazy laughter at the end. They were convinced I had become insane. I shook my head as much as I could because Peter still held my head and quite composedly this time already in Slovak, I said.

"No, I did not become insane. Only somehow I could not resist to saying it out of happiness."

Peter me let go of my head, but Katarina and Nora still scrutinized me, so I said:

"Hurrah, we are already in Austria!"

Peter repeated this sentence after me and threw himself with laughter into the back seat, but Nora and Katarina were still not convinced. Katarina's head was still between the front seats. With my right hand I caught Nora's left hand, softly squeezed it, glimpsed at her and with a modest smile I said:

"Really, I am well. I just suddenly realized all that was already behind us and a crazy gratification got a hold of me. The last year was really full of anxiety for me."

It seemed that this time she believed me and said:

"When you started in Czech, I got really startled. And the laughter at the end . . ."

Katarina's head disappeared from between the seats, she sat down in her seat and said with laughter:

"Dad speaks Czech . . ."

Suddenly the mood in the car altogether changed, and the children started talking again, and anyhow behave like kids yet again. Nora cracked a smile and pointed at the stores outside and said:

"Aha, look at those stores. How much merchandise they have there! We should go have a look in those stores!"

The children also gazed at the stores full of goods and already wanted to go shopping. I entirely understood their enthusiasm. It was a huge contrast to the half-empty stores which they were used to in Bratislava, Prague or Znojmo; these were actual feasts for the eyes to them. Unlike them, I had been in the West before and I did not consider the stores full of goods miraculous. It was very comfortable to shop in them, but otherwise they did not lure me.

"These are only tiny shops in a little border town. Wait until we come to Vienna. There are large department stores and you'll have a chance to walk in those stores to your heart's content," I said.

"Nevertheless, you could stop for awhile anyway," Nora insisted.

"Look, we lost a lot of time at the border and it will take about another hour and a half of driving to get to Vienna. I have never been in Vienna before. As you know, it is a metropolitan city and it will be a bit of a problem for me driving around the city. I would like to get there and find a hotel room for a reasonable price before it becomes too dark," I said.

"All right then," Nora said resignedly and then she added with enthusiasm:

"But when we get a room at a hotel, we will go shopping in Vienna's stores."

"Of course, then we will have plenty of time," I said.

I looked through the rearview mirror at the children. It was quite obvious they were looking forward to shopping in stores where there was plenty to choose from. Both of them had big smiles on their faces and their eyes gleamed with happiness. They knew I would always fulfill my promises. Before we arrived in Vienna, I had to stop a few times and orient myself according to the road map. We passed through the center of Vienna, but there was nowhere to stop. More or less I could not, because by the time I got into the correct lane, we were again somewhere else. Actually we also passed by the US embassy twice. I remembered I had a few acquaintances who resided in Vienna. I met them at technical seminars and they mentioned if I was ever in Vienna sometime to call them. Their names and telephone numbers I had encrypted and written in pencil in my English-Slovak dictionary. Only I knew how to decode them. The list of people with phone numbers written on a piece of paper, or in a notebook, would be a golden fish in the nets of agents at the border crossing. I found a phone booth and succeeded in parking close by. I decoded a telephone number from the dictionary, wrote it on a small card and entered the phone booth. Immediately after I stepped inside, I realized I would not be making any calls until I got some Austrian schillings. In my wallet there were only two American one-hundred-dollar paper bills and some Czechoslovak crowns. I got out of the booth and Nora inquired:

"Did you tackle that so quickly?"

"No, I need some schillings," I said.

Fortunately, we were in the centre of Vienna and a bank was immediately on the other side of the street. They exchanged a one-hundred-dollar bill for me immediately, but once again, I had no change. Somehow I did not think to ask for it when I was at the counter in the bank.

"Just wait a moment; I have to return to the bank and get some change for the phone booth," I said.

"It will take too long. You should just buy us some ice cream over there in the kiosk and you'll have some change," Nora said and pointed her finger at a kiosk.

"Come with me so you can choose which one you want," I said and we went to the kiosk.

"Get vanilla with chocolate for all of us. At least it's going to be simple," Nora said.

"Peter, come along with me so I don't have a problem holding three ice creams and at the same time paying for them," I said. Peter went with me to the kiosk and we came back with three vanilla-chocolate ice creams. They ate their ice cream by the car and I went to call my acquaintance. I dialed the number and Mr. Buchler answered immediately in German:

"Good afternoon, here's Mr. Buchler."

"Good afternoon, Mr. Buchler here's Jan Bielek," I said in English. He immediately responded in English:

"Mr. Bielek, how are you? Where are you?"

"Fairly well, thank you. I am here in Vienna with my family on vacation, as I told you during your last visit."

"Yes, I remember. Where are you at this moment?" Mr. Buchler inquired.

I told him that I was in a red Skoda car and the names of the two streets at the nearest intersection. He said:

"Do not go anywhere and wait for me. I will be there in a few minutes."

"Yes, I will wait for you. See you in a little while," I said.

"Yes, see you in a moment," he said and hung up.

I got out of the phone booth and Nora asked:

"How did you make out?"

"Very well. He asked me to wait for him here and he will be here in a few minutes," I said.

We stood outside by the car in a parking lot and Nora with the children had not finished eating their ice cream when a car stopped next us and Mr. Buchler stepped out of it. I introduced him to my family and he said with a big smile:

"I am really glad that you stopped in our beautiful Vienna and that you called me. This way I have a chance to meet your gorgeous family."

"Thank you, that you came so quickly for us," I said.

"If I may inquire, are in a hurry to go to Italy or would you like to stay a few days here in Vienna?," Mr. Buchler inquired.

Nora and I exchanged glances and then I said:

"No, we are in no hurry. We would like to stay a few days in Vienna," I said.

"If you haven't paid for a hotel, I would like to show you one here close to the centre. It is not deluxe class, but it is a very nice one," Mr. Buchler said.

"We do not need a luxury hotel, just one with a reasonable price is just what we're looking for. Ultimately, we only sleep there and it will fit better into our budget," I said.

"Excellent, just follow me with your car. We can stop by at our company," he said and he got in his car.

We followed him and in about twenty minutes we came to his company. We got out of the car and followed him inside. I had never been there before, so I had at least an opportunity to see what kind of company this was. So far we had always met either in Prague or in Bratislava. The entire company was only a few offices that were sparsely furnished. The company was just a corporate agent, so I did not expect to see any production halls there. He introduced our entire family to two secretaries who were in the entrance office. He opened a door into a conference room and asked Nora:

"Mrs. Bielek, with your permission, I'd like to chat with your husband about business. Ethel and Maria will keep you and your children in the meantime. The two of us will talk in this room for a moment. It will not be long."

I translated to Nora what he said and she agreed. I could not imagine how the secretaries would be company to Nora and the kids. The secretaries knew several languages but not Slovak. Nora and the kids knew only Slovak.

Mr. Buchler and I entered the conference room and a moment later Maria served us coffee and tea. We sat at a huge conference table; he had coffee and I had tea. We talked about current business we enjoyed between the companies and also about new quotations, which were just being evaluated. Finally, after so many years, I could honestly say what I could not before. To my best knowledge, I said the truth about odds for each part because I did not have to follow orders from Prazec or Flak about what I could or could not say to foreign partners. Mr. Buchler was very appreciative of my honesty, and at the end of our discussion, I said:

"Mr. Buchler, for our security, when you go again to Czechoslovakia, we never made contact in Vienna, we did not meet and I did not say anything to you. All this information we will keep only to ourselves."

"Yes, of course. I thank you very much for finding some time for business, even though you are currently here on vacation. I asked Ethel to reserve the hotel close to the center, which I mentioned to you. You are going to follow me again and I will bring you to the hotel," Mr. Buchler said.

"I thank you for all your effort with looking for a hotel," I said.

He handed me an envelope and said:

"This is for your children. Please say "thank you" to them for me for their patience and for allowing you to work despite the fact that you are on vacation already."

When the kids opened the envelope in the car, they found a children's greeting card inside, which said in German:

"Thank you for your patience," and when they opened it a five-hundred schilling bill came out.

We followed his car and in about fifteen minutes we came up to a side street, which started at Maria Hilfer Strasse, one of the largest avenues in the middle of Vienna. There was a small and modest hotel there, exactly what we were looking for. By the time we parked the car and went inside, Mr. Buchler was already there talking to the receptionist, who handed me a key for our room.

"Please, translate to your wife that you are going to take a look at the room and I will wait for both of you down here. Then come down here and let me know how you like the room," Mr. Buchler said.

I translated to Nora what he had said and we went upstairs to our room on the third floor. The room was not really a luxury one, not even a big one. However, for four of us, it was exactly what we were looking for, since we were only going to sleep there. We left the children in the room and went downstairs. Mr. Buchler shook hands with Nora first and said:

"I am really glad I had a chance to meet you and your wonderful kids. I have known your husband too well, but I'd rather not give any details." Then he turned to me, shook my hand and waited till I translated his words to Nora. When I came to the end of his sentence, Mr. Buchler made a long face and also touched his lips with his left-hand finger, indicating he would stay silent with the details. All three of us had a good laugh about that and he said to me:

"By the way, the room has been paid for two nights."

"Thank you, Mr. Buchler for everything. You shouldn't have . . . thank you in the name of my whole family," I said. He just winked with one eye and said:

"Good bye and happy journey to Italy," and he walked off.

"Good bye," I said and Nora joined me also . . . we waved to him until he walked out the main entrance. We went back to our room, where the kids waited for us.

"I am not sure if you understood him, but he said the room has been paid for two nights," I said very quietly when we walked upstairs to our room.

"Really? That's very nice of him," Nora said.

"Now we should make an agreement that we will never tell any of those Austrian guys we are not coming back to Czechoslovakia. After a week, we will leave pretending we are going to Italy and we will get lost forever," I said.

"Of course, nobody needs to know that. Those people have their own business interest in Czechoslovakia and there is no need to include them in our refugee plans," Nora said.

"That's exactly what I had in mind. I don't want them to encounter any problems from it. So, it is a deal?" I said.

"Deal," Nora said and then added:

"We have to wait a couple more days before we let the kids know we are not coming back."

"Deal," I said briefly because we were already coming to the room.

We entered the room and found the kids anxiously waiting for us.

"Where have you been?" Katarina asked.

"Downstairs at the reception desk, saying Good bye to the man who led us here," I said.

"We are going shopping now!" Nora called out with joy and the kids jumped up with happiness.

"We can stop by some place for dinner," I said.

"We can go to McDonald's," Peter suggested.

"Yes, we can," I said and went to the city.

Our hotel was practically in the centre of Vienna, so in five minutes we came up to Maria Hilfer Strasse. It was a very long avenue and we could not see from one end to the other and it was covered with a lot of boutiques and department stores. It was a real feast for the eyes for someone who had not been in the West before and knew stores only from Czechoslovakia. Peter was completely exhilarated when we walked into a huge LEGO store where they sold nothing but construction toys from the company of the same name. Right across the main entrance there was a windmill about fifteen feet tall, which looked like a real one, but when we came closer to it we saw it was made out of small LEGO blocks.

I guess we walked through all floors of every department store and saw every department. Nora and the kids would have liked to shop until they dropped dead, but I had to hold them back. I knew in a few days we were going into a refugee camp. The fewer things we had with us the better for everyone.

As suggested by Peter, we went to McDonalds for dinner. This type of restaurant was not in Czechoslovakia yet and we knew it only from Vienna television. The restaurant looked very good at first sight and a lot of people were there, which indicated it was well accepted. We did not know anything about the meals sold there. We made our choices based on pictures and ordered using German meal names written under the pictures. We brought the tray with our order to a table and smelled a very good aroma. We were already very hungry and anticipated our meals. However, we were really surprised after taking the first bite. The meals were prepared without salt, seasonings or any other flavors. We looked at each other and somehow did not understand. We did not know whether we did not order right or that was the way they sold it there. Whatever it was, those meals were very far from the home cooking we were used to.

We came back to the hotel room about nine in the evening. It was a really busy day and we were all tired. The kids fell asleep the moment they hit the bed.

"This night will be my best night within the last fourteen months. I don't have to chase any signatures anymore, or be afraid of StB showing up in the middle of the night," I said quietly.

"The time spent at the border crossing was a real stress," Nora said silently and added:

"Thank God, it is all behind us."

"You handled yourself excellently . . . and the kids too . . ." I said.

"Good night," Nora said.

"Good night . . . this is going to be a real good night," I said.

In the morning we went for breakfast in the hotel restaurant. We sat at a table and slowly ate breakfast, which was included in the room cost. We all slept very well and were in a good mood.

"After breakfast I should call Mr. Schwartz. He should have those ten thousand schillings for us," I said. We did not have to hide those things from the kids anymore.

"Dad, why is that guy giving you money?" Peter asked.

"A few months ago we met in hotel Panorama and we made a deal that I would give him ten thousand crowns in Prague and he would give me schillings when we came to Vienna for vacation," I said.

"Do you have his phone number?" Nora asked.

"Yes, I do. It is coded in the English-Slovak dictionary. When we go back to our room, I will write it down and call him from hotel reception," I said.

We came back to the room and I decoded the number for Mr. Schwartz from my dictionary. When I was turning the pages in the dictionary, I came across another name. It was Mr. Steiner. I remembered a few years ago I took him into a typical Bratislava restaurant. Since then he had kept reminding me every time he showed up at our company that he owed me dinner. When I saw him the last time in May, I reminded him with a laugh that he would not owe me dinner anymore.

It has been several months since then and I believed he did not forget his promise.

"According to our last discussion, we could go to dinner with Mr. Steiner," I said to Nora.

"What do you mean?" Nora asked. The children looked at me too and they were curious about my answer:

"Awhile ago I took him to dinner in a typical Bratislava restaurant and he kept reminding he that he owed me dinner in Vienna," I answered.

"Did you set up any particular date," Nora asked.

"No, we do not have any particular date yet. He always asked me to give him a call when I arrived in Vienna," I said.

"Do you think he is going to be home now? This is vacation time and most people will be on vacation," Nora said.

"I can call him and we'll see," I said.

"I guess it is going to be boring. You know that the three of us know only Slovak. You and he will talk all night long in English and then you will have to translate every single sentence to us," Nora said.

"No, it is not going to be boring; Mr. Steiner speaks Slovak too," I said.

"Really?" Nora asked with disbelief and then she added:

"Then call him and we will see."

"Where did he learn Slovak?" Katarina asked.

"I don't know, but I always talked to him in Slovak," I said.

I decoded both numbers and wrote them on a card. In luxury hotels phones used to be in the rooms. However, we did not have a phone in the room so I went down to hotel reception and said:

"I would like to make a phone call. It is within Vienna territory."

"Please go into the phone booth. Dial zero and then the number," the receptionist said and pointed to the booth across from reception.

I went in and first dialed Mr. Schwartz.

"Good morning, Schwartz Company, this is Nicole Braun speaking," I heard the secretary say in German, whose voice I remembered from my phone calls in Bratislava.

"Good morning, Ms. Braun, this is Jan Bielek speaking," I answered in English.

"Mr. Bielek, how can I help you? Ms. Braun answered in English.

"I would like to talk to Mr. Schwartz," I said.

"I am sorry, but Mr. Schwartz is on vacation and he will be back in three weeks. Could I help you somehow?" Ms. Braun asked.

"I am not sure . . . I am here in Vienna now and I would like to ask him about something," I said and in spirit kissed my ten thousand schillings good bye.

"Yes, I understand," Ms. Braun said and then she added:

"Mr. Schwartz left an envelope for you here and asked me to give it to you when you showed up.

"Envelope . . . yes . . ." I recovered very quickly and then asked:

"How do I get to your place?"

She told me the address and then briefly how I could get there from Maria Hilfer Strasse. I wrote everything down on the other side of the card and then dialed Mr. Steiner.

"Good morning, this is Hans Steiner," he answered in German.

"Good morning, Mr. Steiner. This is Jan Bielek," I answered in Slovak.

"Mr. Bielek, how are you?" Mr. Steiner inquired in Slovak.

"Thank you, I am very well. Right now I am on vacation," I said.

"Where are you right now?" Mr. Steiner inquired.

"I am going to Italy with my family, as I recently mentioned to you. Right now I am in Vienna," I said.

"In Vienna? This is great. When are we going to meet?" Mr. Steiner asked.

"I don't know, what is on your schedule. We arrived in Vienna only yesterday afternoon and now we are just making plans. We would like to remain in Vienna for a few days," I said.

"How would tomorrow afternoon fit your plans?" Mr. Steiner inquired.

"Yes, that's fine," I said.

"Tomorrow take a taxi and come to my house between four and five in the afternoon. Do not pay for the taxi and let the taxi driver know I will pay him when you get here," Mr. Steiner said.

"Thank you, Mr. Steiner. See you tomorrow," I said and wrote down his address on the card.

"See you tomorrow," said Mr. Steiner and hung up.

I went back up to our room and had not had a chance to close the door behind me when Nora asked:

"How did you make out?"

"Fairly well," I said and told her the details of my phone calls. The children were all ears during my storytelling. I was very glad we did not need to hide anything from them anymore. Almost nothing, because now there was one and only one thing they did not know—we were not returning to Bratislava and we were going to the USA. So far we didn't want to tell them, because we still had a dinner planned with Mr. Steiner. After the dinner there was nothing else left; just to let them know.

"Right now are we going to get the money from Mr. Schwartz?" Peter inquired.

"Yes, only I want to take a peek at a map, so we don't get uselessly lost," I said and took out a map of Vienna. After a little bit of studying, I found out we could get quite easily and simply to the address, which was given to me by Ms. Braun. We got there in about half an hour. I parked the car and Nora said:

"We will wait for you here in the car. You run up for the envelope."

I looked at the list of companies, which hung in the lobby on the wall opposite the main entrance and found that the firm resided on the second floor of a ten-floor building; therefore, I could actually run up there. I didn't feel like waiting for an elevator. I stopped outside the door of the Schwartz Company, took a deep breath, and entered a room opposite the stairway. There was a secretary sitting behind the receptionist counter:

"Ms. Braun?" I asked in English.

"You are Mr. Bielek, aren't you?" she asked in English.

"Yes," I said.

"Here you are," she said and handed me an envelope, which was wedged between a pencil stand and her phone. Then she added:

"Do you have any message for Mr. Schwartz?"

"Yes, please say 'thank' you to him," I said and put the envelope into an inner pocket of my jacket.

"Good bye," I said.

"Good bye," Ms. Braun said and I ran back to the car.

"Did you get it?" Nora asked through an open window.

"I don't know yet, but I got the envelope," I said and jumped in the car.

I took out the envelope and opened it. Nora watched my hands and the kids stood up in the car with their eyes steadfast on the envelope. There was a card on which was hand-written:

"Thank you, Kurt Schwartz" and below the card there were neatly folded ten one-thousand schilling bills.

"So, this came out all right," Nora said with gratification and looked smilingly at me.

"Hurrah," Peter and Katarina shrieked at once and threw themselves back on their seats.

We were all happy my trick with the money exchange came out all right and we went back to the hotel. When we arrived, I asked the receptionist to call a taxi cab for us for four o'clock. We went to the city for lunch, and shortly before four, we came back to reception where a taxi was already waiting for us. I gave the address of Mr. Steiner written on a card to the taxi driver and he studied a map looking for the place. The cab left shortly and in half an hour we came to our destination. Mr. Steiner lived in a very nice and very expensive garden suburb on a hill located at the periphery of Vienna. When the taxi stopped in front of his house, Mr. Steiner came out to welcome us. As he had promised, he also paid for the taxi.

I introduced Nora and the kids to him and this time there was no problem with translation, because he spoke the Slovak language. We entered his house and he brought us into the living room. One wall of his living room was made of glass with a glass door leading to a deck. Because the house was built on a hill, there was a beautiful view of Vienna.

His wife came home shortly after us and then two of his colleagues from the same company, whom I already knew, also joined us. Around 5:30. two taxi cabs came up to the house and they drove all of us to another side of Vienna into a gorgeous wine-cellar restaurant, which was a favorite place of Mr. Steiner and his wife. We spent a wonderful night despite the fact we spoke many different languages. Mr. Steiner spent most of the night entertaining Nora and the kids because he was the only one who knew Slovak out of all of them. The Vienna people spoke German to each other and I stayed with English. I was really surprised how well all Austrians knew English. Apparently it was a part of their business capabilities. We had a lot of fun and nobody wanted to go back home, so we didn't go back to our hotel by taxi until about half an hour before midnight.

It was Saturday morning and we got up a little later than usual. The dinner with Mr. Steiner and his wife was the last meeting with my acquaintances from Vienna. I still had more names and phone numbers coded in the dictionary, but I made a decision to end that search. Our ultimate destination was the USA and continuation with contacts in Austria did not make any sense because we did not intend to stay there. Our journey into the USA was not on a straight line, since we had to go through both the hell and the purgatory combined in one called Traiskirchen. More precisely, it was a refugee camp located in a small and very nice town with this name located about twenty miles south of Vienna. Continuing our vacation in Vienna in the current manner would lead into spending more money, which we might need for our startup in the USA. It was a difficult decision because so far everything was very cool and very vacation-like. In the context of this, I remembered a slogan which practically ruled my life:

"It takes a lot of bravery and courage to live your own life, to be who you want to be, to break off the conventions and rules set by others and go your own way. Only if you are willing and ready to sacrifice all earthly possessions can you break the chains and set yourself free."

After breakfast we came back to our room and planned our program for the weekend. I looked on the map and found we could go sightseeing in the old king's castle called Schonbrunn.

Before we went out, I thought it would be time to tell the children the "whole" truth about our trip to Italy. I had mixed feelings about it because, on one side, I had no idea how they would accept news like that. On the other side, I was extremely happy that we got rid of the shackles of Communism forever and finally we could raise our children according to our imaginations. We would not have to live "double lives" into which we were always forced . . . telling the kids the truth according to our best knowledge and morals and then telling them what they had to say in school or in case someone asked . . . From now on, it wouldl be only one single truth, strong in its transparency and simplicity.

After so many years I was not quite sure how to start, so I said:

"Peter and Katarina, I would like to let you know we are not going back to Bratislava.

Both of them looked surprised at me, then at Nora. She nodded her head I was not kidding and then she added:

"Yes, dad and I made a decision that we are not going back there and we are going to the USA."

Peter still held a LEGO toy in his hand, sat next to his mom, and started crying. Nora put her left arm around his shoulders, put her cheek on his head and said:

"Don't worry Peter, everything is going to be all right."

We could not see any change in Katarina; surprisingly, she jus looked at Peter as if she did not understand why he was crying. Her two pig tails were jumping from side to side as she looked at me, then at mom with Peter. I did not know if she did not care or did not apprehend what was going on.

I came to Peter, kneeled down in front of the sofa, caressed his head and repeated what Nora had said:

"Don't worry Peter; everything is going to be really all right."

Nora and I looked at each other and wondered what to say next. She grabbed the opportunity first and said:

"Peter, do you remember the blue car, which flipped and turned around when it hit an obstacle?" It was being sold in a kiosk at Maria Hilfer Strasse.

Peter just nodded and Nora said:

"Dad will buy it for you."

"Yes I will buy that car for you," I said and then asked:

"Why are you crying? Are you afraid of something?"

"I do not know where I am going to sleep," Peter said.

"Don't worry. You will always have a place to sleep. It might not be a luxurious one, but it will definitely not be under a bridge. In time we will go to the USA and then I will do my best to get both of you a room of your own," I said.

Nora looked at me like I was promising the moon and stars, but she did not say anything. Peter stopped crying as fast as he had started and I wondered if it was due to the promised car or a room of his own. Maybe it was fifty-fifty. However, I hoped it was because he knew me and was confident he would not get lost in the world if he was with me.

"You said we were going on a trip to Italy. We went to the Italian embassy for visas," Peter said with a big question mark on his face.

"The trip to Italy was just a part of my plan to mislead the Communists in order for us to get out. Just to be completely honest I did not plan any trip to Italy. At least not now . . . Maybe in a few years," I said.

"Why did you have to lie to the Communists? Peter asked quite honestly.

"In order for us to get out . . . there was no other way, I would risk that both mom and I would end up in jail or we would get shot at the border. Now it is all behind us and we have come here all right. Lying is wrong and I promise I will never lie again," I said and then added:

"I wanted all of us to get out of that misery and organize our life according to our best consciousness. I did not want you two to go through everything mom and I had to.

Peter looked at me with misunderstanding, so I added:

"The two of you are still too small and did not run across a lot of things . . ." I said and thought about a good example, which would explain my words a little more understandably.

"A few months ago they signed you up in the pioneer organization," said Nora.

"Peter looked at her and said:

"Yes."

"Did you want to go there? Did you like pioneer meetings?" Nora asked.

"No," Peter said with aversion.

"You see . . . You were only in the third grade and Communists had already pushed you with their pioneer organization. It begins like that and then they push you to do something against your will for the rest of your life," I said.

Peter smiled a bit as if he was glad he didn't have to go to any more pioneer meetings. Katarina was all ears the whole time we talked, but she didn't say anything.

"Gradually, we can talk about everything because we don't have to hide anything from you anymore. But now let's go to the Schönbrunn and on the way we can buy the blue car," I said.

Peter jumped up ready for shopping and Katarina asked:

"And what are you buying me?"

"Something you will like in the toy store," I said.

We walked out onto Maria Hilfer Strasse and searched for a small kiosk in the street, which used to sell blue flipping cars. I could've sworn there was one right around the corner when we walked out from our hotel. But right now, just like Murphy's law, it was gone. Peter started to be discouraged, so I said to him:

"I am quite sure the kiosk will be somewhere further down the street because at this corner he has already sold a blue toy car to anyone who was interested."

Peter didn't say anything, only very intensely tracked the street and scanned around. Katarina, on the other hand, was consumed with all stores with toys. When we walked out without avail from the third store, I asked her:

"What are you actually looking for? Tell us what it is and perhaps we can find it in another store." I did not have the slightest idea that her toy would be so scarce.

"Evicka," Katarina said very quiet and sad. The two of us, Nora and I, just looked at each other and immediately understood. Evicka was her most popular doll, which was given to Katarina by Nora's mother for her first birthday. At that time Evicka was almost as big as Katarina. She liked the doll very much and very often they slept in Katarina's bed together. I had a picture of the children's room in my mind when we were leaving and the last time I had passed over our apartment with my eyes. I clearly saw Evicka lying in Katarina's bed and she was covered by her comforter. Evicka was waiting for Katarina till she returned from vacation. It did not occur to either one of us to take her along. If we could only turn back time! It was just five days ago! I squatted down, so that my eyes met Katarina's, took her gently by the shoulders and said:

"When I call grandma, I will ask her to mail Evicka to you. It may take a long time, but one day she will be with you again. Until then you can buy something else."

"All right," Katarina said and she was noticeably satisfied. She believed me because every time my promises came true. Now I was stuck with one of the most difficult assignments in my whole life. I did not know exactly how, but I strongly believed that one day Evicka would come to Austria by mail, nicely wrapped up in a package. But so far I could not undertake anything because we had no address where we would stay for any amount of time. We returned to the toy store and Katarina bought a LEGO. Now she had the dolly from Znojmo and LEGO from Vienna, but evidently neither of these two toys could ever replace Evicka. As we walked outside to the street, I noticed in the distance the merchant with the toy cars, sought by Peter.

"Look there is the guy with the blue toy cars," I said and pointed at the kiosk in the distance. He was at the same side of the street as us and Peter ran toward the kiosk. When we got there, I handed the merchant money and Peter happily took a box with a car, which the merchant handed to him. He had a huge smile on his face and was completely happy. He certainly was not concerned anymore with where he would be sleeping. Peter and Katarina walked in front of us and carried their new toys as we headed in the direction of Schönbrunn.

"It seems that Katarina will really miss her Evicka," Nora said quietly.

"I know. It makes me angry that it did not occur to us to take the dolly along. We didn't have to pack her away anywhere and without a problem she could have sat between them on the back seat in the car. She would not have been conspicuous even to customs officers. So what? A small girl took along a dolly on vacation . . . ," I said.

"We could have taken her without a problem," Nora said.

"Sure, only it did not occur to us and Katarina didn't say anything . . . ," I said.

"Apparently, it did not occur to her either and she did not miss her until today when you told them we were not going back to Bratislava and we were going to the USA; then she remembered her," Nora said.

Sunday we went to Vienna Prater, which is one of the best-known amusement parks in Europe. We spent almost the entire day there and in the evening we returned to the hotel.

Chapter Four

Time of Sorrows

Monday 30 July 1984—Traiskirchen.

Shortly before lunch, we arrived at the refugee camp in the town of Traiskirchen, and unaware of the situation, I entered with our car through the main entrance and stopped in front of a red and white gate. The gatekeeper in a military uniform and with the automatic rifle on his shoulder came up to our car and asked in German through the open window:

"What is the purpose of your visit?"

"Political asylum," I said in German.

"You can not go inside with your car; you have to park in the street," said the gatekeeper.

I backed up the car and parked in the street. From the outside the camp looked like a military base, and as I learned later, once upon a time this was a military base. Following Austria's declared neutrality, the government reduced the size of its army and since then the building has been utilized for refugee accommodations. And there used to be enough of them because Austria's neighbors, Hungary and the former Czechoslovakia, were both Communist countries. Communism in just those two countries alone produced well over ten thousand refugees each year.

We entered the camp, and at a small window by the main entrance, we registered ourselves as refugees who sought political asylum. They took fingerprints of all of us and immediately afterwards one of the armed guards escorted us away to the third floor of the main building where he passed us on to another guard, and when we entered the compound, they locked the door behind us.

The guard brought us to the office door where they signed us in and he returned to the locked door where he stood with the automatic rifle at his chest.

After signing in, each of us received a blanket, pillow, aluminum army gear set of dishes, soap, toothbrush and toothpaste. They sent us to room number 73, which was a huge room with bunk beds. In this room there were about eighty people, families like us, pairs or even people who were alone. We chose two bunk beds next to each other and put the things we had just received on one of them. I looked around and heard people speaking Polish, Czech, Slovak and Hungarian. The room was filled about halfway and new people were coming in every few minutes. I sat down on the bed where Nora sat in the middle of the bed, Katarina on one side of her, Peter on the other side and in front of them was the pile with blankets, pillows, dishes and other things. Nora looked very sad, her big brown eyes fixed absent-mindedly towards infinity. She did not cry, but her eyes were filled with tears. I hugged her and said:

"Right now we have just hit the very bottom of human society. We are at the bottom and it is impossible to go any lower because we are in the refugee camp. From here we are going up and it is up to us how fast we dig ourselves out from here."

"Do you think so?" she asked dejectedly.

"I am sure. We are at the bottom. We cannot go down, we must go just up."

She looked at me, made an attempt at a smile and her eyes returned to the present. She got up from the bed and started preparing them for sleep. Then she also organized all the other things. At the same time I found an empty cabinet with a lock and key and loaded our suitcases and bags in it. It was just an ordinary wood cabinet with an ordinary lock, but locking up our luggage in it was still better than if I left it lying on the floor.

There was only one exit from the room leading to a hallway, which was quite long and there were more rooms like "ours" there. Across the hall were the bathrooms, one for men and one for women, no showers, only ten sinks and toilets in each one with running water. The exit from the hallway was locked and two guardsmen with automatic rifles on their chests stood in front of the door. They did not allow anyone in or out, only if they received an order from the office. We could look out either from the window in the hallway at the rest of the refugee camp, or from the window in our room at the street. We could not communicate with anyone from the outside; the guardsmen watched us. There were no phones and the mail was held up in the office. We were in complete isolation.

For lunches and dinners we went into the dining room at the floor level of the same building, about three hundred of us. They organized us into a line and two guardsmen with automatic rifles on their chests stood in front of the line and another two at the back of the line as they led us. We could not leave our position in line and also were forbidden to speak with anyone from the outside. This way the guardsmen brought us into the dining room and after finishing the meal they brought us back to the fourth floor and locked the door. During our meals there were no other people in the dining room-just the people from the isolation rooms. At first I did not understand why they isolated us that way, but I came to understand when we had our first interview.

To my great surprise, the dining room was much nicer than a company dining room at my last work place. The food was excellent. The "stuff" which was cooked for us by ROH in Bratislava could not compare with what we were getting now. We were also given fruit, yogurt, chocolate, candy bars and other "sweet tooth" items. The portions we received were so big that quite often we could not finish them. Saturdays and Sundays they did not cook; they'd just give out a CARE package for each of us, which was a paper bag filled with cold cuts, cheese, bread, sometimes a can of fish, fruit, yogurt, chocolate or a candy bar. If there was someone "extra" hungry, he was given more food.

For breakfasts, eight to ten men from each room brought in containers every morning with hot coffee, milk and tea. Buns, butter and jam were also carried up to the rooms on trays. Those men were also accompanied by guards every time.

Every morning after breakfast we listened to speakers in the hallway. They read the last names of people who were on the list for today's interview. The purpose of the interviews was to figure out everyone's reason for filing for political asylum status. Only then I understood what the real reason was for such complete isolation from the rest of the world. For the officers filling out our application, it was very important to find out the truth and not stories we could overhear during the week from other refugees who were not in isolation anymore. The turnaround time was about five to seven days, which meant we should get on the list next Monday and with a lot of luck this Friday. Saturdays and Sundays the offices were closed.

We learned from people who were there longer than we that the first interview was very important because what was written in it determined whether someone was or wasn't granted political asylum. People who were not granted political asylum, the Austrians usually did not send back to the country they had come from, but their future was very bleak. Without political asylum, or what they called the "Yellow Card," they were not allowed to obtain employment in Austria and also there were problems with emigration into any other country.

The interview was also a crucial milestone in the life of refugees from another aspect, because right after the first interview, they were released into "free camp," this time without isolation. They could freely move within Austria because they were given a refugee I.D. card, and then they could also get out of the camp and return according to their own will. Armed guards by the entrance legitimized everyone. From the more experienced ones we also heard, that complete families had a great prospect of getting into "family camps," which were all over Austria. The probability of getting into a family camp considerably increased if the whole family obtained the status of political refugees. Supposedly, those who did not get asylum remained in Traiskirchen. It was not an attractive future, because according to what we had a chance to see, the camp in Traiskirchen was full of shady people; many of them looked like criminals. Since it was the main and the biggest camp in Austria, some people who were not accepted for emigration into any other country and additionally had no political asylum, remained there.

Friday morning all four of us stood in the hallway and with anticipation listened to the loud speakers. When we heard our last name being distorted to "Bilek," the children and Nora jumped and shouted in the hallway from sheer pleasure. They were not the only ones; all those whose names were also read, were awfully happy as well. The two of us without the children then went to the office, where along with all the others, we waited until they called us one by one inside. Meanwhile the children waited in "our" room.

"What should I actually say to them?" Nora asked quietly and markedly she was nervous.

"Nothing else but the truth why we left from there. Indeed you know that very well," I said composedly and then added:

"Calm down; if you say the truth, you have nothing to be afraid of."

"Well, you know, that I don't know any German or English, only Slovak," Nora said.

"You don't need to because clerks who do the interview will speak with you in Czech or Slovak," I said.

First they called me inside and when I told my story to the clerk in Slovak he did not ask me any more questions. He had already written three pages. Nora was called in after me and she told them the same story over again. I admired very much that the interview was arranged in the maternal tongue of every refugee. As the officials spoke:

"We can translate; from you we want to hear the truth without being distorted by a bad translation."

Only later we learned that for the right impact of the interview it was very important to provide a consistent story by all family members.

Right after the interview, a clerk from the office gave us papers for our stay in free family camp in Bad Kreuzen. She also said that right now we had to go into the photographic studio in town to have our picture taken for our refugee I.D. cards. She handed me an order for the photographer and also a card, on which was the address and instructions on how to get there. She also recommended to us that, before our departure to Bad Kreuzen, we would need a sponsor for our emigration into another country.

All sponsors were gathered inside of the camp in Traiskirchen and resided on the first floor of the building, which was opposite the main building. During our stay in isolation, we learned from people there that sponsors were not mandatory but very important for gathering emigration visas, and the paperwork was done much faster with their assistance. According to instructions given us in the office, when we got our papers signed by a sponsor, we should come back to the main office next to the main entrance and they would arrange our transportation into a camp in Bad Kreuzen.

We went back to "our" room and heard from the other refugees that this morning two refugees were found dead by the rail track. They were two Russian soldiers who had deserted the army in Afghanistan and came to the camp in Traiskirchen. Thursday morning they were sent to the photographer's studio for picture-taking for their Refugee ID card and Friday morning they were found by railway workers. The rumors said that they were killed by KGB agents in order to discourage other soldiers in Afghanistan from deserting.

We never learned all the details about this incident, but we were really careful during our trip to the photographer's studio. We constantly looked around on our way and made an effort to avoid empty streets. We went to the studio and back with our pictures and were relieved to be back in the camp because it was guarded by the Austrian army.

We literally ran into the sponsor's building because it was Friday and Nora believed we would leave Traiskirchen the same day if we hurried up. We ran inside and did not have the slightest idea which one to choose. There were about twenty of them and we just looked at signs located next to doors and tried to make a decision about which one we should choose, when I spotted a sign with initials AFCR and under it: American Fund for Czechoslovak Refugees.

"This is our organization," I said and we all entered. We were welcomed by a man who spoke Czech:

"Thank you for your decision to choose our organization," he said and asked us to sit down. Then he proceeded to tell us about how the AFCR was currently giving bonus money to all who signed up with them for sponsorship and handed me a slip to sign to receive one thousand Austrian schillings. I looked at him surprised because I was under the impression we had to pay for their services, so I asked:

"You give me a thousand schillings just for choosing you?"

"Yes, you will receive a thousand schillings and we take care of your emigration visas, green card and transportation to the USA," he said with a smile and then he added:

"This bonus is only received once and everything else will be done for you by us."

"Who is paying for all that?" I asked, surprised again.

"The American government, The Austrian government, good-will organizations and also common people in the form of tax-deductible contributions," he said and put the promised money on his desk.

"In that case we chose the right sponsor," I said with satisfaction.

"Certainly," he said and pulled out a sponsorship form for immigration to the USA. In a course of about half an hour, he asked us for personal data, reasons for emigration, our education and other details he immediately wrote on the form. When it was all done, he said, that according to our data, we had a good chance that we would succeed getting accepted by the USA and it would be quite quick, and handed us the form for our signatures. He handed me the promised money and we again ran back to the main office.

We stood in the line where about twenty other happy emigrants stood, who were also going into family camps. In about half an hour we got to the window and I handed our paperwork to a clerk behind the window. She checked our papers and then looked into the schedule of their transportation department and said in Polish:

"Today it is too late; come back here Monday morning."

I heard a big hissing noise behind me as if air had escaped from a balloon. That was Nora, who was very disappointed we did not make it on time to catch transportation into a family camp in Bad Kreuzen. The Polish-speaking clerk noticed Nora's disappointment and said:

"I am sorry, according to our schedule all our cars and buses are gone. You have to wait till Monday."

"Thank you," I said and we all went back to the fourth floor. I stopped in the office and explained our situation. They gave us the finished Refugee ID cards and told us we could stay until Monday in a room on the first floor. We took all our luggage, and this time free and without an army escort, we went down to a room on the first floor. It was quite a big room, but only a few people were there. A pair of young Hungarians, who had lived there for some time and using wood cabinets and bed sheets they had built a small bungalow around their beds. Besides them there was a four-member family from Czechoslovakia. They were ethnic Germans, and under the current regime there, they had experienced too much discrimination, so leaving for the old fatherland seemed to be the only smart solution. They too did not catch the transportation on Friday and had to stay in Traiskirchen over the weekend. They were about our age and their kids just about the same age as our kids. The parents' names were Hans and Gertrude, the kids Ludwick and Johanna.

It was just the beginning of August and the weather was hot and humid. We heard from Hans and Gertrude that there was a public swimming pool in Traiskirchen, so we planned on going for a swim on Saturday. After the five days we had lived in complete isolation, we had an urge to run out and breathe in the freedom. We were looking forward to cool water in a pool.

Saturday early morning Katarina woke up crying and complaining of a sore throat. At that age, she used to have tonsillitis and doctors in Bratislava suggested a few times to have them surgically removed. We resisted and declined because it appeared to us as a too drastic intrusion into such a young body. We tried calming Katarina down and promised her we would go to the doctor in the morning and she would be given Penicillin again. Gertrude heard us and she said:

"I can give you a bottle of Penicillin. We took a few of them with us just in case we might urgently need them and she handed us a brand new, unopened bottle.

"Thank you. It is very kind of you," Nora said and based on our experience with Penicillin from the past, we started giving Katarina the pills.

Katarina took the pills with tea we had in a thermos bottle and then fell asleep again. When she woke up in the morning her throat did not hurt anymore and she was ready to go to the pool. Nora and I looked into her throat and saw that her tonsils were still red and swollen, so we decided not to go to the pool.

"Peter and you can go to the pool and I will stay here with Katarina," Nora said after breakfast.

"No, it would be better if we all stay together. You never know who may wander into this room. There are no guards with automatic rifles standing at the door," I said.

"You are right," Nora said and we just said Good bye to our German friends who were leaving for the pool. All four of us stayed in the room and watched over everyone's luggage.

When the Germans came back from the pool Sunday night, I went to the supermarket in the town and bought a bottle of inexpensive red wine. I put it into a bucket of cold water in order to cool it down a little bit and after dinner we drank with them "To our victory." We were kind of sorry they were going to Germany and not the USA because we all got along very well.

Monday morning we came to the window at eight and waited for our transportation. We were the first there and could hardly wait for our departure from Traiskirchen. We put all our luggage into the car that was supposed to drive us there and then just followed it; all four of us were in our Skoda car. In about two and half hours, we came to camp in Bad Kreuzen, which was located in beautiful hills above the town of Grein, sitting right next to the river Danube. It was the same Danube River which flowed through Bratislava, about a hundred miles downstream.

They gave us a room on the second floor of a three-story building. We had the last room on the left side of the hallway, number 17. It was a relatively large room with three windows and four beds, not bunk beds, and three wood cabinets. In the middle of the room were a table and four chairs. Two windows were on the opposite wall from the door and during nice weather we could see the Austrian Alps through them. Through the third window, which was on the side wall, we could see the camp office building and also the road going up to the town of Bad Kreuzen. We also had a sink with running hot

and cold water, but showers and bathrooms were in the hallway. I looked at the room and said to Nora:

Do you remember when a week ago I told you that we were at the bottom of human society and from now on we were going only up?"

"Yes," Nora said.

"Now you can see I was right. We have a room just for us and we made this little step in seven days," I said.

"We do not have a bathroom," Katarina said.

"I did not say we were going to make a leap and we will have everything immediately. We will go slowly, but surely," I said to Katarina.

The building was the old building of the police academy, and when they built a new and modern building, they started using the old building for refugee accommodations.

It was such a good secure feeling because day and night there were dozens of police officers with cruisers and all other equipment policemen used to accomplish their duties. They were very kind to all of us and we greeted them like good old friends. In the new building of the police academy, there was also a very nice and modern dining room, to which we went for every one of our meals. Every morning Peter and I went for breakfast, carried it into our room and then we all had breakfast together at the table. Breakfasts were very simple; we took pots with coffee, tea, hot milk or cocoa. For each person they gave us two buns, butter and marmalade, or jam.

In the morning the following day after our arrival into Bad Kreuzen, we wanted to call my parents and parents-in-law. It had already been over two weeks since we had departed from Czechoslovakia and we wanted our parents to hear us and also to hear from us what was going on. We knew the situation over there, behind the barbed wire and anticipated that a lot of information which got to them would be at least distorted or completely made up. We went into a phone booth in the town and took along a lot of shillings in the form of change. First we dialed the phone number to my parents-in-law and Nora took the earphone.

"Hi mom. This is Nora," she said into the phone, when her mother picked up.

"Hi Nora . . . ," said my mother-in-law into the telephone and broke into tears.

The two of us were squeezed into the phone booth and I had the duty of throwing coins into the slot, so they could talk without interruption. Peter and Katarina stood outside and over the open door at the booth they followed our phone conversation. Several minutes passed and the conversation did not continue in any way. Nora with tears in her eyes tried to resume the conversation with her mother and constantly repeated:

"Mom . . . Mom . . ."

My mother-in-law did not respond and wept on. About five minutes later, my father-in-law took the earpiece and inquired:

"Nora, where are you?"

"At Bad Kreuzen in Austria," Nora said.

"Come back home," my father-in-law ordered, and immediately after that, he broke down in tears.

"Nora tried to carry on with the conversation:

"Dad . . . dad . . . ," she repeated several times over. My father-in-law did not respond anymore and only wept. Nora and I looked at each other; the kids glanced once at me and then again at Nora. I kept throwing coins into the slot and the amount, which I had in my hand, was consumed very quickly. In a few moments my palm was empty and the minutes left on the display approached zero. The conversation still floundered on with weeping. When there were already only a few seconds remaining, Nora said into the phone:

"Dad, I will write you a letter. Now I must finish because in a moment my minutes will be up . . . ," she still wanted to say more, but the coins made some noise as they fell inside the box and the call was interrupted.

I took another handful of coins, which I had prepared for a conversation with my parents, and dialed the number.

"Hi mom, here's Jan," I said, when my mom picked up the phone.

"Hi Janny," mom said and immediately after she broke into tears.

I tried to go on with our conversation and repeated several times:

"Mom . . . Mom . . . ," but mom didn't say anything more.

After a moment my dad took the phone and said:

"Hi Janny. How are you and where are you?" I could hear in his voice he was repressing his tears.

"Hi Dad. We are fairly well now; we are in Bad Kreuzen in Austria," I said and I was glad I could tell at least someone we were all right.

"Do you have enough food? Do you have a roof over your heads?," my father asked quickly.

"Yes, we have plenty of food and right now we have our own room, where we live," I said.

"I have heard, you were in a refugee camp and you had nothing to eat . . . and you lived in a tent . . . ," dad said.

"No, we've got plenty of food and we live in a building where we have our own room," I reiterated.

Mom took the earpiece from dad and asked:

"Are you staying in Austria? Are you not coming back home?"

"No, we want to go to the USA and we are not coming back home," I said and mom broke into tears again.

"Mom, do not worry about us; everything is going to be all right . . . ," I said but mom did not answer. I had already used all my change and seconds on display were coming to zero.

"Mom, I will write you more in a letter because I have to finish now . . ." I said into the phone and I got cut off.

We came out of the phone booth and wiped our tears. We sat down on a bench next to the booth and tried to regain our spiritual balance. Nora wiped hers and the children's faces and I said quite pragmatically:

"We should write letters because calling is too expensive for us. During those few minutes, we spent more money than we get for the whole month as pocket money and still did not have a chance to talk to them."

"It was understandable that they would cry," Nora answered, also pragmatically.

"Yes, of course. I did not expect they would be laughing and I understand what has just happened. I am just trying to say, that we are going to write letters because calling doesn't lead to communication and then it is too expensive," I said.

Immediately after returning to the camp, we wrote letters to my parents and to parents-in-law, Nora for her parents and I for mine. We wrote about our destiny in Austria in detail: that we had already been granted political asylum from the Austrian government; we were all right; and the children were not missing anything. We also wrote that we had signed up with a sponsor organization, which was doing the paperwork for our immigration to the USA and now we were just waiting for papers to be ready. Into the letter for my parents, I added how Katarina missed Evicka and I would be very grateful if they could send Evicka to us.

Peter also wrote a few sentences into each letter and at the end he signed them. Katarina was not in school yet, but she knew how to sign the letters anyway.

After about two weeks, we received letters from our parents in response to ours. My mom was the letter-writer and dad just signed it at the end. She wrote that it would never have occurred to her even in a bad nightmare that we would make such a decision, and that they will miss us. Despite that, she knew me well and believed I had thought out everything thoroughly and that I was aware of what I was up to. At the end she wished us good luck in the USA, even though they were going to be very sad without us.

The letter from my father-in-law was much more dramatic; in the beginning he wrote that he could not understand how we came up with such a stupid idea. Then the letter focused on a list of all the advantages we had there; mainly, that I had a position of department manager and also was a reserve for the vice president position. Nora was a teacher at the high school and we also had a four-room apartment and two beautiful children. After that was a big question in a sentence:

"What exactly were you missing here?" with four question marks at the end.

Then there were more questions, this time each one with just one question mark: What is Nora going to do in the USA? Wash dishes in a restaurant? Do you think that everything in the USA is just like licking honey?

At the end of the letter were several orders, which we were expected to follow, right away, because everyone had an exclamation mark after it, like these: Come back to your senses and stop stressing out your children! Stop continuing in that stupid idea and immediately come back home! Roasted pigeons don't fly right into your mouth even in America! The-four room apartment in Petrzalka is still yours!

The letters came in at the same time and I read the letter from my parents first and Nora from hers. We were very quiet during the reading and at the end our eyes were filled with tears. Then we exchanged the letters. I started giggling at my father-in-law's letter from the very beginning; at the end I was bursting into laughter.

"What is so funny in that letter?" Nora asked strictly.

"It appears grandpa copied the letter from the Communist newspaper, Pravda," I said. Peter and Katarina peered confusedly at Nora and then at me. They could not understand how it was possible that their mom had cried at the letter and dad had joy from it.

"At least his letter was dictated by the County StB Headquarters," I added with laughter.

"Really, what is so funny about that?" Nora asked again and strictly.

"So read here what he writes . . . Jan had a position of department manager and he was a reserve for the vice president position . . . Nora, you were a teacher at the high school . . .

"He is announcing those things to us as if we were cretins and did not know all of this. He is telling us now this big secret," I said.

Nora looked at the letter again and then admitted quietly:

"I guess you are right . . ."

"He doesn't have to write us what we had there or what we didn't have. We knew what we had there," I said and then asked:

"Can you imagine what your father would say if I asked him whether the word FREEDOM meant anything to him?

Nora twisted her lips and simulating her father's voice she said:

"Please, what kind of stupid question is that, freedom or non-freedom. Where did you come up with that stupid idea?"

I completely lost it and from too much laughter I slipped off the chair right under the table. Peter, who until now did not understand what was going on, lay next to me on the floor and laughed like crazy. Nora and Katarina looked at us really surprised and Katarina said with amusement:

"Mom is crying at the letter and dad is laughing at it. What a pity I don't know how to read, I would like to read it too."

We did not respond to my father-in-law's letter, nor did we return to Czechoslovakia. We got amused by it quite a bit and the kids since then have come to understand that the same letter can be read in different ways. The result could be a weep or even laughter, it all depends from what angle you looked at it. Because we did not react to the letter, about a month later we received another one. Nora read it first and a deep wrinkle appeared in the middle of her forehead as she read it. When she was done with it, she handed it to me with sadness on her face and said quietly:

"Now it is my fault my brothers will not achieve anything in their lives."

"Wait a minute, how is that?" I asked and Peter with Katarina watched with interest. Apparently, they were expecting another cabaret.

"Julo or Miro would not be accepted as Communist Party members because I am illegally in the West. Now Julo could not be a chief physician and Miro could not be a director of the research centre.

"Wait a minute and let's think about it. Leaving the country was made illegal by Communists; your brothers would not be accepted into their party by Communists. And all that is your fault? By the way, aren't Communists the problem in that country? I asked with a smile.

"Well, you know how it is over there," Nora said, really disappointed.

"Just because I know how it is over there . . . Besides that, I am convinced Julo would not make it to the position of chief physician and Miro would never make it to the position of director of the research centre, even if we stayed over there. And what your father wrote in his letter everywhere in the free world is called blackmail," I said.

Mondays through Fridays we went to the dining room for lunches and dinners. Saturdays, Sundays or holidays we had hot meals for lunches and for dinner they gave everyone "take out dinner." From September, when the children started school, having meals in the dining room became a little complicated because by the time they came home from school, lunch time in the dining room was over. So we took their meals in a pot, and when they came home from school, we had to warm the food for them. We heated their lunches first on a propane two-burner camp stove, which we brought along with us from Bratislava and later on an iron. When the propane ran out, I didn't want to buy another refill because it seemed too expensive, so I made a stand for an iron from wood sticks, which we picked up in the woods. Using a pocket knife and pieces of wire I made a stand, which held the iron "upside-down," with the hot plate up. On the iron like that we put the pot with food and using the thermostat we regulated the temperature. When we were departing the camp, I disassembled the stand from the iron and sold it to some people who stayed in the camp.

The food in the camp was excellent and they gave us so much of it, that when we consumed everything they gave us at every meal, we started putting on some weight. We were also given a lot of fruit like oranges, bananas, apples, pears, etc., yogurts flavored with different fruits, chocolates, candy bars and crackers. In the take-out dinner there were little sticks of salami, canned fish or meat. Because the children received the same size bags as the adults, we could not possibly eat it all and after some time the leftovers from bags started to accumulate in the room. In order to prevent all those leftovers from spoiling, I made a refrigerator. It was a cardboard box, which had one side cut out and by this side the box was taped to the window. It was really chilly outside and the box was refrigerated inside by the glass window. The side of the box exposed to the warmth of the room was insulated by a double layer of cardboard. From the room side I made little doors to our refrigerator, which were used for taking out the food and was held closed by a rubber band. Without using electricity, we had a refrigerator for the entire winter. I guess I don't need to tell you the refrigerator was taped to a window which had no direct sunshine.

Some people used to put their leftovers on a window sill from the outside, which accomplished the purpose of refrigerating the food. However, birds from all around the neighborhoods figured out where there was some food, so after some time all the yogurts, salamis or chocolates were pecked over by them. It was not very aesthetic, not to mention the hygienic aspects of such food.

Next to the camp office there was a laundry room where we could bring our laundry for washing. A group of a few rooms had an allotted half-hour segment once a week, when people could bring their laundry and at the same time pick up washed, ironed and folded laundry from the previous week. The laundry was washed, ironed and folded by camp employees and we had no limit as to how much laundry we could bring at one time. The only condition was that every single piece of laundry had to be marked with our identification number by permanent marker. When we came there for the first time, they assigned us the number "52" and gave us a marker. It was our responsibility to have all the pieces of our laundry marked with our number. An unmarked piece of laundry was very difficult to find because there were an estimated three hundred people in that particular camp.

About a week after our arrival at the camp at Bad Kreuzen, an acquaintance who had been there for awhile came to our room and said with excitement:

"Come outside; in a few moments Ivo Zeleny from Prague will come into the camp, who flew into Austria on an engine powered glider."

This was really exciting news and of course we went outside. We joined a big crowd of people, which slowly gathered there. Information flew from one to another and gradually we learned that Ivo was a twenty-four-year-old student of the mechanical engineering college in Prague. During his leisure time he constructed a glider powered by a car engine and a week ago he literally flew out of Czechoslovakia and landed at Vienna Schwechat airport. For awhile he caused confusion in the control tower because he appeared on their radar as a little aircraft without identification. However, Ivo calmly landed at the airport and rolled to one of the hangars.

In a moment the camp's microbus showed up and Ivo, the hero of the day, welcomed by the crowd, got off. Welcoming and shaking hands started. On the faces of all the onlookers, who came from Czechoslovakia, was evident pride of one of them, one who was successful in a real-life stunt. He ran away from the Communists on a homemade aircraft and he had it all thought out to the last detail.

"Ivo, from where did you take off," inquired someone from the crowd and immediately after this an unofficial press conference started with questions and answers, only nobody wrote them down, or recorded them on a tape recorder.

"From south Moravia because I needed a spot which was thickly wooded, near the border, though not too close or too far," Ivo said.

"Why?" someone asked.

"Well, if I was too close, I would be seen by the border guards, and they could shoot me down with automatic rifles. I could not take off very far from the border, because by the time I reached the border, they could follow me with a helicopter," Ivo said.

"So, you had to fly very high, in order for them not to shoot you down?" was the following question.

"No, just the other way around. I flew at a height of about six hundred feet, only a bit above the tree tops. If I had flown very high, they could have found me on radar and have shot me down with a rocket," Ivo said.

The interview lasted over an hour while we learned all the particulars about his adventurous voyage. All that started with a student of a mechanical engineering college who constructed a glider, which was powered by an engine from a Trabant car. The Trabant engine was used because the engine was inexpensive, but also because it was relatively small and for its dimensions rather powerful. He was pleased with flying, so over the weekends he went into the mountains, just to fly around. It became such a hobby for him that he could not stop. However, the Communists did not like it because this again was something they had no control over. A few times he was chased by an army helicopter, but he managed to get away by landing in a dense forest. He took the wing apart and buried it in the woods below tree branches and ran away from his pursuers. After a little while he came back for his wing, laid it on the roof of his car and drove it away. From that time on he had to make any movements with the car only overnight because the wing folded on the roof of a car was not very conspicuous. Later he learned from his house that a warrant had been issued for him, so he had no other choice but to fly away for good. The following night he found a convenient place in Moravia and shortly before dawn he assembled the wing and flew away in the direction of Vienna. He flew at a height of about six hundred feet, at a speed of about thirty miles per hour and the entire flight lasted an hour and forty-five minutes. Right after landing at the airport, he was arrested by Austrian police and when they found out he was just another refugee, they immediately drove him to the camp in Traiskirchen.

He barely finished his story when a box truck with his wing drove into the camp in Bad Kreuzen. Supposedly, Austrian museums offered him eight thousand Austrian shillings and German museums fifty thousand Deutsch marks for his wing. He sold his aircraft to the Germans because it was by far much more money. In a few moments two men drove in in a Mercedes car with German plates and Ivo demonstrated to them how to assemble the wing from transportation form into a flying form.

I carefully watched the assembly of the wing and I was really surprised how all the parts were ingeniously engineered and how nicely and quickly they engaged each other. In about twenty-five minutes, he assembled it together in front of our eyes from something, that before looked like two fabric covered packages with boards. When he was done, the two who came in a car with German plates took pictures of it from every angle. After Ivo took it apart again, he stored it in fabric-covered packages and loaded it back into the box truck.

Ivo stayed in Bad Kreuzen only a few nights and then for security reasons he was transported to an unknown place. He feared that StB agents would find him and kill him, in order to avenge their fiasco. His fear was quite understandable because the border between Austria and Czechoslovakia was guarded only from one side—Czechoslovakia. And the border was only about ten miles from the camp.

Over time we heard about cases where agents came into Austria and attempted to take refugees by force back into Czechoslovakia by car. However, we heard about all those instances only "third hand," so we considered those accounts only gossip. Anyway, this gossip created in every one of us a deep sense of danger, which was too close in order to be completely ignored. Maybe this was just their intention, so none of us would stay close by and rather would run far away to another part of the world.

September the 1st school started and all the children from the camp below eighteen years of age had to go to the local school. Children who knew

German well were sent to grades equivalent to their age with other Austrian children. For those who did not know German and also depending on how many kids they had, the school created a group of grades; for example, from the first to the third grade was one group. One group had an estimated twenty-five children; the teaching language was German and all the children had to learn it. Thus, our Katarina started her first grade in Austria and in Deutsch language. Peter was in another group, where there were schoolchildren from the fourth to the sixth grade. The school was in town, perhaps two miles from the camp and the kids walked there; smaller kids were escorted by parents and bigger ones went by themselves.

The camp completely filled up over time and new refugees kept arriving. The camp management had an agreement with small hotels in the town, in German called "Gasthoff," that they would send additional refugees there. Those lucky people were very happy at first because their accommodations were by far at a much higher level. For example, a family of four got two rooms and a bathroom with a toilet, of course, included with the rooms. People housed in hotels did not get their food in the camp dining hall, but they were fed at the restaurant of the hotel in which they lived. The accommodations and food were paid for from the camp refugee budget, and when rooms inside the camp became vacant, families from the hotels had to move into the camp rooms. Generally, none of them resisted and came to the camp with pleasure. The accommodations were a bit worse, but the food was many times better in the camp.

"A young couple from the USA came into our hotel. You plan on going to the USA; therefore, you should meet them and talk to them," Thomas told me one day.

"Talk to them? About what?" I asked him.

"They could give you a lot of information about the USA, which you will need very much. Particularly in the beginning," Thomas said.

"Information?" I asked and then added:

"And aren't they by chance StB agents, who came here to frighten people with hair-raising stories of the situations in the United States? Then people capitulate and return to Czechoslovakia."

"Nevertheless, I believe you should meet them," Thomas insisted.

I didn't want to meet those young Americans of Czechoslovak origin anyway and I did my best to avoid them. What I had heard in the form of gossip from other people later indicated I was right. But Thomas was very persistent in his efforts and the following Saturday evening he invited the "Americans" for a visit to his place. He also invited us and another two families, so we went there, despite my skepticism. When we arrived at Thomas's place, eleven people were already squeezed into the small room. The young "American" jumped up from the armchair in which he sat and extended to me his hand. I caught his hand with mine and looked into his face:

"Igor Vesely?" I asked surprised instead of saying my name. Once Igor was at the same high school as I. Even back then it was a well-known fact that he was a secret StB agent. Igor was apparently stymied, but and I calmly shook his hand and said:

"Jan Bielek"

Igor again sat down in his armchair and he strove to gain control of the situation. It was quite obvious that my presence was making him nervous. I sat down where I could find a little bit of room for sitting, and at first only listened. I wondered what was so important that this agent, who most likely had never been in the USA, could say to me. Or what was also unlikely, that someone who lived in the US for years would take a vacation and waste his time at a refugee camp in Bad Kreuzen, in order to tell refugees about life over there.

"If somebody falls for such a primitive trick, such a person should definitely not run away from his native homeland. He ought to stay there till his death and at least his tuition fee should be returned to him," I thought, but stayed quiet.

"Where do you live?" someone inquired of Igor and he took out a pen and a paper to write down the address.

"In fact, right now we live nowhere, because they are building a house for us and we do not have an address yet," said Igor. Nobody objected to such a stupid answer and Igor kept on:

". . . that is why we have no telephone either."

I remembered that StB agents never abounded in geniality, but to provide a better answer to such a question did not require genius. It would suffice to make up whatever address, any phone number and his answer would sound much more credible. However, I remained still quiet and listened to the conversation.

Among other rubbish I learned was that every American moved three times a year, all shoes and boots were made from plastic, and leather was completely unavailable. Scented soaps and down comforters were also inaccessible, and when someone wanted to have them, he had to buy those things in Europe. The high point of the entire dog and pony show was that Americans don't know how to eat with silverware and that they have no furniture.

"Cheeses are very expensive, by far more expensive than meat. Eat up plenty of cheeses here in Austria because in the US they will be out of reach for you," Igor reported, uttering another stupidity.

I looked at the people there and wondered whether they failed to take notice that cheeses were several times more expensive than meat also in Austria. I also let this nonsense fly across the small room overcrowded with refugees without any remarks. I listened on and didn't mean to involve myself in the discussion, except when Igor stated:

"American government doesn't care a chip about refugees, and when you come into the US, they will shove you among the blacks." My patience came to its end and I blurted out:

"Wait a minute! Indeed a Welfare Program exists over there and we as people without income would qualify for it as well. The only condition is that we must have a green card. Besides that, as far as I know, around eighteen percent of people in the USA are blacks, so anywhere you go, you find some of them there."

"I don't know anything about Welfare . . . ," Igor stuttered.

"I can see that you don't know the situation in the USA at all," I said.

For a moment the room fell silent and all eyes were on me. It was apparent that everyone waited to see how this conversation would proceed when the silence was broken by a strong bang at the door:

"Open the door, this is the police!"

Thomas jumped up from his chair and opened the door. Two cops stood in the open door and in German they asked Igor and his wife for their passports.

"Where are the passports?" Igor inquired of his wife in Slovak.

"What passports?" his wife asked also in Slovak.

"American," Igor said very nervously.

She reached in her purse and handed them to him. The cops still stood in the door, as Igor handed them the passports. They started to page through the passports and Igor tried to explain something to them in English. Something went very wrong because one of the police officers said the passports were counterfeit and asked both of them to go with them to the police station. Igor tried resisting and claiming he was an American citizen, but the policeman said:

"I advise you, that you both willingly go with us, because I will call for reinforcement."

Igor gave up and the policemen took both of them away.

I opened a window because the air in the room was already unbreathable. Fresh air blew into the room and I said:

"It seems that our discussion with the Americans is already finished. It's time to go home."

"Do you think that these were StB agents?" someone inquired naively.

"Quite sure; indeed, they had counterfeited US passports," I said composedly. We went outside to the street and walked in the direction of the camp. It was nine o'clock in the evening and it was chilly, but from the inside, I was warmed by a good feeling. First, because I was right and second, even more because they were arrested by Austrian police. We never learned how the Austrian police found them, or any other details about their arrests, or when and where they went. We never saw those two again and no more agents after those two showed up. Even though the ending was quite clear, the conversation with the "Americans" left permanent footprints on some refugees. They got a fear of the USA; they were confident that their life would be unbearable there and hence decided preferably to immigrate to other countries. Immediately Monday morning they phoned their sponsoring organization and asked for a change—emigration to Canada. We did not hear about anybody returning to Czechoslovakia as a direct result of StB-agent activities. The only thing they successfully achieved was the fact that some refugees didn't want to go into the USA at all.

When the children started school, the majority of the men started looking for incidental work. There were two types of working opportunities for refugees. Work help at the construction sites or sorting vegetables in the local canning factory. One morning I got up very early and at six in the morning I stood among the other guys in a crowd, which waited for work opportunity. We waited outside the camp until a car drove up, from which the recruiting chief got out. It was a man who knew a few basic sentences in several languages and picked out from the crowd those whom he liked the most. However, when I saw that from a crowd of about thirty guys, only five successfully acquired incidental and temporary employment, I said to myself there had to be another method and chose my own way. I drove the car in the surrounding small towns and searched in window displays of shops for notices offering incidental work. After several days just as I was beginning to think that my own system wouldn't lead anywhere, I found such an announcement in a store window of a small shop with furniture, which was located in Grein. I entered and with my not-very-good German I talked to the shop owner Mr. Plaim, who was about my age. I understood him very well, because from the time I was a little boy, I had watched Austrian television almost daily. There were only two channels we could watch and we still needed special antennas. My conversational accomplishments were very weak because I had never had any conversations with people through the TV screen. Mr. Plaim comprehended that I understood him very well;, therefore, he employed me for a salary, which was only a quarter of the lowest pay in Austria.

I started working for him immediately the next morning and it was in his house, which was about fifteen miles from Grein. It was a very nice house, but it was also quite evident the house had been built about three hundred years ago. At the time the main source of family income was agriculture, specifically breeding cows and selling their milk. It appeared to me as if Mr. Plaim married into this house because every day I saw his wife, sister-in-law and their mother milking the cows. Instead of milking cows, he decided to go his own way and started selling furniture and other furnishings.

He brought me into the old part of the house, which once was a cow house. Right now he had furniture storage and a workshop for furniture repair there. The front end of this building was turned into the street and regular windows were replaced with big showcase windows. He had state-of-the-art type of furniture on display there. With chalk he drew on the wallpaper two lines about seventy five feet long and told me to chisel out there a groove for water pipes. He gave me a hammer and a chisel and when I carefully cut out the wallpaper I found out I would be cutting into a wall, which was built using granite blocks joined with cement concrete. It took me the entire day to finish it, because the wall was really hard. When I was done with it, a professional plumber laid pipes into my groove supplying warm and cold water to a new bathroom. The following day, when the plumber was finished, I fixed the wall again and finally put new wallpaper up. After that, I worked every day for Mr. Plaim and performed work such as repairs and spraying paints and colors on furniture, repairs of locks and handles, repairs and concrete work for sidewalks in his back yard, helped during the furniture transport to customers or laying new floor in his shop. He always found something, what needed repair or a make up. I liked the work I performed, and every time I achieved something new, I was proud of my "professional" approach and level.

Life in the camp flowed with its specific pace. Our accommodations and food were fairly good and our minds were focused on one sole thing: the loudspeaker in the hallway in the morning.

"Achtung, Achtung. XY family come immediately into the camp office."

Following the first "Achtung," the door of every room opened and people breathlessly waited to hear their name. The lucky one, whose name was read, then hurried into the office. It meant only two things: either the family got a date when they went for their interview at an embassy, or when they would leave camp and depart for their new country, which they picked for their emigration. The less lucky ones, whose name didn't get read, then somewhat envied others and hoped that one fine day they would also hear their name through the loudspeaker.

On a day following an "Achtung," they said our name for first the time, I was not at home because I worked. Nora ran into the office and took the instructions for our interview at the American embassy. As I arrived back home at half past four, she waved to me from the window, her eyes shining with pleasure and she called:

"We are going to our interview . . . we are going to our interview . . ."

By the time I raced up the stairs, she stood in the room door together with the children and waved a paper from the office, on which were written instructions and other particulars about our interview. It was dated for October 31, 1984. Transportation to the embassy and back was provided for us from the office and the paper said the camp microbus Mercedes would leave about 5:30 in the morning.

"Now you should buy me the boots which you promised in Prague," Nora said, and then she added:

"I have nothing I can put on my feet for such an important occasion."

"All right, Saturday we will go into Amsteten and purchase boots and clothing we need for the interview," I said

Early morning Wednesday October 31, we boarded the camp microbus in the best and prettiest clothing we had. They transported us to the US embassy in Vienna, where we had a ten o'clock interview. At first they fingerprinted all of us and then they led us into a room, where an embassy clerk via interpreter inquired for reasons and other particulars of our departure from Czechoslovakia. I didn't see into his papers, but according to his questions, I figured out the clerk was looking at a record of our first interview in Traiskirchen. Then I perceived again how important our first interview was and comprehended, why we had to be in complete isolation. After the interview they sent us for medical examinations to a physician in Vienna, where we were again transported by the camp's microbus. We were awfully happy because a long time ago we had heard from someone that when the Americans send you for health examinations, it means our emigration into the USA was already certain. I did not know if that statement was true, but we were awfully happy anyway. After the medical examinations the microbus drove us back into camp in Bad Kreuzen.

For the day of our American interview I took a day off work, of course unpaid. The following day, I went back to "work." Since the very beginning of my employment I took note, that Mr. Plaim did not endure stress very well; at the beginning of every new project, he was very nervous and at the same time he used me as a lightning rod for his anger. Initially, I tried ignoring it, but after some time it started bugging me and his smile at the end of a well-done project did not let me forget his yelling and swearing at the beginning. Somehow it accumulated inside of me. At my first working day after the interview with the US embassy, when I worked on a new floor at his shop in Grein, he again started screaming and swearing at me without any reason. I put the tools down, stood up and I said to him very composedly right in his face in German:

"Then, I am finished here," and walked away.

He noticed that this time he had overshot. He stood in my way and started begging me for forgiveness. I said to him it wasn't the first time; that he screamed and used bad language at me without reason and within those two months I had had enough of it. I walked away and never returned.

It was about half-past ten in the morning when I arrived back in camp.

"Why are you home so early? What happened?" Nora regaled me.

I told her what had happened and that for us I had no appetite to suffer through daily screaming and swearing for $1.50 per hour. She laughed:

"Since when do you figure out your income in dollars?"

"When I calculate using the current exchange rate of schillings to dollars, I am being paid $1.50 an hour," I said.

"You're right, stay home. We will be together and we can take some English classes," Nora said sensibly.

I liked her proposal because a while ago we had heard about a few Americans who taught English courses and they came into Bad Kreuzen. They were volunteers sent by religious and sponsoring organizations, such as WCO or AFCR. Courses were held in the building of the police academy, so it was very close. We registered for them. Nora for a beginner's course; I for an advanced course, and we went regularly. We did not miss a single class, until our teachers went back home for Christmas.

Every day after lunch we went in the office to check for mail. The list of people who received mail was pinned up on a bulletin board. If your name was listed that day, you would go up to the window and the camp staff handed out the mail. We didn't have to say our last name anymore; they knew everyone by name. Mostly, we got letters or postcards, but once in early November, they handed us a package. Nora and I looked at each other and said at once:

"Evicka."

Immediately, we opened the box and, sure enough, Evicka was there. We went upstairs to our room and we could hardly wait for the time when we went to meet the children outside the schoolhouse at the end of the day. Nora laid Evicka in Katarina's arms and we went to school. We stood opposite the exit of the school, and when Katarina appeared in it, Nora raised Evicka over her head, Katarina noticed her, dropped her bag on the pavement, and when Nora handed her Evicka, she hugged her with both arms and at the same time swung around. She was quite delirious with happiness. The following days Katarina played exclusively with Evicka. We bought some clothing for her and Katarina was fully occupied with changing her and washing her in our room sink. Every evening she lay in bed side by side with her; otherwise, she couldn't fall asleep.

"Evicka needs her own crib," Nora said one day, when the children were at school.

"Are you serious?" I asked startled.

"Yes, because Katarina sleeps side by side in bed with her and many times I find her lying on top of her. It is not good for Katarina, because she doesn't sleep straight and Evicka is also sort of distorted," said Nora.

"I can make her a crib," I said.

"You mean buy," Nora said.

"No, I can make it," I said.

"How? You don't have tools for it," Nora said.

"There is not too much I need for it. I will make it the same way I made the stand for the iron. By using just my pocket knife," I said.

"Do you think so?" Nora asked in disbelief.

"Sure," I said.

As we walked with the children home from school, Nora said:

"Dad will make a crib for Evicka."

Katarina looked at me with a wide smile and asked:

"When?"

"We have to go into the woods for some sticks, let them dry, and then in a week the crib will be ready," I said.

When we came back to our room, Katarina asked:

"Are we going to the woods for sticks"?"

I looked outside through a window. It was still light out, but I knew in about half an hour it would be dusk. I remembered I had seen nice straight-branched hazelnut bushes right under the camp by the river.

"Let's go," I said.

"Isn't it too late now? It will be dark in a moment and it is too far to the woods," Nora said.

"We don't have to go too far, just under the camp by the river," I said.

"All right, then you can go," Nora said.

Katarina caught my hand and we walked out. When walking down the hallway, Nora called:

"Just be careful, so you don't fall in the water!"

In about ten minutes we came to the place I remembered. Almost all the branches of those hazelnut bushes were nice and straight, exactly what we needed. The bushes grew at the river bank, but the best branches grew far into the water.

"Stay here at the bank, so you don't fall in the water. I will hand you sticks," I said to Katarina and climbed on the bush. I cut some sticks and handed them to her and she sorted them by size. In about ten minutes we had enough material for building the crib. I jumped back on the river bank, took the sticks from Katarina because they were too heavy for her to carry and we went back. We were holding hands; I held the sticks on my shoulder with my left hand and we walked up the hill in the direction of camp.

"Now, we have to let them dry and then I can start making the crib," I said.

"How long does it take until they dry," Katarina asked.

"Three to five days. We can store them under the bed and check them in three days," I said.

By the time we came back to our room, it was almost dark out. We carefully laid down the sticks under the bed and went downstairs for dinner.

Five days later the sticks were dry, so I could start the crib manufacturing. During all that time I was making the crib, Katarina sat next to me. It looked like she was playing with her toys, but she very carefully watched the whole process. I measured Evicka and drew a crib design on paper. Using a pocket knife I cut single sticks for each part of the crib and at the end glued them together with glue I bought in a store in Bad Kreuzen. Within the next two days the crib was done. Nora sewed a mattress for the crib. She used a cloth from shirts the children had grown out of and the inside she made from the polyurethane foam which Evicka was wrapped in when she came in the package from grandma. Katarina laid Evicka into her new crib and she slept in it every night after that.

Camp employees treated all of us very nicely, and when the holidays came, they showed us that they did not forget us at all. December 6, on St. Nicholas day, two men dressed up. One of them looked just like St. Nicolas and the other one just like a devil. Those two then went from room to room, St. Nicolas jingling a bell and the devil making a lot of noise with chains he held in his hands. They entered every single room in the camp and every kid received a St. Nicolas bag from them, which was filled with oranges, apples, bananas, chocolates, peanuts, candy bars and candies. The devil looked really convincing. Katarina was very scared of him and did not want to stand next to him for picture-taking when I tried to take a picture of them in between the devil and St. Nicolas. I could take a picture of them standing next to St. Nicholas only.

The destiny of the cars in which people came to the refugee camp was very unusual. It was impossible to sell the car and at the end it ended up in a metal scrap yard. Towing a car to a metal scrap yard had to be paid by its owner, which was about fifty US dollars. I just could not admit that our car would end up in the scrap. It was relatively new, only one and half years old. I did not want to pay for towing and I was convinced I would get some money for it.

I chose again my own approach. It did not take too long to figure out the car could have any value for people who immigrated into European countries because transporting the car over the ocean would be uneconomical. I was swayed to believe that I would be able to find someone who was focusing on Germany because it was just the closest country neighboring Austria. It was not a big deal to figure out who was going where since nobody made a secret of it. Following a few conversations with future Germans, I found a young married couple who claimed to be ethic Germans and who had come from Czechoslovakia, Johan and Ingrid. They expressed a real interest in our car and asked their uncle in Germany to send them money for the car. About a week after our conversation about the sale of the car, they both came to us and said they would buy it. However, they had three conditions. The first one was that the car had to pass a technical inspection; the second that it would be officially registered at the Austrian registration of motor vehicles under their name. And the third was according to the law: car insurance was mandatory on all registered vehicles. Obviously, I agreed, because in no case did I mean to sell our car to someone illegally. Johann and I took the car for its technical inspection, then to an insurance company, and ultimately, to get the registration. They took both old registration plates and I had a tinge of regret of selling the car as I watched them unbolt them. I wanted to take one of them as a souvenir. When the car was registered and transferred to Johann, he gave me the amount we agreed upon—eight hundred marks. This was no way near the vehicle's value, but it was definitely much more than if I had to pay for hauling the car to the scrap yard.

It was interesting to observe people's behavior when they learned that we successfully sold our car. Some of them congratulated us because we succeeded in something no one had done before. However, there were also people who did not try to conceal their envy and said we were going to have some trouble due to sale of our car.

At the beginning of each month, we obtained pocket money (Taschengeld), which they paid to the head of the family, picked up in the camp office. It wasn't too much money, around twenty American dollars. After signing a column on a payment release form, we were given the money in cash. Also once a month, we were given toiletries for the entire family, which we again received upon signing a release document. We received these items according to some rules established by the camp management, but it was always more than we were able to use up within a month. After a few months of stockpiling all the extras, most people took only those things which they needed. It did not make any sense to store extra soaps, or toilet paper only because they were given to us for free.

On weekends and holidays after lunch, we always went for a walk around the neighborhood. First, we started only walking in the closest neighborhoods, so we would not get lost. Later, as we got to know the area, we'd venture out further and further. We hiked on foot in the woods in the vicinity of the camp; after some time, we knew all the paths, forest and field walkways. It was an exquisite and picturesque country, with small hills and winding roads, which in one spot went steeply up, and a bit further, down again. If we had not lived in a refugee camp, but in a hotel in town, we would have thought we were on vacation. Even just outside the camp, there were ruins of ancient castles, from which we could see the countryside like it was in the palm of our hand.

Christmas and the end of the year approached. We wanted to celebrate them the best we could, given the circumstances. We knew it would be no way near the level to which we were accustomed. However, we were confident that, despite the circumstances, it would be filled with its usual Christmas charm and, in its own way, it would become an unforgettable one. In the building next door, just by the kitchen, there was a little chapel, which was used for Christian religious services. Two Catholic priests, one Slovak and the other Czech, alternated in holding Catholic mass. A few hours before mass they went together from door to door and let people know when the following mass would be starting. They concentrated largely on the Czechs and Slovaks in the camp because they knew that the other nationalities, like Polish, or Hungarians, had their priests, who held religious ceremonies in the same chapel, but in their native languages. People like us who came from atheistic Czechoslovakia, gradually got up the courage because we realized that now we had freedom of religion, and more and more people came to mass. Among them was also a five-member family we had known in Czechoslovakia. Four members of the family had been in the Communist Party. A requirement of membership in the Communist Party was that one had to be at least eighteen years of age. This particular family of five would have had five members had it not been for the age of the youngest who was only twelve. It was a bit vicious, but true gossip. However, the priests did not discriminate against anyone and accepted everyone with open arms because they believed that the path to Christ frequently deviates.

As Christmas approached, the people's willy-nilly mood changed into one that was more jovial. Maybe they realized that their way out of the country, no matter how adventurous and courageous, was relatively easy compared to what Christ went through. Perhaps we would never forget the words of the priest who said during the Christmas mass:

"Each of you, meditate about the moment when you left from there and how you were led by zeal for liberty. If you will be honest with yourself, you will perceive that above every one of you there was a divine arm, which safeguarded you in your every step. Your arrival here wasn't accidental, but you came here only due to the Divine support. Now you are free and from now on you'll proceed in your free life."

The camp employees, especially the cooks made us really happy because they made Christmas dinner and served on Christmas Eve for lunch. We were served deep fried fish and potato salad, which was our Christmas dinner our entire life growing up. We thought it was very nice of them and we understood that the camp employees also wanted to be home with their families for dinner and that was why they served us the dinner for lunch. For dinner we received bags of "take out" as it was already the custom for weekends and holidays.

We bought some toys for the kids and we were given the top of a tree from the saw mill in Bad Kreuzen, which was given for all the refugees from the sawed off tops of pine trees that were used for lumber. It was about three feet tall and we used an empty pickle jar as a Christmas tree stand. I removed some branches on the bottom of our tree and put it inside the jar. In order to hold the tree straight, I filled the rest of the jar with stones. Then I poured water over the stones to prevent the tree from drying out. The children drew Christmas ornaments on paper and we covered the outside of the pickle jar to hide its unsightliness.

We went to the store and bought a few chocolate Christmas ornaments, chocolate filled coins and small tree candles including clips, four tall purple candles for the Advent wreath and a small package of sparklers. We put all the ornaments and coins on a tread and hung them on the tree including paper decorations Katarina and Peter had crafted from colored paper.

We also crafted our own Advent wreath from branches of spruce trees, which we brought from the woods. We bound them into a circle using a thin wire and then attached the four purple candles on the top. We didn't want to buy any additional decorations for the wreath, so we picked a few pine cones in the woods during our most recent hikes. We lit up one candle for the first Advent Sunday, and then every following Sunday we lit an additional candle. The last Advent Sunday all four candles were burning and lit up the whole room without turning on the room lights. The soothing flickering candlelight in our room announced the arrival of Christmas holidays.

For Christmas Eve we dressed up in the best clothing that we had. The snow was falling outside and at dusk we lit the candles and a few sparklers on our Christmas tree. The room was lit only by the candles on the Christmas tree and the Advent wreath; our faces shined with the blinking lights of sparklers. We sat at the table and silently watched the sparklers burning up. There was no stove to cook dinner on and we were not hungry yet because only recently we had finished our Christmas dinner in the dining room. We had a few plates on our table filled with fruit, chocolates and nuts. Peter and Katarina started eating them and Nora and I poured a glass of Martini and clinked glasses "To our victory."

We went for the Midnight Mass to a church downtown. We left a little early because we expected a full church. We arrived at the church about half an hour earlier and we were lucky we could get inside. We stood very close to the main entrance and a lot of people who came later did not get in. They stood outside and watched the mass through the open main entrance.

On our way back home, the snow started falling again. Snow flakes silently flew in the air and created a sparkling ball around every street light. It was Christmas, not only in our spirit but also in the country. It was our first Christmas in the free world!

Right after Christmas the real winter started. Temperatures dropped well below freezing and it snowed frequently. Children had school vacation, so we were all together again. We did not have to go anywhere and looked out the window at the falling snow. Our hikes into the woods were less frequent and much shorter, because we did not have enough winter clothing. Time went by really slowly and only infrequent visits to the dining room for lunches and dinners broke the boredom.

For the New Year party we had several acquaintances in our room. As usual we told each other stories of our lives back in Czechoslovakia, of our journey across the border, many of them already repeated many times over and over. Every one of us hoped after the New Year our "cases" with the sponsoring countries would start moving again. We had only a very foggy idea about the countries into which we were preparing to immigrate to. We absorbed very quickly all the information we heard about the country we had chosen and strove to find truth in any of it. It was not very easy though because we knew so little about them. Time ran really quickly during our discussions, which was very important.

We all expected to leave the camp soon, but no one knew when. One time we heard from someone:

"You will leave for the USA really quickly because you are a complete family. Besides that, chemists are very welcomed there."

Then we heard from someone else:

"You've got plenty of time; you have only been here half a year. A family that lives across the hallway from you has been here for three and a half years . . ."

It was very difficult to find out who was right and there was absolutely no way to verify any of the information. Uncertainties about our future made us nervous and fully occupied our consciousness and also sub-consciousness. We lived in the most beautiful vacation country and despite the fact we had plenty of time, we could not enjoy the surroundings. If only there was someone who would say:

"You are going to be here until this time . . . and then you will go to this place . . . and this is what you can expect . . . ," we could focus on the beautiful country. No one like that existed and every day we heard new information, which completely contradicted what we had heard the day before. We decided to ignore all the "information" and not to listen to anyone and just wait and hope.

Chapter Five

Time to Get Freedom

The New Year of 1985 started and the kids went back to school. Every morning Nora and I listened very carefully when the loudspeakers in the hallway started:

"Achtung . . ."

We again waited breathlessly to hear if they would say our last name, no matter what the pronunciation they used. During the last half a year, we got used to different pronunciation variants of our name and most of them were not correct. This time our name coming out of the loudspeakers would mean we would travel over "the big lake." Three weeks after the New Year, we finally heard it, among the others:

"Bilek" sounded throughout the deserted hallway and the two of us happily ran into the camp office. We learned that on January 31, we were going for an orientation to a camp in Maria Schutz and we were flying to the USA on February 21. They informed us they would take care of our transportation and we just had to get ready for it and all the information about our travel to the USA would be shared with us during our stay in Maria Schutz. All of a sudden all the uncertainty we had disappeared; at that moment, we knew more about our future fate than at anytime during the last two years. We were extremely happy that we were going to the USA and I was also awfully delighted that my plan came out just the way I had wanted. This was the plan, which was born inside of me in a fragment of a second, when before the party meeting, Prazec splattered me with saliva, right after he machinated my position of technical sales representative for ICI Company. I spared him my fist into his jaw and began preparing for my family a new, free life. I was so confident with it that I did not have a plan B in case this one failed. Now I would never need it, the US had already welcomed us with open arms . . .

The office also gave us a few copied pages with detailed information about how and when to prepare for the trip; when they would drive us away from the camp; how to turn in our key to the room; and to let the school know our children would not be coming there anymore, etc . . . We still had a week left in the camp and we could easily handle everything. We got back to our room and smilingly I said:

". . . and at poplars by the rocks, a green hobbit applauds . . ."

Nora only smiled and this time she didn't say anything about the poem. She sat at the table, laid down a piece of paper and a pencil, and pensively said:

"I will make out a list of things, which we can take with us. Things which we don't need, we can donate to someone."

"Clothing, which the kids have outgrown we can donate, but belongings like appliances, we will sell for a "tiny" sum as "used," I said.

"All right, you take care of the appliances and I will sort through the clothing," Nora said.

"Don't forget we only have four suitcases and three bags. We can take only what will fit," I said.

The following week was possibly one of the best which we lived through at the camp of Bad Kreuzen. Somehow consciously we felt that our following life gathered certain direction and from now on it would be only up to us how we arranged it. From now on, we didn't have to wait for paperwork, sponsors or someone's decision at an embassy. From February 22, only we would make decisions as to what would be next. I sat down at the table opposite Nora and started studying in detail the papers which were given to us at the office. Among them was a letter from AFCR, which informed us we were going into Boston, Massachusetts. I smiled and said:

"We are going to Boston . . . Maybe ICI Company will also be there and they will need a technical sales representative."

"It is undoubtedly true. They are already waiting for you . . . ," Nora said sarcastically.

"Look. I know I am not stupid and I recognize I will work in a chemist's position even in the USA. Maybe it will take me some time until I achieve this. I am quite sure I will not tank gas at a gas station, or wash dishes in a restaurant," I said composedly.

"Are you sure?" Nora asked.

"Totally sure," I said with confidence and read through the rest of the papers, in order not to forget something important. We were fully preoccupied and did not notice it was lunch time already. I looked at my watch and said:

"It is already half past twelve. Let us go to lunch."

"Come along," Nora said, fully absorbed by the list of clothing and she added:

"We can finish that when we come back. We can sell our appliances only the last day. We will still need the coffeemaker and lunch heater made from our iron as well."

"Of course . . . Till the last day . . . and this time nothing will happen if we don't sell them . . . we will certainly live through without those few schillings," I said and we went to lunch. We took lunch for the kids in a pot and, as usual, we heated it up on the lunch heater made from our iron.

"A week from today we are leaving," Nora said with pleasure, when Peter and Katarina appeared in the door.

"Where?" Peter inquired.

"Into Maria Schutz and then from there to the USA," I said.

"Hurrah," Peter exclaimed and jumped up. He looked as if he did not know what to do with all the excitement and threw himself on the bed. He lay on the bed, laughed, and waved his arms in the air.

"We are taking Evicka along," Katarina said, lifting Evicka from the crib and hugging her.

"Of course, from now on, Evicka is going with us everywhere," Nora said.

"Also with her crib," Katarina said.

I squatted to Katarina, caught her by the shoulders, looked into her eyes and sought the appropriate words:

"Katarina . . . it will be a problem with the crib . . . it is too big . . . it will not fit into our luggage . . . if you carry it in your hands it will fall apart on the way . . ."

"Will you make me another one in America?" Katarina interrupted with a spark in her eyes.

"No, I will buy you a new crib in a toy store," I said.

Katarina laid Evicka on the bed, took a hold of Evicka's crib and looked at it from all sides. It was as if she was estimating whether the crib would withstand transportation into the USA. Maybe she was just saying good bye . . . Then she turned to me and said:

"All right, you will buy me a new one."

The last evening before we left, we sold the coffeemaker and the iron; from which I removed the twig stand, and a propane two-burner camp stove, for which there had been no more propane for a long time. We still kept the hair dryer because we needed it for Maria Schutz. We decided we would give it to someone after that because it was made for European voltage and was unusable in the USA. We said our farewells to all our acquaintances, with whom we became friends over the past half year.

We promised each other that, when we arrived at our destination, we would get in touch somehow.

In the morning we got up really early and everyone who was scheduled to leave that day had an arranged early breakfast—six o'clock. After breakfast we brought our luggage out. One more time we looked at the room, locked the door, and I brought the key to the camp office. We boarded the camp's Mercedes microbus, where there were more people with whom we left for orientation to Maria Schutz. Also Jano and Klara were there, a young couple we became friends with. The microbus started moving and our eyes filled with tears. We waved good bye to people who stayed there. We also waved good bye to the whole camp and town . . . So long Bad Kreuzen and thank you for everything you have done for us . . . we will never forget how you took care of us . . . another chapter in our journey ended and the next one was about to begin.

About 9:30, the microbus came to the camp in Traiskirchen where a lot of people and a few buses had gathered. A clerk from the main office read names from a list and this way directed people to the right bus. The bus we were sent in filled quite quickly and at about eleven o'clock we got on our way to Maria Schutz. The rest of the ride did not take too long and we knew all the people on this bus were going into the USA, but we had three weeks of orientation ahead of us.

We came to the hotel in Maria Schutz shortly after lunch. Based on the number of members in each family was how we got arranged into rooms. We were waiting for our turn when we were awakened from our lethargy by Klara's voice as she said to the receptionist:

"Please give this room to the Bielek family. They have two small children."

We were very pleasantly surprised . . . it was very nice of her. She voluntarily surrendered the last room with a bathroom to us and preferably took a smaller room without a bathroom.

"Thank you, Klara," Nora said to her and went to the receptionist for the key.

"Thank you, Jano," I said to Jano, who stood next to me and shook his hand.

"We will always remember that," I added.

Klara and Jano used to come for a visit quite frequently. They did not have children yet and they treated our kids like their own. I was pretty sure they heard Katarina saying:

"Little Thomas is lucky because they have their own bathroom."

Katarina repeated the sentence every time she had to go to the bathroom or in the shower in Bad Kreuzen. The common showers and bathrooms in the hallway did not suit Katarina at all.

"After you bring your belongings into your rooms, immediately come down to the dining room for lunch," our bus guide said before we ran upstairs into our rooms.

We brought our luggage into our room and Katarina ran into the bathroom.

"We have our own bathroom, we have our own bathroom . . ." she called from the bathroom and stared into the tub. Then she turned to me and said:

"Now we should buy bubble bath and then I will fill the tub and take a bath in the bubbles."

"All right, but now let's go to the dining room for lunch so we are not late," I said.

A moment after we sat down at a table we were served a tureen with chicken soup with noodles. We scooped the soup into our bowls and started eating hungrily. We were really hungry since the last time we had eaten was at breakfast at six o'clock in the morning. We had not eaten anything since then and it was already 1:30. All four of us were silent and stared into our own bowls when Katarina interrupted the silence and said:

"I cannot get this one." All three of us looked at her and started laughing. Katarina finished all her soup and was chasing the last noodle around the bowl with her spoon. She could not scoop the last noodle with her spoon!

"So, let it go," Nora said with laughter and Katarina gazed at us and could not apprehend why we were laughing so much.

During lunch our course instructors came to the dining room and gave us a schedule for our orientation. They were Czechs and Slovaks who had lived a few years in the USA and now they worked for the American Embassy. Therefore, all courses were in the Czech or Slovak languages, which, was a big advantage for those of us who did not know any English. The following two weeks we had daily courses from eight to noon and then again from one to four. The courses focused on information about the USA, which was meant to prevent "Cultural Shock" of immigrants after arrival to the country. We had no courses on the weekends and we could make any plans our hearts desired.

Maria Schutz was a small town located in the mountains approximately fifty miles south of Vienna and it was well known to all skiers from Austria as well as the rest of Europe. At that time it was a very cold winter and the whole countryside around the hotel was covered with a thick layer of snow.

We did not have any ski gear, so we only went for our hiking trips to the hills in the neighborhood.

At the end of our courses, they again let us know we were leaving Maria Schutz on February 21, 1985 and the bus would leave at 4:00 in the morning. The bus would drive us back to Traiskirchen, where we would receive instructions and documents for our flight to the USA. The breakfast was served at 3:00 in the morning, so we had to get up at 2:00 in the morning. It was relatively early and we had a hard time waking up, especially the children.

After having breakfast, we boarded the bus, and after about two hours, we came back to the main refugee camp in Traiskirchen, where refugees from different parts of Austria had gathered. It was early in the morning, still dark and cold; all of us were sleepy and cold. Then they directed us into other buses which brought us to the Vienna airport in Schwechat. Shortly before our arrival at the airport, we passed a road sign, which said "Bratislava 30 km"

Someone in the bus yelled:

"They are driving us back to Czechoslovakia" and some people started panicking. For them it was still a terrible thought to be able to laugh about it. The clerk from the camp office, who accompanied us, stood up, turned to the back, and said in German:

"No, we are not going to Bratislava, but to the airport in Schwechat." And then he sat down and laughed about it. A few minutes later we really did stop in front of an airport building with all signs written in German. It was clear we were in Austria. We came off the bus, took our luggage, and the clerk led us into the airport building. Then he gathered everyone and checked against his list to ensure that we had not lost anyone. He also distributed our documents shortly before everyone's departure. We received en envelope and he asked us to check the contents of it. Our Austrian refugee passports were there for Nora and me and they were valid only for a few months. The USA visas were already stamped inside and the children were written in Nora's passport. Besides that we found our green immigration cards there and also four air tickets to New York and then to Boston. As the planes were departing to fly to different parts of the world, our group was shrinking. Our turn came around ten o'clock; we checked our luggage and said goodbye to the friends we had met in the camps. We walked through the detectors and one last time waved to the shrinking crowd behind the glass in the airport hallway. The Pan American flight to New York was scheduled for eleven o'clock.

The aircraft sped up the runway, took off, and everything below us faded away. The four of us sat in the middle row, but I looked down through the closest window and thought:

"Thank you, Austria. Thank you for everything . . ." and my eyes filled with tears.

The flight was very interesting for Peter and Katarina because it was their first one. They could hardly wait until the aircraft got to cruising altitude. They wanted to walk around the inside of the aircraft and check everything out.

"You must be seated and buckled up until that little light goes out," I said and pointed at the sign saying "Buckle up."

The moment that little light went out, they both unbuckled themselves at the same time and stood up. They hesitantly started walking down the aisle between seats and inquisitively viewed the aircraft from the inside. After a few moments they came to a window, which was in an aisle by the bathrooms, and looked down at the ocean. Along with us there were more families in the aircraft, and, therefore, also more children, with whom they had chummed around with during the stay in camp. On each side of the aisles, flight attendants pushed carts with beverages in front of them. Nora tipped to me and she said:

"Go get the kids and bring them here, let them sit in their seats; otherwise, they will stand in the way of the flight attendants."

I brought Peter and Katarina back. As we were just sitting down, a flight attendant came to us with the cart and inquired what we would like to drink. Nora and the children asked for orange juice and I asked for beer. The flight attendant handed us the beverages and as she gave me a bottle of beer, she said:

"Five dollars."

I looked at her surprised because I had flown before many times and I had never paid for beer. However, I didn't mean to reject the beer because she already held an open bottle in front of me. Therefore, I handed her five dollars and took the beer.

"You could have rather taken orange juice," Nora said.

"If I had known this beer would cost me five dollars, I would have taken the juice. I had beer aboard a plane before, but never paid for it. It was included in the price of the air ticket," I said.

"Never mind, right now we have five dollars less," Nora said.

"It bothers me too, that now we have five dollars less. In our situation this amount is a great deal for us," I said.

"So, drink this beer and do not ask for a second one," said Nora.

"Definitely not . . . ," I said.

"We don't know what kind of air tickets we have because we did not buy them. Most likely ours would be the cheapest air tickets out of the entire aircraft . . . and alcohol isn't included," said Nora.

"I guess you're right," I said and glanced at her. Her head was leaning against the headrest and her eyes were closed.

"Are you not feeling all right?" I asked.

"My head hurts and the smell of the food, which they serve here, is turning my stomach," Nora said.

"Do you want a pill for your headache?" I asked.

"No, I have already taken some. I can hardly wait until they finally come to an end with those meals," Nora said.

When the flight attendant came to us, Nora rejected the food and, with her eyes closed, she sat still in her seat. After lunch our children fell asleep and we covered them with blankets, so they would not be cold. Nora and I had already flown before, but they were usually only short flights within Europe, mostly one to two hours. But we had never flown over the Atlantic before and a seven-hour flight was unusually long for us. We had mixed feelings. We were looking forward to going into the USA, refugee life was over for us and we couldn't wait to start a new life. On the other hand, we felt anxiety and were a bit nervous because we did not know what we were getting ourselves into. We had only a very foggy perception about the country to which we were flying. We knew it was not a devilish country and not full of criminality, as it was interpreted by the Communist propaganda. Maliciousness, with which propaganda portrayed absurdities about the USA, always provoked an impression in us that they were doing it out of jealousy. Somehow, subconsciously, we felt life in the US would be better than in the country we had left, dramatically, but with pleasure. Even though we did not have the smallest apprehension where we would live, how we would find work, or what we would live off, we had no regrets about leaving that dreadfully oppressive place we called home for so many years; at least I knew I had no regrets. For a long time it was no secret to us that we would get the welfare support, but that wasn't what we were going after. Above all, America was for us, a symbol of liberty, which in our minds was symbolized by the Statue of Liberty in New York. In a couple of hours we would see her with our own eyes. We were shivering just thinking about our future life under the Statue of Liberty.

Apparently, it was these kinds of feelings and thoughts which caused Nora's headache, which could not be suppressed by pills. Her awareness that she didn't know too much English did not help her feel any more at ease. I caught her hand, leaned my head against hers and said silently:

"Don't worry. It is going to be all right. The beginning will be a little hard, but it will not take too long and, with our will and hard work, we will move up rather quickly. In a few years, when we talk about this flight, we are going to have a good laugh about it."

Nora opened her eyes, turned her head toward me and said:

"I am thinking about the kids . . . how they are going to school if they don't know a word in English . . ."

"Exactly the same way they went to school in Austria. They will be placed in the grade according to their age and in a short time they will both know English much better than we. We, the "old" people, will have to study a bit harder than our kids. They have a much better ability for learning than we do," I said.

"It is going to be easier for you than me, because you know English," Nora said.

"What I know is not too much, but at the beginning it is going to be an advantage for all of us because we will not need someone else to translate for us. You know how much time and energy I put into learning that language the best I could in the last few years," I said.

Nora had her eyes closed again and her head rested on the seat. She squeezed my hand slightly and said:

"I know . . ."

"You will learn English as well and it will not take a long time. When I used to go to courses, it was only a few hours a week and the courses were held only once a month. Beginning today, we will have English courses twenty four hours a day . . . Anyhow, for learning any language, geniality is not needed. Anyone can learn it. The effort in learning will reflect in how well one masters it. Anyway, there are two hundred eighty-six million people who learned it somehow," I said.

Nora opened her eyes, looked at me, but did not say a word and just smiled. Then she peeked over at Peter and Katarina, who slept next to us. She tidied the blankets they were covered with and again rested her head and closed her eyes. Then she said quietly:

"I hope someone will be at the New York airport waiting for us."

"Certainly . . . I am convinced someone will be standing in the hallway right behind customs holding a big sign "AFCR" (American Foundation for Czechoslovak Refugees) in front of them. But we are not going to get lost even if no one is there. Somehow we will find the flight to Boston," I said.

"According to what they wrote us from AFCR, someone will be waiting for us also in Boston," Nora said.

"I am quite sure. AFCR is a professional organization, which is making its living by helping refugees with their beginnings in the USA," I said.

"I would be glad if we were already there," Nora said.

"Me too, but now we have to wait a couple more hours," I said and then I added:

"Now let's make a plan what kind of meals we are going to cook."

My suggestion was met with success because Nora woke up from her lethargy a bit and started mentioning meals, which we missed so much during the last couple of months. The food in the camp was excellent and we were given a lot of it, but it wasn't exactly the type of cooking which we were accustomed to and grew up on. We missed meals such as roasted duck, beef with mushrooms or sheep cheese noodles. When she said sheep cheese noodles, she turned to me and asked:

"Do you think we can buy sheep cheese there?

"Most likely not . . . but I am quite positive we can buy a cheese there from which we can make a concoction similar to sheep cheese," I said.

"How do you find that cheese?" Nora asked.

"It is very simple, by the smell," I said and laughed.

We continued talking about cooking our Slovak meals for a long time. We did not know what town we were going to live in, or the shape of our new apartment, which was provided to us by the AFCR. However, we knew that this time we were going to have our own kitchen and bathroom.

"Do you remember, when at the end of July last year you sat on the bunk bed so unhappy and I suggested that from now on we were going only upwards?" I asked.

"Yes, I remember . . ." Nora said quietly.

"Now we are going to be another step higher. We cannot expect we are going to get a luxury apartment. It will be an apartment of the lowest price range, but we will have much more than the room in Bad Kreuzen," I said.

Nora did not say anything and just leaned her head on my shoulder. We sat like that for a moment and then the kids woke up. In the first moment they did not recognize where they were and surprisedly looked around.

"In about an hour, we will land in New York," Nora said to the kids. When she said it, one of the pilots just walked by us in the aisle and heard something other than English. Being surprised, he stopped and pulled two Pan American pins from his pocket and gave them to Peter and Katarina and then he asked in English:

"Would you like to come to the pilot's cabin?"

The two of them did not understand and looked at me. I translated the pilot's question into Slovak and they agreeably nodded their heads.

"They do not understand English but they would like to go into the pilot's cabin," I said in English to the pilot.

"Excellent, If you don't mind, I will take your kids into the pilot's cabin for a moment," the pilot said with enthusiasm. Apparently, he was glad at finding someone who would understand him.

"Go with him, the pilot is taking you with him," I said to the kids in Slovak.

Both of them jumped up from their seats and went with the pilot. About fifteen minutes later he brought them back. Their eyes were lit up when they described what they had seen inside the cabin.

"Now, say to the pilot "thank you" in English I said to the kids when they were getting back into their seats.

"Thank you . . . thank you," both of them said.

"You are very welcome," the pilot said.

It was very nice of you. Thank you," I said to the pilot in English.

"You are very welcome," the pilot repeated and went to the back of the aircraft. He was looking for other kids he would take into the pilot's cabin. After a few moments he found some and when he passed us with Peter's friends, Peter said:

"We have also been in the pilot's cabin. It is fantastic . . ."

I turned to Nora and whispered:

"It is really very nice of him. It seems that he is looking for kids of new immigrants and to take them on a field trip into the cabin."

"The Americans are very nice people," Nora said with a smile.

Shortly after that almost all the kids went into the cabin, the door of the cabin closed again, and the voice of the chief pilot sounded in the loudspeakers:

"In twenty five minutes, we are landing at JFK Airport in New York. The weather in New York is very nice, sunny and the temperature is about forty degrees. Local time at our destination is 1:45 in the afternoon."

"What did he say?" Nora asked.

I translated the pilot's announcement and she asked very surprised:

"Forty degrees . . . ?"

"Yes, Fahrenheit . . . it is about five degrees on the Celsius scale," I said.

"Cold . . ." Nora stated disappointed.

"It's February . . ." I answered.

When the plane flew in a circle above New York, I looked out through the closest window, watched the city and waited for a sight of The Statue of

Liberty. I said to myself I had to see her before we landed. When I spotted her I called;

"Aha . . . look—The Statue of Liberty," and I was as happy as a little boy.

As the pilot had said, we landed in a moment. We went out of the aircraft, went through Immigration, where they stamped our Austrian passports and checked our "green cards." Then waited at the carousel for our luggage and loaded it on a cart. We walked through Customs without stopping because the customs clerk on duty just waved at us to keep walking. We came out of Customs and spotted a blonde-haired lady who held a sign in front of her: "AFCR."

We stopped by her and I said:

"Good afternoon, we are the Bielek family."

"Good afternoon, my name is Martha and I work for the New York branch of the AFCR and she looked on a list she had.

"Bielek . . . Jan, Nora Peter and Katarina," Martha read from her list and made a check mark at our names.

"Please, just wait a minute with me. I will bring you to the terminal from which you are going to fly to Boston. I am waiting for another two families who flew on your plane," Martha said.

"Yes, of course . . ." I said and she shook hands with each of us, saying:

"Welcome to the USA"

"Thank you," Nora said first.

While we were waiting for the other two families, Martha informed us that AFCR had sent her along with a colleague to meet families flying in today and they were both going to lead them into other terminals for connecting flights. However, she was the only one at the airport now because her colleague had stayed home with a sick child. So she had to come up with some sort of organizational scheme because each family was flying out from a different terminal.

"Bohdan and Krizan?" I asked.

"Yes, how do you know that," Martha asked surprised.

"We were all in the same camp in Bad Kreuzen and we all just flew in the same plane," I said.

"I appreciate that you know them. We can find them easier," Martha said.

Moments later the other two families showed up and Martha welcomed them and checked them off on her list. Then she addressed the whole group:

"Excuse me, I am here alone today and that's why we are all going together. Each family flies out of a different terminal and I will show each one of you where to wait for your connecting flight."

Martha looked into her papers again, lifted her arm and called:

"Follow me, please."

We all followed her and she brought us to the terminal with our connecting flights. She also showed each family where to check their luggage and the display with the number of their flight and boarding time. All of us were also asked not to leave their particular terminal in order not to get lost.

"Happy journey, good luck in the USA and so long," Martha said at the end.

We stayed at "our" terminal and with sadness looked at the display. It was only 2:30 and our connecting flight to Boston wasn't scheduled for departure until 6:30. We had a full four hours of waiting!

"How long is a flight to Boston?" Nora asked.

"About an hour," I said.

"So by the time we get to Boston, it is going to be two o'clock in the morning in Austria.

"Yes, by the time we get to Boston it is going to be twenty four hours since we got up in Maria Schutz," I said.

We sat in the airport terminal and it was quite obvious we were tired. The initial excitement about coming to the USA had worn off and sleepiness hit us really hard. Nora very carefully studied the display with plane departures, which was very close to us and asked:

"Look, there are three other flights from here to Boston before ours. Could we fly a different flight?

"I don't think so. During our flight, you said the air tickets we had were the cheapest on the whole plane. They are non-exchangeable for anything else," I said.

"We could try it anyway and maybe we won't have to wait here for four hours," Nora insisted on her idea.

"Look, even if we were able to obtain an earlier flight, it is not going to help us at all. Whoever is expecting us in Boston is not going to be there four hours sooner. He wouldn't know we were flying with an earlier flight and he would be expecting us according to our original one. Besides that, the luggage we have already checked in and it will be loaded into the originally scheduled flight and then we would have to wait for it anyway, even if we fly in sooner," I patiently explained, to show why it would not be a good idea.

"We could at least try it anyway," Nora repeated.

I did not answer that. We all were very tired and it wasn't very wise to continue our dialogue concerning different ideas about the flight to Boston. I set an alarm on my wrist watch. In order to prevent missing the boarding time in case we dozed off. It was forty five minutes after our arrival, so "only" slightly over three hours before our departure.

The kids were in seats, their eyes were closing, and they yawned very intensively. If there was a place to lie down, they would fall asleep instantly.

"Look at that big bear in the display window over there," I said and pointed to a window a short distance from us.

"Let's go take a look at him," Katarina said and ran across the hallway to the window.

"Do not go too far, so you don't get lost," Nora said and yawned at the same time.

"We will be only at that display," I said and went to join the kids at the display. We watched the bear and could not believe someone had actually made such a huge stuffed bear. I have never seen a real bear, but I was convinced that the one in the display window was at least as big as a real one in the wild if not bigger. We walked around several display windows and peered at the merchandise. Nora stayed in her seat and held a bag we were taking on board the plane and she watched us with her eyes half closed. We came back to her and sat down again. I looked at my watch and found out the time was moving along brutally slow. We had killed only twenty minutes by peeking at the display windows.

"It is so interesting how slowly time goes when one is waiting for something. Sometimes it appears years go by so quickly, we don't even notice them. Now we cannot wait for a few hours," I said.

"Because, we are paying too much attention to it . . . Now let's go for a little walk, the two of us," Nora said and then she turned to the kids and said:

"You two stay here now. We are going to take a close look at the bear."

We walked up to the display windows and I looked back at the kids. They sat in the seats and their heads nodded up and down. Just about falling asleep . . .

"Let's go back, because if Peter and Katarina fall asleep now, we will not be able to wake them up. I don't know how we are going to board the plane," I said.

Nora looked at them also and said:

"We have to come up with some kind of entertainment."

We walked back to our seats and I said:

"Who would spot a man with a black top hat on his head, will get a dollar."

My sentence really worked because Peter started laughing and Katarina asked with interest:

"What is a top hat?"

"A black tube-like hat with a small brim at the bottom. When you see someone with a black hat, let me know. If it is a top-hat, you win and at the same time you will know what a top hat looks like.

The game really worked and the kids were not sleepy anymore. They diligently watched the crowd of people around us and looked for a man with a top hat on his head. I hoped that people from Friends of the Black Top hat Club would not go by now because it would cost me a lot of money.

The time was going by unbearably slowly, but we finally heard a voice from the loudspeakers which asked travelers from our flight to board the plane. We entered the plane and the moment the kids hit the seats, they instantly fell asleep. We covered them up with blankets, put pillows under their heads and Nora said very quietly, just to herself:

"Let them sleep for a little while."

"When we arrive in Boston, I can carry Katarina in my arms, but we have to wake Peter up," I said.

The aircraft taxied to the runway and quickly became airborne. Peter and Katarina were already in a deep sleep. They were not awakened by the takeoff or by the roar of the engines. Nora and I also dozed off for just a little while, because in what seemed like a moment, we were landing in Boston. The aircraft went all the way to the terminal and people started leaving the plane, but Peter and Katarina were still in a deep sleep. I lifted Katarina in my arms; she just looked at me with one eye, put her head on my shoulder, and kept on sleeping. Nora took her purse and a bag we had on board and tried to wake up Peter. She gently rubbed Peter's left cheek with the fingers of her left hand and whispered into his right ear:

"Peter, wake up . . . we are already in Boston . . . Peter wake up . . ."

Peter just opened his eyes, looked at Nora, turned his head to other side, and kept on sleeping. Nora started rubbing him on the other cheek and again whispered into his other ear:

"Peter, wake up . . . we are already in Boston . . . Peter wake up . . ."

This time Peter really woke up a little bit and surprised looked around in the plane. Nora took him by the hand and said:

"Let's go, we have to get out . . . we are in Boston . . ."

Peter stood up, still rubbing his eyes with one hand and Nora pulled him by his other hand out of the plane. This way we walked all the way to the carousels for our luggage. I gave Katarina to Nora for a moment and she again looked around with just one eye open. When she saw Nora, she laid her head on her shoulder and kept on sleeping. After a minute of waiting, our luggage came out. I took it from the carousel and laid it on a cart and then took Katarina back into my arms. We pushed the cart together with Nora; she also pulled Peter behind her and he looked half asleep.

We came out into the airport hallway and not too far from us spotted a young couple. She held a sign "AFCR" in front of her and he stood next to her.

"Good evening, are you waiting for us?" I asked when we approached them.

"Could be, we are waiting for the Bielek family," the blonde said . . .

"That's us," I said and shook her hand.

"Welcome to Boston. My name is Nada. I had to come with my friend because I don't have a car now because it is being serviced," Nada said.

"It appears the traveling wore down your kids. My name is Roman," Nada's friend said and extended his hand.

"We have been traveling for more than twenty four hours and the kids are sleepy. My name is Jan," I said when shaking his hand.

Nada and Roman helped us by pushing the cart with our suitcases and bags to their car in the parking lot. Nora pulled the semi-sleeping Peter and I carried Katarina. The car toward which we were walking was not exactly built for transporting four adults, two kids and additional luggage. When the trunk of the car filled up, we could not do anything else, but lay the bags and two suitcases under our feet in the car. Somehow we managed it and Roman drove. Nada let him know which way to drive and then she turned to Nora and me and said:

"We found you an apartment in a small family house in Chelsea. You will have two bedrooms, hall, kitchen and bathroom. Above yours there is another smaller apartment, which is so far vacant. We also reserved it for a father with his son, who should come next week."

"Thank you," I said; the car stopped at a small street. We did not see too much because it was already dark. Nada opened a door into the house and then a door into an apartment on the ground floor and we all went inside. I put Katarina on a couch, which was in the room right next to the entrance door. She was surprised by our new apartment and immediately woke up.

"Where do we have a bathroom?" Katarina asked, sat up and slid down from the couch.

"Come and look," Nada said and escorted Katarina to the bathroom. We followed them and then we made a complete examination of our new apartment. Everything was remodeled, painted, newly carpeted and even the ceiling was new. In the bedrooms there was no furniture, only mattresses laid on the floor; everyone had just one blanket and a pillow. The kitchen was very small; even the, kitchen table would not fit there, so it was in the next room, along with four chairs and a couch. This room was between the two bedrooms, Nora and I had a front side bedroom with windows to the street. The children had their bedroom on the other side, with windows in their bedroom to the back yard. That was the entire apartment, small and cozy.

"How do you like it here?" Nada asked.

"It is very nice. Much better than one room without a bathroom in a refugee camp," I said.

"You are a bit different than other people, whom I've met here till now," Nada said pensively, but smilingly.

"In which way?," I asked.

"All people before you, when I brought them to any apartment, were dissatisfied and did not like anything," Nada said.

"But we really like it here. Not that it would be called luxurious, but it's nice and cozy here. As I suggested before, much better than in a camp," I said.

"I can see in the faces of all of you that you are happy people. Other people were not as smiley as you," Nada said.

"If I have to say the truth, we expected much less," Nora said.

The others were always angry and swore that they had not gotten any furniture," Roman said, joining our discussion.

"Over time we will buy some furniture. We did not come here to be given everything. For a start this will be enough for us and later we will arrange everything according to our imagination," I said smilingly.

"That's exactly the difference in which you differ from the others," Nada said and also smiled.

"Here are your keys. You have three keys for the front entrance and three for this apartment," Nada said and handed me a bunch of keys.

"We still have to arrange tomorrow's program. I will come here tomorrow morning about 8:30 and take you to the Social Security and Welfare offices, so you can be given support and food stamps. We also bought you some food, so you have something to eat before you get to a store. In the kitchen there are two brown bags with food from the supermarket," Nada said and then she added:

"Rent for this apartment has been paid to the end of March. Beginning in April, you have to start paying, "but do not be afraid; you will be getting some money from Welfare."

"Thank you for helping us and for the food purchase, as well as everything else," I said.

"Have a good night; tomorrow I will be here again. See you tomorrow," Nada said.

"Once more thank you and see you tomorrow," Nora and I said. Nada and Roman left and we were just by ourselves. We were tired; therefore, we did not unpack our luggage. We prepared our beds, which were actually four mattresses laid on a carpet and we went to bed. We fell asleep very quickly.

I awoke when I felt that I had had enough sleep and I didn't want to sleep anymore, but it was still entirely dark outside, so I looked at my watch. It was four o'clock in the morning.

"You can't sleep either?" Nora asked quietly, when she saw me looking at my watch.

"Perhaps our bodies are still on European time. Over there it is right now already ten o'clock in the morning," I said.

"I am going to take a look in at the children," Nora said and tiptoed into the kid's bedroom.

"Good morning," I heard Nora say aloud.

"Those two might also be up," I thought and went there.

"I am hungry," Peter said.

"Me too, Katarina said.

"I will make you breakfast," Nora said and went into the kitchen.

"We already have our own bathroom," Katarina said with a big smile and jumped out of her bed.

After breakfast we viewed our new apartment a bit more carefully. The house was about a hundred years old and it was quite obvious it had only recently been remodeled and they made two little separate apartments from a small family house. From outside it was painted brown, the door frames and windows were yellow. It looked like only recently the house had a new owner and he had bought it as an investment.

The bathroom was brand new, including bathtub, sink, shower and toilet. However, everything was covered with a thin layer of dust, as if handymen who made the bathroom left only yesterday. The kitchen looked likewise; therefore, Nora started cleaning. Fortunately, we had a small bottle of detergent, which we brought along from Austria. In both bedrooms we had new wall-to-wall carpets and even though they had covered the entire floor, according to Nora they needed to be vacuumed. However, we did not have a vacuum cleaner.

"When you go to the offices with Nada, ask her where the closest stores are around here. We should buy some appliances, in order to clean this place a little," Nora said.

"Do you mean a vacuum cleaner?" I asked.

"Yes, a vacuum cleaner, but we will also need some others, like a toaster, coffeemaker, hair dryer and iron. But I will also need other things, such as a bucket for water and a mop, so I can wash the floors," said Nora.

"All right; when I return, we can make a list and we will go shopping," I said.

Nada came at 8:30. and this time she arrived with her car. First we went into the Social Security Office, where I filled out applications for Social Security numbers for the four of us. The office was in Chelsea, just a couple of streets from the house we lived in. It was on the back side of a business complex, in which were stores like Market Basket, Osco Drug, Radio Shack, Stuarts and others. Their names did not mean anything to me and I asked Nada where we could buy some appliances and groceries.

"Stuarts has miscellaneous articles, like clothing, household items and appliances. Market Basket is a sizable grocery market. But they also have other household needs," Nada said.

"It is good because this complex is relatively close to where we live now," I said.

"Yes, on foot you will get here in about ten minutes," Nada said.

In the Social Security Office there were only a few people; filling out the forms did not take me long and in about an hour the applications for our numbers were handed in.

"Your Social Security cards will be mailed to your home address in about two weeks. If you do not get them in three weeks, come back here," said the clerk at the counter, as she checked our applications and filed them.

"Yes, thank you," I said and Nada and I went outside.

"Right now we are going to the Welfare Office, where you will get support in dollars as well as stamps for food, which are called Food Stamps. Besides that you can also get assistance with heating your apartment," Nada said.

"I have already heard about Welfare support and Food Stamps, but not about heat assistance," I said.

"Yes, that's a new program right now. It usually works like this: They give you a phone number which you call when you need heating oil. The oil company fills your tank and sends the bill to the Welfare Office. In case someone has gas or electric heat, he has to send the heating bill to the Welfare Office and they will pay it. In any case the expenses are paid by them," Nada said.

"It is very well organized. People who have no money for heat don't have to freeze to death," I said.

The Welfare Office was also very close. By car we got there in about five minutes and I estimated that on foot it would take another ten minutes to get there. I watched the road there very carefully and tried my best to remember how to get there, if I needed to next time. It was a pretty sunny day and I had no problem with orientation.

Inside the Welfare Office, there were a lot of people and right after walking inside I knew we would be there for a long time. Nada tore off a numerical ticket from a dispenser on the wall right by the entrance and she advised me to remember to always take a ticket, if I ever needed to go back there by myself next time. The waiting and processing took about two hours.

"This is a check and stamps for this month. Because you came at the end of the month, right now you don't get the full amount. Beginning in March you will get the full amount for both assistances mailed to your home," said the clerk at the counter and then she added:

"Here is a phone number which you will call when you are going to need oil for heat. Monday morning you come back here for ten o'clock and register at the Department of Work Assistance. I have already signed you up in their schedule for Monday."

"Yes, thank you," I said and Nada and I went outside.

"I would like to ask you for one more thing. Where does one go when he needs to hook up a phone line?" I asked Nada after we came back to her car.

"Someone has to call the phone company, so they will hook you up with a phone line," Nada said.

"Would you be so kind and call them, please?" I asked.

"All right, I will call them. I think Chelsea is covered by New England Telephone. What kind of service would you like?"

"Something not very expensive . . . More or less, just to have a phone, when I am looking for a job," I said.

"All right; I will call there today and in a few days your line should be connected. Just one thing in connection with the phone line . . . You can buy a phone from New England, but if you don't want to pay a lot of money, you should buy your own telephone," Nada said.

"Where can I buy a phone?" I asked.

"Radio Shack, Stuarts and sometimes you can also get it at a supermarket like Market Basket.

"Look at it in several places and then purchase it according to the best price," said Nada.

"Thank you, I said.

"It was about 12:30 after lunch when Nada drove me back home. I held in my hands a check for a few dollars, food stamps and a business card with a phone number for heating oil. On the way home she told me that we now had everything we needed for our beginnings in the USA. However, in case we needed anything, I should give her a call and she gave me her AFCR business card for that purpose.

"I am really thankful, and thank you for the entire family that you have been so providing at our beginnings here. Now we already have a place to live, we have enough food to eat and we are not going to freeze to death either," I said smilingly.

"Do not forget that your children must attend school, because school attendance is mandatory here until sixteen years of age," Nada reminded.

"Of course . . . Today is Friday; perhaps it is too late now. But right away on Monday morning we will go to school with them," I said.

"A short distance from where you live, is a school which is named Williams School. All grades are there, from the first grade to the twelfth grade of high school, so both your kids may go there," Nada said.

Nada just turned her car from Broadway to a side street and stopped. She pointed over one street and said:

"There is the Williams School."

I could clearly see a big brick building from the car and on top of it was a sign: "Williams School."

"Do you know how to get there?" Nada asked.

"Of course, without problems . . . I have a good sense of orientation," I said and then added.

"Right now I remembered I must buy something. I would be grateful if you could drive me to the shopping centre where the Market Basket s."

"What do you need," Nada asked.

"Flowers. Today is the tenth anniversary of our wedding," I said.

"Really? That is unbelievable. Yesterday you came into the USA and today you have your tenth wedding anniversary?" Nada exclaimed surprised.

"Yes, we got married February 22, 1975. Today it has been ten years," I said.

"Congratulations. It is very kind of you that you did not forget despite all the preoccupation after your arrival in the USA. I must drive you back home and congratulate your wife," Nada said and stopped her car outside the Market Basket. We went into the supermarket together and she helped me find a bouquet of roses. I had never seen the inside of that store before and I did not have the slightest idea where to look for flowers. I paid for the flowers at the register and we went to my apartment. When we got out of the car in front of the house, I went first and Nada followed me. I opened the door, handed Nora the bouquet of roses and said:

"Best wishes."

"Thank you . . . you did not forget even today," Nora said with tears in her eyes.

"No, I did not . . . just like all those years before," I said and hugged her.

"Let me also congratulate you and for many more years to come," Nada said and then she hugged Nora and then me.

"I have to admit that he did not forget all those years, not a single time," Nora said.

"That's really lovely. This year you would forgive even if he forgot, wouldn't you?" Nada asked.

"Yes. But I am glad he did not forget today either," Nora said smilingly.

Nada said good-bye to us and left. Nora unwrapped the bouquet from its paper and inquired:

"Where will I put it now? We have no vase."

"We don't have a pile of other things . . . Let's go to the kitchen; maybe we can find some sort of jar from bottled fruit or pickles," I said.

After a few moments of opening cabinets in the kitchen and searching, we found an empty pickle jar. We dipped it in warm water in order to remove the sticker and then filled it with cold water. Nora inserted the bouquet in it and placed it in the middle of the table; the only table that we had.

"For lunch I made sandwiches with the food which the AFCR had bought for us. Now we can eat," said Nora and next to the bouquet of flowers she laid a plate with sandwiches.

After lunch we took the list of appliances and household items, which Nora had made and we went out to Stuart's. I took the money—dollars in cash, which we saved in Austria and walked in the direction of the shopping plaza I had gone by with Nada, as best I could remember. Judging by the position of the house where we lived and where the shopping centre was, I guessed that there must have also been a shorter way, but I did not want to chance a short cut on the first try. We arrived at the plaza in about twelve minutes, even though it was not the shortest way. The first item on the list was a vacuum cleaner, then a coffeemaker, hair dryer, toaster and iron. I added a phone to the list. Besides that there was a bucket, detergents for cleaning, rags, sponges and laundry detergent. Everything we had on the list we purchased at Stuarts and went back home, again not through the short cut. At the time we did not know that people like us, without a car, routinely took a shopping cart home. We came out of the store and everything in the cart we divided among us, depending on how much each of us could carry. I got most of it—all the heavy things and Nora took quite a bit also. Peter got one shopping bag and Katarina, the lightest of all, had only an iron. We went back home by the "long" twelve-minute route; with every step the bags got heavier and heavier, but I thought that somehow I could carry my part of the shopping all the way home. After about five minutes Katarina handed me her bag with the iron and said:

"It is too heavy for me. I have no power left to carry it any further."

"All right; give it to me then," I said, took her bag and attached it to all the others, which I was carrying. The iron was really light and it felt like nothing was added to my total load. I started laughing and looked at Nora. She looked once at Katarina and once at me and at the same time she laughed. In a couple of minutes, we were back at the house with our shopping and we noticed a shopping cart from Market Basket in the street close by.

"When we go shopping for groceries, we should take the shopping cart all the way home like these people. Lugging all the shopping bags in our hands has no logic," Nora said.

"When we go shopping for groceries, we will not walk around, but will go by a short cut. And we will go with the cart, so we do not stretch our arms out," I said.

"Do you know any short cut?" Peter inquired.

"Not yet, but I guess if we go up that street, we should come straight to the shopping centre," I said and pointed to a street in front of us.

"We will drop these shopping bags at home and immediately after we can go shopping for groceries," Nora said.

I opened the door to our apartment and we laid down all the bags on the floor immediately at the door in the hallway. We were all happy this was all over and we could put the bags down.

"Let's go to the supermarket for groceries," I said.

"Wait a minute; let me take my list from the table that I wrote this morning," Nora said and then she added:

"Tomorrow is Saturday; it is necessary to purchase groceries for the weekend as well. The groceries which AFCR gave us are almost gone already."

"If we take the cart all the way home, we can buy groceries for the entire week," I said.

This time we went grocery shopping by way of the short cut I had shown Peter earlier. It was really much closer that way. It took us only seven minutes and the street led straight to the shopping centre. We bought all the groceries on the list and we had almost a full shopping cart. We had so much of it we would never have been able to carry all of it in our hands. We pushed the shopping cart all the way to the house, and after we carried everything inside, I said to Peter:

"Come along with me; we will push the cart back to the parking lot in front of Market Basket."

"But why? You can leave it in the street, just like those people there," Nora said and she pointed at a cart, which stood about two houses away.

"Perhaps you're right, but I'd rather push it back to the parking lot. If we leave it here in front of the house, it may stand there the entire week. Peter and I will get a little walk and in the meanwhile you and Katarina can sort out the stuff we bought," I said

"Almost in front of every house there is a car parked, and where there isn't a car, there is a shopping cart," said Peter, when went with the cart up the street. I looked back at our street and I was very surprised by Peter's talent of observation.

"You are right. People who don't have cars walk with the shopping cart all the way home," I said.

"And we are not going to purchase a car?" Peter inquired curiously.

"I think so, that's why I saved money in Austria," I said.

"Are we going to buy a new car?" Peter inquired.

"No, we do not have enough for a new one. Money we have will be enough for only a used one. It doesn't have to be beautiful and shiny, it can also be a bit rusty. The most important thing is, it must be drivable," I said.

"When are we going to buy it?," Peter inquired.

"I don't know what you need to buy a car here, and I also do not have an idea how much it will cost us to get an insurance policy. We will also need driver's licenses. I want to talk to someone who has been here longer and can give me some advice," I said and then added:

"I will not be able to find work if we don't have a car. A car is very important for finding a job and to start earning money. The probability of finding a job so close that I could walk there, is minimal."

"You and mom have already got your driver's licenses," said Peter.

"Yes, we do, but those are from Czechoslovakia. I have to find out how we can get American driver's licenses," I said.

Busy with our discussion about buying a car, we did not notice we were almost back at the Market Basket. We crossed the street to the other side, left the cart in the parking lot in front of the store and went back home.

"Monday we will go to school with you," I said.

"Katarina and I don't know any English," Peter said.

"I know, but you will both learn it. School is the best place for learning," I said and then I added:

"I understand it will be very difficult for you until you learn a bit of English. Just remember, the better you handle it, the better it is going to be for your life."

Peter did not say anything, but just silently walked next to me. I did not know whether he was thinking about what I had just said, or he was just spiritually preparing for school. For a little while we walked this way until we came up to our street. From a distance we saw Katarina who watched us from the window.

"We are going to buy a car," Peter said to Katarina when we walked up to the house and then he ran up the stairs.

"We are going to buy a car," Peter repeated to Nora when he found her in the kitchen.

The two of you should open the boxes with the appliances and assemble the vacuum cleaner, so I can vacuum the carpets," Nora said and completely ignored the notion about a car.

"Peter, please try to assemble the vacuum cleaner for mom," I said.

Peter jumped up from joy and opened the vacuum cleaner box. He took out the directions and, following the pictures, he put it together in a moment. He plugged in the cord, stood up the vacuum and turned the switch on its handle. A screechy noise echoed in the hallway, the dust bag blew up and the room filled with the typical aroma of a new vacuum cleaner.

Saturday morning we had just finished eating breakfast when we heard someone knocking on the outside door. I walked out from the apartment and I saw Nada through a little window on the door. I opened the door:

"Good morning. How are you doing?" she asked and, as she walked in, she handed me a small card.

"Good morning. Thank you. So far everything is fine," I said and looked at the card.

"Your new phone number is written on that card and your line should be all set by now. If you bought a phone, you can start calling," Nada said.

"Yes, we bought it yesterday, but we have not plugged it in yet," I said.

I plugged the phone into the phone jack we had in our bedroom and picked up the phone. I heard the dial tone.

"We've got a phone," I called out with happiness.

"Excellent," Nada called out and then she continued:

"On the card I gave you, there are a few names and phone numbers. Those are people from Czechoslovakia who have been here for some time and they will certainly help you with questions and information for your start up here and maybe you will find some friends among them. If you agree, we can also add your name and phone number to the list and new immigrants will contact you in the future," Nada said.

"Yes, thank you. You can add our name to the list," I said.

"I've got to go. Good luck and see you later," Nada said, shook Nora's and my hand and left. I waved to her from the door when she was getting in the car and locked the door.

We were sitting at the table and eating lunch when the phone rang. I went into the bedroom, picked up the phone and said:

"Hello"

"Good afternoon, this is the technical service department of New England Telephone and we are just checking out your phone line. Are you satisfied with the line?" a female voice asked in English.

"Good afternoon. We have not made any calls yet, but I can hear you all right. So I guess everything is OK," I said.

"Thank you; if you need anything just dial zero," the female voice said.

"I thank you too," I said and hung up.

I went back to the table and I had not even sat down, when the phone rang again.

"New England is checking on it again . . ." I said to myself and went to the bedroom. I picked up the phone and said:

"Hello."

"Good afternoon. AFCR gave me your name and phone number," said a male voice in Czech.

"Good afternoon," I said in Slovak

"I am going along with a Czech friend to Chelsea. If you give me your address we can stop by your place in about an hour. My name is Jaro."

I looked at the card given to me by Nada and found Jaro's name and phone number there.

I told him our address and he said:

"We will see you at four."

"Yes, it is going to be my pleasure," I said and hung up.

"Who was that?" Nora asked when I sat down at the table to finish lunch.

"Someone who's name is Jaro and he was contacted by AFCR," I said.

"Is he coming here to see us?" Nora asked.

"Yes, about four o'clock . . . along with another friend," I said.

Shortly after four o'clock, a grayish van stopped in front of our house and two tall men got out of it. They looked to be just a few years older than us. When I opened the door, the first one shook my hand and said:

"My name is Jaro and call me Jaro."

"My name is Jan and I am for first names as well. It is much simpler" I said and shook Jaro's hand.

"My name is Thomas and call me Tom," said Jaro's friend and shook my hand.

"My name is Jan and call me Jano," I said.

Then both of them met Nora and the kids. They both were really tall, almost a head taller then me.

"Welcome in our house," Nora said and then she asked:

"Coffee anyone . . . ?"

"Yes," they both said at the same time and Nora went to the kitchen and turned on the coffeemaker, which we had bought only the day before. In a moment the nice smell of fresh coffee filled the whole apartment. Jaro and Tom sat on the couch and we sat at the table. Both of them were very friendly and it was a very pleasant discussion. My questions were mostly focused around the car, mostly how to buy one, driver's licenses, insurance and registration. Nora looked very grouchy and she said:

"A car is not the most important item we need right now."

Jaro and Tom looked at her very surprised and Jaro said:

"Indeed, a car is the most important item you need here in the USA. Without a car you will not be able to find any work and shopping is almost impossible, because public transportation is very thinly covered. You cannot even get to some places without a car.

Now Nora looked very surprised at the two of them, but did not say anything.

"Distances from place to place are in the USA much longer as the ones we were used to in Czechoslovakia. Very often it is impossible to walk because walkways are not everywhere, like they were in Prague or Bratislava. Quite simply, you must have a car," Tom said.

"If you had a car, Jano could help me with my work of painting houses and he would make a few dollars. At the beginning, every extra dollar into a budget is welcomed," Jaro said.

It appeared that this time Nora understood how important a car in the USA was. Until now I was the only one talking to her about it and she considered it only as a useless luxury, for which we did not have any money now. At this moment people who lived a few years in America told her from their own experience how important having a car was. She listened to the discussion with interest and she did not look grouchy anymore. We learned the price brackets for cars, where we could buy one, how much was needed for insurance and so on. When we let Jaro know how much money we could spend for a car, he said:

"For that money you can buy only a used car, no luxury . . . but it will serve you for a year or two and during that time you save money for a better one . . . Next week I will take a look at a dealer who sells those kinds of cars. Those dealers are called "Behind a fence." If he has something in your price category, I will pick you up and then you can choose . . ."

"That would be fantastic . . . thank you," I said and was really glad the problem of the "car" was solved in our family.

When we talked about driver's licenses, Tom said:

"I know a guy from our country, who came here in 1968 and he could help you with driver's licenses. He has a license as a notary public and he could type you a translation of your license into English and then put his signature and notary stamp on it. You just take the translation into the Registry of Motor Vehicles and they will give you Massachusetts licenses based on the translation," and he handed me his business card.

"That would be the second fantasy . . ." I stated with a lot of joy and then added:

"With your help we can really speed things up here quite quickly . . ."

"We will gladly help you, with whatever we can . . . I know you just came here a few days ago and you need a lot of things," Tom said and then he asked:

"Right now what would be the most important item you would desperately need?"

"A washing machine . . . we have a hookup installed in the kitchen. Nora is washing everything by hand and they are in bad shape," I said without thinking.

Jaro and Tom looked at each other and for a moment it was really quiet.

"I just said that because the washing machine will be the first item we have to buy. Washing everything by hand is simply unthinkable," I said into the silence.

"Wait a minute," said Thomas and then he added:

"I've got an old washing machine in the garage. When I go back home, I will test it and if it still works, Jaro and I can bring it here in his van at the beginning of next week."

"I think it still works because the kids played with it last week. They kept turning it on and off and they had fun with it," Jaro said.

"I hope they did not break it," Thomas said disappointed.

"If it still works, we will bring it here Monday evening," Jaro said.

"Thank you . . . I am not going to wash everything by hand anymore," Nora called joyfully.

Jaro and Thomas also told us a lot of other information that was very important to us, such as where the nearest Registry of Motor Vehicles was, how we could get there, how much we were going to pay for a car insurance policy and that according to the law it was mandatory in Massachusetts to have insurance, and about the vehicle inspection sticker, which had to be stuck on the front windshield and how we could get it. We did not have the slightest apprehension about all these matters and if we had to figure them out without their help, it could take us a very long time. We had a very good time and we were extremely happy the AFCR had sent those two guys to our apartment, and when they were leaving, we walked them all the way to the van.

Monday morning we went to school with the children. We took along their baptism certificates we had received in Austria because those were the only legal documents of their birth which we had. Their real birth certificates were left behind in the apartment in Bratislava together with all the other documents and at that time we did not know whether we would ever get to them. We went to Williams School and walked into the office of the school principal:

"Good morning, my name is Bielek and I'd like to sign up our children to your school."

"Good morning, my name is Smith," said the school principal; he shook my hand and then said: "I need your address and birth certificate of the children."

I told him our address and handed him the certificates of baptism from Austria. He glimpsed at the documents written in German and gave me a startled look.

"Last Thursday we came to the USA; we are from Czechoslovakia and the children don't know any English," I said and handed him their "green cards."

"I am here as their father and at the same time as their interpreter," I said.

"Do not worry; they will master English without any problems," the principal said.

"I know, very soon they will know it better than I," I said with a smile.

He looked at them and then he turned to Peter:

"You must be Peter" and shook his hand.

"And you must be Katarina," he said to Katarina and also shook her hand.

"This is Nora, my wife and their mother," I said and introduced Nora.

"I am glad to meet you," the principal said and I translated the sentence into Slovak for her.

"How do you do," Nora said in English, which she remembered from English courses in Bad Kreuzen.

"The children will be placed in grades according to their age; accordingly, Peter will be in the fourth grade and Katarina in the first," the principal said and he asked us to follow him. First he led us to the first grade, where we handed Katarina over to her teacher. The principal told her that we had only recently come to the USA and Katarina belonged in her classroom. She offered Katarina her hand and very slowly said in English:

"Good morning. My name is Ms. Ferranti."

"Good morning. My name is Katarina Bielek," Katarina said in English.

We will be good friends because Katarina is a quick learner," Ms. Ferranti said.

"See you later," said Ms. Ferranti to us and took Katarina to her classroom.

The principal then led us to the fourth grade and again told that teacher we had just recently come to the USA and Peter belonged in her classroom.

"Good morning. My name is Ms. Brown," the teacher said to Peter slowly and shook his hand.

"Good morning. My name is Peter Bielek," Peter said in English, when shaking her hand.

Ms. Brown said good bye to us and the principal led us back to his office.

"Come with me to my office; we have to sign your kids into the bus schedule," he said on our way there.

"I don't think it will be necessary. We live really close by and Nora can walk them to school and after she will bring them back home," I said.

"So, then I just need you to sign the kids admission paperwork and everything will be taken care of," the principal said. We went to his office and signed the paperwork.

"Thank you," I said to him and shook his hand.

"I thank you too and in case you need anything just let me know," the principal said and said good bye to us.

Nora and I went out of the school, we held hands and slowly walked back home. Nora looked at me with her eyes filled with tears and said:

"I felt so sorry for them when they took them into their classrooms . . . just like that . . . They do not know any English."

I stopped both of us and gently grabbed her by the shoulders. I hugged her and asked very quietly:

"I guess you are not going to cry now?"

"I felt so sorry for them," Nora repeated.

"Indeed, they went to school just to learn that English," I said.

"I know, but it happened so quickly," Nora said.

"And should they have made a small picnic before they led them to their classrooms?" I asked with laughter.

"No, but it was somehow too quick," Nora insisted on her idea.

"Don't cry. You will see everything will be all right," I said, grabbed her hand and we walked on.

I walked Nora back home and then I went to the Welfare office where I had an appointment scheduled at the Work Assistance department. Inside, there were a lot of people again, waiting for assistance. As Nada advised me before, I took the ticket from the dispenser, even though I was not quite sure I was going to need it. On the right side, all the way at the end of the hallway, there was a sign saying "Work Assistance." That part of the hallway was completely vacant. I came up to the window and said:

"Good morning, my name is Jan Bielek and I've got a meeting scheduled here for job assistance."

"Good morning. Could you please spell out your last name?" the receptionist behind the window asked.

I spelled out my name and she wrote it into a note book in front of her and then she said:

"Just a moment please, I will get you someone."

In a few seconds the door next to the window opened wide and a very nice lady appeared in it, shook my hand and said:

"My name is Jackie and from now on you and I will be a team, until we find work for you."

"My name is Jan Bielek and I am glad we've had a chance to meet," I" said.

She very carefully watched my lips and then she asked:

"Which one is your first name?"

"J a n" I said slowly.

She still watched my lips and then she hesitantly repeated after me:

"J a n"

"Yes, Jan," I repeated my first name.

"Call me Jackie," she said.

She opened the door which closed in the meantime with the automatic door closer, showed me inside and said:

"Jan, please come in."

We both walked inside and she led me to her desk and asked me to sit down. She sat down behind her desk and asked me:

"Jan, now tell me briefly about yourself, when you came here, about your family, if you have one, your occupation and what you imagine your future to be."

In a few sentences I told her about our arrival in the country, about Nora and the kids, that I was a chemist and had a master's degree in chemical technology from a university. In the near future I would like to go to school for English and continue working in my career as a chemist.

Jackie looked at me surprised and asked:

"Do you want to teach English?"

"No, I just want to learn it better," I said.

"You do not need any English courses; you know English very well. The only thing you need is work," Jackie said very decisively. Her voice was so persuasive I agreed with her immediately and said:

"All right; then let's go looking for work for a chemist."

"You see, this is the kind of answer I like. We are going to look for a chemist job," Jackie said and then she asked:

Tell me in a little more detail what you did in Czechoslovakia as a chemist."

I told her what I did just recently, what kind of job it was and what sort of position I wanted. Jackie wrote everything into her note book, which lay on her desk in front of her.

"It is definitely a very interesting career. But be aware it will be a problem to find exactly the same position in a short time," Jackie said and then she asked:

"Would you be willing to accept also a different chemist position, even if it is not exactly what you have done before?"

"Yes, I would, as long as the position is at a certain level. I did not come to this country to live on Welfare assistance. I want to work and provide for my family at the level we were used to before," I said.

Jackie winked at me with one eye and said with a big smile:

"The longer I know you the better I like you," and led me into a small room, which was across the hallway. I looked at the equipment there and realized it was a reading room for "microfiche" cards.

"Sit down here and I will bring you an envelope with some microfiches containing lists of job opportunities for chemists. There are a lot of jobs, so take a good look and when you find something applicable write down on this paper the number of the advertisement and the phone number listed in it. When you are done, bring the paper to my office," Jackie said, walked away and shortly after came back with the envelope.

"Do you know how to operate the reader?" she asked as she was handing me the envelope.

"Yes, we had exactly the same model at my university library," I said. I took out the first microfiche from the envelope and laid it down into the reader. I turned on the light and set the reader on the first advertisement record. Jackie watched me for a while and when she saw I did not have any problems with the reader, she said:

"Good luck. Before you leave just stop by my office with your list," and she walked away.

"Thank you, Jackie I will stop by your office," I said.

I stayed alone in the reading room and diligently studied the microfiches. I had a whole bunch of them and at the beginning it looked like I would need the whole day to read through them. After some time I noticed that all the advertisements were not only numbered but they were also coded depending on the type and level of the job available. I figured out a few of the codes for the types of positions I liked and the process of reading them sped up substantially. Instead of reading the complete advertisement I just looked for "my" code numbers. When I did not see "my" code, I jumped over on to the next microfiche without reading it. This way I spent only one and a half hours to go over all the microfiches Jackie had given me. I came to her office and handed her the paper with the advertisement numbers and phone numbers, which I had selected.

"Did you already read all the advertisements?" she asked in disbelief.

I explained to her how I figured out the coding system and codes, and picked the ones which fit my image for a job. She looked at me surprised and said:

"You are really very smart. It is very good because we can find a job for you much faster. Sit down here and I will call the numbers to see if those positions are still available."

I sat opposite her and observed how she made the phone calls. I thought that it would be an unbelievably gigantic miracle, if we were successful in finding something immediately on the first shot. However, I liked the entire system and was quite confident that if we continued this way, with Jackie's help I would have a regular job very soon. At this thought I was flooded with the feeling of happiness from within, and something muttered in my head:

"Shortly I will have a regular job in the USA . . . that's a fantasy!"

While I raved about the thoughts of having a chemist position, Jackie called all my numbers and ultimately she said:

"Unfortunately, all these positions are already reserved. Never mind, come to see me again Wednesday and we will fight on. By then we're going to have a new shipment of microfiche cards."

"Certainly. Wednesday morning I will be here again," I said.

"When you get a phone, give me a call at this number, so I can write your number down," she said and handed me her business card.

"We already have a phone," I said and told her our number. When she wrote it down in my papers, she smiled and at the same time she shook her head. Then she lifted her head, still smiling and shaking her head in disbelief:

"Thursday you came here . . . and Monday you already have a phone . . . ," she said and then she added:

". . . that is unbelievable . . . see you Wednesday at nine."

"See you Wednesday at nine," I said and went home.

Jaro and Thomas came back just like they promised, Monday at about five o'clock in the afternoon. They brought along the washing machine and laid it down in the kitchen, where we had connections for cold and hot water, as well as the plug for electricity. We hooked it up immediately and of course tested it out. We filled the washing machine with water, put in detergent and Nora brought some laundry. We set it on a cycle, turned the washing machine on and as it started spinning and turning, all four of us jumped up and down from the sheer excitement of having a working washing machine. When we stopped jumping, the house still shook. With surprise we looked at each other and then at the washing machine, which was jumping around a bit. Out of curiosity, we lifted the washer lid and noticed that the washing machine worked a little strangely. The drum, instead of turning from side to side, jumped up and down.

"That's a little strange, how this washing machine works," I said.

"This is an old type of washer, but the laundry is washed okay," Thomas said.

"That's actually all we need right now; a washing machine that washes the laundry. We can handle the shaking of the house and after some time we'll get used to it anyway. Thank you," Nora said. When she took out the laundry about twenty minutes later, it was really washed okay.

Perhaps a week later Jaro came to us again. This time he came alone, not with the van, but in a car. When he stepped inside, he declared with pleasure:

"I found a car for you; exactly what you wanted. If you want I can drive you there."

The children were already home from school, so all four of us went with him. On the way there he told us that he knew this dealer of used cars very well and recommended him to other people as well. He also prepared us for the fact that in the price category, which we chose were cars with a few rusty spots on the body, but mechanically were in good condition.

"So far, all the people who have bought a used car there have been satisfied," Jaro said.

"I am assuming that right now we're not going to have a perfect car. We just want something we can drive and will not need a lot of repairs," I said.

After an estimated half an hour, we came to a shop, which was just a flat parking lot with sections overgrown by grass and with some muddy sections. It was surrounded by a high fence, over the fence there was barbed wire and in the middle of the grounds was a little trailer, where the dealer had his office. When he saw us coming, he came out for a moment and shook hands with Jaro.

"We are here to take a look at the Chevrolet I saw yesterday," Jaro said.

"Please, come in," the dealer said and he shook my hand and introduced himself:

"My name is Jerry," he said and then he met Nora and the kids.

"Take a look at all the cars, and in the meantime, I will be in my office. If you need anything, let me know," Jerry said and went back to his trailer. It was quite cold outside and I saw smoke coming out of the chimney of the trailer.

"It must be comfortably warm inside," I thought.

The Chevrolet which Jaro selected for us was about an eight-year-old brown car and there were a few spots on the body where rust was "blossoming" through the brown paint. Jaro noticed that the car did not impress me too much. He lifted the front hood and said:

"The engine looks quite good. It will last at least for another two-three years."

We looked inside the engine and Nora with the kids went inside the car, sat down and scanned the interior of the car. The engine really did not look bad, but I was unable to make a judgment about how many years it would last just from looking at it. I did not say anything, so Jaro suggested:

We can take it out for a ride and you will see I am right."

You know these cars better than I do, but if you don't mind I would like to take a look at some other cars," I said.

"Of course . . . You are buying the car, I am here just as an adviser," Jaro said.

"Nora and I are very grateful to you for helping us this way," I said and then I asked:

"What do you think about that blue car over there? I pointed at a car a short distance from us.

That is an AMC Pacer. Those cars are also good. They were very popular a few years back," Jaro said.

We walked up to the car and Nora with the kids ran up to us. We walked around the car and I liked it.

"Judging by the price written on the windshield it comes out a little more expensive, but it would still fit our budget," I said.

Let's go inside and ask Jerry how much he would want for this Pacer," Jaro said and we both walked into the office. It was really nice and comfortably warm inside.

"How much would that blue Pacer be?" Jaro asked.

"The same price as the Chevrolet," the dealer said and my heart started racing with joy.

"Could we take it out for a ride?" I asked.

"Certainly," Jerry said and took the keys out of a small cabinet behind him and handed them to me. He walked out with us and wiped off the car price from the windshield, which was written in a white water resistant marker. We opened the doors and Nora with the kids again went inside and looked at the interior.

"This car is more expensive than the brown one we looked at before. I don't know if we are going to have enough of money for it," Nora said.

"The dealer said he would sell it to us for the same price as that Chevrolet," I said.

"Let's buy it," Peter called with excitement.

"We have to take a look at it first," I said.

Jaro opened the front hood and we both looked inside at the engine.

"Wait here, I will try to start it up," Jaro said, sat down in the front seat and turned the key. The engine started up with the first attempt.

"That is a good sign," Jaro said with a smile through the open window.

"Yes, so let's go take it for a ride," I said also with a smile.

"I will take Nora and the kids inside, so they are not freezing here till we come back," Jaro said.

"How long will it take you till you come back?" Nora asked.

"About ten minutes," Jaro said and led them to the trailer. By the time he came back I closed the hood and sat inside in the passenger seat.

"You don't want to drive it?" Jaro asked surprised when he came back and did not find me sitting behind the steering wheel.

"No. You drive it now. First, you know this neighborhood better than I do. And also you know cars here much better, so you can make a better assessment," I said.

Jaro sat down behind the wheel, the car came out from the lot and we drove down a few streets. He commented while driving:

"Motor is working very well . . . brakes are all right . . . power steering is working just fine . . . it sits well on the road when taking a turn . . . and look—the windshield wipers are also working . . ."

"Do you think it is a good buy? I asked him.

"I think so," Jaro said.

Maybe ten minutes later we returned to the dealer. Jaro parked the car next to the trailer and we went inside.

"How did you like it?" Jerry asked when we entered.

"Yes, it is a deal . . ." I said.

Jerry opened a filing cabinet, for a moment he looked for something and then he pulled out the Title for the car, laid it in front of him and said:

"Let's do the money transaction first and then I'll write up the Title."

I handed him money in cash and Jerry counted the money and laid it in front of him in piles of a hundred on the desk. He then counted the number of hundreds, made just one pile and grabbed the money and laid it inside a small safe and locked it up. He wrote up the Title and handed it to me along with two sets of keys.

"Thank you for buying the car in my store and I wish you good luck," Jerry said with a big smile.

"I thank you too," I said and we all left the trailer. It was cold outside and it was already getting dark.

"Have you ever driven a car with an automatic transmission?" Jaro asked me.

"No, not yet," I said with a smile.

Jaro went into our car, started up the engine and said:

"You start it up without touching the gas pedal, step on the break and shift it into drive. Leave it in drive until you want to park. You start driving by releasing the brake under your right foot and push down the gas pedal with your right foot. And when you are parking, hold down the brake and this way you switch the gear box to "P"—parking. Your left foot you put all the way to the side, you don't use it while driving," Jaro said.

"And what about at traffic lights . . . ?" I asked.

"Hold down the brake," Jaro said very briefly and my fifteen-second course for automatic transmissions was done.

Jaro turned to Nora and said:

"You and the kids come with me. Jano will certainly be nervous during his first time."

He turned to me and said:

"Follow me, I will bring you all the way to your home."

"Just do not lose me because I don't know which way to go," I said.

"Don't worry, I will be watching you," Jaro said and he, Nora and the kids went into his car.

By the time they got in the car, I had tried the blinkers and practiced shifting into drive the way Jaro had shown me. It took me a little while to locate the switch for the headlights. Everything worked all right and a little nervously I slowly started following Jaro's car. After a few minutes of driving, I got used to the automatic transmission, and the nervousness melted away, because I did not have to watch out for switching gears. It was much simpler than manual transmission, which I was used to for years. During the whole time driving, Peter and Katarina watched me through the rear window in Jaro's car and frequently waved to me. When we stopped in front of our house, I stepped on the brake and switched the transmission to "P" as Jaro had shown me. I had not even turned the engine off when Jaro ran to me, opened the door to the car and said:

"You drove very well."

"Getting used to it is quick and easy," I said and turned off the engine.

"Look, you also have air conditioning here," Jaro said with enthusiasm and added:

"Start up the engine and let's try it," Jaro said.

I started it up again and Jaro pushed up a lever below a sign that said A/C. He turned down the heat, held his hand at the blower vents and said:

"Look it works!"

I held my hand next to Jaro's and he said:

"Do you feel the cold air? It is not cold air from outside, but from the air conditioning. In the summertime you will appreciate the air conditioning in your car because summers here are very hot and humid."

"This is great, even the air conditioning works on this car. We did not know it was there when we bought the car," I said with eagerness.

I turned off the engine, locked the car and we went inside our apartment.

"Jaro, would you like coffee?" Nora asked immediately at the door.

Jaro looked at his watch and then said slowly:

"Yes, I would . . . it is not too late yet . . ."

We sat down at the table and I said:

"Jaro, thank you for helping us. It is hard to find words to say what I have on my mind . . . many times thanks . . .

"Not at all," Jaro said modestly and added.

"Don't forget to register the car at the Registry of Motor Vehicles and buy an insurance policy. Without those two things, you should not drive it."

"Of course, Tomorrow morning I will go find an insurance policy and then to the registry," I said.

"When you are done with it, give me a call. We can make arrangements when you will help me paint houses, which I am working on right now. The first time I will come for you, so you will learn how to get there. But only once, then you have to remember the way there," Jaro said.

"Twice a week I must go to the Job Assistance office, where they are helping me search for work. All the other days I am free for now so I can help you paint," I said.

Immediately the next morning I went looking for an insurance company. I remembered that during my first trip with Nada I saw an insurance company on Broadway in Chelsea. It was just a short distance from us, so I went there on foot. I took the papers for the car, money and perhaps in an hour I was back at home with an insurance policy valid for a half year. On the way

back I bought a detailed map of eastern Massachusetts, which became very helpful during initial difficulties with orientation and for finding places and locations that were all new to us. Jaro and Thomas told us that the Registry of Motor Vehicles office was just a short distance from us in Medford. In the phone book I found the address of the Registry and looked at the new map, which I had just bought, to find where it was and map out how to get there. It was just a short distance—by car. If I went there on foot, it could take me hours. After studying the map for awhile, I memorized the way there and said to Nora:

"Let us go to the Registry now. We can get our driver's licenses there and right after we can register the car."

"Do you know how to get there?" Nora asked.

"I studied how to get there from the map and in case we get lost we can take the map with us," I said.

After about twenty minutes, we came to the office with no problems. I remembered the way there all right and there were no problems with orientation because it was a nice sunny day. There were a few people inside and first we stood in a line in front of the "Driver's Licenses" window. When our turn came, I handed the clerk our driver's licenses from Czechoslovakia along with an English translation signed by the Notary Public, just like Jaro and Thomas had advised us. She looked at each of us and compared us with the photo inside the license. Then she only browsed through the English translation and it appeared to me she had done it before, because she did not

ask for anything and just took our pictures with a Polaroid camera and I paid
the fees. A couple of minutes later, she handed us our new drivers' licenses.
We could not believe it was so simple.

Now we stood in a line in front of a window "New Registrations." This
line was a bit longer and after about twenty minutes we got to the window.
I handed the clerk papers for the car, my new license and the certificate for
the insurance policy. I paid the car sales tax and in a moment we were also
finished with the registration. The clerk handed me a registration plate and
we went outside to the parking lot. I looked at my watch and said:

"It took us less than an hour. We would need two days of vacation for
the same kind of paperwork in Bratislava. One day for license and one day
for registration. Nora also looked at her watch and said:

"We still have plenty of time before the kids come back home from school.
Now we can go grocery shopping and we don't have to push the shopping
cart all the way home.

At the beginning of March, we received the Welfare assistance check,
and together with what they had given us at the start, we had a few hundred
dollars that needed to be cashed. I thought the best way of handling all the
checks would be by opening a checking account in a bank. That would make
cashing our checks much easier and then as I understood it we also had to
start building our credit for the future. On Broadway there were three big
banks, so I went there to try my luck. My luck started by finding a parking
spot right in front of one of them, it was called Bay Bank. I went inside and
stood in the line. When I got to the window the teller smiled at me nicely
and asked:

"How can I help you, sir?"

"I would like to open a checking account," I said.

"Yes, how much money would you like to deposit on the account now?"
she asked.

I handed her two Welfare checks and said:

"That would be all today."

She stared at the checks surprised, and then she stared at me and said:

"I am sorry sir, but with this you cannot open a checking account at our
bank," she said and handed me back the checks.

"But I need a checking account now," I insisted.

"I am sorry sir, but this is not a bank for you. The best you can do now
is try opening a checking account at Broadway National Bank," she said and
her smile was not friendly anymore.

"Broadway National Bank?" I asked confused, because I still could not understand how come a bank teller could send a future customer into a competing bank.

"Yes, Broadway National Bank," the teller at the window repeated. This time completely without a smile and her eyes were saying perhaps this:

"Get lost man and do not bother me anymore."

I took back my checks and went out. When I got back to my car, I turned my head and looked at the blue-green sign: Bay Bank. I incomprehensively shook my head over it and I did not even try my luck at the other big banks, which were just next to it. I felt like I had just wandered into a big supermarket, tried to buy something small and they chased me out and sent me into a small shop at the end of the street.

At Broadway National Bank everything was different, much more professional. When I walked up to a window the teller asked me exactly the same way:

"How can I help you, sir?"

"I would like to open a checking account," I said.

"Yes, sir," she said and opened a door between the windows, came out and added:

"Please follow me, sir" and led me into the bank vice president's office.

"Welcome to our bank, sir" the vice president said, shook my hand and asked me to sit down. He filled out the paperwork and at the end he asked me to sign it. There was no problem with my Welfare checks and the checking account was opened. The vice president handed me a new check book and an Express24 card for cash withdrawals and said:

"Thank you for choosing our bank and I wish you good luck."

"Do you know that I was actually sent here from Bay Bank? I wanted to open the same kind of checking account as here and they told me their bank was not for me and sent me here," I said.

"Did they?" the vice president asked surprised and then he added:

"What they did to you there is against the law. We are just a small bank, but we are glad having you as our customer. We treat every account equally, small one or big one."

"That's the way it should be!" Thank you," I said, I said good bye to him and went home.

Twice a week, Mondays and Wednesdays, I went to see Jackie at the Work Assistance office. I read the microfiche cards, wrote down the advertisement numbers and phone numbers and then Jackie called those places. I sat across the desk from her and watched her calling. After three weeks of our already routine collaboration, luck smiled down on us. It was Wednesday March 20, exactly one month after our arrival in the USA. As she phoned someone, the voice on the other end told her the position was still available because they had placed the advertisement only the previous day. A big smile appeared on her face and she lifted a hand to attract my attention. It was not necessary because I was watching her really sharply and already understood from her conversation that she had found something.

"Here in my office there is sitting the best and the most intelligent chemist I have ever met," Jackie said, over-rating my qualities, and then she continued:

"He is a very nice and hard-working young man. If you give him the job you are advertising here, you will never regret it."

I heard a voice on the other end, but I could not understand what he was saying. Jackie then went on with more praises on my account. When she put down the phone, she stared at me with a big smile and said:

"Tomorrow you are going to a company in Waltham for your first interview. Now tell me how you are going to get there."

"Very easy . . . by car," I said

"Do you have anyone who will drive you there? Jackie asked. "No, I will go there with my car," I said.

"Do you have your own car? You came here just a month ago and you already have your own car?" Jackie asked and at the same time she looked at me in complete disbelief and also amusement. Then she looked at the ceiling, shook her head and repeated:

". . . he has his own car . . . he has his own car . . ."

"Yes, it is a used car, AMC Pacer from 1977," I said.

"Well, anyway . . . ," she stopped mid-sentence. After that, she leaned both elbows on the desk, gave me a stare, and said:

"Let me tell you something. You will never have a problem with looking for a good job here in the USA, a place to live or anything else. You are very conscious of your goals, you follow them very quickly, restlessly and accomplish them fast."

"Thank you Jackie," I said with a smile.

"All right, you are going with your car. How will you find the place?" Jackie asked.

"Using a map, which I bought recently," I said.

"Show me on your map how you are going to drive to Waltham to Bacon Street?" Jackie said.

I opened the briefcase I carried with me and pulled out the map. I looked at the page with the Waltham street listing and following a moment of searching I said:

"Either there is no Bacon Street in Waltham, or this map is wrong."

"Let me see," Jackie said surprised and I turned the street list to her. She ran her finger down the list looking for Bacon and when she could not find it picked up the phone and called the company I was going to for the interview. When she hung up, she said:

"It is not Bacon but Beacon Street.

I looked into the street list again, found Beacon Street and using a pencil I marked which way I would drive from home to the company. I turned the map to her and said:

"This is the way I would be going. When I get to Beacon, I can find the number easily."

"Excellent," Jackie called and then she added:

"You must show up there on time and professionally dressed. White shirt, tie, suit pants and suit jacket."

"I've got a white shirt, a few ties and two three-piece suits, which I used to wear to work in Czechoslovakia. Those are the newest ones and they are both in perfect condition," I said.

"Did you bring two three-piece suits with you?" Jackie asked surprised again and then she added:

"You are just unbelievable!"

"Yes, those two suits I took with me to wear for job interviews in the USA," I said. I lifted the briefcase and asked her:

"Where do you think I got this briefcase from?"

"Did you bring it also with you?" Jackie asked and clasped her hands in excitement.

"You guessed it," I said.

"It looks really professional. Tomorrow take it with you as well," Jackie said.

"I most certainly will," I said.

"So I wish you good luck for tomorrow and when you come back home call me to tell me how you made out," Jackie said.

"Thank you Jackie, for your help and also the good word you said on my behalf when you called," I said. I told her good-bye and went home.

When I arrived at home and told Nora that the next day I was going for a job interview, she shouted with pleasure.

"Wait, I will serve us lunch and as we eat you can tell me everything in detail. I want to know how it happened," Nora said and started serving us lunch. I helped her with the tableware and then as we ate at the table I told her everything that had happened at the Work Assistance office. Nora carefully listened and laughed with me when I portrayed for her our discussion about the car, the suits and the briefcase. When I came to the end she asked:

"Do you think you will get this job?"

"When she spoke about me on the phone, she portrayed me as the best chemist in the world. I think that was the best introduction I could have wished for," I said.

"Right after lunch I will iron your shirt and suit pants so you will look spiffy tomorrow," Nora said enthusiastically.

We went together to school to pick up the kids. We waited outside in front of the school in our usual spot, and when they came to us, Nora said:

"Tomorrow you have to keep your fingers crossed for dad, because he is going for his first job interview."

Peter and Katarina looked at us surprised and Peter shouted:

"Hurrah . . ." and at the same time he jumped up off the ground.

"I will hold both of them for you. Like that," Katarina said and raised both hands to me. The thumb on each hand was covered with four fingers.

"Where are you going?" Peter inquired curiously.

"To Waltham. It's only about fifteen miles from here," I said.

In the evening I looked at the map one more time to remember the way to Beacon Street in Waltham and then inserted it again into my briefcase, just in case I would need it. Nora prepared my shirt, tie and suit, hanging everything up on a hanger outside the closet, so I wouldn't have to look for them in the morning. I polished my shoes and laid them at the door below the hanger with my clothing.

In the morning I left very early because I did not know how much time I would need for driving there. In cases like this, I usually gave myself plenty of time, so that I wouldn't be late. I got to Beacon Street in Waltham too early, without problems. I drove up to the place and pulled into the parking lot in front of the company. I looked at my watch and saw that I still had fifty minutes till my interview. I didn't want to park so early in front of the company, so I drove back one street and parked outside the supermarket at the end of the street. I waited there a long forty minutes and then returned to the company where I had the interview. I looked at my watch again; it was 8:55.

"Perfect," I said to myself and stepped inside.

"Good morning. My name is Jan Bielek. I have an interview with the lab manager at nine," I said to the receptionist.

"Good morning. Yes, I will let him know right away," the receptionist said and picked up the phone. An older gentleman walked in a few minutes later, shook my hand and said:

"Good morning. My name is Mark. Come with me into our laboratory."

"Good morning," I said and followed him.

Mark led me through a chemical laboratory and he stopped for a while at every instrument. I immediately comprehended what he meant by this process and when he showed me an instrument, I started talking about it, what kind of instrument it was, on which principle it worked, what it was used for, and what were the detection limits. He was very impressed by my knowledge because when we came to the end of the laboratory and we sat down in his office, he said:

"You have made a very good impression on me with your knowledge about analytical instruments. Where did you learn all that?"

"I have a master's degree in chemical technology. I still remember a lot from school and one time I was a part-time teacher of analytical chemistry at a Chemical Professional High School. When I wanted to teach the analytical chemistry, I had to relearn everything, I have already forgotten from my schooling," I said. Later we talked about classical analytical methods and I made a good impression on Mark again. I was surprised too, how much I still remembered from the analytical chemistry. Years which I had spent at a Chemical Professional High School as a teacher of analytical chemistry perhaps was not a waste of time.

When we parted about an hour later, Mark said:

I have to talk to the president of our company and I will call you Monday.

"Thank you," I said, gave him our phone number and we said good bye to each other.

When I drove back home, I was in a very good mood and I felt that my first job interview in the USA went very well. The certainty with which the lab manager told me he was going to call me Monday gave me confidence that the position was already mine. I must have had a big smile on my face during that thought, because when I came back home, Nora said:

"When I saw you through the window, parking the car in front of the house, I could see that you made out well. But you have to tell me everything to the last detail. I will have some coffee and make tea for you."

We sat down on the couch. Nora sipped coffee from a mug and I held a cup of tea with both hands. I described to her every single detail, beginning with waiting in front of a supermarket all the way to Mark's promise to call me Monday.

"So, in a week you are going for the second interview," Nora said when I finished my monologue.

"Most likely, but I have to wait until they call me," I said.

"Now you can call Jackie. She will be glad when you tell her how you made out," Nora said.

I finished my tea, which was slowly cooling down because when I was so busy talking to Nora that I completely forgot about it. I dialed the Work Assistance phone number:

"Hi Jackie. This is Jan," I said when she picked up the phone and then I just briefly repeated what I had already told Nora.

"Excellent . . . My congratulations," Jackie said and then she added:

"Monday you are staying home because you are going to wait for the phone call. If they don't call you or you do not get another interview, come to see me Tuesday morning. We will go on with our search. If you are going to the second interview, call me after and let me know how you made out."

"Yes, Jackie. Thank you for your help because I credit you a lot with my success," I said.

This time the weekend went by again very slowly; we could hardly wait for Monday. Nora walked the kids to school and I stayed home because I did not want to miss the phone call. When she came back home, we both impatiently waited for the phone to ring. I picked it up just to check if it was working. I heard the dial tone. Around ten o'clock the phone rang.

"Hello," I said when I picked up.

"Jan?" the voice asked and I recognized it as the laboratory manager.

"Yes, good morning Mark," I said.

"Good morning Jan. I talked to the president of our company about your interview. He suggested that you come here for the second interview Thursday. Would ten o'clock fit your schedule?" Mark asked.

"Yes, of course," I said.

"So, we are all set. We will see you at ten on Thursday. Besides the president whose name is Lou, there will also be our vice president Norm and of course myself.

"Yes, thank you. Thursday at ten o'clock . . . ," I said

"Good bye," Mark added and hung up.

Nora watched my phone call with Mark with a lot of tension. She already understood some English and apprehended what we had talked about. When I put the phone down, she grabbed my hands and she started dancing with me in our empty bedroom.

". . . Thursday you are going for the second interview . . . . Thursday you are going for the second interview . . . ," she yelled and at the same time we were dancing in a circle. When our heads started spinning, we stopped and hugged.

Thursday I went to the company shortly before ten. The receptionist showed me a conference room and asked me whether I would like some coffee.

"I would prefer tea. Black without sugar . . . Thank you," I said.

Exactly at ten all three of them came into the conference room. When I was introduced to Lou and Norm, the receptionist brought a tray with two coffees and two teas. They all sat down at the table across from me and took their drinks. When I took my black tea, Mark said:

"I can see the right chemists drink tea."

We all laughed at his remark because Mark also had a cup of tea. I briefly repeated what I had already told Mark. When I was done, Lou said:

"Mark told me about your first interview and he put a lot of weight on the fact that he was really surprised with your knowledge. He suggested that I give you an offer," and he handed me a card, which was folded in the middle.

I opened the card and saw my annual pay written inside.

"This is our offer and you don't have to give us your answer immediately. We will wait for your answer till Monday," Lou said.

"I believe there is nothing to think about. As you may know I have been looking for my first job in the USA. I like this company and the people I have met so far are very sympathetic and the work in the lab is exactly what I am looking for. I am accepting your offer," I said.

"Excellent. I really like your approach, the way you think and the way you make decisions. I welcome you to our company. You can start Monday April the first; the work hours are from eight until four," Lou said and then he added:

"Here in the USA we are all on a first-name basis. Call me Lou" and he shook my hand. Norm, who until now had not said anything, just smoked his pipe and exhaled smoke, also shook my hand and said:

"Norm."

"Mark," said my future boss, shook my hand and added:

"I am really glad you accepted our offer and you will be working with us. It appears to me that we will understand each other very well.

When Mark and I were going downstairs, Lou asked me:

"How long have you been here in the USA?

"Five weeks. I came here with my family February 21," I said.

"I can see you are one of the successful ones who knows what he wants. Allow me to tell you something. You are going to be successful at your job; in a short time you will have a big salary and also your own house because you've got all three basic features: you are young, highly educated and appropriately aggressive."

"Thank you, Lou. I can see you have read me very quickly. We did not know each other just two hours ago," I said.

"Anyone, who talks to you for ten minutes must notice it; otherwise, he doesn't have any observational skills," Lou said.

Mark and I went down to the lab and he suggested to me:

"Monday you don't have to wear a suit or a tie. Look at me. I have jeans and a flannel shirt. We will give you a lab coat Monday.

"Mark, a phone call on line two," we heard the receptionist say through the paging system.

"I have to go back to work . . . see you Monday," Mark said and shook my hand.

"See you Monday," I said quickly and Mark ran to the phone.

When I drove away, I could not wait until I got back home and could tell Nora and the children the good news. I was extremely happy that, shortly after our arrival, I was able to obtain a full-time job at the level I wanted and with good pay.

I looked retrospectively back . . . it was only a year and tem months since I had said to myself I was fed up with Communist scheming with Prazec in the lead . . . exactly a year ago I was still waiting, with my head leaning down, for signatures from ROH and the Communist Party . . . it was less then nine months since we had crossed the border at Znojmo with a resolution of never returning . . . it was only thirty five days since we had come to the USA.

"We are going to be on welfare assistance for only thirty-eight days," I thought.

I just had just come up to a big intersection in the town of Medford, and on the left side, there was a huge liquor store called Kappy's.

"Today Nora and I should celebrate and clink our glasses "For our victory" as we used to do it in Bratislava," I thought and drove into the left lane for a left turn. I went into the Kappy's store and looked for red wine. It wasn't so simple because the type we were used to was unavailable there. Beside that they had so many different types I could hardly make a decision. Finally I made a choice and bought a bottle of red wine.

When I drove up to our house, Nora again looked out the window. Judging by my face, she recognized everything had come out fine, and by the time I parked the car and came out, she already stood outside on the stairs. I ran upstairs, hugged her and said:

"Monday I am going to work."

"Excellent . . . congratulations . . . ," Nora called and then she asked:

"What is in the brown bag you're holding in your hand?"

"Red wine, so we can clink glasses 'To our victory' tonight," I said.

During lunch, I told her in detail about the second interview with Lou, Norm and Mark. After lunch I called Jackie.

"Congratulations," Jackie said.

"Thank you again for your help. You told Mark I was the best chemist in the world and now they all think that way," I said with laughter.

"Don't tell them otherwise and let them believe it. Good luck," Jackie said and hung up.

"Do you think we will get the welfare assistance for April? Nora asked when I concluded my phone call with Jackie.

"I doubt it. Jackie works at the welfare office and, most likely, they stop our benefits immediately," I said.

"We will need it because you won't get your first check for a week and we will not have any money," Nora said.

"Two weeks later . . . but we have to pull through somehow. I know we will need it . . . . It is to our disadvantage that I am going to start working the first day of the month. If I started a week later, we would have received financial assistance and also food stamps," I said.

They did stop our assistance immediately and we never got a cent from welfare again. Most likely, no one at the office was concerned what we were going to eat for two weeks till I got my first paycheck because we did not get food stamps either.

When we needed heating oil in the middle of April, I did not use the card given to me by welfare. I supposed there would be problems with paying our bill, so I bought heating oil from the first paycheck as well.

"I just cannot imagine how we are going to catch up with heating bills during the next winter. Indeed we are going to burn off your entire income here," Nora said.

"Who said we are going to live here during the next winter, or that I will be the only one bringing home money?" I asked.

Nora did not say anything but just looked at me like I had just fallen off the Moon. Moving, or that she would go to work, when she knew only a little English, were simply things she had not considered yet. We knew our heating system was very ineffective. Someone stuck a new oil burner into an old hundred-year-old boiler, which was originally built for coal. The hot air from the boiler was conducted into the apartment through ductwork and gravity, without a fan. It was a very cheap approach for someone who owned the house, but definitely not for someone else who was paying for the heating oil.

When I got the second paycheck by the end of April, our financial situation improved drastically. Even though the first half of April we lived on a very tight budget, by the end of April, we started systematically planning what kind of apartment furnishings we would buy. We needed furniture, most of all beds, because we were still sleeping on mattresses laid on the floor.

It was no secret at my company that we had just recently come into the USA and all the people tried their best to help us. The receptionist, Barbara, brought me two complete used beds and a few cabinets. Mark gave me a couple of chests and a reclining chair. We gave the beds to the children, so they had their mattresses on frames, not on the floor. Nora and I agreed that we could sleep on the floor a month longer and bought a new color TV set instead. We were convinced it was needed for all of us in order to learn English. We paid half in cash and the other half we charged on a Master Card, which we received from Broadway National Bank. We wanted to start building up our credit and also we did not have enough money to pay for the TV in cash. We paid off the Master Card immediately after receiving the monthly statement and we did not pay any interest. About a week after we paid off the bill, I called the bank and asked for an increased maximum credit, which was just three hundred dollars. The bank approved my request and we built a two-thousand-dollar credit limit within one month. We put the TV set on a chest which was given to us by Mark.

From the middle of April, Nora started English courses, which she heard about through Peter and Katarina from their school. They were called "English as a Second Language" and courses were held in Chelsea close to our house and she went back and forth on foot. They lasted from nine in the morning until twelve noon. At the time we had only the one car I used to drive to work and I left the house about seven in the morning every day.

In May we wanted to buy some furniture for our bedroom, but destiny decided otherwise. The washing machine, which Thomas had given us, broke. It lasted for two months, and in that time, it washed really well. Most likely, the motor burned out because when we turned it on, it did not move at all. It still filled with water, but the drum did not jump up and down and did not shake the entire house. At the end of the cycle, the water also did not get pumped out. We had no choice but to buy a new washing machine. We bought furniture for our bedroom in June.

With the end of June also came the end of the school year, and the report cards the children brought home were very good. When we considered that both of them had started the school year in Bad Kreuzen, Austria in German and finished at Williams School in Chelsea in English, we felt that their report cards were outstanding. As their parents we were very proud of them, because it was quite evident that they both realized that the more they learned at school, the better off they would be in their life. It was the sentence which they heard from me many times over and at which they surely rolled their eyes on each occasion.

In July, Nora decided that she had had enough of the English courses. Not because she already mastered English perfectly, but because all the others in her course were only beginners, who were just learning how to pronounce "sh," "j" or "g." She already knew how to pronounce those speech sounds. At the same time she decided that she would rather go to work because two incomes per family are better than just one.

"Do you have any perception about what you would like to do or where you would like to work," I asked.

"In a nursing home," Nora said with conviction.

"But that means you are going to start as a nursing assistant. That's quite hard work," I said.

"I know that, but eventually, I will learn better English and gradually I will work up to a higher position," Nora said.

"It would be better if you went to school and graduated from a school of nursing and be a nurse. You would have a higher salary and also a better position," I said.

"No, I do not want to go to school because I have had enough of going to school. I want to go to work," Nora said.

"Since you were a little girl you have wanted to be a nurse, and if your parents had not been against it, you could be one right now," I said.

"You're right, but I want to go to work." Nora insisted on her idea.

So, we started looking in the newspapers for openings for nursing assistants. It did not take too long and Monday August the fifth we went to her first interview to a nursing home in Wellesley. I took a day of vacation because we had only one car. Nora didn't want to drive by herself because she was sure she wouldn't be able to find it. She also feared that she would have difficulties with her knowledge of English and she wanted me to go with her to the interview and be her interpreter; therefore, we both went.

The interview turned out very well and the nursing director said at the end:

"Nora, tomorrow morning you can start working here."

When I translated to Nora what the director of nursing had just said, Nora grabbed her head and said:

"For God's sake, that's too soon. I am not ready for that yet."

I turned to the nursing director and without a blink of an eye I said this as a translation:

"So far we have only one car. We will buy another car and Nora will start working here next Monday.

"Excellent; we are all set. Nora will start next Monday," the nursing director said.

When we went out to the parking lot, Nora asked:

"What did the nursing director say?"

"That we agreed you start working next Monday," I said.

"That's too soon; I did not have the second interview yet," Nora said.

"You don't need the second interview because they gave you employment immediately at the first one," I said.

"But I'm not prepared for it yet," Nora insisted.

"Look, this company gave you the job for tomorrow and then I said that you would start next Monday. They agreed and now you have two choices. Either I will call them and tell them you changed your mind and we will seek a position for you somewhere else, or you start working there next Monday. They will not hold that position for you for a long time. Ultimately, what do you want to prepare for?" I asked. We got into the car, Nora thought for a moment, and then she said:

"All right, I will start work next Monday, but you have to teach me how to get here because I will not make it on my own."

"Of course. Saturday and Sunday you'll drive with me from the house to the nursing home and you will do this as many times as it is necessary to memorize the way there and back," I said.

"The second car we buy should be brand new," said Nora.

"Yes, I am also thinking about a new one. What kind of car would you like?" I asked.

"I like the Ford Escort, but I want a red one with automatic transmission and air conditioning too," Nora said.

"There is a Ford dealer just a short distance from here. We can go there to take a look," I said.

We went to the Ford dealer, parked the car and went to the section of the lot where the new Escorts were parked. We could see from a distance there were different colors—blue, green, black, silver and other colors, but not a single red one.

"Let us go somewhere else; they do not have a red one here," I said.

"Just wait a minute until we look around," Nora said.

"Do you want red, or don't you?" I asked.

"Yes I would like a red one the most. Exactly such a red color, as was our Skoda car," Nora said.

"They have all the Escorts parked here but I do not see a single red one," I said.

Nora did not respond and went on inspecting the cars. There were about forty of them and she went from one to another and looked inside.

"Let's get out of here because, if a car salesman catches up with us, we will not be able to get rid of him," I said, but Nora still did not reply.

"Good morning. How may I help you?," I heard a voice behind me. I turned around and noticed one of the salesmen walking toward us. He had a big smile on his face, and when he came closer to us, he first shook hands with Nora and he said:

"My name is David. How could I be of assistance to you?"

"Nora," Nora said and looked at me. The salesman was a little confused, he did not discern that she looked at me to say what she wanted. I shook hands with the salesman:

"My name is Jan and we are looking for a red Escort for her, with automatic and air conditioning."

The salesman now looked at me because he comprehended that I would be the one with whom he would need to converse. When he heard what we were looking for, he scratched behind his ear and slowly said:

"Red . . . Escort . . . automatic . . . air conditioning . . . It seems that we do not have such a car right now . . ."

"Maybe it would be better if we went somewhere else . . . Allow me to translate to my wife, about what we just spoke," I said and translated to Nora our dialogue into Slovak. As I ended my translation to Nora, the salesman said:

"Ah, no, no, no . . . I will find you a car with a better price than somewhere else. What language do you speak? Where are you from?"

"It's the Slovak language and we came from Czechoslovakia," I said.

"Stastny Brothers," David said and then he added:

"Czech hockey players."

"Slovakian . . . in Czechoslovakia there are two main nationalities Czechs and Slovaks," I said.

"Czechoslovak hockey players," David corrected himself and it was quite obvious that my explanation about two nationalities did not mean anything to him. I did not intend to stretch out the car purchase with conversations about nationalities or sports and I asked:

"What about the car we are looking for?"

"Stastny? What does it mean in Czechoslovak.?" David asked.

"Happy . . . ," I said in English.

"Come with me," David said and he led us into his office.

When we were walking by some of his colleagues, he said to them enthusiastically:

"These two are relatives of Stastny brothers . . ."

He brought us to his desk, we sat down, and he asked us to excuse him for awhile, so he could bring a list of cars, from which we could choose one. I grabbed the opportunity and said to Nora:

"Let's get out of here now. It is not going anywhere. We have already talked about hockey players and nationalities, but it is still unclear what kind of car they want sell to us."

"Where are you off to in such a hurry? You cannot wait for a moment?" Nora asked irritated.

"By Friday we need the second car and it seems to me that we are uselessly killing time here. In the mea time, we could be finding a car somewhere else. And it would be a red one . . . There are more than enough car dealers around here," I said. Nora did not have a chance to answer because David returned with the list of cars, laid it in front of him and started to page through it. He looked at Nora and said:

"We have green, brown, black, grey and silver. Which one would you like the most?

I translated his offer of cars to Nora and she picked out silver.

"Silver," I said to David and I inquired:

"That silver one . . . does it also have an air conditioning?"

"No, none of those have air conditioning. Those are Escorts with automatic transmission . . . but no problem, we professionally install air conditioning in it," said David.

"How much extra will the air conditioning be?" I asked.

"It will cost you nothing extra, only as much, as you would pay for an Escort with air conditioning and automatic," David said. I translated to Nora, what he said and she decided for the silver one, but only if it was with air conditioning. However, she wanted to see it first.

"Nora would like to take a look at the car," I said.

"Of course," David said and led us outside to the parking lot. On the way out he picked out the car keys from a cabinet on the wall. When we came to the car and David unlocked the door, Nora looked inside and she pointed at a car, which stood at a distance:

"Aha, there is also a silver Escort, but it has seats, covers and the whole interior in red. Ask him whether we could see that one. The one he just opened has the whole interior in black," she said. David looked at me and waited until I translated to him, what Nora said. According to her gesticulation, he estimated that the car, which he showed to us, she did not like. When I told him what the problem was he said:

"Of course. However, that car is not a Ford Escort, but a Mercury Lynx. In essence it is the same car as the Fort Escort, only it is produced by Mercury, which is another division of the Ford Motor Company. I'll go get the keys, you stay here," said David and ran off to the office. While he was getting the keys, I translated to Nora what he had said. Nora sat inside behind the steering wheel and it was pretty obvious she liked the red interior much more than the black one.

"I will not have a red car from outside, but it will be red from the inside instead," Nora said and I automatically translated her sentence to David.

"Excellent, so the car has been chosen," David called with a big smile on his face, locked the car and lead us back inside. We sat at his desk while David filled out papers for a loan, registration, sale, insurance, etc. When he was done, we gave him a hundred-dollar security deposit and signed the papers. With the additional installation of air conditioning, the pickup time for the car stretched a bit, but David pledged we would have the car by Thursday. He said he would call me at work when we could pick up the car.

I was very surprised when David called me at work the next morning and said they could not sell the car to us because we did not have satisfactory credit.

"All right, send me back our hundred dollars and we will buy a car somewhere else," I said quite composedly. In essence, I was fairly glad because the after-market fitting of air conditioning into a brand new car appeared to me as a needless complication. I knew it was not going to be a problem finding another car dealer where they would have what we were looking for.

"The money you gave me yesterday is non-refundable because the business transaction did not go through," David said fairly imperiously. I comprehended that he wanted to play a "tough guy," so I changed the tactics a bit:

"The business transaction did not go through from your side, not from of mine. I want the money back," I said.

"You don't have good credit . . ." David started and I interrupted him in the middle of his sentence:

"Wait a minute . . . We have very good credit and it won't be a problem to prove it, if I wish to. You canceled the transaction, then the fault is from your side. And then I am a kind and pleasant man, until someone burns me. I will get those hundred dollars from you even if it costs me five hundred dollars," I said with an already raised voice and hung up the phone.

"What happened?," Mark inquired, because he saw and heard me on the phone. I told him the entire history of purchasing a car at Ford. He draw a big line in the air with his hand and announced:

"Do not worry about it. As we go home the two of us will stop at a car dealer, where I bought some cars. It is Chrysler, not Ford . . ." and in the middle of his sentences he was interrupted by the receptionist's voice paging:

"Jan, line three please . . ."

I picked up the telephone and it was David again from the Ford dealer. Immediately from the beginning he apologized to me and said he did not mean it that way and also begged me not to hang up again and listen to him. I said to myself that I would give him one more chance; therefore, I promised not to hang up and let him speak. Allegedly, their secretary placed somebody else's paperwork, who did not have good credit, in our folder. They had already found the papers about our credit, everything was OK and we could pick up the car Friday.

We actually picked up our brand new Mercury Lynx Friday and Nora was really happy about it. However, her pleasure did not last too long because the air conditioning malfunctioned and I had go back for a repair the following week. We could not understand why a brand dealer like Ford, who should have the best shops for installations and repairs, could sell a brand new car to someone in such a condition. The unpleasant event with David and unworkable air conditioning in a brand new car left permanent distaste in our mouths. The loan, which we received from them, we refinanced at the first opportunity to another bank with lower interest. From that time on, we avoided dealers under the blue Ford sign and never bought another car from them.

Saturday and Sunday Nora and I had training drives from Chelsea into Wellesley and back. We made two rounds on Saturday, one on Sunday and Nora said it would be enough because she had already memorized the way back and forth. For safety's sake she drove the Pacer because we were afraid of using a brand new car for a beginner's driving.

"Monday when you come to work, call me from a phone booth so that I know you arrived all right," I said, when we came back from the training drive.

"All right, I will call you," Nora said.

Monday all day I was at work sitting on pins and needles waiting for her call, but the morning call from Nora never came. I hoped she had gotten to work without problems and she did not get lost on her way. When she finally called me, it was already after one o'clock in the afternoon.

"Hi, I am already home," she said.

"Hi, why didn't you call me in the morning?" I asked.

"I tried calling you several times, but the phone booth we have at work must be broken. Every time I dialed the number, some woman intruded on my phone call. I did not understand what she said so I'd hung up. I dialed the number again and the woman was there again. Accordingly, I could not call you.

"But that was no woman, but only a woman's voice from a machine telling you how many coins you had to drop in the phone slot for the call which you had just dialed," I said with laughter.

"I could not understand her at all and I thought the telephone was broken because some other line was intruding on my call," Nora said also with laughter because now she comprehended the voice, which she did not previously understand.

"Why are you home so soon?" I asked.

I did not know I should come to work dressed in white like a nursing assistant, so the nursing director let me wear her white coat and I worked the whole morning and she sent me home at noon. She told me I have to come in at six not at eight as this morning . . . and already dressed in a white uniform," Nora said.

"Are they going to give you those uniforms?" I asked.

"No, I have to buy them on my own. And I have to come in all ready with the uniform on. When you come back home, we will go uniform shopping," Nora said

The income Nora brought to the family not only substantially changed our financial situation but also our overall point of view of life. Moving into a bigger and nicer apartment wasn't as unimaginable as it had been in March when we talked about it. This time she was actively involved in a search for it.

There was a young couple that lived on the same street just a short distance from us and they had a little girl named April. The husband had Polish origins after his parents and he could speak Polish a little bit. Because Polish is a very similar language to our native Slovak, he tried speaking Polish to us every time we met him. This way he learned from Nora that we were looking for a new apartment and he advised her that he knew a family who lived just a short distance from us and had an apartment for rent in their own house. The house was in the same city—Chelsea, but it was in a much nicer part of the city, on the other side of US Route 1. We liked the apartment a lot, agreement with the owner was easy and then, thanks to Nora's activity and his advice, we moved at the end of August.

We thought about renting a truck for our moving, but all rental places in our neighborhood already had all their trucks spoken for. We did not know that the end of August—beginning of September was the worst time in the whole year for renting trucks because college students were moving back into their dorms. When it came to the date of moving, we already had everything arranged in the old and new apartment and by pushing the moving date up we would lose the new apartment. There was nothing else to do but to find an alternative transport. At that time we already had some furniture and therefore our cars were unusable for it, so we asked Jaro to help us with his van. He again helped us with a lot of enthusiasm and moved all the big pieces of furniture. He had to make three trips until we moved all of it and we just could not believe how much stuff we had accumulated in less than six months. Smaller articles were moved in our cars and again we could not do it at once, but had to make six trips. At the end of February, we arrived with four suitcases and three bags, which all fit into one car!

At the beginning of September, the children went back to school, Peter into the fifth grade and Katarina into the second. Because we had moved in the meantime, they did not go back to Williams School but into the Prattville School, which was just on the next street over. They were very sad not to be going back to Williams School because they had gotten used to the teachers and had found some friends. It was also true for children what grow ups said:

"Meeting someone is easy, saying goodbye is difficult."

Prattville School was very close and they walked to school on foot, just like a lot of the other children from that part of Chelsea. Over time they found new friends instead of those "they had left in the old school" and also became friendly with new teachers.

Nora drove the Pacer into work for about a month when she called me at work one morning:

"Something is wrong with the car. Every time I push the brake pedal, something in the front, like it is on the front wheels, makes a big noise," Nora said very startled.

"When did it start? I asked.

"I don't know, first time I noticed the noise this morning," Nora said.

"Brake pads are worn and they must be replaced," I said.

"But I am afraid of driving that car," Nora said.

"Don't worry, that is not a big deal . . . you will come back home without problems and tomorrow you will take the new car. I will take the Pacer and have the brakes fixed," I said and from that time on we stayed with that change, because it was much easier for me to handle "illnesses" of an old car. After all, the Mercury Lynx was chosen by Nora. It was her car.

Shortly after fixing the brakes, a hole burned in the muffler and the car was making noise like an army tank. I had the muffler fixed and then the battery went. None of those repairs were complicated ones or too expensive, but after the winter, the fixing up started piling up and there was something to be fixed twice a month. We said it was time to buy a new car and at the beginning of March 1986 we bought another new car—Chrysler LeBaron GT . . . of course with automatic transmission and air conditioning. We did not want to forfeit the driving convenience we got used to after buying the Pacer car.

In connection with the purchase of that car, a little event happened, which I will not forget for the rest of my life. I perceived again what an unfathomable and at the same time a fragile thing the soul of a child is. The night we went to pick up the LeBaron from the dealer, Katarina had a cold and did not feel good. Peter went with us to the Chrysler dealer, but she didn't want to go with us; therefore, we left her in bed and told her, that were we going to pick up the car and in a short time we would return home. The dealer was a short distance from the house, just over in Medford, the next town from Chelsea. Besides, Katarina was not alone in the house; the owners lived downstairs in the house and at that time they were home. We were on very good terms with them and sometimes they watched our kids. We expected that it would take us only a few minutes, but the proceedings with signatures and paper work took about three quarters of an hour. When we finally got the car and were getting ready to go home, Nora proposed:

"Supermarket Heartland is very close to here . . . let us go shopping and we'll save driving back and forth."

"But right now we have two cars with us, which we will drive back and forth," I said.

"Never mind, it is only a little bit from here," said Nora.

"All right, then let's go," I said.

Peter rode with me in the new LeBaron and Nora drove behind us in her Lynx. We purchased some groceries in Heartland, loaded the bags into the car and went back home. Nora ran upstairs first, Peter and I brought up the bags with the groceries.

"I am going to take a look, how Katarina is feeling," Nora said as she was going upstairs. She stepped into Katarina's room and found her there weeping.

"Katarina, what happened? Why are you full of tears?" Nora asked, squatting by her bed and embracing her. Nora lifted and seated Katarina in bed, still embracing her;, with her left arm she held Katarina around her neck and with the right hand gently rubbed her back:

"Katarina, don't cry . . . tell me, what happened to you . . ."

Katarina still wept and when she relaxed a bit, so she was able to say something, the two of us with Peter stood in the door and stared stunned and uncomprehending at them.

"I thought, that you . . . you went away and left me . . . left me here on . . . on my own . . . ," Katarina said brokenly. At that moment I comprehended . . . tears gathered into my eyes, I squatted down to them and hugged both of them at once.

"Without you we wouldn't go anywhere . . . we didn't leave you in Bratislava but took you with us," I said.

"Katarina, we would never abandon you. You're indeed ours and all of us love you.," Nora said, still embracing Katarina and still gently rubbing her back. Peter also joined us and hugged Katarina around her head, which rested at Nora's shoulder:

"I love you too . . . indeed we wouldn't leave you just like that . . ." Peter said.

Our attention to Katarina markedly soothed her; after a few moments she calmed down, stopped crying and it was possible to communicate with her.

"How did you come up with such nonsense?" Nora asked.

"You said you were going to pick up a car and would be back in a few moments. You were gone for a long time," Katarina said.

I looked at my watch. We were gone for an hour and forty five minutes. Nora winked at me and with her hand she indicated to me, not to say anything.

"We then stopped at the supermarket to buy some groceries and that's why it took us a little longer," Nora said guiltily.

Following some initial difficulties with the English language Nora, put herself very quickly into her new job, and thanks to her abilities and willingness to help others, she became a favorite with everyone. Her bosses realized very quickly that she did not avoid work and she always finished her daily duties a hundred percent. She must have been completely overwhelmed by sickness in order to take a sick day. I would call it a "personal humanity," which did not allow her to stay home on days she did not feel all right or there were severe weather conditions. She recognized, if she did not come to work, then the patients she cared for would not have anyone to take care of them. The patients were not just patients to her, but old people who desperately needed to be cared for, helped out of their beds and fed their meals. She also successfully completed the Certified Nursing Assistant course in order to improve and simplify her work by discerning theoretical knowledge.

One and a half years after she started working there, she was offered a Rehabilitation nursing assistant position, which she gladly accepted because she felt that her everyday hard work was highly appreciated.

She always maintained a very good relationship with all the patients and, therefore, they loved her for it. Every Christmas the list of people for whom we bought presents became longer and longer with people from the nursing home she cared for because they did not have anyone who would buy presents for them. In some cases the people had their own relatives, but Nora was simply afraid, they would not bring them any presents.

There were some changes also in the laboratory where I worked. About one and a half years after my joining the company my boss Mark retired and his position of the lab manager was offered to me. I accepted it with gladness. Being a manager I was responsible for the whole lab in all aspects, professional, organizational and also financial. I did not have any problems handling the job because I used to be a manager before and that was of an even much larger group of people, it was very interesting work, but after some time I noticed that a lot of analytical work, which we performed for our customers became repetitive. Somehow I was missing that imaginary and not completely marked straight road, which I used to draw in front of me when working on research. Then I had to walk on it very carefully, so it would not brake, or would not end up in a dead end. When my road ended at a solid wall, there was nothing else to do and just take two steps backwards, stop and start with making out and drawing another road.

Before I used to think up something brand new all the time and now I just followed analytical chemistry work according to "old" and very proven and written methods. When we left Czechoslovakia I already had three patents and a few applications I never finished; all of them were related to plastics, or more precisely to paints and coatings. The longer I thought about it the less willing I was to stay faithful to analytical chemistry, which I used as the closest and fasted way of obtaining my first job in the USA. At that time there was no point of considering that if I wanted to switch back to paints and coatings in the future, it would be much harder because all my credits and experience in the USA would be in just analytical chemistry. Then I wanted a job . . . a job quick, so we would not live on Welfare.

The situation was totally different now. We both had full time jobs and the family was taken care of. There was no need to hurry up with anything and there was plenty of time for job searching in "paints and coatings." I prepared my Resume and started mailing it to places with job openings, which I selected this time with much more critique, because I knew exactly what I wanted. I went to Harvard University library and searched for and had printed my patents from Czechoslovakia and translated them into English during nights. The originals along with my translations found their permanent storage in a briefcase I carried with me to interviews. I pulled them out at appropriate moments as proof of my profession. I have to admit they always made a very good impression.

After about a half a year I received two similar job offers within the same week. Both of them were from companies located in Rhode Island, one of them a large company in Pawtucket and the other one a small company in Central Falls. After a long and difficult deliberation I made a decision for the small company in Central Falls.

At that time we still lived in Chelsea, so I had to travel every day to Rhode Island. Every morning I drove south on interstate 95. It was an advantage because most cars were going the opposite direction, from the south to the north to Boston. Going back home it was again a benefit for me because most cars were going in the other direction.

We had no permanent tie to the apartment in Chelsea and I already had my job in Rhode Island and we both believed that after some time Nora would find a similar job in a nursing home down there, so we decided to move to Rhode Island. However, finding an appropriate apartment was not so easy. We wanted a residence at least at the same level we already had, which meant three bedrooms, as they say in the USA. So I started looking at advertisements in the local newspaper and after work I went to take a peek at those places. I was really surprised that for double what we paid for our apartment in Chelsea I could not find anything I would be willing to move into. I kept on looking and searching but at the same time there was no need to hurry. The gas was very inexpensive those days and my daily commute did not come up expensive.

A few months went by and I still did not find the right place. Sometimes I mentioned at work that I was still looking for an apartment in the neighborhood and some colleagues started looking around for me. From time to time they gave me a hint and this way I learned from one of my co-workers who lived in Mansfield that he saw a condominium complex being built close to his house and just recently he noticed a sign saying they were ready to rent. I called the number he wrote down for me and made an appointment with the owner for five o'clock to see the place. When I came to the place I was pleasantly surprised how beautiful and modern those condominiums were. Just from the outside there was a huge difference from the others I had seen so far. I walked up to number twelve, which was the unit we talked about with the owner over the phone. It was a little too early, only quarter to five, but I saw a light on inside, so I rang the door bell. I heard a bell making noise right behind the door, which opened in a moment and a very sympathetic gentleman appeared in it:

"Good evening, I am a little early; we made an appointment for five. My name is Jan," I said.

"Good evening . . . it doesn't matter . . . come in . . . my name is Rick," the gentleman in the door said.

I walked in. The condominium was maybe even more beautiful from the inside, than from the outside. There were three bedrooms, a big dinning room—kitchen combination, a living room and everything was clean and smelled brand new. I had to use my internal power not to divulge my excitement. Compared to what I had seen so far, this was a real stunning apartment inside and out. It was something I was willing to move into immediately. Under the apartment there was a garage for a single car and in front of it a brand new driveway.

"How do you like it?" Rick asked after we walked around the whole apartment and came back out from garage.

"It is really beautiful," I said without hesitation and then asked:

"How much would the monthly rent be?"

"One thousand four hundred fifty dollars," Rick said without hesitation.

When I heard the amount it shook the inside of my whole body and for a moment I was unable to speak. When I regained my senses, I asked in disbelief:

"One thousand four hundred fifty?"

"Yes, one thousand four hundred fifty," Rick repeated.

"It is a really gorgeous apartment . . ." I said quietly.

"Brand new, we just finished it a few days ago," Rick said and then he added:

"Beginning next month I am start to paying the mortgage . . . the bank is already waiting for me," Rick said with a smile.

"How much is the mortgage?" I asked.

"One thousand four hundred fifty dollars," Rick said again without pause.

"So . . . one thousand four hundred fifty is the monthly rent and one thousand four hundred fifty is the monthly mortgage . . . ? I asked slowly.

"Yes, my wife and I made this our investment," Rick said a bit grouchy.

". . . I will pay his investment . . . I would rather take the mortgage on my own and will pay my own investment . . ." I thought, but did not say anything to Rick. I felt like a bulb lit up over my head. Until now we did not think about buying our own house. We still searched for an apartment to rent. We were here just for a short time, less than three years and we did not know any conditions for taking a mortgage . . . and we didn't even know where to start.

I just comprehended that we would have to pay much more money for living in a decent place. However my internal instinct was telling me that if we had to pay much more I would preferably pay it into my own pocket.

"Rick, thank you very much for your time, showing me the apartment and everything else," I said and shook his hand.

"So, did you make a decision?" Rick asked and then he added:

"Talk to your wife, or you both can come here and take another look. It may be easier to make a decision."

"No, thank you. It has been decided, we are not interested in this apartment house," I said and went home.

When I came back home I had not closed the door yet and Nora asked:

"How did you like the three bedroom condominium?"

"Dazzling . . . brand new . . . everything smells like new . . ." I said.

"How much is the rent?" Nora asked.

"The rent is also dazzling . . . one thousand four hundred fifty a month . . ." I said.

"What?" Nora asked and then she added:

"You are not serious!"

"Exactly what you heard . . . one thousand four hundred fifty dollars monthly," I said.

"Do you want to pay so much a month?" Nora asked with reservations.

"Yes, but not into someone else's pocket," I said.

"What do you mean?" Nora asked.

"It is fairly simple, the owner said to me the rent was one thousand four hundred fifty monthly and the mortgage was also one thousand four hundred fifty a month," I said.

"Do you want to buy a condominium" Nora asked.

"I don't know yet, not condominium . . . I want to see how much we would pay for our own house. Or better yet, whether we could get a mortgage for a house for that kind of money a month," I said.

"Do you think we can handle that?" Nora asked.

"That is what I don't know. I have to figure that out," I said.

From that time on we did not look for an apartment for rent anymore, but I started figuring out the details around buying a house. I knew completely nothing and began inquiring with people at my company. I can imagine my questions were sometimes considered funny. I did not mind, because I said to myself there was no such thing as a stupid question, because if someone did not know something, the best way of finding out was asking a question. Only a stupid answer could be funny . . .

I paid attention to free brochures commonly available in grocery stores or real state agencies and began studying houses for sale. I chose the towns of Cumberland and Lincoln, because I became somewhat familiar with them during my previous search for an apartment and I admired those locations the most.

I found mortgage information at banks . . . how they are open . . . for how much we would qualify for . . . etc.

In the mean time another colleague of mine got me in touch with a realtor. I did not have all the details cleared up yet about what was involved in getting into a mortgage, or how much we would qualify for, but I thought it would not hurt to see a few houses in the neighborhood over the weekends. Some days later a realtor called me, her name was Mary.

"Your colleague Steve told me you were looking for a house in Cumberland—Lincoln.

"Yes," I said.

"I could show you a couple of houses. When would you like to do it?'" Mary asked.

"I guess Saturday would be the best. I would come with my wife and kids," I said.

"If you would like this coming Saturday I could show you a couple of houses in Lincoln," Mary said.

We agreed to meet in front of a bank in Lincoln on Saturday, even though it appeared to be a little too early. I had a feeling I needed more time to orient myself in real property. Mary showed us four houses in the chosen territory. It was a real nice location, but the houses she showed us we did not like at all. They were either too small or not even in the category we were looking for. They gave the impression of being too cheap, not by price, but by their appearance. Some of them were right on a busy and noisy main road, others were stuck in the back of another house and the only access to it was through the property of the owner. We thought the owner just built an additional small house in his back yard in order to make money for the one in the front. When the situation repeated itself again the next Saturday, we said to Mary it was not the way we liked looking for a house and fired her. However, we did not want to go home because there was the whole afternoon for the house search. We went into a Chinese restaurant for lunch. During the lunch we laughed about the houses Mary showed us. There was no way we would buy anything from her collection of houses. We just could not believe there would not be a better choice of houses in the neighborhood. I recalled seeing a real estate agency, which I remembered including the sign, because we have already driven by several times. It was located next to interstate highway 295, right down across the exit ramp to Cumberland. We decided we would return to that real estate office and tried our luck there before we returned back home to Chelsea.

Thanks to my sense of orientation we had no problems locating the agency and a few minutes after leaving the Chinese restaurant we parked the car in front of it.

Immediately after entering the office Irene welcomed us at the door and asked us to sit down at her desk. I explained to her, what type of a house we were looking for, so we would not waste anybody's time. She very carefully listened to me and then she pulled a few listings of houses and handed them to us.

"Take a look at those pictures and let me know which type would fit your interest and I will drive you to them. If you don't like them, I will find others for you," Irene said.

"That is an excellent idea. At least we will not waste time driving to a house we would not like," I said to Irene and then added:

"This morning we just fired Mary, a realtor from another real estate agency, who showed us houses according to her choices. It was just a waste of time."

"Now you are in the hands of a professional of this real estate office and I will find you such a house that you are looking for," Irene said with a big smile on her face.

"That sounds very promising," I said also with a big smile and laid three pictures of new listing in front of her, which we chose.

"Leave your car here and I will drive all of you in my car," Irene said, when we walked outside to the parking lot.

First she drove us to a house which was located on the same street as her office, just a few blocks down the road.

"Irene, this house is very nice from the outside. It is exactly what we are looking for, but it is located on a street, which is too busy and noisy," I said and Nora nodded her head.

"So, we are not going to waste our time by going inside," Irene said and drove on. In just a moment we drove up to the second house, which we chose by its picture. It was a new construction and the inside of the garage was just being finished.

"If you choose this one, you can have your own choice of carpet colors, kitchen cabinet color including your own preference for appliances and so on, because they will custom finish the house for you," Irene said.

We went inside the house and took a look, but we found out the rooms were relatively small. It appeared to us we would not fit in the furniture we already had. When we glanced outside the windows, we saw the same houses all around.

"It reminds me of a housing development," Nora said.

This type of house is too small and we could not fit our furniture in it. I am also afraid that one dark night I could wander in my neighbor's house by mistake, because all the houses look the same," I said.

"I take that as a no . . . let's go on," Irene said.

We came up to the third house we chose by the picture. The house was built on a curve of a very quiet street. During the whole time we stayed there not a single car went by. It was a very nice house.

"I am very sorry, but we cannot go inside, because the owner moved out and I don't have a key with me. If you are interested, I will get a hold of the key and we can make an appointment for the inside inspection for some other day," Irene said.

"Yes, we like the house and we would like to see it from the inside," I said. Nora and even Peter and Katarina nodded their heads. It was pretty obvious this was a big candidate.

"This part of Cumberland is called Arnold Mills and it is considered the most beautiful part of Cumberland," Irene said and then added:

"I just recalled there is a house a short distance from here, which you would most probable like. It is listed with another real estate agency, but I can call there and ask them if they would not mind us looking at the house."

All of us nodded our heads in approval and Irene drove us to the house. She parked on the driveway in front of garage and asked us:

"Please wait out here and I will call the real estate office."

We stayed outside and glanced around. It was the best looking neighborhood we saw so far.

"Look, there is a two car garage. Exactly what we wanted," I said.

"The house looks very nice from the outside, but I don't like the color of it. It is too dark," Nora said.

"We can paint it to another color," Peter said.

"Look, we can sled down from that hill in the winter," Katarina said and pointed at hill, which went down from the neighbor's house to where we stood.

"The color is really dark. I would prefer a white one much more," I said.

Our repainting plans were interrupted by Irene's, who stood in the open door and called us to come in:

"Everything is OK, come in. The owners are home now and they agreed to having you take a look inside, but they beg you not to wake up the baby, which fell asleep just a moment ago."

We walked in. The first room was interesting, but relatively dark, because it had very small windows and a high, cathedral type of ceiling.

"This could be a dinning room," I said.

"It is the family room for the current owners, they watch TV here," Irene said.

"There should be a sliding door right there. It would bring in more light," Nora said and pointed to another side of the room, where there was a deck from the outside.

We eyeballed the room and found out there was no problem fitting our dinning room furniture there. We walked into the kitchen and Irene showed us the stove, oven and dishwasher. That kitchen was the biggest one we saw so far in any house, with three windows and kitchen cabinets running around almost the entire kitchen.

We went through a hallway into a living room and we were so surprised at how huge that room was, we just stopped and gazed. There was a big fireplace right in front of us, a big window to the street on our left and two windows to the back yard on our right. Irene led us through the living room to a door next to the fireplace and she put her finger on her lips and said silently:

"This is one bedroom and now the baby is sleeping there. I will open the door for you to see, but please be quiet and don't wake up the baby."

When she opened the door we were surprised again. The room was really spacey, with three windows and two closets.

Then she showed us a bathroom and another two bedrooms. First we saw one smaller one and behind that one, there was a huge bedroom with a bathroom and a walk in closet, which was so big, it was practically a small room. The view from the windows was attractive, mostly into the back yard.

We evidently admired that house and Irene noticed it. We all went back into her car and she drove us back to her real estate office. She looked at us and said:

The house you just saw has been on the marking for a long time and I believe the owners would be more flexible . . . they would certainly consider an even lower price than listed."

"Irene, excuse us for a moment, we would like to discuss the house just between the two of us," I said.

"I promise I will not listen," Irene said with laughter.

"You can certainly listen to us. But you will not understand a single word, because we are going to speak in Slovak," I said also with laughter.

Irene looked at us surprised and said:

"Of course . . . Go ahead."

"What do you think," I asked Nora.

"I actually liked that house very much. And what about you?" Nora asked.

"I also liked it very much. I don't know, whether we should search further and then decide," I said.

"This house was indeed the best looking . . . nicest and biggest we've seen so far. I think if we find something better the price will also be much higher," Nora said.

"If we say we are taking it, we will not be able to see any more houses. Only, if they decline our offer," I said.

"I suppose, this house would be suitable for us," Nora said.

"All right, if you agree we will offer them ten thousand less than it is listed for and we will see, what will be their answer," I said.

"I agree," Nora said.

I turned to Irene and translated to her our deal, to English.

"Fantastic . . . tomorrow I will announce your offer to the owners and then I will call you back with their decision," Irene said.

Irene called me the next Monday morning. Immediately, after I picked up the phone and introduced myself, she called enthusiastically:

"Congratulations, the house is yours."

"I see the owners already accepted our offer," I said and in spirit regretted, that we did not give a lower offer . . . right now it was already too late . . .

"Yes, your offer was accepted. Right now you have to pay a deposit, so you officially confirm that the purchase is legally binding. Thereby you also insure that the house can't be sold to anybody else," Irene said.

Later Irene and I decided to meet in her office the next Saturday morning and Nora and I would bring the deposit for the house. It was the end of November 1987.

During December, I was able to successfully conclude the mortgage process for the house and for Friday, the twenty-ninth of January 1988 at 10:00 a.m. our mortgage closing was scheduled at the bank. Everything ran smoothly, and perhaps an hour and a half later, Nora and I walked out of the bank as the new owners of the house.

The next day, Saturday, we moved. The company rented me a big truck, including the driver, and with the help of a few friends we loaded it with furniture early that morning. I just could not believe my eyes that in less than three years after our arrival in the USA, we had accumulated so much stuff, which completely filled the truck. It was all furniture and other furnishings. Glass, porcelain and other fragile belongings were wrapped in boxes and loaded into seven personal cars. Shortly before noon, we departed from Chelsea in the direction of Cumberland and I sat in the big truck next to the driver. When we came to Route 93 with the truck, I looked into the rearview mirror, just to make sure we did not lose anybody from our convoy of cars. Behind us there was Nora with Katarina in her Mercury Lynx and behind her car yet another six personal cars. Peter was in a car of one of our friends.

"Exactly three and a half years ago we were at the refugee camp in Traiskirchen and today we are moving into our own house," I thought and in my mind I could see the picture of Nora when she had sat on the bunk bed with her big, sad eyes. My eyes filled with tears . . .

www.ingramcontent.com/pod-product-compliance
Lightning Source LLC
Chambersburg PA
CBHW061335280526
45784CB00001B/25